RUSSIA, THE WEST, AND MILITARY INTERVENTION

Russia, the West, and Military Intervention

ROY ALLISON

OXFORD
UNIVERSITY PRESS

OXFORD
UNIVERSITY PRESS

Great Clarendon Street, Oxford, OX2 6DP,
United Kingdom

Oxford University Press is a department of the University of Oxford.
It furthers the University's objective of excellence in research, scholarship,
and education by publishing worldwide. Oxford is a registered trade mark of
Oxford University Press in the UK and in certain other countries

First Edition published in 2013

Impression: 1

British Library Cataloguing in Publication Data
Data available

Library of Congress Cataloging in Publication Data
Data Available

ISBN 978-0-19-959063-6

Printed and bound in Great Britain by the
MPG Printgroup, UK

To Olga and Maria

Acknowledgements

This book could not have been written without the strong intellectual and practical support provided by the Department of International Relations at the London School of Economics, which provided me with a term of sabbatical leave in 2011, and St Antony's College, Oxford. Colleagues working in Russian and East European Studies at the University of Oxford have been particularly encouraging. However, this project draws on discussions, interviews, and materials gathered over a long period of observation and study of Russian international conduct and foreign policy. During that time I benefited greatly from working at Chatham House (the Royal Institute of International Affairs) for twelve years, as Head of the Russia and Eurasia Programme, and from an attachment as a Senior Research Fellow in the Centre of International Studies, in the Department of Politics and International Relations at Oxford during 2001–5.

I have drawn inspiration from discussions with a large number of academic colleagues in recent years. A very few may be mentioned here: Pavel Baev, Vladimir Baranovsky, Archie Brown, Barry Buzan, Chris Davis, Edmund Herzig, Lena Jonson, Bob Legvold, Dov Lynch, Margot Light, Neil S. MacFarlane, Marie Mendras, Vitaly Naumkin, James Nixey, Alex Pravda, Stephen White, and Andrei Zagorski. I have benefited from frequent conversations with Western diplomats and officials with interests in Russia and other CIS states, as well as their counterparts in the region, who have provided important insights, but who cannot be attributed individually. Two anonymous referees for Oxford University Press provided detailed and most helpful suggestions for my preparation of the book, for which I remain indebted. I am most grateful also for the patient commitment shown throughout by Dominic Byatt on behalf of Oxford University Press in shepherding me from initial book proposal to final manuscript. Lastly, for their firm belief that I would complete this study despite all distractions, and for supporting me in so many ways to allow that to happen, this book is dedicated to my wonderful wife Olga and daughter Maria.

Contents

1

Military Intervention, Norms, and the Case of Russia

Since the closing days of the Cold War military interventions by major powers have reverberated through the international system: in the Gulf, 1990; Kosovo, 1999; Afghanistan, 2001; Iraq, 2003; Georgia, 2008; and Libya, 2011. These interventions have been less dangerous to global order than many earlier ones in an era of bipolar confrontation. Yet the coercive use of force against sovereign states, often accompanied by efforts to alter political arrangements in the target states, has deeply divided the post-Cold War international community. Controversies have flared over the legal, normative, and political rationales of these operations. They have weakened the common ties of international society and challenged established principles of international order.

The dividing lines between states in these controversies have varied. However, Russia has distinguished itself as a frequent and vocal, if not consistent, critic of Western-led intervention. Russia has also been embroiled in disputes over its own use of force in neighbouring post-Soviet states. Since the early 1990s, especially since the end of that decade, Moscow has been one of few major states with the political will and some influence, at least through its permanent membership of the United Nations Security Council, to shape or maintain norms and law regulating the use of force. This can be traced discursively though the justifications, claims, and responses of Russia and other states around major interventions. The wider political context to key interventions has also impacted on the evolution of norms constraining and enabling the use of force.

Russia's engagement and influence in international debates over military intervention and the use of force has been understudied. Moscow's role has puzzling inconsistencies but also intriguing continuities, and an examination of these over more than two decades, from the first Gulf War in 1990 to intervention in Libya in 2011, reveals a complex interaction between domestic state, regional, and global political and normative processes. It reveals adaptation as well as resistance to wider normative currents and the evolution of customary international law. It also shows how Russia, as a former superpower, has struggled to adjust to dramatic changes in its relative power, to strong challenges to international rule-making, as well as to efforts to loosen constraints on the use of force led by its erstwhile superpower rival the United States.

Through a close examination of the Russian role this volume contributes to the wider study of norms and the politics of international law related to the use of force, as well as the politics of international security around major military interventions. It also presents a novel analysis of the perspectives, policies, and influence of contemporary Russian international relations.

MILITARY INTERVENTION: THE ROLE OF INTERNATIONAL LAW AND NORMS

In studying military intervention we should consider initially the theoretical assumptions which inform different understandings of the role of international law and norms in the international system. A starting point could be realism. Realist scholars focus on the salience of power in the structure of international relations. They have tended to regard the influence of international law and norms, therefore, as inherently limited, especially in matters of national security and military affairs.

Our analysis of intervention accepts that the power relationships of states have been a significant shaping and constraining influence on the evolution of norms and customary law with respect to the use of force. Indeed the structures of power politics, especially since the early 2000s, would seem to be in serious tension with what could be termed the constitutionalist order of international law and institutions. It is also relevant for our study that Russia is a state whose leaders have traditionally paid great attention to power in the wider international system and the exercise of it in their neighbourhood.

This volume, however, is not based on a realist view of the world, with its belief in the inherent vulnerability of states in an anarchical system. Rather we rely on insights about the constraints on power drawn from the alternative approaches of constructivism and the English School. Constructivists point out that even when powerful states fail to comply with international law 'they seek to justify their actions as consistent with prevailing law, and if they fail to do this persuasively they often pay high costs to their reputation and perceived legitimacy'.[1] Law and norms, therefore, are not just instrumentally harnessed to the interests of powerful states. Indeed, we argue that justification, through persuasive argumentation, has been central to state engagement in and response to military intervention.

Constructivists go further, however, to claim that states may internalize international rules and norms over time, so as to reconstitute the identity of states and shape their interests. In this respect Russia has displayed a remarkable continuity in its underlying attitudes to the use of force. We suggest below that this may be explained by locating Russia within the pluralist group of states in international society, as presented in English School thinking. Moscow perceives itself as bound by common rules, as other states, but perceives a thinner set of common values than many others in the society of states. This pluralism in turn has been reinforced by particular and traditional Russian conceptions of regional and domestic state order rooted in the thinking of domestic political elites.

Military intervention defined

Military intervention is defined for this book quite broadly. This allows the selection and examination of the legal and normative discourse and political responses around a variety of high profile cases of the use of military force. Military intervention is viewed first and foremost, however, as a political act with the use of military means. Legal or normative claims are used to justify this political act and we investigate how far this discourse contributes to norm formation.

The central feature of the phenomenon of intervention, defined from this political perspective, is an effort to change or preserve the structure of power and authority within a foreign state. Attention is focused on 'the direct and coercive application of military force in internal conflicts to affect their course and outcome'.[2] The core element found in legal definitions of intervention, on the other hand, is action that is neither requested nor approved by state authorities; consent is critical. This is incorporated in the definition of military intervention offered by Finnemore, as the deployment of military forces by a foreign power or powers for the purpose of controlling domestic politics in the target state, 'in ways that clearly violate sovereignty'.[3]

On the other hand, if we are to take military coercion seriously as a criterion and we recognize that it may be problematic to establish sovereign decision-making in civil conflicts, then the scope of our analysis should be enlarged. It is necessary also to cover those cases, which do not constitute UN peacekeeping, where a government invites or accepts intervention from outside by a state to militarily coerce its domestic opponents. This focus on coercion, or enforcement, means our analysis includes Russian-style 'peacekeeping' in regional CIS conflicts, such as in Tajikistan in the 1990s.

Then humanitarian intervention can be defined as a subset or offshoot of military intervention, aimed at protecting the lives and welfare of foreign citizens. In such cases coercion for self-interested material goals or for altering the political balance in the state involved may not be foremost and is seemingly replaced by human-focused and ethical principles and motivations, at least in the discourse supporting such intervention. But in practice it is difficult to argue that political and material objectives are quite absent in such cases. The operation in Libya in 2011, which was exceptional as a UN authorized enforcement operation, may also be viewed as an intervention. It lacked host country consent and changed the course of the internal conflict.[4]

In the post-Cold War era in practice major states have preferred to avoid formal declarations of war in conditions where military interventions still represent acts of war, regardless of the strength of self-defence or other justifications for military action that are used. For our analysis there is little to gain, therefore, in distinguishing between full-fledged 'war' and 'military intervention', whether in the Gulf (1990), Kosovo (1999), Afghanistan (2001), Iraq (2003), Georgia (2008), or Libya (2011).

Finally, to explore further the changing context to debates on the use of force, our analysis moves a little beyond wide-scale or high-intensity conflict or efforts to reconfigure internal conflicts. Some attention is paid to Russian and Western discourse over a grey area at the lower end of the spectrum of coercive military action—limited 'pre-emptive' military strikes. Such strikes may be more or less transparent and intended to replace wider conflict rather than act as its precursor. They may take the form of a reprisal. Such strikes may be defined as an illegal use of force, but not as interventions from a political standpoint. In practice they have little chance of altering political structures in the affected state. In contrast this study does not address targeted killing associated with strikes by drones (remote-controlled, unmanned aerial vehicles), as developed especially under the US administration of Barack Obama. The legal and normative issues involved overlap with those posed by limited strikes with less advanced technologies.[5] But the complex controversy over the use of drones would divert us too much from our core focus on military intervention as a political act.

International law and core restrictions on the use of force

If international law and norms both constrain and enable state behaviour then the United Nations Charter has represented the foundational source of legal restraint on the use of force since its signature in 1945. Most international lawyers, including Russian ones, have considered that the right to use force is restricted under the Charter, as a core treaty obligation, strictly to the purposes of self-defence: the 'restrictionist' interpretation. Article 2 (4) of the Charter enjoins member states to refrain from the 'threat or use of force against the territorial integrity or political independence of any state'. There are only two legally recognized exceptions.

First, Article 51 of the Charter acknowledges states' 'inherent right of individual or collective self-defence' in the case of an armed attack against a UN member. Any force used, however, should be both 'necessary and proportionate'. In essence this means such military action should be a measure of last resort and not be excessive with respect to the goal of abating or repelling the attack. Secondly, force may be authorized by a decision of the UN Security Council, acting under Chapter VII, in response to threats to international peace and security.[6]

The restrictionist case is supported by reference to customary international law. Customary law is not formed by written agreements between states, but depends on two different requirements. First, most states, especially the most powerful concerned with the matter at hand, should conform to the practice. Secondly, the states must also be engaging in such practice because they believe there to be legal obligation to do so, as opposed to some other reason.[7] The justifications they offer for the practice, described as *opinio juris* by lawyers, are key to identifying the customary rules that become legally binding upon states.

As regards the use of force, it is generally claimed that state practice and *opinio juris* have allowed for no exception to the foundational principle of non-intervention, besides the two cases noted above. It is noted that this expression of customary law is found, for example, in various standards on non-intervention declared by the UN General Assembly. Customary law may evolve and adapt, however, in a discursive and politically charged environment. With this in mind we explore the legal justifications, framed in terms of customary law, offered in various cases of military intervention. These justifications are centred on various interpretations of self-defence and UN authorization. In contrast, the weight of legal opinion has continued to rule out any legal right of unilateral humanitarian intervention.

What role might this leave for international norms in constraining or enabling the use of force and military interventions? If we define norms initially as shared principles and expectations about proper behaviour (see below), this raises the question of whether and how to demarcate norms from international law. Research on norms has built bridges between scholarship on international relations and international law. Some have asserted that customary international law, as defined above, *is* norms and note that such 'legal norms' have powerful behavioural effects and are also bound up inextricably with the workings of international institutions, as studied by IR scholars.[8]

For our analysis, however, it is preferable to differentiate norms which are emerging from legal precepts. Such norms form single standards of behaviour that are not yet consolidated and recognized broadly through state custom as rules, although such norms may shade into customary international law as an evolving process. However, contestation (discursive debates, as we discuss further below) and state practice underpin both normative change and the adaptation of customary international law. As a result, in addressing international law, this volume focuses on legal debates in a political context, on the politics of international law, rather than legal rulings and detailed juridical interpretations.

Norms and military intervention

In broad terms norms are shared principles and expectations describing what states generally do and how they should or should not act in particular situations. A norm can be defined more concisely as a standard of appropriate behaviour for actors with a given identity.[9] What role do standards of appropriate conduct then play in relation to state behaviour and the understanding of how states 'ought' to act? Finnemore argues persuasively that 'norms create permissive conditions for action but do not determine action'. In other words 'new or changed norms enable new or different behaviors; they do not ensure such behaviors'.[10] Norms also constrain behaviour by offering standards of judgement and the option of censure or sanction by other states.

Norms are closely connected to the idea of an international society, they help form the rules and structure enabling a sense of community to emerge from the system of states. Widely held norms develop and are shared inter-subjectively among states. Since they are not idiosyncratic in their effects, they leave broad patterns for social science analysis and scholarly study.[11]

Normative context also shapes conceptions of interest of international actors both at the systemic and sub-systemic levels (this opens up the regional dimension which we explore below). However, do norms as defined above take sufficient account of the role of states' self-interest? A focus on self-interest, especially among neo-realists, has led many to argue that what matters in military intervention is state motivation.

Yet it is very likely that the motivations of the states participating in interventions, such as in Kosovo or Iraq, included a mix of politically driven self-interest, alliance interest, and the pursuit of normative principles. Similarly both self-interest and normative concerns seemed to infuse the Soviet and Russian cases we investigate, such as Soviet approaches to the Gulf War in 1990 or Russian involvement in CIS conflicts early in the 1990s. In admitting a role for *Realpolitik* we can still recognize the constraints that arise from the regulating effect of norms and law.

The key insight here is that states seek international legitimacy for their actions and 'for intervention to be legitimately mandated, it must be justified in terms of normative principles that are generally accepted in international society', even if 'such justifications may to some extent be spurious and mask power-political or other self-centred motivations'.[12] We should note also that a striving for legitimacy explains the importance attached to the role of international organizations, especially the United Nations, in *interpreting* norms and authorizing intervention. As noted below, such bodies also act as sounding boards for states seeking to justify their actions. A multilateral imprimatur enhances legitimacy both in relation to the action and discourse of states.

Therefore norms matter in relation to interventions. They may enable action but they can also enmesh states in a network of constraint. Such constraint is built into the balance of interests and policy choices taken by state leaders. So it is consistent with recognition of the role played by states' material capabilities. The role of material power and the self-regarding predisposition of states and their leaders does not negate the importance of norms, whether they are only acknowledged by part of the international community or have gained the broad support necessary to evolve into customary international law.

Nonetheless, power and structural change in the post-Cold War international system has clearly influenced the interventionary conduct of states and the *choice* of norms referred to or justifications advanced in cases of intervention. Dominant states in the international system have historically been at the forefront of major normative change and the associated codification or adaptation of customary international law. Some would go further to argue that power tends to create a normative framework convenient to itself.[13] Keeping these concerns in mind considerable attention is paid in this volume to American discourse on norms, especially when this has appeared to contest not only Russian legal and normative positions but also the wider constitutionalist order, as reflected in controversy over US hegemony.

Justifications and normative change

Justifications for interventions are primary indicators for normative change and the emergence of norms around such interventions. This proposition is built into the methodology adopted for this study. Finnemore explains that 'norms embody a quality of "oughtness" and shared moral assessment' and therefore 'prompt justifications for action and leave an extensive trail of communication among actors that we can study'.[14] We draw heavily on such discourse in the following chapters.

Finnemore observes that 'when states justify their interventions they are drawing on and articulating shared values and expectations held by other decision-makers and other publics in other states'. This is an attempt to 'connect ones actions to standards of justice or . . . to standards of appropriate and acceptable behavior'. State leaders may of course display double-standards. However, the fact that states 'may violate international norms and standards of right conduct that they themselves articulate', should not deter us from looking at aggregate behaviour and 'seeking patterns that correspond to notions of right conduct over time'.[15]

Our study follows this reasoning, but seeks broad regularities in what is perceived as right conduct. This reflects the principal focus on the discourse of a single state, Russia, and its interaction with other powers during just two decades (1991–2012). In the case of Russia the process of articulating shared values and expectations mainly has engaged top decision-makers and sometime elites rather than the wider public. Finnemore investigates humanitarian intervention, as well as norm contestation and change, over a much longer time period. Her findings show that the consensual basis of certain norms has been challenged by others and especially by humanitarian claims.[16] The discourse we assess involves a wider typology of interventions during a narrower time frame. We also explore the grey area, or transitional process, between norms and customary law. We appraise a variety of legal claims to justify action, for example, ones based on new understandings of the preconditions for self-defence.

Change in both norms and customary law is a discursive process. Contested interpretations are played out and compete on the international stage for the benefit of wider audiences and to persuade them, most prominently in the UN Security Council. This body is not just a decision-making body but also 'a key venue for deliberation and justificatory discourse—a place where the rules about the use of force are defined, debated, interpreted and reinterpreted'. Deliberation on the basis of agreed standards injects some impartial argumentation into the process, at least slightly mitigating calculations of national interest and vote-trading or buying.[17]

Yet the discourse of the Security Council, which we will study closely, clearly does not express a competition just driven by logic, reason or jurisprudence, since it is underpinned by political and state interest. The playing field is far from level, moreover, although Security Council veto rights have some levelling effect between the privileged five permanent member states. Norms and customary law evolve discursively in an environment where major powers wield particular influence and may exercise coercion. They hope to attract and often succeed in attracting other states to their claims over what is appropriate, legal, and indeed legitimate and their persuasiveness often reflects their political clout.

That said it remains difficult for states to challenge established parameters over the use of force. Even powerful states struggle to advance claims which operate at the expense of basic principles of state sovereignty and non-intervention (which we might also regard as comprising collections of norms).[18] They need to take account of not only the reactions of other states but also the possible backlash on their own interests and on their own state immunity of such claims in the future. This is demonstrated by the way the US under the administrations of George W. Bush eventually reined back its claims over military pre-emption.

This confirms that the process of justification over interventions, even if cast in legal terminology, or the language of emerging norms, is fundamentally political, that norms and customary law develop in a political context.

Therefore the political response to interventions and the politics of the discursive process around them are important subjects of analysis in many of the ensuing chapters. They help provide a thick narrative for understanding normative and legal evolution in the post-Cold War era.

For our study of state discourse around interventions there is a politically consequential legal distinction between *jus ad bellum* (justice to resort to war) and *jus in bello* (justice in war). In contemporary international law the former represents the justifications states offer for resorting to the use of force against other states, which should essentially be articulated at the time of that action or before it, and should not be in the form of *ex post facto* rationales. We study Russian legal justifications of this kind and normative justifications, as well as Russian responses to the justifications advanced by other major powers. In contrast, *jus in bello* legal claims, which are not our concern, refer to the body of humanitarian law applied to state conduct in war. Exceptionally, however, we consider Russian conformity to such law in Chechnya for the broader insights it offers on Moscow's attitude to the use of force and sovereignty.

As explained, this volume focuses on the justificatory discourse before and at the start of interventions, to assess legal and normative claims, rather than on later efforts to recraft these initial justifications. Then the Russian political and strategic responses in each case are analysed. We acknowledge that the evolution of norms and customary law can be influenced by the state practice of intervention and other studies may be consulted for insights on such influences.[19] Space restricts us, however, to refer only briefly to the operational content of interventions and the way the conduct of operations has been rationalized and justified. The state practice of intervention becomes more relevant for our analysis in those cases when there has been a UN Security Council mandate: in the Gulf, Afghanistan, and Libya.[20] Russia has argued, as we show, that strict consistency with such mandates, as interpreted in Moscow, is required for the continued legality and legitimacy of the unfolding operations.

This leaves the questions of whose discourses and for whom. The justifications we study are most clearly present in the discourse of state leaders, senior diplomats, and leading politicians; it is an elite communication. The inter-subjective understandings that develop or are contested are ones essentially between different nations' political and foreign policy elites. They form an 'interpretative community' over those aspects of law and norms we address. However, three caveats should be noted.

First, conceptions of appropriateness and right conduct among foreign policy decision-makers are influenced by the wider social and political milieu of their states. This has been true for Russia, especially during periods of active domestic political struggle (the Gorbachev period and the early 1990s). So it can be revealing to study the opinions of various specialists and opinion-formers on appropriate conduct in relation to the interventions analysed. Nevertheless, detailed or legally framed debates on relevant topics have remained confined mostly to limited circles within Russia and usually have been confidential. These tendencies increased as the Russian state became more rigid and centralized under President Putin. The approach we adopt, therefore, focuses more on the discourse of the Russian leadership than on the input of broader domestic political constituencies.

Secondly, the discourse may deliberately be intended to have a variety of separate or overlapping audiences—domestic state, foreign state peer groups, regional as well as global. It may also be aimed at particular groups of allies or subsets of states in the international community. This can generate inconsistencies or contradictions in the argumentation, which should not simply be dismissed as double-standards. Third, the legal justifications and principles favoured by leaders cannot be divorced from wider conceptions of position, status, and recognition within the international system. This is an important consideration for Russia, which we develop later.

The challenge of legitimacy

As observed previously, justifications in terms of normative principles generally accepted in international society and as customary law, are advanced by states seeking legitimacy for their interventions. Legitimacy in this sense 'is what people accept because of some normative understanding or process of persuasion' based on justification and reason-giving. This is critical even if normative acceptance and the process of justification are often based on law, including 'the lawfulness of a legally-structured constitutional order within which day to day politics takes place'.[21]

If the role of normative understanding is accepted, other means of assessing the legitimacy of the use of force in international politics appear insufficient in themselves: adherence to the provisions of international treaties and conventions (drawing on public international law); or moral criteria (drawing on international ethics).[22] Moreover, the emergence of norms and customary law itself is inherently political. They arise out of contested discourses between major states and are influenced by disparities in power between these states. So our study addresses the politics of international law rather than the interpretation of treaty law, recognized standards in international society rather than moral principles, as well as the political contexts to the interventions examined.

For this study legitimacy is considered as it is traditionally conceived in the disciplines of international relations and international law, as an issue among *states*. The analysis does not follow the more recent normative literature which focuses the legitimacy debate on the relationship between citizens and international or supranational organizations.[23] Anyway, taking domestic factors into account, it has become problematic since the early 2000s to identify transnational norm diffusion at the societal level or transnational societal consensus in Russia. Greater political centralization of the Russian state has been accompanied by decreasing citizen participation in politics (at least until 2012). Another claim in recent literature is that perceptions of the legitimacy of global norms and rules partly depend on fairness in the distribution of costs and benefits domestically within states.[24] Although this could offer insights for a broader study of Russian interaction with global norms, norms related to interventions have not raised such domestic distributive pressures for the Russian authorities.

There remain contentious debates over how states perceive legitimacy with respect to the use of force.[25] The proposition that serious tension has grown between legality and legitimacy is particularly controversial. The argument has been made that the international provisions related to force in the UN Charter are inadequate to deal with contemporary problems, as revealed by the furore around the 1999 Kosovo and 2003 Iraq interventions. This has given rise to the fundamental question of whether the use of force might be assessed within some alternative, non-legal framework comprising principles of international legitimacy.[26]

A further step is expressed in demands that the exercise of power and the workings of international institutions 'should be subject to appropriate standards of democratic legitimacy', that is standards applied within liberal democratic states.[27] This amounts to a strong challenge to the procedural legitimacy of established institutions, especially the United Nations. The lines here are drawn since procedural legitimacy, that is legitimacy founded on generally accepted principles of 'right process', in this case the process by which a decision to use force is made, conforms naturally with pluralist notions of international society.[28] Pluralism, in the form expressed by states such as Russia and China (as described below) has cherished the minimal regulation offered by the UN, especially the foundational principles of the UN Charter system.

One response to this debate would be to observe that even with some non-legal framework assessing the use of force, legitimacy would still be sought through discursive efforts, as analysed in this volume. It would require the persuasion of others about right and appropriate actions or rules, through the language of claim and counter-claim which arguably occurs most prominently and authoritatively in the UN Security Council.[29] This is a politicized activity, but is expressed through presenting normative principles. To evaluate such legitimacy, therefore, it would remain relevant to focus on the identification of norms.

More fundamentally, Clark makes a powerful case that legality should not be set against legitimacy as alternative variables, since there can be no separate legitimacy scale of values and legality forms no more than one of the elements of which legitimacy is composed, alongside morality and constitutionality.

Constitutionality broadly forms the political constraints voluntarily entered into in international society, through conventions as well as informal understandings. Legitimacy then represents a composite. It is necessarily political and dynamic, as well as being influenced by distributions of power.

This is expressed well in the function of collective legitimization offered by the UN. Clark argues that this is not mainly a matter of legality, though international law is involved. Rather the core elements of UN legitimization are its *collective* nature (the need for consensus) and *political* aspects (the arbitration between interests and multiple, often contested, norms). The challenge is to reconcile legality, morality, and constitutionality and 'legitimacy encapsulates that political perception of where the balance lies at any one time'.[30] We study this process of political accommodation and contestation, especially Russia's involvement, in relation to different interventions.

Finally, we could note that in relation to the triad of legality, morality, and constitutionality, morality features little in Russian debates. Russian discourse equates legitimacy often with lawful conduct in terms of the legal system. But it has conceived of legitimacy especially as conduct in compliance with a legally structured constitutional order, as expressed in the UN Charter system. For Moscow this has been essentially about 'who makes the rules'—a matter of utmost concern. Constitutional orders may be defined by shared agreements about the principles and rules of order; authoritative limits on the exercise of power; and the entrenchment of these rules in a wider political system.[31] In all these respects Russia has emphasized constitutionalist procedures in the operation of the global system. This is claimed to offer general benefits, but is consistent with the political goal of constraining US hegemony. Meanwhile, Moscow has sought to cultivate an order more hierarchical than collective within the CIS regional order.

SOURCES OF RUSSIAN INFLUENCE

Cold War era Soviet attitudes and approaches to the use of force and military intervention mattered greatly for the stability of international society and the bipolar world order. After the collapse of Soviet superpower did Russian positions on these issues continue to reverberate in the international community? During the 1990s Russia suffered a sharp decline in many dimensions of international influence, However, this study argues that Moscow has retained significant leverage over the legal and normative regulation of force, not only within its neighbourhood but in the international system at large. Studies to date have focused on aspects of Russian involvement in the conflicts of the 1990s in the CIS region. They have neglected the 'Russia factor' as an influence on law and norms around the major Western-led military interventions.

Russia above all has continued to impact on global rule-making through its 'top table' presence as a permanent member of the UN Security Council. This gives Moscow leverage and the blocking power of its potential veto. There exists an 'anticipatory veto' effect, which has enabled Russia to engage in vigorous political bargaining with other P5 states. Russia has maintained a presence also in key groupings for regional crisis management, such as the Contact Group for the Middle East, the Four-Party talks on the Korean Peninsula, and the Six-Power talks on the Iranian nuclear programme.

Moscow has sought to persuade and argue its case about the appropriateness of military force within these forums; this is their discursive function. However, Russian claims have leant on Russia's continued status as one of the two principal global nuclear heavyweights, as the signatory (inherited from the USSR) of the Conventional Forces in Europe (CFE) agreement and of Soviet era and post-Soviet nuclear arms treaties, and as the possessor of one of the world's largest (if decaying) inventories of conventional arms. Since the early 2000s Russia may also have derived structural power indirectly through its position as a globally influential, and within parts of its neighbourhood regionally dominant, energy exporter.

In the global political bargaining around military interventions, moreover, Russia's Eurasian geographical location and political heritage have provided singular leverage in post-Soviet conflict zones. Its Central Asian neighbourhood and proximity to the Middle East have also offered the means to influence scenarios for forceful action in Afghanistan and Iran. Furthermore, Moscow has relied on traditional ties with states such as Serbia, Iraq, Iran, and Syria, dating back to Soviet years, buttressed in some cases with more contemporary arms trade. Russia has used such ties to claim special relations to influence these states or to mediate between them and the wider international community. These are all states which have experienced or feared Western-led military interventions. Finally, Russia's geographic proximity to unstable regions, or responsibility for such regions in the case of the North Caucasus, has provided Moscow with access and a sense of entitlement in debates on the use of force linked to the global campaign against transnational terrorism.

Russia has also mattered in debate and policy on the use of force because of the proactive political and discursive role it has projected, for much of the period since 1991, as a bulwark of the traditional legal order centred on the UN Charter framework. This role was rather muted in the early to mid-1990s, as well as during 2001–3 when Moscow sought to reposition itself in the mainstream of the 'war on terror' and even inclined towards American thinking on military pre-emption. Otherwise Russia has tended to outflank China as the Security Council member most insistent in the defence of a pluralist, sovereignty-focused view of international order (as explained further below).

With mounting self-confidence in the mid-2000s, the Russian leadership campaigned against American and NATO 'hegemony' and condemned their efforts to appropriate UN authorization for the use of force. For many both in Russia and Western states, the vigour of this campaign restored more than a trace of the East–West Cold War era polarity. It seemed difficult to envisage shared understandings among major powers about norms to justify intervention, drawing on universalist principles or new conceptions of legitimacy which sidestep traditional legal prohibitions. However, to identify the room for manoeuvre, scope for agreement, and variation in this apparent normative rift a deeper analysis of Russian as well as Western discourse and policy is required.

Russian decision-making

This study often uses the shorthand, 'the USSR', 'Russia', or 'Moscow', for those representing the official policy of the Soviet and Russian state. However, this is not an undifferentiated, unitary state. As previously noted, in certain periods in Moscow legal or normative positions and political responses to interventions have been influenced by vigorous political debate between domestic elites and institutional interests. This is the case especially with the build-up to the Gulf War in 1990, CIS conflicts in the early 1990s, and responses to NATO's campaign against Serbia in 1999.[32] These debates have broadened Russia's 'interpretative community' on law and norms.[33]

In contrast, during the Putin and Medvedev presidencies in the 2000s the Russian leadership was more determined itself to shape domestic public and elite attitudes to the use of force abroad. This could be attempted through increased political centralization and control of the Russian state, as well as media management. In this period, therefore, it is the perspective and discourse at the apex of the decision-making structure, especially that of the president (and the Foreign Minister as reflecting presidential opinion), about appropriate or lawful international conduct that has real salience. At the same time this presidential perspective, and the normative basis it represents, is unlikely to be stable and consistent over time if it is not rooted domestically in a wider elite consensus.

Russian leaders rely on expertise in formulating such legal and normative positions, as well as in developing their broader policy around interventions.[34] Relevant departments of the presidential administration (such as the head of the legal department) and advisers within that top body (such as the longstanding adviser on foreign policy for Putin and Medvedev, Sergei Prikhodko) are first at hand.[35] More detailed and varied expertise is available in the Russian Foreign Ministry and its various departments.

For example, the justifications and legal claims presented by Russia and foreign states in the Security Council are likely to be scrutinized in the ministry's International Organizations and Legal departments, as well as the

Russian mission at the United Nations itself.[36] Sergei Lavrov (appointed in 2004), the Russian Foreign Minister most skilled in debate on international legal issues, previously spent a decade as Russia's UN representative. However, in the Russian system the Foreign Minister and Ministry essentially implement rather than devise policy. They are responsible for the conduct of Russian relations with other states, but may have to put the best diplomatic face *ex post facto* on decisions beyond their control and not of their choosing.

The practice of Russia's own interventions and assessments of Western interventions naturally have drawn on professional security and military policy expertise. The Russian Security Council is available for the president to consult (he chairs this body). Russian security agencies are influential, especially the Foreign Intelligence Service (SVR), since they can gather and channel specialized information and have direct access to the president, especially during Putin's presidencies. The Russian Ministry of Defence and General Staff, particularly its Main Intelligence Directorate (GRU), have been important sources of analysis and expertise and significant influences on Russian approaches to interventions.[37]

Arguably a stronger Russian military input in framing policy reduces perceived constraints on the use of force. Detailed research on Russian statements during 1998–2008 has found that 'although military elites are significantly less likely than political elites to embrace an interventionist foreign policy agenda, they also display attitudes that are considerably more permissive to the use of force as an instrument of foreign policy'.[38] We show later, for example, how a Russian military interest in the notion of military pre-emption seeped into policy statements during 2002–3, even if this complicated Russia's broader foreign policy stance. However, overall in the 2000s the 'siloviki' elite in the 'power ministries', which gained political prominence at the centre of the Russian state, was drawn from the Russian security services, rather than the professional military.

RUSSIAN PLURALISM IN INTERNATIONAL SOCIETY

The preceding discussion on the principles of legitimacy and the constraints of law reflects the tensions which divide the pluralist and solidarist variants of international society as framed by English School theorists.[39] These alternatives involve competing claims about the 'thickness' of the normative content of international society. For solidarists this content is quite thick, in the sense that the degree of solidarity between states over norms, rules, and institutions is rather developed. Solidarists contend that individual human beings are members of international society and are viewed as subjects of international law. This understanding is reflected in the human-oriented 'universal values' built into the foreign policy agendas of Western states.

Pluralists conversely perceive the solidarity over international norms, as well as rules and institutions, as significantly 'thinner'. They recognize only rather minimal norms, especially those codified conservatively by international law and reciprocal rules like non-intervention, which enable the orderly coexistence and competition of states. From this perspective the consensus that underpins international society is procedural rather than substantive. Pluralists insist that states not individuals occupy the centre ground of international society.[40] This is expressed in the Russian emphasis on state sovereignty, non-intervention, and territoriality.

The alternative trajectories of solidarism and pluralism are reflected in core controversies about intervention, especially whether there exists an emerging solidarist norm justifying humanitarian intervention to protect civilian populations in internal conflicts, and what is meant by the responsibility to protect, or whether it is becoming 'legitimate for international actors to use force to promote particular forms of internal state arrangements'.[41] An international society approach, which directs attention to such questions, is used in this study to clarify the normative interplay between Russia and other major powers.

Since the late Soviet period the USSR and Russia have vacillated along a pluralist–solidarist continuum, but Russia has been positioned primarily in the pluralist camp. Towards the end of Gorbachev's rule Soviet foreign policy was distinguished by forthright solidarist and universalist language and policies. This emphasis was carried forward to some extent in the statements of Russia's new leaders during 1991–3, but was soon diluted. Since then it has largely been displaced by a reversion to the language of sovereignty and non-intervention. As regards the normative underpinnings of solidarism and pluralism, Russia appears as a somewhat *hybrid* state. It has been unwilling to position itself outside the Western, especially European, community of states and so has been reluctant to fully reject the normative language associated with it, including that related to the use of force.

Russia's qualified pluralist position has been easier to sustain in international society because of perspectives it shares with China, India, the Group of 77 developing countries and other states. Meanwhile the Western transatlantic community has not been uniformly or harmoniously solidarist over global norms or approaches to the use of force, notably during the administrations of George W. Bush. Gaps, or disagreements about use of force issues, that potentially could shape global norms in significant ways, have not only formed between the world's biggest states. There has also been a transatlantic gap and an intra-European gap.[42] This has made it easier for Russia to contest solidarist themes in international policy and has helped Moscow also to challenge the assumption that the (non-unified) West has some mandate or the legitimacy to establish the normative agenda in universalist terms, let alone to drive it forward.

The question of who should define international norms or rules emerged as a major theme in official Russian discourse after 2006. Russia insisted that it had the right itself to define what was normatively acceptable and that its voice should count seriously in global rule-making. This insistence fuelled a vociferous Russian campaign against the 'hegemonic' international order sustained by the US and NATO. Moscow evoked a world instead where privileged great powers (including Russia) collectively, and at least notionally also equally, would define the substance and normative underpinnings of the international order. This resembles the original institutional logic of the UN Security Council reaffirmed and writ large in the contemporary international political setting.

From its pluralist perspective Russia has presented international law as a source of stability in this contested normative environment. Like other states it understands that material and reputational costs may be attached to non-compliance with widely held norms of international conduct as with international law. Yet Russian leaders tend to emphasize the obligatory nature of international legal demands and legal prohibition. They talk in terms of fixed legal principles and the UN Charter system. Moscow is certainly aware, however, that customary international law is not static but evolves and that this happens in a political context. The sense of obligation to legal rights and duties ultimately 'is developed in an international political process involving instrumental, normative, and ideographic reasoning and action by states'.[43]

The influence of instrumental motivations means that Russian state practice, as that of other major states, may be selective in its interpretation and application of law. But such action involves costs and as for other states it is not in the Russian interest to do this too much. Instrumentalism clearly influences Russian legal arguments in the cases of intervention we study. For example, it pervaded Russia's position in 2008 in the clash with Georgia. The contested legal discourse in these cases is important, however, in adapting or constraining legal precepts and the sense of obligation felt by states, including Russia, towards them.

It can be argued, however, that for Russia a synergy has developed between law and particular notions of international and state order. As regards international order, Moscow traditionally has not viewed international law in terms of a framework of responsibility (except rather briefly during Gorbachev's leadership), although Russian diplomats sometimes use the language of international responsibilities. One question is how far a Soviet era tendency remains, that is to regard international law as codifying attributes of structural power in the international system, including the preservation of Russian (and inherited Soviet) gains. Russia's robust defence of the authority of the UN Security Council and its veto rights could be interpreted in this light.

Secondly, we should note Russia's preoccupation with its own state structure. Since the early 1990s Russia has tried to interpret international law and use its Security Council membership to counteract human-focused normative universalism where this is seen potentially as challenging its own state and political order. Since the end of that decade Moscow has wielded the principle of non-intervention more explicitly as a shield against foreign involvement in Russian domestic state order. Russia has explicitly rejected American normative claims about its role as an instrument of democratic change in the international system.

The Russian focus (shared with China) on the UN Charter framework as indispensable in rule-making seems starkly at odds with any suggestion that coalitions of democratic states possess sufficient legitimacy to justify the use of force in cases where support of the Security Council permanent five is not forthcoming. Nor does the Russian preoccupation with sovereignty, shared by many other non-Western states, dovetail with claims that democratic governance and human rights should be central to a new standard of international legitimacy. Such claims give rise to the image of an exclusive club of liberal democratic states, a club denied to Russia.

REGIONAL, GLOBAL, AND DOMESTIC ORDERS

An important hypothesis of this book is that the Russian view of global norms and law related to military intervention interacts in significant ways with conceptions of regional and domestic state order. Here we outline the argument.

Norms, as inter-subjective standards of appropriate behaviour, form shared assessments. How widespread should the assessment be shared among states before it can be designated as a norm? Certain norms may command agreement in a significant part of the international community of states, but not be necessarily global and so may or may not be shared for example by Russia. Where such norms are contested, this signifies that they are only partly incorporated in international society and therefore lack confirmation as a global norm. If a norm is weak, arguably its domain may be confined to a region. Or it may be promoted, defined, and interpreted for that region by a regionally preponderant or hegemonic power. That regionally focused (and recognized) norm may be inconsistent with other norms that claim or seek global recognition but have been accepted so far by only part of the international community of states.

These questions suggest that our previous discussion of norms simply as emerging and sometimes contested emerging *global* standards of conduct is insufficient. It is also necessary to consider the way major states' commitment to global standards may be influenced by standards of conduct defined within and for a region, where these exist. There is also the question of how far states accept that their own regional order can be shaped by global order normative evolution. They may try to reinterpret how such norms apply to their region or use other ways to selectively resist such 'external' constraints.

This volume analyses interventions in the region of the former Soviet Union. It is a region defined by varying degrees of Russian preponderance and normative commonality, though whether those norms have arisen more consensually or coercively can be debated. It is a fluid regional order, which Moscow often has referred to as the 'near abroad' or (excluding the Baltic States) the 'CIS space'. We suggest this order has been structured hierarchically, but has reflected fluctuating levels of Russian influence since 1991. We pose the question whether the norms accepted by Russia and other CIS states, particularly those related to the use of force, have been shaped by this regional order or have evolved separately within it.

It is reasonable to hypothesize that Russia's sovereignty-focused pluralist stance towards the global system at least partly reflects Russia's relatively weak position in the distribution of global power. Could the specific power hierarchy in the CIS region, which favours Russia, be reflected then in a more interventionary Russian approach in this regional order, buttressed by normative and treaty principles mainly defined by Moscow?

Moscow may seek (domestically, among CIS states and wider afield) approval for or assent to principles to legitimate aspects of its policy towards CIS states related to the use of force, for example mandates for Russian-style peacekeeping or the protection of Russian citizens abroad. We may question, however, whether these actually represent cases of regionally defined norms seeking wider international recognition.

Could Russian claims around these areas of policy, as we describe in later chapters, imply instead that Moscow is thinking in terms of a dual normative order—global and regional? A third order could engage elements of the global and regional. In practice what these distinctions imply is that Russia, despite its pluralist rhetoric over global principles of sovereignty and non-intervention, exercises discretion whether or not to apply these principles in the CIS regional order. On the other hand, it may appeal to these principles to prevent perceived Western 'intervention' in this regional space (including the projection of a human rights focused solidarist agenda).

In this context it is interesting to consider whether the notion of a single international society, varying along a continuum from pluralism to solidarism, can be qualified and differentiated at a regional level.[44] Criteria for the use of force are unlikely to contribute much to the formation of a CIS regional international society. However, by identifying more abstractly a regional level of international society, and asking how social structures at that level interact with each other and the global level, Buzan has reframed the issue of intervention in the form of three questions.

First, how legitimate/legal within the global rules and norms is intervention in any part of the system? This forms the lowest common denominator of interstate society. Secondly, how legitimate/legal is intervention within the rules and norms of a given regional interstate society (such as the EU-Europe or, we may add, the CIS region)? Thirdly, how legitimate/legal is intervention *across* the boundary between distinctive interstate societies (here we may suggest from the West into the CIS region)? Buzan concludes that 'it is absurd to confine a discussion of the *de jure* aspects of intervention by imposing an assumption that interstate society is a single global-scale phenomenon'.[45]

The notion of separate interstate societies with distinct legal and normative characteristics resembles that of 'regional public orders'. The latter has been developed as a critique, in policy-oriented jurisprudence, of efforts to find universal norms to address questions of political or normative conflict. Borgen argues that the world is composed of 'nested public orders', various regional public orders, and at least one global public order (the UN system where the use of force is constrained by a Security Council-led managerial system). Accepting the reality of pluralism, this world is defined as multi-normative.[46] It is a world significantly influenced by the role of hegemons in different world regions (with the United States simultaneously acting as a superpower with global reach). Hegemonic states play a crucial role in defining the 'rules of the game' for state relations within their regional realm, but also seek to cultivate a belief in their legitimacy, their legitimate domination, through reference to universal norms and institutions. At the same time, it is argued, each actual or potential hegemon has a particular conception of norms that it enforces and tries to socialize others into viewing as legitimate, within its sphere of influence—a form of normative regionalism.

A further hypothesis we offer is that there exists a decisive relationship between Russian strategic priorities and normative preferences with respect to international order (CIS regional and global) and Russian perceptions of order at the domestic state level. This proposition is considered central to understanding Moscow's overall stance on military intervention and emerging global norms. In brief, the Russian state has long been preoccupied with order and the concentration of power at the domestic level, and Russia's conception of international society has strongly reflected the priority of preserving its own domestic structure of power. As MacFarlane argues, Russia has insisted on the primacy of order over justice domestically and 'its privileging of order over justice at the international level is in many respects an external projection of this internal preoccupation'.[47]

This is expressed in Moscow's pluralist emphasis on state sovereignty as a principle and its rejection of any claims that external actors have a right to shape or judge that domestic state order, whether in relation to the conflict in Chechnya or Russian political structure. Russian leaders are loath to accept that 'traditional international law' (or the 'law of nations') is being displaced by some 'new international law' which asserts that the domestic practices of states must conform with emergent global norms of conduct. The concept of 'sovereign democracy', promulgated by Russian officials during Putin's second presidential term, expresses a statist rejection of the transference of 'external' norms to the Russian domestic order. At the same time it was used by Moscow to foster a regional public order among CIS states opposing 'external' (supposedly Western) agendas to foster 'coloured revolutions' in these states.

The Russian domestic order has another influence on the normative context to military intervention. States quite often seek to legitimize their conduct not by reference to some international or even regional standard, but in terms of their own national culture, traditions, and norms. This is true for both Russia and the United States. The debate on American exceptionalism has thrown up discourse similar to Russian claims about the policy imperatives of its 'constitutional rights', as well as about Russia's unique history, culture, and traditions, which form a constituent part of 'sovereign democracy'.

Justifications referring to national traditions or history can also reflect a sense of entitlement at the expense of other states. For example, the embedded experience of the Soviet period in the mindset of post-Soviet Russian leaders and elites seems to underlie claims for special rights or 'privileged interests' in defining appropriate Russian conduct in the CIS regional order. However, a nationally derived rationale of this kind will not easily translate into wider international legitimacy for expressed norms. It also poses the risk of clashing national narratives and claims with other states in situations of conflict.

CHAPTER STRUCTURE

The following chapters analyse the evolution of norms and customary international law related to the use of force, as expressed in military interventions, with a particular focus on Russian discourse and influence. Politics and power relations between states shape this analysis, so the chapters also explore the political and security policy context of Russian attitudes to and claims about these interventions. The chapters reveal an international landscape of contested understandings about rightful conduct, punctuated by interventions of different kinds over two decades. In this contest Russia appears sometimes but not always or consistently arrayed against Western powers.

The cases of military intervention we examine are not selected in order to identify one or more key variables to explain the process of normative change or resistance to such change. This is not possible since the cases vary in numerous ways, across different criteria. They are chosen instead to include the major military interventions since the late 1980s which have been driven by Western powers and/or Russia. The method is probabilistic.

A large body of discursive and empirical evidence is used to frame key arguments. These identify underlying perspectives and influences, in different periods and political contexts, which help explain Russian approaches to interventions and the role of norms. This requires us also to trace norms associated with the use of force more generally. However, the intention is not to focus on how far norms or customary law have constrained or enabled state behaviour before or during these interventions. This would require a significantly different research agenda.

Several major themes frame the volume and the positions the USSR and Russia have occupied within international society: divergence between pluralism and solidarism; the related tension between traditional legal principles and emerging norms; the broad juxtaposition of constitutionality and power in the international system; and the variation or interaction between Russian perceptions of order at global, regional, and domestic state levels.

Chapter 2 presents the background of the Soviet and Cold War era, when interventions and the claims surrounding them were powerfully conditioned by the structural constraints of the bipolar system. Changes under Gorbachev and the experience of the Gulf War offered a new prospect of normative convergence. Chapters 3 to 5, however, reveal stark contradictions as well as substantial consensus between Russia and major Western states over the rationales for major post-Cold War interventions. Chapter 3 scrutinizes the clash over humanitarian intervention in Kosovo and beyond. Chapter 4 explains how Russia acceded to expanded notions of self-defence, in the context of intervention in Afghanistan, but soon was at odds with the US over the wider demands of global counter-terrorism. Chapter 5 argues that a Russian interest in the notion of military pre-emption soon was displaced by acute concerns over the process of international rule-making with the launch of the Iraq War.

Chapters 6 and 7 address the CIS regional dimension of Russia's own interventions. We identify a longstanding Russian inclination to interpret global legal and normative standards over the use of force by assessing their potential application to CIS regional and Russian domestic order. Russian efforts to develop regional principles between CIS states for the use of force are explored in Chapter 6. Chapter 7 addresses the anomalous and controversial case of Russia's only post-1991 major use of force against a CIS state, the Russian–Georgian war of 2008. It reveals how Russian state interests and instrumentalism can sometimes quite eclipse norms and law, even if the need to justify action in terms of the latter remains.

This was ironic, given Russia's acerbic campaign against the US-led 'hegemonic international order' and its impact on rule-making. Chapter 8 examines this campaign, with other aspects of Russian global diplomacy in the 2000s, as they relate to disputes over the use of force. The chapter then analyses Moscow's discursive and political responses to two contemporary controversies: the threat of intervention in Iran and the UN mandated intervention in Libya in 2011. The latter case briefly offered some hope for normative convergence between Russia and Western powers over the legitimate use of force. This was quickly dashed. Moscow's criticism of the Libya operation has reaffirmed how problematic it is to achieve common understandings between Russia and the principal Western powers over the use of force against states.

2

The Soviet Union and Cold War Interventions

The Soviet Union and Western powers intervened in states militarily quite often and in contentious ways during the Cold War era. The global theatre for such use of force was one divided into two spheres of influence, supported by extensive alliance networks, in which the two superpowers sought to structure political and economic arrangements according to their ideologies.[1] This bipolar international system had a strong imprint on interpretations of the fundamental norms of sovereignty and self-determination, which were contested. Even when there was formal agreement on principles this was still routinely subsumed under the logic of superpower competition.

In this bipolar system the maintenance of spheres of influence and the ideologies that defined them was the *sine qua non* of international order. Each superpower regarded challenges within states to the core ideological principles of its sphere as justifying intervention to prevent political changes, especially to avert the defection of states to the opposing camp.[2] Any intervention that spilled over the sphere of influence divide was viewed as especially threatening and unacceptable. It even posed the threat of major war if it was overt, especially in the European theatre.

In contrast, much of the Third World was not firmly anchored in one sphere or another. For the rival blocs it formed a grand theatre of competition for the allegiance of the regimes and peoples of states, through both overt and covert methods.[3] Military intervention in many cases meant an effort to repress or support struggles for self-determination, depending on how the outcome was expected to affect the bipolar balance sheet. The inadequate regulation of superpower competition in the Third World, which was not constrained or intended to be constrained by the Soviet proclamation of 'peaceful coexistence', contributed to the collapse of détente in the late 1970s.[4]

However, some 'norms of competition' emerged, whether these were tacit or verbalized, and reflected patterns of restraint. Such norms developed in an evolutionary way, which codified existing practice and built upon it. They were not legal or quasi-legal, in the sense of international law, but 'analogous to a "common law" which develops through experience and offers useful precedents or benchmarks'. They formed quite simplistic rules of prudence rather than of law or morality, for example a general respect by the superpowers for each other's sphere of influence.[5] By providing some predictability in the Soviet–American relationship they could help to limit interventions that threatened to escalate to a direct inter-systemic confrontation.[6] But such norms of competition could not change the contested nature of fundamental norms of sovereignty and self-determination and the instrumental approach of the powers to them.

In this system of self-interested interventions by major powers seeking to enlarge their blocs, or at least to sustain or restore intra-bloc allegiances, there were two important effects on the basic norms applied to the use of force. First, the development and diffusion of solidarist human-focused norms was blocked; sovereignty clearly took precedence over human rights concerns. There was considerable *de facto* agreement that once states had been positioned in a particular sphere then the manner they treated their citizens was a domestic issue, that 'a state's ability to be a reliable ally maintaining peaceful relations with other states could be decoupled from its internal behaviour towards its own citizens'.[7]

Secondly, UN Charter principles on the use of force were devalued by state practice but not discarded. To be sure both superpowers rather openly defied UN Charter principles where these clashed with their wish to retain ideological and substantive hegemony in their sphere of influence. However, this deviance from the normative strictures of the UN Charter was never allowed to consolidate into a licence to intervene. In the expanding international community of states the majority of states still condemned most interventions, usually through the UN General Assembly (since Security Council member states' veto rights prevented this body from issuing collective resolutions on the most egregious interventions). Moreover, superpower interventions, even if unabashedly self-interested in motivation, were still justified by Moscow and Washington using UN Charter system claims, alongside their more ideological arguments.

For example, when the Soviet Union deployed its forces in Hungary (1956), Czechoslovakia (1968), and Afghanistan (1979) it did not rely exclusively on ideologically derived justifications such as the notorious Brezhnev Doctrine, which was centred around defence of the 'socialist commonwealth'. Moscow also claimed a legal basis for its actions by invoking the necessity of repelling aggression or external interference, and claimed that it had been invited by the lawful government. This recourse to traditional legal principles should not be dismissed out of hand, even if these Soviet claims were vitiated by the actual circumstances of the interventions and were overshadowed by ideological rationales.

Similarly the US relied on the justification of an invitation from a lawful government as the basis for intervention, along with self-defence, the rescue of citizens, and the decisions of a regional organization. This is illustrated by Washington's intervention in its Latin American zone of influence, in the Dominican Republic in 1965 and in Grenada in 1983, even if US legal claims were not convincing to most states. In the case of Grenada, eleven members of the UN Security Council and 108 members of the General Assembly deplored the American invasion as breaching fundamental principles of international law.[8] In another controversial intervention, during the closing days of the Cold War, the US justified its dispatch of troops to Panama in December 1989 by recourse to Article 51, among various other claims.[9]

The legal and normative justifications for these superpower interventions were not merely legal shadowboxing or cynical efforts to play to the gallery of global opinion among states. In the grand ideological and political contest of the time the claims of such powerful states mattered. Such claims could shape or even recast basic interpretations of principles and norms on the legitimate use of force among the wider community of states, which in turn could be used to sustain and enlarge spheres of influence.

The justificatory claims of the superpowers were also interactive. In a bipolar world neither side in reality could expect that military action by one side which flouted traditional understandings of basic international norms would be accepted as a unique scenario, rather than as a precedent or potential model for expedient use by the other side. A detailed study has shown the way the Soviet rationalization of its 1968 intervention in Czechoslovakia closely tracked the language used by the United States to rationalize its own 1965 intervention in the Dominican Republic. In this 'echo phenomenon' the superpower engaged in similar interactive verbal strategies.[10] Referring to President Lyndon Johnson's claims to legitimize intervention in the Dominican Republic, a group of American lawyers similarly referred to 'Brezhnev's promulgation of a reincarnated version of the Johnson Doctrine' to justify his own invasions.[11]

Such reciprocity between superpower doctrines on intervention was not, however, an inter-subjective process, in the sense of developing genuine shared understandings about appropriate conduct. To the extent that it occurred it was a politically expedient effort at justification through imitation. Nor is it confined to the Cold War period. Some parallel could be made with the way post-Cold War Russia eagerly adopted the American discourse on military pre-emption after 2002 (as discussed in chapter 5) to rationalize military action that it might wish to take in the future.

In 1986 the International Court of Justice (ICJ) issued an authoritative reaffirmation of legal norms governing the right to self-defence which clearly gave precedence to juridical norms over ideological and political doctrines. In the renowned case of *Nicaragua v. United States of America* the ICJ asserted, among other important findings, that it 'cannot contemplate the creation of a new rule opening up a right of intervention by one State

against another on the ground that the latter has opted for some particular ideology or political system'.[12] This was a forthright rejection of the Reagan Doctrine, expressed in a series of speeches by President Reagan and actions by the US in the 1980s, which had stipulated that 'support for [pro-US] freedom fighters is self-defense and totally consistent with the OAS and UN Charters'.[13]

The *Nicaragua* ruling equally repudiated the Brezhnev Doctrine that had been used to justify Soviet intervention in Czechoslovakia and to some extent in Afghanistan in 1979. The ruling was timely since it was just in 1986 that the Soviet leadership began to advance its New Political Thinking, which eventually diluted the ideological basis of Soviet policy and replaced it with a growing emphasis on international legal regulation based on universalist principles shared with Western states.

IDEOLOGY AND SOVIET INTERVENTIONS

Soviet ideology should be understood primarily as a cognitive framework influencing policy, rather than as the prime determinant and motivation of Soviet intervention behaviour. This behaviour to a considerable extent reflected *persistent factors* linking Tsarist, Soviet, and Russian policies, which have shaped their strategic culture and understanding of international order.[14] Such factors of continuity in strategic, historical, and psychological outlook help explain, for example, why quite soon after the end of the Cold War differences multiplied between Russia and Western states over intervention in regional conflicts, although the new Russian foreign policy was pragmatic rather than ideologically framed.

To reinforce the point that ideology as such did not drive Soviet and Russian approaches to intervention, we could refer back to the preoccupation of the Russian state with order and the concentration of power at the domestic level. This enduring focus on domestic state order, which conditioned the development of attitudes on sovereignty, was fuelled by the historical experience of interventions by other states in Tsarist Russia and the USSR Russian and Soviet leaders have rather persistently feared potent challenges from other states. But they have also focused on the challenges that could arise to the internal structures of their state from within, as well as the possibility that domestic uprisings could be provoked by foreign states.

These preoccupations also have had a regional expression. For the USSR, regional order in the Cold War era, as in earlier periods of Russian history, 'was perceived to be predicated on the internal arrangements of states'. Ultimately this explains the record of Soviet intervention in Eastern Europe to sustain pro-Soviet regimes and its readiness to abuse the sovereign rights of states located here, even as Moscow has insisted on recognition of the sovereign rights of the USSR itself.[15]

Ideology as a cognitive framework

During the Cold War Marxist-Leninist ideology not only shaped Soviet justificatory rhetoric around its military interventions, but more basically as a cognitive framework influenced the Soviet world view. The universalist objective of world proletarian revolution, which vindicated and could be advanced by forceful means, might be viewed as a basic justice-based challenge to international order. On the other hand, 'it differed substantially from what later became liberal solidarism in its emphasis on classes rather than individuals and its devaluation of political as compared with social and economic rights'.[16] Moreover, we have noted that in the self-interested sphere of influence system defined by the Cold War the diffusion of human-focused solidarist norms anyway was blocked.

The Marxist-Leninist world view reinforced the constraints on what remained a 'thin' international society during the Cold War. Moscow referred formally to international law, but its approach tended towards legal positivism, that is 'a readiness to accept only that to which agreement was manifested', and 'this practice limited the creation of customary norms'.[17] In the wider frame as well there was no chance of developing any substantive shared normative framework with Western states, beyond tacit norms of competition as discussed above, before the late 1980s.[18]

It was a core assumption of Marxism-Leninism that capitalist and socialist states were locked in an epic hostile struggle. Once the USSR proclaimed the rather deceptively termed doctrine of 'peaceful coexistence' following the death of Stalin, Moscow no longer considered war between these systems of states as inevitable. However, the outcome was still viewed as foreordained—socialist victory. The global 'correlation of forces', a distinctly Soviet concept, admitted no other outcome.[19] Therefore 'societal' cooperation between the competing systems of states could only be tactical and temporary. Ultimately, as MacFarlane argues, Soviet participation in the primary institutions of international society, such as the balance of power, international law, and diplomacy, remained expedient and had little intrinsic normative value.[20]

Marxist-Leninist ideology provided categories and a discursive framework that could be used to craft specific justifications for Soviet military interventions.[21] This was less obviously done in the case of Soviet relations with non-socialist states where Moscow formally upheld the (traditional) non-intervention norm. However, the USSR's *interpretation* of self-determination in the Third World was such that any state that hinders the movement of a people towards self-determination was held to be acting in an illegal manner, while one that assists such a movement was acting legitimately (though in practice these determinations were qualified by the competitive dynamic between the superpowers). This affected which newly formed governments Moscow recognized as legitimate and therefore as competent to issue invitations for interventions (such as to protect them from external aggression or to restore order).

In Soviet relations with socialist states ideologically crafted justifications framed the discourse around interventions. A core element was an effort to claim for socialism exclusive rights over the principle of sovereignty. This was done by postulating a direct relationship between 'external' or international sovereignty and the location of internal sovereignty (i.e. domestic political supremacy, or from the Soviet Marxist perspective, class rule). The Soviet Union equated genuine or 'people's sovereignty' with proletarian supremacy, which in practice meant rule of the Communist parties of the USSR and of Eastern Europe. Any threat to Communist rule, *ipso facto*, then became a threat to the genuine sovereignty of the people.[22]

This had the effect of creating a distorting mirror, so that 'what may look like a *prima facie* case of aggression (e.g. a military attack upon another socialist state) is said to be a defensive altruistic action undertaken out of respect for the sovereignty principle'.[23] Not surprisingly, the politically malleable concept of 'people's sovereignty' carried little conviction outside the Soviet bloc, particularly since there was no evidence that the sovereign 'people' were ever consulted on decisions affecting their sovereignty. The concept was expressed in justifications for Soviet interventions in Eastern Europe and Afghanistan, which consolidated a Soviet doctrine of limited sovereignty in its immediate sphere of influence.

SOVIET INTERVENTIONS IN EASTERN EUROPE AND AFGHANISTAN

The first major step in developing this doctrine was during the large-scale Soviet military intervention in Hungary in November 1956. This was justified by Moscow, probably as window dressing for other states, on two traditional legal grounds. First, the USSR claimed that it had been invited in (though there certainly was no such invitation by the national leaders of the government headed by Imre Nagy who might have been empowered to make such a request). Secondly, Soviet leaders claimed it was permissible under the Warsaw Pact Treaty as an act of collective self-defence (although the Warsaw Pact clearly contemplated attack only from the outside and not 'internal' threats, and needed an explicit request by the Hungarian government to come into force).[24]

However, already in 1956 Moscow claimed that military action had been needed to defend socialist achievements. Soviet officials came to describe this as a principle of 'socialist internationalism'. It was given fuller expression after the USSR and some of its Warsaw Pact allies invaded Czechoslovakia in August 1968. In this case Moscow again unconvincingly referred to the right of self-defence under Article 51 of the UN Charter and an alleged invitation by the Czech authorities. But the invasion of Czechoslovakia was also justified in Moscow more specifically as an expression of the duties and rights of proletarian internationalism, mandating Soviet 'fraternal military assistance'.[25]

This rationale for intervention, as further developed in several official statements, was branded in the West as the Brezhnev Doctrine. Its essence, expressed in an address to the UN General Assembly in October 1968 by Soviet Foreign Minister Andrei Gromyko, was that 'the socialist states cannot and will not tolerate a situation which infringes upon the vital interests of socialism and encroaches upon the inviolability of the boundaries of the socialist commonwealth'. Next month Soviet leader Leonid Brezhnev confirmed that 'a threat to socialism in [one] state' was viewed as 'a threat to the security of the entire socialist commonwealth'.[26]

The 'socialist commonwealth', as an ideologically defined Soviet legal and normative space, equated with the Soviet East European sphere of influence or security zone. But actual Soviet coercive control over East European states and the effective 'unity' of the socialist camp varied, as therefore did the effective geographic application of the Brezhnev Doctrine. Some East European Communist leaders made the political risks of military intervention too high for the USSR, especially where they could credibly threaten to lead their nation to war in defence of its sovereignty.[27] The interventions Moscow actually undertook, once Communist-led 'people's democracies' had been established, were aimed essentially at preserving the status quo in terms of domestic political arrangements. For the USSR this was an imperative for regional order, although the real strength of Soviet hierarchical control in that order varied from state to state.

In contrast to Eastern Europe, according to the unwritten superpower code over spheres of influence, Soviet intervention in Afghanistan in December 1979 was anomalous.[28] This was the first direct large-scale Soviet military intervention outside the East European security zone since the 1940s. However, although Soviet motivations for this intervention varied, Moscow had important similar concerns to the Czechoslovakia case.[29]

In both cases local regimes had become politically unstable and unpredictable, which Soviet leaders believed threatened their regional strategic influence (although in Afghanistan deeper Soviet influence only dated back to the 1978 coup by the People's Democratic Party of Afghanistan). Moscow perceived the Afghan and Czech leaders just before the interventions, Hafizullah Amin and Alexander Dubček respectively, as both charting independent courses in domestic politics, heedless of Soviet advice, and Moscow feared this could spill over into their foreign policies[30]

To justify its invasion of Afghanistan, Moscow called again on traditional legal principles as the first line of defence: Article 51 of the UN Charter, together with the December 1978 bilateral treaty of friendship, good-neighbourliness, and cooperation, as well as an invitation by the official authorities in Kabul. Yet the request for Soviet military help came after Soviet troops had arrived and overthrown Amin and his government. Therefore the invitation and the 1978 treaty were irrelevant in terms of legitimizing the intervention (and anyway 'collective self-defence' would not have required a treaty relationship). That this was legal window-dressing is only reinforced by the fact that during the Cold War the USSR had always officially supported a narrow interpretation of the term 'armed attack' in Article 51, and therefore of self-defence. So the Soviet leadership should not have relied on it even had there been foreign interference before December 1979 in the form of armed bands and aid to the opponents of the Kabul regime.

World opinion outside the Soviet bloc was not at all convinced by Soviet claims. A draft UN Security Council resolution, which condemned the presence of foreign troops in Afghanistan and called for their immediate removal, received thirteen votes for and two against (the USSR and the German Democratic Republic) and was duly vetoed by Moscow. In the emergency special session of the UN General Assembly that followed on 14 January 1980, 104 governments voted resoundingly in favour of a similar resolution (with eighteen against and eighteen abstentions). Led by the non-aligned members of the General Assembly, the large majority of world states that voted denounced the 'foreign armed intervention' as inconsistent with fundamental UN Charter principles.[31] This raised the question whether Cold War alignments were shifting, as Third World states appalled by the Soviet action drew closer to America.

Such fulsome condemnation in the non-aligned world, in addition to China and the Western camp, was likely to have been a factor dissuading any expansive Soviet ideological claims to support the occupation of Afghanistan, even by those in Moscow who still believed that the global 'correlation of forces' was tilting in favour of the USSR and its allies. Many in Western capitals, fearing the worst, did indeed view the invasion as a further calculated expression of socialist internationalism, as an 'apparent Soviet decision to give global and universalist application to the so-called Brezhnev Doctrine'.[32] Yet in the 1980s the USSR did not characterize its intervention in Afghanistan in this way. Had Moscow done so, it would have posed an open challenge to the sovereignty of a wide set of Third World states. The USSR certainly called for the defence of the revolutionary cause in Afghanistan. But this was done with growing frustration as it found itself mired in its most protracted and damaging Cold War counter-insurgency war.

Ultimately, the Afghan intervention proved to be *sui generis*, rather than the precursor of renewed efforts to extend the parameters of the Soviet bloc by force, and in the long run it contributed to pressures that led to the dissolution of the USSR itself.[33] Well before this collapse of the bipolar order, however, once Mikhail Gorbachev took office as general secretary of the Soviet Communist Party in 1985, the legitimacy of selective military intervention as a Soviet policy instrument began to be reappraised fundamentally. A new approach to regional conflicts was gradually adopted, with a serious search for an exit strategy from Afghanistan as its centrepiece.[34]

GORBACHEV, A NEW UNIVERSALISM, AND NORMATIVE CONVERGENCE

The New Political Thinking on foreign and security policy that began to unfold after Gorbachev's accession to power brought with it the prospect of revolutionary transformation of the bipolar ideological confrontation. The tendency on both sides to subsume norms of conduct, including UN Charter principles, to the logic of the Cold War spheres of influence, gradually eroded and a new form of Soviet universalist, globalist thinking offered normative convergence with Western states in a manner inconceivable since the brief high hopes for cooperation under the UN system (at least among some Western leaders) were dashed in the early post-war years.

The determinants of the New Thinking have been exhaustively studied, as part of efforts to explain the end of the Cold War and the challenge this represents to structural theories of international relations. To identify changing norms for the purposes of this volume it is not essential to determine the extent to which the New Thinking motivated key policy changes, at least in offering a new de-ideologized cognitive framework for them, or simply rationalized them for various instrumental reasons. There is significant evidence that ideas acted to socialize Soviet leaders (rather than just to sell their policies) and to persuade them to assume new identities and new policies. Regardless of Soviet motivations, however, international norms in the sense of standards of appropriate behaviour that create permissive conditions for action, did seem to evolve remarkably under Gorbachev.[35]

The policy changes associated with this, as regards the use of force, were undeniable by the end of the 1980s. These included the Soviet rejection of force to maintain Communist domination in Eastern Europe in 1989 (or to attempt to prevent the dissolution of the USSR itself in 1991), Soviet support for UN-mandated international peacekeeping, and the active Soviet search for solutions to regional conflicts, including in the Persian Gulf in 1990.[36] Such innovative policies, as expressions of a new universalist outlook in Moscow, gave substance to the discourse of New Thinking. In the late 1980s this helped to establish common ground between East and West on fundamental norms of sovereignty and non-intervention, and beyond this to offer hope for the promotion of an increasingly human-focused solidarist international order.

Gorbachev's New Thinking developed a set of interrelated premises that over time breathed new life into traditional normative constraints on the use of force, among other transformative outcomes. The foundation stone was the burial of the Manichaean Marxist-Leninist vision of irreconcilable class struggle, through a gradual process of 'de-ideologization' of international relations, as of domestic politics, in the late 1980s. This meant that inter-systemic rivalry was no longer conceived as preordained. By establishing the premise that class values should be subordinated to 'all-human' values, Gorbachev framed policies to promote global identity and solidarity instead and opened out new horizons for Soviet decision-makers. Such solidarity could be realized, for example, through disarmament and developmental goals.

These goals were also presented as expressions of a foreign policy agenda of mutual security and interdependence—concepts at the heart of the global vision of New Thinking on security. They were grounded in idealism, but also in a pragmatic recognition of the mutual vulnerability of East and West to nuclear catastrophe and the belief that the ensuing security dilemma meant that powerful states should aim at common security rather than the unilateral pursuit of security. A corollary was that the resort to force or threats of force could be regarded as neither efficacious nor legitimate as a means to resolve interstate disputes. There was also a new imperative to overcome existing military conflicts in the Third World since these posed the ever-present danger of escalation regionally and vertically to open confrontation between the nuclear powers.[37]

Debates continue over whether the new international outlook of Soviet leaders reflected the adoption of a new identity. However, a major implication was that the structural intervention expressed in the Brezhnev Doctrine and its constraints on (or reinterpretation of) sovereignty could not endure. The logic of the universalist message of all-human values promoted by Gorbachev, which was both normative and expedient, was that 'political orders that are held in place by military force are both morally illegitimate and politically unstable', and that a new framework of legitimacy based on the will of the governed should be established.[38] In essence, once intervention in Eastern Europe of the 1968 variant had been delegitimated in Soviet society, the use of force or its threat became very difficult, as events in 1989 confirmed.

This reaffirmation of the non-intervention norm in practice may have been encouraged in other ways. It has plausibly been argued that Gorbachev's interest in joining the Western 'community of nations' (reflected, for example, in the language of 'a common European home') and the gradual strengthening of civil societies in Eastern Europe inhibited the USSR from using force to stop the revolutions of 1989.[39] Moreover, Gorbachev and Foreign Minister Eduard Shevardnadze personally seemed to be fundamentally averse to the use of force. Arguably this reflected a cognitive process of learning lessons from the ongoing military interventions in the 1980s in Afghanistan, Angola, and elsewhere.[40] At the same time, the novel Soviet acceptance of human rights in Eastern Europe, or even in the USSR itself, as a subject of legitimate international attention, suggested a more fundamental process of normative evolution towards a thicker international society.

The evidence for the new Soviet universalism could also be found in attitudes to the United Nations, (traditional) international law, and collective security. The UN had been used by previous Soviet leaders as an instrument to defend and promote the rising influence and status of the USSR at Western expense and to assist the strategic denial of the non-aligned states to the Western bloc. Gorbachev in contrast came to regard the UN as the essential site for developing a cooperative, comprehensive security system, ideally based on the rule of law.

Speaking at the UN in December 1988 with more than a tinge of idealism, Gorbachev appealed for 'an accord within the UN framework on a uniform understanding of the principles and norms of international law, and their codification, taking account of the new conditions, and also the formulation of legal norms for new spheres of cooperation'.[41] Such high-flown language certainly seemed to mark out Gorbachev's ambition to overcome the normative dissonance of the Cold War and to frame new areas of legal cooperation, even if he was still striving to ensure that his rhetoric rested on a solid bedrock of support in the Soviet diplomatic and security establishments.

From 1987 specific proposals by Soviet leaders followed the rhetoric, notably those for an expanded UN role in conflict resolution and mediation, as well as for the prevention and settling of conflicts.[42] In October that year Moscow decided to meet its outstanding debts for international peacekeeping since 1973. It suggested reactivating the Military Staff Committee of the Security Council, and offered a Soviet armed forces contingent for that purpose, as well as material support and training for UN forces. The UN Security Council revived its functions in holding practical consultations over unresolved conflicts, including ones engaging the superpowers such as in Angola and Central America. The Soviet commitment to UN peacekeeping was extended through an agreement on the terms governing Soviet military withdrawal from Afghanistan. The Geneva agreement in April 1988 was assisted by the mediation efforts of the UN Secretary-General and his Under-Secretary for Special Political Affairs.[43]

The new Soviet enthusiasm for UN peacekeeping and conflict resolution in the late 1980s was a case of principles meshed in with pragmatic requirements. It reflected the Soviet decision to scale down foreign commitments, especially in costly and unsuccessful counter-insurgency wars, and to search for forms of disengagement from regional conflicts that could be presented as achievements rather than humiliations.[44] A rise in Soviet political prestige could offset a decline in Soviet status in material terms, or so it was hoped. Moreover, strategic gains could be made for the USSR not just by retrenchments where it was overextended, but through promoting a multifaceted, legally bound international order. This kind of regulation might well constrain American superpower impulses at a time of significantly declining Soviet material resources.[45]

The existence of such self-interest, however, does not vitiate the idealism expressed at the apex of the Soviet leadership—the benefits perceived from a more harmonious, positive-sum international security and political environment.

Nor does Soviet self-interest plausibly explain the choice of the more human-focused, liberal international agenda advanced under Gorbachev rather than a policy of retrenchment or scaling down of Soviet foreign policy ambitions. This new agenda included attempts to reinforce the jurisdictional authority of the International Court of Justice, an acceptance of international obligations and international scrutiny with respect to human rights in the USSR, and an exploratory readiness by some Soviet officials to consider UN involvement in resolving inter-ethnic conflicts within the USSR. Such policy shifts indicate a growing normative congruence with Western states over the balance between state sovereignty and individual rights, with potential major ramifications for understandings of extra-territorial intervention.

THE GULF WAR AND THE PROMISE OF NORMATIVE CONSENSUS

Soviet New Thinking acted as an impulse for innovative policies and created a permissive environment for major international transformations: the end of Communist rule in Eastern Europe, the dissolution of the Warsaw Pact, and the unification of Germany. However, it was not until the seminal international crisis of the 1990 Gulf War that Cold War competition was set aside sufficiently to achieve East–West consensus over the large-scale use of force in a regional theatre. This encouraged hopes at the beginning of the 1990s that common approaches to universalist principles might provide the basis for some new world order. Such hopes proved to be transitory. The Gulf War set a high-water mark for cooperation between Moscow and Western states over the restoration of international order by force. However, if this was a high point of normative congruence between the two sides, it was one built around a pluralist defence of sovereignty. In retrospect it appears as an exceptional case of response to the particularly egregious and unambiguous case of Iraqi aggression against Kuwait.

International law, justifications, and the Gulf War

The Iraqi invasion of Kuwait in August 1990 was singular as an attempt by one UN member state to terminate the sovereignty of another member state by annexation. Such action had been common in the pre-United Nations international legal system, but outlawed by the modern system represented by the UN Charter.[46] Iraq essentially offered various spurious political justifications for its action. The UN Security Council quickly rejected Iraq's claim that it had been invited to intervene by a provisional revolutionary government in Kuwait, and in Resolution 660, adopted by a vote of fourteen to one, focused on Kuwait's sovereign rights and demanded that Iraq withdraw from Kuwait immediately and unconditionally.[47] For the international community this was a case of blatant aggression in breach of an elemental rule of international order.[48]

For its part the US administration of George H. Bush from the outset deplored Iraq's blatant military aggression and violation of the UN Charter. Thereafter the US leadership rather consistently emphasized the need to respond in terms of international law and norms; this was at the core of its justificatory discourse. Bush appeared to regard it as imperative to reverse the Iraqi invasion as a threat to the foundations of global order, even if he was also motivated by American oil and economic interests.[49]

In such a clear case of Iraqi repudiation of international law, the US did not need to struggle to find a compelling legal case for military action, were Iraq to fail to comply with Resolution 660. Kuwait and its allies could have resorted to armed measures in collective self-defence against Iraq, based on the Article 51 inherent right of self-defence. In this event, in legal terms Washington could easily have opted to defend Kuwait and Saudi Arabia upon a request from their governments.[50]

However, another legal route, the one chosen, was preferable: to follow the UN Charter procedures and seek a multilateral imprimatur for war. This offered a more powerful justificatory framework and for the US promised greater international political legitimacy and more domestic support. It was the appropriate way for America to present itself as combating aggression through leading a broad international coalition with other powers and as advancing a new international order in the wake of the Cold War. Using the UN route American leaders could link force to law through an international decision-making mechanism. Moreover, it did not preclude a Plan B: if the US failed to obtain a Security Council mandate to use force, it reserved the right to fall back on the collective self-defence provisions of Article 51.

Once embarked on the UN track, what was needed to justify war was a Resolution authorizing 'all necessary means' to ensure Iraq complied with prior resolutions and a specific ultimatum date. These conditions were provided for in Resolution 678 on 29 November 1990 adopted under Chapter VII of the UN Charter. This resolution, following the passage of twelve previous resolutions on the Kuwait crisis by autumn 1990, represented a triumph for the politics of international law, and provided strong procedural legitimacy to reinforce normative legitimacy for the military offensive eventually launched by the US coalition in January 1991.[51]

Soviet views on legal claims

The Soviet legal and normative position in the crisis was crucial for this unprecedented unanimity in the Security Council. The emphasis Moscow placed on international law and the role of the Security Council reflected aspects of Gorbachev's New Thinking. So did the universalist thrust of Soviet policy in autumn 1990, and this universalism had an ardent exponent in the person of Eduard Shevardnadze, Soviet Foreign Minister until his resignation in December 1990. However, as noted later, the New Thinking also acted as a brake on the march to war and its effect was diluted by Soviet domestic policy wrangles and wider strategic concerns.

From the outset of the crisis Gorbachev was unwavering in his support of the principle of Kuwaiti sovereignty.[52] Moscow tried to channel away expectations that the US might act unilaterally to defend Kuwait, outside of collective UN action. The Soviet hope was that UN-led diplomatic pressure, sanctions, and perhaps Soviet mediation would compel Iraqi compliance with UN resolutions to avoid a track towards war. However, as Iraq flagrantly flouted successive UN resolutions between August and November 1990, the Soviet leadership came to accept that it would be legitimate for UN collective action to assume a military form.

In the space of a week in September 1990 Gorbachev shifted from a warning that 'any resort to military force is unacceptable', to issuing a joint statement with President Bush that warned Iraq of additional steps under the UN Charter since 'we must demonstrate most convincingly that aggression cannot and will not yield benefits'.[53] On 25 September, speaking on the same day as a trenchantly worded and unanimous Security Council condemnation of Iraq (Resolution 670), Shevardnadze reminded the General Assembly of the UN's 'ample powers to suppress aggression'. He warned that these 'will be exercised if the illegal occupation of Kuwait continues' and presented the challenge dramatically: unless a way is found to respond to Iraq's action 'our civilisation will be thrown back by half a century'.[54]

In the spectrum of opinion among Soviet leaders, Shevardnadze was one 'new thinker' who saw the Gulf crisis not just as a threat to core UN Charter norms, but as an opportunity for states to think beyond them. Responding to threats by the Iraqi leader Saddam Hussein, he told the UN General Assembly there was 'an urgent need to institute a new norm in international law that would declare the threat by any individual, for purposes of blackmail, of using weapons of mass destruction, hostage taking, or mass terror, to be a crime against humanity'.[55] This proposal gained no traction at the time, but to an extent it prefigured American concerns about 'rogue states' more than a decade later. The difference was that Shevardnadze placed the management of these threats squarely in a multilateral normative context.

Since Saddam Hussein refused to yield to the Security Council despite all political efforts and a flurry of Soviet diplomatic manoeuvring, the track towards the authorization of force in Resolution 678 and Soviet acquiescence with the subsequent military action unfolded with a grim logic. In the first official reaction to the outbreak of war on 17 January 1991 the new Soviet Foreign Minister Alexander Bessmertnykh reiterated Soviet support for Resolution 678. He set the tone for subsequent Soviet government statements on the core justification for war, observing how 'it was very important to avoid a precedent in which a large country swallows up another one while bearing no responsibility to the world community'.[56]

The onset of war, however, brought a new legal issue—how extensive could military operations be and remain consistent with the goal of enforcing Security Council resolutions? Already ten days into the air campaign Bessmertnykh referred to fears that the conflict was entering a grave phase. In his view it was exceeding the requirements of these resolutions, which he defined as the liberation of Kuwait, and proceeding to subject Iraq to very serious destruction.[57] The US-led coalition seemed indeed to be embarking on wider goals, beyond removing Iraq's forces from Kuwait, those of degrading Iraq's long-term military potential to make future aggression less likely, including elements of civilian economic infrastructure, and the destruction of Iraq's nuclear research facilities. It was a matter of judgement whether this exceeded the requirement of 'necessity' in the terms of Resolution 678 and in general international law.[58]

Moscow was alarmed by the expansion of targets. On 9 February Gorbachev warned the coalition that 'the logic of military operations and the nature of the military actions' were threatening to exceed the Security Council mandate.[59] Senior figures in the Soviet military establishment voiced their opinion that the destruction of non-military facilities exceeded this mandate.[60] By 28 February, when a land offensive had just routed the Iraqi army, Gorbachev's military adviser Marshal Sergei Akhromeyev noted that the UN mandate had definitely been overstepped, though he did not know whether it was 'deliberate' and pointed out that 'there are various degrees of overstepping, because war is war, and in a war you cannot measure things in inches or pounds'.[61]

A deeper Soviet concern from early in the conflict was the scenario of an occupation of Iraq and the possible adoption of regime change as an American, if not coalition, war goal. The Soviet ambassador in Ankara insisted that the future of Saddam Hussein was a matter for the Iraqi people alone and that 'the Soviet Union will not allow any of the powers involved in the conflict to attempt to put a placeman in Saddam Hussein's place'.[62] For his part Akhromeyev emphasized that an advance of US ground forces to Baghdad 'would be a direct violation of the Security Council decisions'.[63]

However, regime change was neither built into the US justificatory discourse for the war, nor into its military planning, so in the event this challenge for the legal framing of the US-led coalition's war effort did not arise (although the issue became politically controversial in the West later when Saddam Hussein brutally suppressed Kurdish and Shi'a resistance movements in Iraq). At the end of the campaign a senior Soviet official even praised the US since it had 'subordinated its military machine to the restraining supervision of the United Nations and, in the end, had halted its advance at the outer bounds of the UN mandate it had received'.[64]

Overall, the consensus between Moscow and the US-led coalition on the legitimacy of extensive military action to liberate Kuwait, vested in the resolutions of the UN Security Council, held despite severe strains. However, these strains were less about interpretation of legal norms per se, since this was an unusually clear-cut case of response to state (Iraqi) aggression, which united the Security Council in a period when Cold War barriers had been lowered. More complicated was the political management of the Soviet Union in the process that legitimized the Gulf War.

The Soviet political response to intervention in the Gulf

Soviet support for a succession of Security Council resolutions enabled President Bush to mobilize an international coalition; it helped legitimize his route to war against Saddam Hussein among the American public and the wider international community. If Moscow had vetoed any of these resolutions in the months preceding the onset of war in January 1991 this would have undermined that consensus building and could have jeopardized the overall operation. But Soviet solidarity with Western states in the Security Council was far from predetermined.

From the outset, the Soviet policy of aligning with the US-led coalition in the Gulf was fraught with difficulties. Some arose from basic precepts of Gorbachev's New Thinking: that military force had little useful role in international statecraft, that negotiated settlements and political solutions were the best response to regional crises, that the risks of military conflicts should be avoided, and that the UN and other international bodies could be used effectively to prevent the escalation of local wars. These beliefs constrained Gorbachev when deciding whether to support calls for the use of force in the Gulf, as did perhaps his receipt of the Nobel Peace Prize in October 1990. On the other hand, as noted previously, the focus on international law in New Thinking had the contrary effect, when confronted by Iraqi obduracy, of encouraging Moscow along the track towards Resolution 678.

Soviet policy was also subject to significant constraints at the level of domestic politics.[65] First, there was the effect of a post-Afghanistan syndrome in Soviet society—a distinct aversion to foreign ventures, which reflected disillusionment with the whole experience of a decade of military intervention in an intractable regional conflict.

Second, more significantly, for much of the Soviet political and military elite it was impossible to overcome the psychological legacy of Cold War bipolarity sufficiently to approve of Soviet military alignment with the US against Iraq, a country with which Moscow had long maintained close trade and military ties (although the USSR also had longstanding ties with Kuwait). Most of the Soviet military establishment in particular framed the Gulf crisis, as well as the military implications of US strategy and tactics in the war, in bipolar terms.[66] For the Soviet Communist old guard and the military, the USSR should strive to maintain its regional positions and influence and they feared the introduction of Western power into the Gulf. From this perspective Gorbachev's Gulf policy, following the sudden loss of the Warsaw Pact, was leading to the loss of Soviet power over yet another region.[67] Moscow's special Crisis Committee to monitor events in the Gulf was dominated, moreover, by doctrinaire security and defence chiefs.[68]

Both New Thinking and its counterpart, old-style competitive geopolitical thinking, could be accommodated by Gorbachev's search for peace plans to avert war in the Gulf. Gorbachev sought to delay and dilute, if not prevent, Security Council decisions permitting the use of force against Iraq in the apparent hope that alternative diplomatic pressures and UN sanctions might force Iraqi compliance.[69] Gorbachev fervently hoped to secure some diplomatic success to restore his crumbling domestic reputation, as the Soviet economy rapidly declined, although he was also driven by principled motives and genuinely seemed to wish to avert a devastating conflict with large loss of life in the Gulf. The domestic political context was reflected in Gorbachev's choice of the geopolitically minded Yevgeny Primakov as his special envoy for the Gulf, as well as in Primakov's efforts first to pre-empt coalition military action and then to halt operations before the start of the US-led ground offensive.[70] By the end of 1990 Gorbachev's room for manoeuvre over foreign policy narrowed after Shevardnadze resigned as foreign minister in response to conservative pressures.

If both old and new thinkers in Moscow shared unease about the slide to war against Iraq, they were more divided about the desirability of even a limited Soviet military commitment to a UN-authorized intervention. At one end of the spectrum, in September 1990 Shevardnadze reminded the UN that two years previously Moscow had proposed reactivating the work of the Security Council's Military Staff Committee. He suggested now that the Soviet Union could contribute forces of its own to action in the Gulf, provided they formed part of a collective UN effort under this committee.[71]

Counteracting this, however, Soviet Defence Ministry sources had insisted that Soviet troops would not take part in any intervention in the Gulf, citing Moscow's earlier 'unfounded decisions' to commit troops in Czechoslovakia and Afghanistan to carry out their so-called 'internationalist duty'.[72] Shevardnadze's cautious interest in new collective military measures under the UN was stifled by this backlash against Soviet material participation in any form of 'internationalism' and by persistent geopolitical concerns. Even if the US-led coalition had welcomed some Soviet contribution, the Soviet old guard could not envisage the commitment of its forces to combat under what appeared as American leadership against a former protégé armed with Soviet weaponry, and was unwilling to associate its forces too closely with expanding American Gulf war plans.[73]

By December 1990 Shevardnadze was forced to backtrack, stating categorically that Soviet diplomatic actions 'even with the most unbridled fantasy...could not imply any participation by Soviet combat, auxiliary or any other forces or formations in any military actions in the region of the Persian Gulf'.[74] A week later he resigned in 'protest against the onset of dictatorship' in the USSR, and in his resignation speech bitterly complained that attempts to forbid the Soviet leadership to send troops to the Gulf had 'filled to overflowing' his 'cup of patience'.[75] Shevardnadze's departure ensured that Moscow would remain on the military sidelines of the campaign in the Gulf, and care was taken to remove all Soviet military specialists (those linked to earlier Soviet arms sales) from Iraq before combat operations commenced. Soviet diplomatic efforts to avert war failed, but politically the USSR remained a fully signed-up member of the Security Council consensus that collectively legitimized the recourse to war.

CONCLUSION: THE AFTERMATH OF THE GULF WAR

The rapid coalition force victory over Iraq blunted complaints by Soviet military 'old thinkers' that America had irresponsibly brushed aside the chances of achieving a peaceful settlement to the crisis. As a *fait accompli* it also helped set aside the diplomatic friction between Moscow and

Washington over widespread Soviet reservations about the land campaign to drive Iraq out of Kuwait. Indeed, at the end of military operations Foreign Minister Bessmertnykh enthused that 'for the first time, the international community has demonstrated its united will when confronted with the seizure of one state by another'. He described this as a 'historic precedent' that 'may prevent similar situations in the future'.[76] It was hoped that the normative consensus over force the Security Council had demonstrated could endure beyond the Gulf crisis.

At face value these hopes matched President Bush's discourse, during the crisis, of a new world order. He spoke of a 'vision of a new partnership of nations... based on consultation, cooperation and collective action', governed by international law and based primarily in the United Nations.[77] However, this rhetoric was not accompanied by any American re-evaluation of its efforts to strengthen unilateral power through its global military reach. Nor was there any reinterpretation of former American interventions, such as in Panama in 1989, which had not been legitimized by the UN. In reality this was a time when US capabilities were expanding in stark contrast to the precipitous decline of Soviet global influence outside the formal voting structure of the Security Council.

In the regional context of the Gulf the prospects for a cooperative vision were mixed. Bessmertnykh overplayed the Soviet hand at the end of the war in proposing the creation of a new regional security system for the Gulf, effectively asserting the Soviet right to play a significant role in post-war diplomacy in the region.[78] Moscow did not achieve this role. However, agreement was at least reached for the UN to monitor and enforce the terms of the Gulf War ceasefire. In April 1991 Moscow also voted in favour of Security Council Resolution 687, placing key elements of Iraq's internal affairs under UN inspection. This was followed by approval of Resolution 688, which condemned the repression of the Iraqi civilian population, 'the consequences of which threaten international peace and security in the region'.[79]

The prospects for Moscow buying into future collectively legitimized military interventions under Chapter VII of the UN Charter, however, seemed uncertain. There was already a problem with Resolution 688, which did not authorize the (renewed) use of force against Iraq, but soon after it was passed the US deployed forces to establish safe havens and no-fly zones to protect Iraqi Kurds. Moscow made clear it viewed this action as limiting Iraq's sovereignty and undertaken without a legal mandate. But this was related to the deeper problem of whether, regardless of the norms or legal principles at stake, the USSR and later Russia would be prepared in future cases to delegate authority to enforce UN decisions militarily after the experience of the Gulf crisis.

The question, reinforced by Moscow's unsuccessful peace missions during the Gulf crisis, was whether Moscow could tolerate the inability to control the implementation of a Security Council use of force resolution by major

Western powers once that resolution is passed. In the Gulf crisis the Security Council, having no forces of its own, delegated the responsibility to enforce Resolution 678 to the coalition of states cooperating with the government of Kuwait. However, after granting legal authority the Security Council lost control over the subsequent course of events. It was virtually excluded from decision-making and even from consultation throughout the last period of the crisis.[80] Moscow lost this channel of influence and found no other during the five weeks of the coalition's air campaign, even as the war goals expanded beyond those specified in Resolution 678.

This question of whether to associate itself, through Security Council approval, with an apparently inevitable Western-driven military intervention, was a dilemma that recurred for Moscow in different guises over Kosovo (1999), Afghanistan (2001), Iraq (2003), and Libya (2011). This mixed considerations of status, principle, and pragmatic statecraft.

The Gulf crisis did confirm that the Soviet leadership was at one with the major Western powers over the inviolability of foundational UN Charter norms, even to the extent of alignment against an erstwhile military protégé. However, it also showed that the acceptability of such alignment, regardless of the principle of defending Kuwait, was highly controversial domestically. There was deep opposition and sensitivity in Soviet elites to any Soviet military participation in action against Iraq (including in the naval blockade of Iraq approved by Resolution 665). Even months after the war the Soviet Defence Ministry found it necessary, in reply to a query by a group of People's Deputies, to stress that 'no action of ours on the international arena... even under the most unrestrained fantasy could be understood as any sort of participation of Soviet combat, support, or any other troops or formations in combat operations in the Persian Gulf region'.[81]

What emerged during the Gulf crisis, and in the months after it leading to the conservative coup attempt in August 1991, was that influential political and security elites in Moscow had abandoned neither their competitive geopolitical orientation, nor their country's longstanding protective attitude to national sovereignty. In other words the 'all-human' universalist message of New Thinking was far from entrenched among such elites. For them domestic state order and the maintenance of Soviet status as a great power still trumped globalist responsibilities. As regards the use of force, Gorbachev was also unable to overcome the deep imprint of the earlier ideologically derived 'correlation of forces' thinking on the foreign and security policy establishments in Moscow. The persistence of these attitudes, together with the economic crisis of the new Russian state and the collapse of its wider international influence, leaving the US as the sole superpower, help explain why the normative potential of Gorbachev's vision of common security faded so quickly from Moscow's world view in the 1990s.[82]

3

Humanitarian Intervention, Kosovo, and Beyond: Divergent Norms

In the post-Cold War era the clash between Russia's pluralist orientation and emerging solidarist principles in international society has been graphically revealed in controversy over the legitimacy of humanitarian intervention. This division was most starkly expressed over NATO's first large military operation in Europe: the campaign to subdue the Federal Republic of Yugoslavia (FRY), Operation Allied Force (OAF), which commenced in March 1999.[1] NATO's central justification for its intervention—the need to protect the Albanian population of Kosovo from gross human rights violations conducted by Serbian forces—was rejected outright by Moscow as a cover for an illegal aggressive war motivated by power politics.

The deeply polarized discourse over this intervention reverberated for years in Russian relations with leading NATO states and NATO as an organization. It was the most serious rift between the two parties since the Soviet period and quite unlike formal cooperation during the crisis leading to the Gulf War in 1990, when the legal principles involved were quite clear and the procedural legitimacy of military action was grounded in UN Security Council resolutions. In the Kosovo crisis neither international law, nor the UN Charter process, nor established norms, offered clear support for the case presented by NATO and major Western powers, and Russia did not recognize alternative claims for legitimacy made by the participants in OAF.

Ultimately, however, Russia's leaders were most antagonized by the raw expression of NATO power in asserting principles, humanitarian or otherwise, to justify military action in the European zone (which NATO may not have been ready to apply elsewhere). For Moscow, OAF seemed all the more provocative since it commenced a few days after the Czech Republic, Poland, and Hungary joined NATO as new member states. As with the case of the Iraq War in 2003, Russia viewed Western challenges to rule-making over Kosovo as a measure of Moscow's international authority and status and of its ability to avert potential intrusions into its more direct zone of interests in the future by stronger powers and coalitions of powers.

The hostile Russian reaction to OAF abated in autumn 2001, when there arose new unexpected opportunities to cooperate over global counter-terrorism, as discussed in chapter 4. However, as we discuss in this chapter, Moscow remained cynical about justifications for humanitarian intervention; it trenchantly contested the military enforcement of liberal principles and similarly remained cautious about efforts, even under UN auspices, to consolidate emerging international norms on humanitarian responsibilities more generally at the expense of state sovereignty.

OPERATION ALLIED FORCE: INTERVENTION IN YUGOSLAVIA

The virulent Russian criticism of the OAF campaign, of NATO's violation of legal principles and the UN Charter framework, expressed its pluralist world view. But it can only properly be understood by taking account of the wider structural context. Moscow feared its declining influence in the shaping of the European security environment, and relied all the more on legal constraints and sovereign rights to limit the adjustment of power on the continent. Russia was shocked, therefore, by NATO's readiness to bypass Russian objections and its UN Security Council veto and to present legally dubious justifications for the military enforcement of humanitarian responsibilities in the Balkans.

The impact of the NATO campaign on Moscow was all the greater since Russia itself was a state locked in ethnically complex conflicts within its borders, and CIS states and Moscow perceived NATO as an organization both dominated by the US and intent on expanding its strategic remit in new undefined geographic zones. As a participant for years in the SFOR and IFOR peacekeeping operations Russia was no stranger to the complexity of Balkan conflicts, or to the intransigent, belligerent, and ruthless policies of the Yugoslav president Slobodan Milosevic. But looking at the crisis around Kosovo, the Russian elite fixated on the threat of tectonic shifts in Russian influence and status, on principles of international order slipping from their grasp, rather than on the imperative need for international action to counteract large-scale injustices and human rights violations in Europe.[2]

International law, justifications, and the OAF intervention

The justifications presented by NATO and its leading states for the threat and actual use of force against FRY were not principally cast in terms of international law (despite the debate later among international lawyers). The legal basis for NATO action was not properly explained, although it was claimed to be legally supported. This reflected the difficulty of justifying OAF in conventional use-of-force terms, and also, it seems, a feeling among the majority of NATO members that 'it would not be helpful to expand on the exact nature of the justification, to avoid a precedent for the future'.[3] It also expressed the strong value attached to normative, political, and strategic arguments in the discourse around this unprecedented major military operation for NATO on the European continent.

The debate in NATO occurred essentially in the period between the Security Council vote on Resolution 1199 on 23 September 1998 and NATO's threat of force in its Activation Order of 12 October 1998, which authorized NATO's Supreme Allied Commander in Europe to launch air strikes within four days if Milosevic failed to comply with the requirements of this resolution. The resolution had been prompted by operations by FRY forces in summer 1998 across Kosovo, supposedly against the Kosovo Liberation Army (KLA), which had led to the eviction of over 250,000 Kosovar Albanians from their homes. The resolution demanded, *inter alia*, the end of acts of violence against civilians and the withdrawal of FRY security units used for civilian repression.

The US, the lead state pressing for military action against the FRY, actually made little effort at the time to explicate this in legal terms. Yet NATO states still needed to present some legal case for intervention in the FRY. It was not credible to invoke self-defence under Article 51 of the UN Charter, as the FRY represented no direct threat to any of the NATO members. Reference might be made instead to collective security under Chapter VII. There was also an effort to refer to previous Security Council resolutions on the developing crisis. This was accompanied by an effort to invoke international customary law. An argument revolved around whether there existed a rule of customary law permitting an armed humanitarian intervention, and whether that rule could justify action in the Kosovo case. Overall, NATO and its major states tried to generate legitimacy for OAF by recourse to a variety of arguments that merged legal and normative claims, but the emphasis on the lawfulness of their action was lukewarm.

At a basic level, the procedural legitimacy or formal legality of OAF was clearly problematic in the absence of an explicit authorizing resolution by the Security Council, let alone the ability to cite self-defence. At one point US Secretary of State Madeleine Albright talked of NATO's actions as justified and operating 'within what we believe are legitimate parameters' by reference to Yugoslavia's flagrant ignoring of the mandatory obligations of Security Council resolutions 1160, 1199, and 1203.[4] This failed to convince most lawyers at the time or later. Both Resolutions 1199 and 1203 defined the threat in Kosovo as 'a threat to peace' in UN Charter Chapter VII language, but neither authorize the use of force. Some NATO states found an *implied* authorization by the Security Council in these resolutions. But German Foreign Minister

Klaus Kinkel was dissatisfied with this claim. Russia and China, he noted persuasively, both accompanied their votes for these resolutions by legally valid declaratory statements spelling out that the resolutions should not be interpreted as authorizing the use of force.[5]

The clash over OAF with Russia, China, and many non-aligned states was deepened by Western justifications expressly based on humanitarian claims, which were not consensually embedded in customary law and went to the heart of pluralist/solidarist tensions. Some NATO states were more drawn to these claims than others. Notably, after an internal debate the Clinton administration rejected the explicit use of a doctrine of unilateral humanitarian intervention as a legal basis for action against the FRY. One concern of US legal advisers was the risk that this precedent might be used by others to undermine international order to the detriment of US interests. They also sought to avoid expectations of similar American action in other crises, which could restrict American freedom of action.[6] For Washington, humanitarian claims were instead part of a diffuse normative discourse in favour of OAF.

On the other hand, a humanitarian rationale for force against the FRY was set out explicitly in a UK Foreign Office paper in October 1998. This justified force 'on the grounds of overwhelming humanitarian necessity without a UNSCR', if such a resolution could not be obtained, subject to certain criteria. One criterion was the existence of 'convincing evidence, generally accepted by the international community as a whole, of extreme humanitarian distress on a large scale, requiring immediate and urgent relief'.[7] This implied a situation when most but not necessarily all Security Council members accept that they are faced by exceptional humanitarian demands. At the launch of OAF, the UK claimed unequivocally that 'military intervention was justified as an exceptional measure to prevent an overwhelming humanitarian catastrophe'.[8]

Other justifications by NATO states were essentially strategic or political. President Bill Clinton claimed at the start of the air campaign that US and NATO forces acted not only 'to protect thousands of innocent people in Kosovo from a mounting military offensive', but 'to prevent a wider war; to diffuse a power keg at the heart of Europe that has exploded twice before this century with catastrophic consequences'. He evoked the Kosovan challenge to 'a peaceful, stable, free Europe'. NATO action was justified here by the potential disruption in European security that could be triggered by the FRY assault on the Kosovar Albanians. Clinton also described inaction in Kosovo as discrediting NATO (in formal terms as a guarantor of the October 1998 ceasefire that Milosevic had signed), the cornerstone of US security. The credibility of NATO was supposedly at stake.[9]

However, Clinton's address also implied an assertion of special NATO responsibilities in the European theatre beyond the self-defence of NATO members. This became explicit in the context of NATO's 50th anniversary summit a month after OAF began. An American statement affirmed that future NATO missions should include 'out-of-area' contingencies such as Bosnia and Kosovo, 'which threaten the overall strategic stability of Europe'. It specified that 'in taking any such NATO action, it is our strong belief that the UN Security Council resolutions mandating or authorizing NATO efforts are not required as a matter of international law', although NATO's actions would 'remain consistent with the purposes and principles of the United Nations'.[10] Therefore, the regional mandate offered by NATO and the collective judgement of the nineteen NATO nations on the necessity to use force, at least in the European theatre, was presented as eclipsing authorization in the UN Charter system.

In this sense, for Washington, OAF in proceeding outside UNSC authorization should not be viewed inherently as unique (a point we return to below). This posed wider questions for the management of regional order. An American international lawyer duly noted that 'other states may in the future create artificial groupings in order to claim a greater scope of authority to use force'.[11] The US and NATO claim certainly offered Russia more leeway in efforts to claim that CIS mandates for the use of force within its *own* asserted sphere of responsibilities carried weight even when lacking a UN mandate (as discussed in chapter 6). It also encouraged Russian expectations in the early 2000s about the authority it could derive for putative interventions from working within the format of regional subgroups of CIS states. However, as analysed in chapter 6, the uncertain scope of the strategic interests of both NATO and Russia-led CIS structures meant that this fuelled a structural competitive dynamic.

The Russian rejection of justifications for OAF

It should have been no surprise that Russia trenchantly refuted these Western justifications for OAF, since Russia had staked out its position on the use of force against the FRY quite clearly the previous year. In June 1998, when NATO foreign ministers grew alarmed that the Serbian army could be conducting a policy of ethnic cleansing in Kosovo during its operations against the KLA, the NATO Council resolved to study how NATO troops might be deployed on the territory of Albania and Macedonia as a preventive measure. Russian Foreign Minister (and Prime Minister after September 1998), Yevgeny Primakov, responded in terms identical to Moscow's central accusation over OAF: 'any forcible methods that NATO might employ outside its zone of responsibility must without fail be authorized by the UN Security Council'.[12]

This stance held fast to law as vested in the procedural power of the Security Council. Over autumn 1998 Russia threatened to veto the use of force against the FRY if the matter were taken to the Security Council, and (together with China) it watered down Resolution 1199 so that it should not be construed as enabling military intervention. On the other hand, Russian leaders refused to be drawn out about the circumstances under which their state might vote in favour of the military enforcement of Security Council demands of Milosevic.[13] The diplomatic stakes continued to rise as Moscow dug in its heels and downplayed the extent that Serbian actions in Kosovo amounted to, in UN Charter Chapter VII terms, a threat to peace in the region, so ultimately no vote to authorize force was placed before the Security Council.

The launch of OAF evoked Russian protestations of outrage. President Yeltsin described OAF as 'an act of open aggression', violating both the UN Charter and the Founding Act on Mutual Relations, Cooperation and Security between NATO and Russia, and by rhetorical extension 'the Russian Federation has been violated as well'. In the Security Council debate on 24 March 1999 the Russian representative, Sergei Lavrov, presented a scathing critique cast in terms of international law, norms, and the UN Charter process, and lambasted the *Realpolitik* motivations of NATO action. Setting the tone of Russian statements for years, he accused NATO of 'subverting the Charter and other norms of international law and for attempting to establish in the world, de facto, the primacy of force and unilateral diktat'. For UN members, he reminded, UN Charter obligations should trump those of any other international obligations.[14]

Russia argued that no authorization for the use of force could be drawn from Resolutions 1199 and 1203. Moscow had already spelt this out in the formal record of its views in the Security Council debates at the time.[15] This Russian interpretation of any 'implied' Security Council authorization was reaffirmed later in the discussion of Resolution 1244, which on 10 June brought the conflict around Kosovo back into the remit of the UN. Russia took care to insist that the reference in this Resolution to Chapter VII of the UN Charter 'contained no hint of the possibility of any type of use of force except that set out in the peace agreement'.[16]

Russia dismissed the claim that OAF was justified to avert humanitarian catastrophe on two grounds. First, as a matter of principle, this claim was 'in no way based on the Charter or other generally recognised rules of international law'. Secondly, in practical terms, 'the unilateral use of force will lead precisely to a situation with truly devastating humanitarian consequences'. On the first, Lavrov asserted that Russia had no wish to condone violations of international humanitarian law (implicitly admitting transgressions by Serbia), but the response should be with 'clean hands', otherwise 'lawlessness would spawn lawlessness'. In this reading, traditional legal norms overrode any solidarist ambitions or putative emerging norms unconsolidated in customary law. But a fear of the expanding threat of such norms to a pluralist order, to a strict view of the sovereign rights of states, was implicit in Lavrov's warning against the 'virus of illegal unilateral approaches' spreading not just 'to other geographical regions but to spheres of international relations other than questions of peace and security'.[17]

Moscow also disputed the reality behind humanitarian claims, claiming that the refugees fleeing Kosovo were actually escaping the bombing commenced by OAF rather than Serbian forces, and this was the analysis offered by the Russian media to the Russian public. The logic was 'NATO itself first creates a humanitarian catastrophe through its air strikes, and then launches a land operation in order to head off that same humanitarian catastrophe.'[18] As Russian rhetoric escalated, OAF was described as 'a ruthless war to extinction against the peoples of Yugoslavia'.[19] Foreign Minister Igor Ivanov dismissed the Western 'accusation of genocide' against the FRY as a calculated pretext to effect change in Yugoslav politics and to widen the NATO presence in the Balkans. He observed that anyway the 1948 international convention on combating genocide 'does not authorise states to use armed forces spontaneously for the prevention of genocide', and that this is the prerogative of the Security Council.[20]

Beyond disputing these explicit justifications by NATO states for OAF, Russia put great energy into refuting the more indirect Western, especially American, assertion that NATO was acting out of special responsibility for security and stability in Europe, even if this exceeded the Alliance's traditional geographic remit. In terms of law in the UN Charter system, Lavrov pointed out, Article 53 spells out 'the inadmissibility of any enforcement action under regional arrangements or by regional agencies without the authorization of the Security Council'.[21] However, NATO's readiness to sidestep this clear rule and entrench its claims regarding regional security order at its 50th anniversary summit was driven by a political and strategic logic. Russia's strong reaction is only intelligible in the overall context of its political response to OAF. This shaped Moscow's discourse on law and norms around the use of force for years to come.

The Russian political response to the OAF intervention

The NATO onslaught on the FRY and Russia's reaction threatened a rupture over important ordering principles of international society. However, the fact that this serious controversy continued to be played out in debate in the UN Security Council and other international institutions, despite Russia's suspension of most of its ties with NATO, that the Russian leadership resisted domestic pressures for active military association with the FRY in resisting NATO, and that NATO states opted to present OAF as *sui generis* rather than a precedent, averted a much deeper confrontation.

It is notable that the Russian leadership and its representatives appealed to primary institutions of international society—sovereignty, international law, diplomacy, and UN multilateralism—in channelling its attack on NATO. Indeed, it was important for those with a broadly liberal outlook who remained in the domestic power play in Russia that they had the option of articulating opposition to NATO action quite persuasively in terms of (traditional) international norms and law, a line of attack with considerable popular support in Russia. In this way they could counteract radical alternative appeals by Russian nationalists and communists to decisively end security cooperation on a whole series of issues with Western states, especially the US, and to militarily assist the 'fraternal' Serbian people.[22]

Therefore, Russian official rhetoric that 'all norms of international law were being flouted', that 'the humanitarian slogan was being used to cover up NATO's attempts to destroy the world order',[23] coupled with Russian efforts to use international institutions for leverage on Western governments, ultimately helped preserve substantial continuity in Russian policy with key Western states. It left space for the restoration of a Russian–Western sense of international community in the aftermath of OAF. This outcome would depend, however, on whether OAF proved to be an exceptional case of NATO or the US stepping outside established rules. Moscow remained nervous so long as it was uncertain whether OAF, especially as a form of intervention in Europe in a zone of expressed Russian interests, might instead become a precedent.

Nevertheless, the Russian leadership struggled to develop a policy around the crisis on Kosovo that would preserve some leverage on the course of events and help it to resist the anti-Western thrust of domestic nationalist and communist political forces. This effort was not assisted by a Russian tendency, in a period of declining capabilities highlighted by its financial crash of August 1998, to misread the extent of its diplomatic influence and to underestimate the resolve of NATO states. The Russian diplomatic approach in the year and a half before OAF had aimed to preserve negotiations between NATO and the FRY, despite Milosevic's intransigence, so that Moscow could continue to exert leverage as the only state on quite cordial terms with both parties. When this collapsed in March 1999 Russia was left as an affronted bystander to OAF.

The Russian balancing act was apparent during the 'pre-crisis' during September–October 1998, as NATO indicated it was preparing to use force if Milosevic did not make concessions to international demands. Russia worked with the Security Council, which approved Resolution 1199 on 23 September, which expressed grave concern over the excessive and indiscriminate use of force by Serbian security forces and the Yugoslav army. NATO then ratcheted up the threat of force to compel Milosevic's compliance with UN demands, eventually issuing an ultimatum that extracted sufficient concessions from Milosevic to avert NATO strikes.

During these diplomatic tensions, Russian leaders were careful to reject outright radical anti-Western responses, proposed by Russian opposition and some military figures, were NATO strikes to occur without UN authorization. These included full-scale military cooperation with Belgrade, in contravention of the international embargo on arms sales to the FDY, or providing Russian volunteer forces to assist the FDY.[24] In the rising domestic clamour Foreign Minister Ivanov insisted that any Russian 'response entailing the use of force' to such a NATO strike was out of the question, and that overall 'there are no strategic disagreements' between Russia and the West.[25] This implied a continued sense of community with Western states.

Milosevic's climb-down averted NATO strikes in autumn 1998. However, status-conscious Russian leaders inflated their role in defusing the crisis, partly with domestic politics in mind. 'Look how other countries have to reckon with Russia', boasted Prime Minister Primakov. The 'determining argument', he claimed, was Moscow's threat that in the event of a strike 'there would be a dramatic shift in Russia's relationship with NATO and many changes in our orientation'. As tensions mounted again next year, Yeltsin went public that he had told President Clinton 'we will not allow anyone to touch Kosovo'.[26] In this way he set himself up for a fall.

Moscow refused to endorse NATO's threats of air strikes against the FRY in the first half of March 1999, before the critical Rambouillet meeting. This undermined NATO's coercive diplomacy, since NATO's threats failed to resonate in Belgrade, and reinforced Milosevic's intransigence.[27] Yet ultimately Moscow failed to avert OAF, and was left affronted by the collapse of the role it claimed as an indispensable player in security management in the Balkans.

With the launch of OAF, the radical Russian response could have been a deeper association with Milosevic, excusing his refusal to comply with previous Russian efforts at persuasion. However, the Russian leadership, along with more liberal-minded Russian politicians, constructed a discourse of opposition to NATO's action 'not as an outgrowth of fraternal love for the Serbs, but as a violation of international norms'.[28] This approach enabled Yeltsin to level a strong critique against OAF yet to avoid dangerously escalatory measures. Russia suspended a variety of contacts with NATO and bilateral military links with the US, but maintained diplomatic contact with NATO governments. The vociferous and emotive calls in Moscow for radical responses to OAF failed to derail Yeltsin's policy of gradually re-engaging with NATO and the US.[29]

In April 1999 such radical responses were vigorously debated among Russian politicians. They included possible forms and methods of delivery of Russian military assistance to Serbia.[30] Scenarios of Russian involvement in a large-scale war, such as an escalation from a limited Russian naval commitment to the conflict zone, were aired. This was not wholly fanciful at a time when the Russian naval commander-in-chief was himself quoted as saying that 'Russia simply must provide military-economic assistance to Yugoslavia.'[31] Attention was drawn to the potential flashpoint of a Russian refusal, as a 'neutral' country, to recognize a possible naval blockade of the

FRY in the Adriatic Sea.[32] Unofficial 'patriotic' organizations in Russia were said to be recruiting volunteers to travel to Serbia to assist its military efforts.[33] However, Yeltsin dismissed such bellicose speculation and proposals, declaring that 'Russia's participation in hostilities in the Balkans is inadmissible.' He declared that Russia was ready to offer humanitarian not military aid, and to all affected people in the region not just to the Serbians.[34]

The risky and notorious march in June 1999 to occupy the Kosovan airport at Slatina, by some 200 troops from the Russian SFOR peacekeeping forces in Bosnia, could be interpreted as the exception that proves the rule of overall Russian constraint. This bold gambit probably had the strategic goal of seeking to ensure some Russian military presence in the centre of Kosovo at the beginning of the post-conflict phase of OAF. The intention, therefore, was to avoid Russia being frozen out by NATO and to exercise leverage in the days just before the conclusion of negotiations on the Russian involvement in the KFOR peacekeeping force in Kosovo.[35] Yeltsin himself probably approved the dramatic move on Slatina also as a deliberate gesture to assuage Russian nationalist and military critics of his Kosovo policy, to counteract their sense of humiliation over OAF.[36] Even so, Yeltsin was committed to working through international institutions as his main response to the NATO campaign.

For the initial Russian response to OAF, the Security Council was the most authoritative institutional platform to contest OAF on normative as well as legal grounds. But the Council reflected the deep political divisions over the crisis. This was shown when Russia introduced a resolution on 26 March, with Belarus and India, affirming that the NATO unilateral use of force against the FRY constituted a flagrant violation of the UN Charter and a threat to international peace and security. Lavrov contrasted support for the UN Charter with 'tolerating a situation where gross force was the norm'.[37] The rejection of the Resolution by a vote of twelve against and three in favour (China, Namibia, and Russia), was surprising since it would have been only necessary to abstain from voting to defeat the text. If anything, this offered a degree of tentative support for the combined justifications for OAF by NATO states.[38]

At this stage Moscow had to consider the risks of this polarized rhetoric in the UN leading to more confrontational interstate relations. In pondering their options two core questions about the international system seemed particularly to trouble Russian leaders. First, was NATO's attack on the FRY confirmation that Russia was being sidelined from the core of international decision-making in some emerging 'oligarchic' Western-driven international order? Secondly, if this was happening, should Russia choose pragmatically to side with the dominant powers and avoid further estrangement from them, or at least revive its role as mediator in the conflict over Kosovo, or should it actively challenge the 'hegemons' and seek partners outside the Euro-Atlantic zone?[39]

At first Russia was inclined to lean on likeminded opposition to OAF by China in the Security Council. The Chinese response became more vehement after NATO inadvertently bombed the Chinese embassy in Belgrade on 7 May, a violation of China's sovereignty, Beijing fumed, on top of OAF's violation of 'the basic norms of international relations'.[40] However, despite calls for an anti-Western alignment in Moscow, Yeltsin did not believe that a temporary policy of bandwagoning with China over Kosovo could be transformed into a feasible strategy. This was confirmed when Moscow sidestepped China on 6 May to reach agreement with the other G8 foreign ministers about the principles for a political solution to the Kosovo crisis. These principles were only afterwards taken to the Security Council and proposed in a draft resolution, which was approved (with a Chinese abstention) in Resolution 1244 on 10 June.

In fact, as early as mid-April, when he appointed Viktor Chernomyrdin as his special envoy, Yeltsin seemed focused on restoring Russia's international role in the crisis, as well as its self-esteem, through a process of engagement, through mediation efforts towards a political settlement, which could then be brought under the remit of the United Nations. By June Moscow clearly was eager to bring the conflict, especially the presence of international civil and military contingents in Kosovo, under the remit of the Security Council, to capitalize on Russia's role as mediator, and to explore what influence could be extracted from a Russian contribution to a Kosovo peacekeeping force. After protracted haggling, this eventually led to Russian participation in the KFOR operation in Kosovo, though without a dedicated sector for the Russian troop presence as was sought.[41]

Yeltsin's wish to return Russia to its position as an insider state influencing the diplomacy around Kosovo, in coordination with Western states, was encouraged by its failure to orchestrate a joint platform against OAF on a CIS-wide basis. Russia could not convincingly present itself as at the forefront of a regional defence of principles of international law and order. The differing interpretations of NATO action against the FRY by CIS states reflected their own interests and relations with NATO states.

This emerged from a meeting of six CIS defence ministers on 25 March, which failed to adopt a resolution Belarus suggested 'condemning NATO aggression against Yugoslavia'. A senior Georgian official even suggested that the concept of NATO using force for humanitarian purposes without the need of any special UN Security Council mandate might become a powerful instrument for settling local conflicts.[42] The Georgian President, Eduard Shevardnadze, claimed that NATO had no choice faced by 'ethnic separatism and extreme separatism'. He portrayed Abkhazia as in an almost identical position to Kosovo. Armenia responded to OAF by stressing the right of peoples to self-determination, and claimed that it had a similar problem in Nagorno-Karabakh. The Azerbaijani leadership also related Kosovo to Karabakh, but tended to view the Kosovo scenario (the use of force) as a model for resolving its own protracted conflict over Karabakh, and was unequivocally pro-Western and pro-NATO.[43]

Elsewhere in the CIS region, where the issue of subnational units was less sensitive, Russia gained some support. The leaderships in Kazakhstan, Kyrgyzstan, and Tajikistan expressed solidarity with the Russian position. The Uzbek president, Islam Karimov, criticized military solutions to disputes, but also stated that Milosevic should be called to order to prevent confrontation and war. Belarus firmly allied itself with Serbia and Russia, and severed ties with NATO. The Ukrainian president, Leonid Kuchma, acknowledged the humanitarian crisis in Kosovo, but argued that legally this did not justify the use of force, especially without UN backing.[44]

A CIS summit on 2 April 1999 confirmed that Russia could not mould this spectrum of response to OAF into some common normative front. All that emerged next day was a declaration by the low-level Inter-parliamentary Assembly of CIS states, which condemned NATO military operations without Security Council authorization as a challenge to the current system of international relations and a real threat to peace and stability. But Georgia, Azerbaijan, and Uzbekistan failed to join this plea, which anyway only expressed the critical attitude of CIS state parliaments rather than state leaders.[45] These variations in CIS policy were clearly a challenge to the special role Russia had claimed in the CIS region, especially over the modalities of peacekeeping. For Moscow, the parallels drawn between Kosovo with its example of NATO power and CIS conflicts were especially disturbing in light of uncertainty about NATO's changing missions.

NATO's 'out of area' responsibilities and regional interventions

For the Russian elite the diverse response of CIS leaders to OAF ended their hopes for rallying a collective CIS political counterweight to the collective will of NATO states. As previously noted, a basic Russian concern was the threat of falling outside the core group of states of an emerging and consolidating 'oligarchic' international order. In this scenario these states would adopt key decisions, including on the legitimate use of force, regardless of the UN Charter system.[46] For Moscow, OAF was evidence that its ability to use UN Security Council primacy to constrain NATO decision-making was crumbling.[47]

Before OAF in 1998 Foreign Minister Ivanov had also used the NATO–Russia Permanent Joint Council (PJC) and the OSCE to resist NATO attempts to assume greater responsibility outside the territories of its member states. In December he proposed that a European Security Charter should include a 'Code of all-European Peacekeeping', drawn up mainly by Russia and NATO in the PJC, to ensure 'genuinely equal partnership between states and organisations'.[48] Ivanov claimed that 'the Balkans have always been a zone of special strategic interest for Russia' on account of 'the region's geographic proximity and access to the Mediterranean'.[49] OAF, however, left these Russian positions in disarray and seemed a graphic illustration of the extension of NATO's reach and military ambitions in Europe.

This outcome appeared to be reinforced by the new Strategic Concept, adopted at NATO's 50th anniversary Washington summit in April 1999, which set NATO new tasks beyond collective defence. The Allies undertook the promotion of security and stability across the Euro-Atlantic area (which was left undefined) through non-Article 5 crisis response operations. Such operations could be 'distant from their home stations, including beyond the Allies' territory'.[50] Ivanov repudiated the Concept's 'obvious claim to apply NATO's activities on a global scale'.[51] Russia interpreted the Concept not only as a doctrinal expression of OAF and as an official abandonment of NATO's 'purely defensive strategy', but also as a proclamation of NATO's position at the apex of international security decision-making.

For Russia, the predictability of global rules was at stake, as well as its ability to leverage these rules to keep stronger Western powers in check, especially in and around Europe. This was clear in elite and official discourse. Mikhail Gorbachev castigated the Washington summit for revealing that 'NATO's will is above the UN, the OSCE and the Council of Europe', that 'the US intends to offer the world its military intervention in any internal conflict, in exchange for the principles of international law'.[52] Ivanov declaimed that the Balkan region had been chosen to road-test 'a "NATO-centrist" concept of world order, in which a group of states would arrogate the right to dictate, by force if need be, its will to the international community'.[53]

This trenchant critique, cast in terms of threats to international order and legality, helped deflect the more radical anti-Western proposals in the Russian political debate. Yet it reflected real concerns and some fear about developments in and around the European theatre. In this vein Defence Minister Igor Sergeev warned of the 'very dangerous precedent' of 'a massive use for force in the centre of Europe... beyond the framework of international law, bypassing UN regulations'. For him the precedent was not just abstract, however, but an encouragement to ethno-separatist tendencies, since it 'validates armed conflict aimed at separating regions from existing states'.[54] This referred obliquely not just to the Balkans, but also to potential scenarios in the CIS region.

Before considering such scenarios we should note a different connection between the NATO campaign against the FRY and Chechnya. Before OAF, Russia had insisted that political and diplomatic means to a settlement over Kosovo had not been exhausted, that force was unjustified. Nevertheless in practice the Russian authorities came to conclude that the precedent of NATO action, as evoked by Sergeev, had made the use of force in general 'less unjustifiable', including in Russia's own domestic conflicts. In this sense the 'Kosovo model' had some influence on Moscow's decision in November 1999 to commence its military offensive in Chechnya, though in this case Russia could rely on the persuasive legal justification that it was applying force to its own territory. Therefore OAF 'contributed to eroding the political and psychological obstacles reducing Moscow's freedom of action with respect to Chechnya'.[55]

Another potential connection between OAF and Chechnya was more challenging for Russian policy-makers. Might the normative justifications by NATO states for OAF, given NATO's expanded role, be expressed in pressure for some form of military intervention in Russian domestic state order in Chechnya, as evidence mounted of widespread human rights abuses and extensive refugee flows in and around the republic? A popular belief among many Russians was that Chechnya was indeed vulnerable to NATO intervention, as captured in the alarmist catchphrase 'Serbia today, Russia tomorrow'. Russia risked NATO 'punishment', it was suggested, for its efforts to suppress separatist movements in the northern Caucasus. Russian nationalist politicians and many military officers conjured up 'forces in the West ready to play the North Caucasus card with the goal of weakening Russia'.[56]

It strains credibility that the Russian leadership itself really feared such a dangerous NATO violation of Russian sovereignty, not least given Russia's nuclear deterrent. Neither is there the slightest evidence of any official Western thinking about intervention in Chechnya. But Russia–NATO tensions mounted as the prospect of mass civilian casualties in Chechnya's capital Grozny loomed in December 1999. NATO rebuked the 'disproportionate and indiscriminate' use of force by Russia and called on Moscow to ensure the conflict would not spread to other states for the sake of regional security. Russia's response, true to its acerbic post-OAF discourse, was to denounce 'the impression that NATO has seriously decided to try to try on the uniform of a "world policeman" and intervene where no one invites the Alliance to intervene'.[57]

The Russian Foreign Ministry sought to deflect NATO criticism of Russian abuse of international humanitarian law in Chechnya by arguing that it was unacceptable for NATO to 'suddenly recall "rules of international behaviour"' after having argued post-OAF that the UN Charter and documents of pan-European forums 'are not mandatory'.[58] This rhetorically conflated international law *in bello* and *ad bellum*. However, with the humanitarian claims around OAF still resonating, Moscow was becoming increasingly resistant to any notion of applying solidarist norms to its national jurisdiction. 'Internal matters' such as Chechnya, Moscow insisted, 'are not and cannot be and will not be a subject of our international dialogue, and the more so with NATO'.[59]

It was somewhat more realistic for Russia to speculate about NATO intervention in the CIS regional order rather than in the Russian Federation itself. As noted previously, the Georgian and Azerbaijani leaders invoked the Kosovo scenario as a possible model to address their own separatist conflicts. Beyond these cases some Russians speculated about the vulnerability of the Ukrainian region of Crimea, as a result of its own ethnic tensions. Russian analysts and military specialists claimed that the US had worked out 'a Crimean version of the Balkans scenario', that 'a further intensification of the situation in Crimea could lead to a humanitarian intervention according to the scenario worked out in Yugoslavia'.[60] It was argued that various military and political leaders in CIS states were interested in the presence of NATO troops on their territory, hoping in this way to resolve their local conflicts, and that Western states could achieve their own military and political goals there through forceful interventions.[61] The lack of evidence for any such plans failed to dampen down nationalist Russian discourse of this kind. It was rooted in pervasive cynicism in Moscow about humanitarian motivations or norms in Western policy

HUMANITARIAN INTERVENTION AS A CONTESTED NORM

The justifications of NATO states for OAF triggered debate about the possible consolidation of a solidarist trend towards the legitimacy of humanitarian intervention. This could be influenced by the discursive and political responses of major states such as Russia. In the aftermath of OAF Moscow showed some interest in discussing the legal aspects of the use of force, but proved to be a relentless critic of normative claims based on the model of the NATO campaign.

An emerging norm of humanitarian intervention?

OAF stimulated a wide-ranging discussion among specialists and the policy community about whether a norm enabling humanitarian intervention was in the making, or had been revived, and if so how it might qualify established rules on the use of force.[62] According to a minority legal opinion, the legality of OAF could be assessed on the basis of a previously existing customary norm which allowed for the use of force in the case of humanitarian necessity, a norm which had re-emerged since the UN Charter came into force. Despite considerable variation in legal opinion, however, this is disputed by most international lawyers, in Western states and beyond, who are agreed that the current law of the UN Charter cannot accommodate NATO's attack on the FRY.[63]

After OAF, however, many of those who regarded the campaign as contrary to UN Charter law noted a trend in the international community towards a better balance between the security of the state on the one hand and the security of people on the other. This was expressed clearly by UN

Secretary-General Kofi Annan early in NATO's bombing campaign against the FRY. He affirmed that 'emerging slowly, but I believe surely, is an international norm against the violent repression of minorities that will and must take precedence over concerns of sovereignty'. He insisted that the UN Charter should 'never [be] the source of comfort or justification' for 'those guilty of gross and shocking violations of human rights'.[64]

Annan envisaged a process of normative evolution. It seems that NATO was only staking out a normative claim through humanitarian justifications for OAF itself (the dominant state in OAF, America, rejected the option of relying legally on a doctrine of humanitarian intervention). However, if this claim were to have growing international resonance, over time it might form the basis of new customary law. This would require state practice consistent with the norm as well as *opinio juris*—states justifying the practice as legally permitted.

It is revealing that Russia's draft resolution of 26 March 1999, which sought to condemn OAF, was unequivocally defeated and that in this case six non-Western states (non-permanent Security Council members) 'either legitimated, excused or acquiesced in the use of force on humanitarian grounds' which lacked express Security Council authorization.[65] However, Russia was among other influential states that rejected all justifications for the NATO campaign. Overall a sufficient number of states formally and directly opposed any purported justification of humanitarian intervention to make it impossible to 'to render its induction into the corpus of international custom'.[66]

Moreover, specialists noted that even limiting the time frame to the post-Cold War period, there is little evidence of humanitarian arguments actually being invoked to support the interventions that occurred. In the case of OAF itself, neither NATO nor the UK, in referring to 'overwhelming humanitarian necessity', systematically supported their claims by referring to past state or international practice. NATO officials appeared to suggest instead that this crisis was exceptional, *sui generis*, rather than offering guidelines for the future.[67] This pointed to the shakiness of any claims on humanitarian grounds that might be invoked as precedent.

It also suggested, however, the reluctance of NATO states to 'loosen' the law, to stretch the interpretation of legal standards (*internal* to the domain of legality). It would better preserve the core constraints of law (the basic prohibition on non-defensive force), the NATO position implied, by acknowledging the limits of law and creating 'an *external* domain of exception, labelled "legitimacy"'.[68] Indeed the basic appeal was to so-called legitimacy, in what might be viewed as a very specific case of the use of force beyond legality.

This was essentially the conclusion reached by the high-level Independent International Commission on Kosovo, reporting to the UN Secretary-General in 2000. It emphasized the 'need to close the gap between legality and legitimacy', seemingly taking the view that OAF was not strictly legal, but still should not be condemned, and was legitimate because of its effective response to an imminent humanitarian catastrophe.[69] From this perspective, an appeal to the legitimacy of OAF, despite Russian accusations of NATO stepping outside established law, actually represented an effort to avoid challenging the core constraints of law. This understanding has a surface plausibility, but as we argue in chapter 1 it presents a false dichotomy between legality and legitimacy and obscures the way legitimacy is derived in international society.

Michael Glennon offers a quite different and provocative argument about the Kosovo war. He views the whole legal framework of constraint enshrined in the UN Charter as 'sufficiently superseded by the present global setting to lose its restraining force'. This allowed behaviour to be authoritatively shaped by 'coalitions of the willing' until 'a new legal regime responsive to current realities of power and values can be established by the consent of major states'.[70] This interpretation of structural power, in practice US power in particular, as trumping law is one that fits Russian cynical claims about the underlying *Realpolitik* impetus of OAF as well as later Russian claims, centred on the American prosecution of the 2003 Iraq War, about trends towards a 'lawless world'.

Clearly strategic and security considerations were involved in the mix of motivations which animated NATO states' decisions to support OAF, especially the wish to avoid the spillover to other European states of any wider destabilization of the Balkan region. This prompts the question whether OAF represented an attempt to develop new rules, without a Security Council resolution or Russian endorsement, valid for intervention specifically in the *European* region.[71] This regional focus might be suggested by American claims in the context of the Kosovo crisis about the imperative need to prevent a wider war in Europe, and NATO's expanded missions post-April 1999. Jackson has also argued that as a war of democracy against one of the last remaining dictatorships in Europe the Kosovo war was 'strongly suggestive of a geographical sphere of influence where Western norms and values shall prevail'.[72]

On the other hand, one could point to NATO's rejection of OAF as forming any precedent, whether in Europe or elsewhere, and to the dangerous impracticality of trying to freeze Russia out any rule-making in Europe related to intervention. Given the security policy dimension to OAF, it could also be concluded that outside the Balkans NATO was unlikely to be faced again by a similar combination of humanitarian emergency and core security interests. What this suggested, Wheeler observed in 2001, was that 'Kosovo does not mark the beginning of an era in which NATO will act as a global enforcer of humanitarian norms.'[73] This was prescient since it was a full ten years before the closest analogue to OAF, the intervention in Libya in 2011. However, this was not evident to Russian leaders at the time, who continued to condemn militarized humanitarianism without Security Council approval.

Russia qualifies its critique of humanitarian intervention

Russia viewed the model of OAF as anathema, but this did not mean it viewed the UN Charter principles on the use of force as beyond debate. Indeed at the G8 summit in Cologne in June 1999 Russia proposed a discussion on the legal aspects of the use of force. This may have been a sideswipe at the legal basis of the NATO campaign. But it also seemed to be motivated by a wish for debate, within and outside the UN, to achieve 'collective decisions that would legitimize and multilateralize the use of force across national boundaries'.[74] Russia hoped to reinforce traditional mechanisms of response to mass human rights violations (with the central role of the Security Council, etc.). But this did not mean that a more flexible formula could not emerge through negotiations over time.

The subject of humanitarian intervention was debated in the UN General Assembly in September 1999. UN Secretary-General Kofi Annan raised the need for the international community to intervene more decisively on behalf of peoples badly maltreated by their own governments. Foreign Minister Ivanov reaffirmed Russia's view that coercive measures should only follow endorsement by the Security Council (subject to Russian veto rights), since 'unlawful means can only undermine rightful ends'. He held to a pluralist emphasis on national sovereignty and the need for the UN to move 'resolutely to put an end to all manifestations of separatism' (with clear implications for Kosovo). But then he showed flexibility in seeming to indicate Russian interest in clarifying the criteria for intervention.[75]

After the initial polarized discourse with NATO states over OAF, Russian officials clearly did not wish to appear on the international stage as inherently opposed to norms inducing the military protection of human beings, not least since they knew that the Security Council had adopted a number of resolutions in the 1990s connecting human rights violations with a threat to international peace and security. In this vein the Russian UN representative affirmed that 'we are far from insisting that the principle of the non-use of force should block practical implementation of other fundamental principles of international law, including respect for human rights and protection from genocide, war crimes and crimes against humanity'.[76] The tenor of these remarks contrasted notably with the blunt Chinese view that 'the sovereignty of a country was the precondition and foundation on which the people of a given country enjoyed human rights'.[77]

In Moscow it was left to specialists in Russian Foreign Ministry institutes to assess further the legal and normative aftermath of OAF.[78] One argued that law should follow emerging norms. There was an urgent need for 'a new and much more detailed and unambiguous definition of the legal aspects of the use of force in international relations in the context of globalization and democratization'. Another way of putting it was 'more criteria for the use of force according to the UN Charter, including in extraordinary humanitarian situations'. Special attention should be devoted to developing a clear international legal interpretation of humanitarian crisis.[79] Failing such legal innovation, another specialist underlined the dilemma under the current system: there may be situations when on account of the political position of some of its permanent members, 'the Security Council cannot make a decision on the use of armed force to curb human rights violations, even if it should really be used'. Yet in his view 'it would be fraught with far too serious consequences to regard this as grounds for breaching international law in the name of humanity'.[80]

Such nuanced analysis was absent unfortunately in top-level Russian discourse, or in official documents such as Russia's new Foreign Policy concept of June 2000.[81] A central problem for any serious discussion of the possible criteria for human-focused military intervention was the inclination of the Russian leadership to view the entire subject primarily in terms of world order and geostrategic competition.

This problem was reinforced by President Yeltsin's selection of Vladimir Putin as his heir apparent in September 1999 (setting him on course to be elected president in March 2000). Putin's personal background in the security services oriented him strongly to order and state authority rather than to justice, which was soon graphically displayed in the brutal prosecution of Russia's second campaign in Chechnya. As Director of the Federal Security Service, he had positioned himself as an fervent critic of NATO action during OAF, branding it a threat not just to Europe but to the whole world: 'a unilateral attempt is being made to scrap the world order which has been created since World War II under the aegis of the UN'.[82]

As acting Russian president, it is notable that Putin singled out Russian objections to humanitarian intervention in one of his first statements on foreign policy and presented it as a geostrategic challenge for Russia.[83] He had already expressed this in zero-sum terms in spring 1999, in his other role as secretary of the Russian Security Council, when he promised a reaction to Western humanitarian intervention in Russia's new national security concept, which duly took a more anti-NATO thrust.[84] After becoming president, he met top-rank Russian officers in summer 2000 and stressed the role of armed force for Russia in response to attempts to 'reshape the world map' under the guise of humanitarian intervention.[85]

This was part of a post-OAF renewed Russian emphasis on upgrading military defences, influenced partly by scenarios of intervention in the CIS regional order, as previously discussed. The new Russian military doctrine issued in 2000 was not explicit about military threats to the state.[86] However, some Russian military studies spelt out the potential threat of armed humanitarian intervention. If this took the form of 'international peacekeeping forces', sent to CIS states without UN approval, it could provoke Russia to respond by fulfilling its defence obligations under the CIS Collective Security

Treaty.[87] The US and NATO were accused of hoping to use such means to extend their influence into the CIS region and to counteract Russia-centred integration there.[88]

Russian criticism of humanitarian intervention not only assumed the form of grand rhetoric about challenges to world order and legality, and nervousness about regional order among CIS states, as previously discussed. In the Balkans itself humanitarian intervention was blamed for encouraging the principle of secession in Kosovo, and of creating the danger of the 'export' of secessionism, with adverse consequences for other regions, including Chechnya.

In June 2000 Russia complained of 'a clear tendency to separate Kosovo from the FRY, fraught with serious and long-term destabilization in the entire Balkan region'.[89] By the next spring Russia accused 'extremist and separatist forces of the Kosovo Albanians' of setting up a 'network of terrorist groups' in Kosovo, southern Serbia, and Macedonia. Moscow even called for international action to prevent a new spiral of conflict engulfing several states in the region.[90] This scenario was avoided. Yet in subsequent years Russia accused Western states of bias in overlooking the destabilizing activities of Kosovar Albanians and of underwriting Kosovan secession, up to the clash over formal recognition of Kosovo in 1998.

Finally, we should consider whether the Russian leadership's strong rejection of humanitarian intervention reflected not just the privileging of order in terms of the UN Charter legal framework over justice, and differing views of justice to Western states (the rights of the FRY and Serbs versus those of Albanians in Kosovo), but also a resistance to the perceived projection of Western values more generally by force of arms.

A well-informed Russian specialist reported that after OAF humanitarian intervention was widely perceived in Russia, not solely in leadership circles, as the forcible dissemination of democratic and human rights standards. It was considered that such 'humanitarian messianism' would inevitably provoke strong resistance from non-democratic parts of the world, and for Russians it brought back uncomfortable memories of Soviet attempts to 'make others happy against their will'.[91]

This reaction also reflected a growing disenchantment among Russians over the economic and social results of democratization in their own state in the 1990s. Even those in Russia who supported the normative paradigm on offer for the Balkans, it was argued, mostly opposed the forceful methods of advancing it.[92] This was especially so since the supposed forcible projection of values largely involved American firepower. Although the European Union had decided to support OAF, Russia muted its reaction to the EU in this crisis. Russian rhetoric was also almost entirely focused on the US, among NATO states, with the implicit assumption that America's NATO allies had succumbed to American pressure, in some cases reluctantly.

The way Russia linked Euro-Atlantic values, rather than global norms on human rights, with OAF's display of power in the Balkans was also reflected in Moscow's denigration of NATO's new Strategic Concept. The document included a strong emphasis on democracy, human rights, and the rule of law, and also characterized Euro-Atlantic security as based on democratic institutions. At the same time it held out the prospect of NATO out-of-area missions.[93] As explored in chapter 6, the Putin leadership would gradually develop a narrative that the Western promotion of democracy and human rights norms concealed hostile US-led *Realpolitik* strategies for the CIS regional order and domestic state order in Russia itself.

Responsibility to Protect and Russian responses

The post-OAF debate left uncertain whether this crisis had consolidated human-focused norms in international society, and under which conditions force could legitimately be used to protect populations from gross human rights' abuses. This grey area was explored by governments and NGOs during 2000–6 to shape a wider consensus among states, in coordination with the UN Secretary-General Kofi Annan.[94]

A particular debate developed over the criteria for a 'responsibility to protect' (R2P), a concept intellectually derived from the notion of 'sovereignty as responsibility'.[95] UN Secretary-General Kofi Annan encouraged this discussion as an approach to reconciling the principles of sovereignty and fundamental human rights. The hope was that R2P could overcome the divisive militarized discourse over 'humanitarian intervention' and move beyond the controversy about 'world order' provoked by OAF. However, many states including Russia adopted conservative interpretations of R2P, influenced by the legacy of OAF and the reality of pluralism within the international community at large.[96]

The R2P notion was first explored extensively in a report by the International Commission on Intervention and State Sovereignty (ICISS) presented to Annan in December 2000.[97] The Commission's ideas fed through a High-Level Panel on Threats, Challenges and Changes, set up by Kofi Annan in 2003, to the report 'A More Secure World' in 2004. Annan used this for his own report the following year, 'In Larger Freedom', which was a background document for the important 2005 UN World Summit. This established the baseline view of the global society of states on the matter.

The proponents of the R2P initiative in ICISS sought to identify a new norm or 'emerging guiding principle', based on the growing practice of states and regional organizations, as well as Security Council precedent: the responsibility of states to protect not only their own citizens but also the citizens of other states. It highlighted a shift in emphasis from the right of states to intervene, to human individuals' rights to some protection. The core proposal by ICISS was that states, rather than making claims for humanitarian intervention, should assume a responsibility to protect the human rights of those who deserve protection. The initial assumption was that governments are responsible for preventing large-scale losses of life and ethnic cleansing in their own populations.[98] But the further proposition was that if a national government were unable or unwilling to prevent such atrocities, the international community, acting through the UN, in 'extreme cases', should accept a responsibility to protect the suffering population, whether or not it had the consent of the recalcitrant government.

ICISS also considered how to avoid OAF's adverse example of states bypassing the Security Council in cases of potential humanitarian catastrophe. It proposed that agreement should be reached with Security Council permanent members that they refrain from exercising their veto rights unless their vital national interests were engaged.[99] One legal specialist has referred to this as the 'Chechnya clause'—so dubbed since in the hypothetical case of a proposal for international intervention in Chechnya, Russia could legitimately issue a veto. But in the case of Kosovo (absent a vital Russian national interest) Russia should have abstained in any Security Council vote to authorize a Chapter VII action, a 'constructive abstention'.[100] Arguably this is what occurred in practice much later over intervention in Libya (see chapter 8).

The R2P initiative was primarily sponsored by interested Western governments and NGOs, but in the 2000s major Western states were cautious about it, which limited its traction as an emerging norm. The United States under the Bush administrations, from its position as a hegemonic power, was opposed to establishing criteria for the legitimate use of force, which might tie its hands in the future or entangle it in interventions that do not directly affect its national interests.[101] From a different perspective, Russian caution reflected the qualified pluralist position it had staked out in autumn 1999.

Together with other influential states, including China, India, and the Philippines, Russia was reluctant to accept further erosion of the principle of non-intervention through empowering the international community at the expense of the domestic jurisdiction of states. However, this group of states did not reject as such the underlying purpose of R2P, the prevention and halting of genocide and mass atrocities.[102] Their caution about how R2P might be used was reinforced by the abuse of humanitarian language by the US in the context of the 2003 invasion of Iraq (see chapter 5).[103]

At the first Security Council discussion of R2P in 2002, Russian diplomats reacted coolly, arguing that R2P by countenancing unilateral intervention risked undermining the UN Charter.[104] For Moscow, it was essential to retain a veto over proposed action. By the time the September 2005 UN World Summit approached, the Russian Foreign Minister accepted that force could be used against a state without its approval to preclude and prevent massive and grievous violations of human rights, if authorized by the Security Council.[105] Moscow also agreed with the idea of 'continuing a UN discussion on the theme of the permissible limits of the use of armed force, of devising criteria for its authorisation by the UN Security Council'.[106]

It was by insisting on this authorization that Moscow aimed to prevent the expedient use of the R2P concept, by Western states, 'coalitions of the willing', or NATO. It claimed that 'the UN should, as it copes with "humanitarian catastrophes", be a kind of guarantor for the prevention of the use by states or regional structures of either unauthorized repressive measures or their military intervention'. Russia also insisted on a high threshold in defining a crisis that could trigger a R2P response: the Security Council should define the situation as posing a Chapter VII threat to international peace and security.[107]

In the event, at the UN World Summit the General Assembly unanimously endorsed an outcome document that declared the 'responsibility to protect populations from genocide, war crimes, ethnic cleansing and crimes against humanity'. It expressed the international community's agreement to stand 'prepared' to take collective action in those cases where national authorities 'are manifestly failing to protect their populations' from these forms of extreme abuse. [108] However, this specific language was chosen to water down the Security Council's responsibility to protect. In fact 'the idea that the R2P implies responsibilities—even obligations—on the part of international society and especially the Security Council was all but removed'. A higher threshold was set also for a transfer of R2P from the host state to international society than proposed by ICISS, which had proposed this would occur merely when the host state is 'unable and unwilling' to protect its own citizens.[109]

A General Assembly resolution like this could be indicative of the evolution of law, but was not legally binding by itself. Even so, in further debate on how to proceed, a number of states including Russia argued that the only commitment made had been one to deliberate further on R2P. A group of 'Westerners', including the EU, Canada, Japan, and South Korea, pressed for adoption of R2P by the Security Council. However, Russia claimed this was premature, and together with China and major developing countries it tried to rein in this process.[110] This was accompanied by the continuation of American opposition to R2P criteria. Ultimately the Security Council reached agreement only on a watered-down brief reference to R2P in April 2006, which merely reaffirmed the provisions on it contained in the World Summit Outcome Document.[111]

It left the criteria justifying the use of force for humanitarian purposes unspecified, and any military intervention under R2P would require Security Council authorization.[112] This in turn left Moscow's veto over any putative R2P actions intact. In the second half of the 2000s Russia entrenched itself in a group of mainly non-Western states, including China, which tended to constrain practical steps to further extend the R2P norm beyond the limited consensual agreement in 2005–6. In the June 2007 Security Council debate on the protection of civilians, Moscow insisted the Council should strictly adhere to the R2P parameters offered by the 2005 World Summit and not widen their scope.[113] Likewise at the UN General Assembly debate on R2P in July 2009, Russia claimed it was important 'to avoid rash, hasty steps or broadening the interpretation of the concept'.[114]

In the period after OAF, Russia consented exceptionally to Security Council authorized interventions for humanitarian purposes in East Timor (1999) and the Ivory Coast (2003). But during Putin's second presidential term Moscow was increasingly wary about Security Council pressure against states for humanitarian ends, even when military intervention was not officially contemplated. In autumn 2007, for example, Russia and China thwarted an attempt by Western states to discuss sanctions in the Security Council against Burma for the violent suppression of protests there.[115] This was a Chinese priority, and the two states were also united in rejecting the imposition of sanctions against Sudan over the egregious and large-scale human right violations in Darfur.[116]

Another illustration of openly clashing claims over the Security Council's role in humanitarian crises occurred in July 2008, when Russia and China vetoed a draft resolution, sponsored by Western states, with token African support (Liberia and Sierra Leone), to adopt sanctions against the leadership of Zimbabwe. The draft defined the situation in Zimbabwe explicitly as posing 'a threat to international peace and security in the region'. This arose, in the words of the UK representative, from the fact that Zimbabwe faced not only a political crisis, but also 'a grave humanitarian crisis, for which the Government of Zimbabwe bears full responsibility'.[117]

The Russian veto was probably intended to forestall any possible Western use of the resolution to claim authorization for actions beyond sanctions, or to initiate a process which might slide towards an intervention. Russia viewed Zimbabwe's domestic human rights situation as insufficient to justify such responses. Moscow complained of 'illegitimate and dangerous' attempts 'to take the Council beyond its Charter prerogatives and beyond the maintenance of international peace and security'.[118] It remained a priority of Russian Security Council diplomacy to maintain a high threshold in defining a humanitarian crisis as a threat to international peace and security, with all the implications of this for potential intervention within states.

This expressed the pluralist position Russia shared in the decade after OAF in general with states like China and India. But it also reflected and relied on wider international cynicism of the US tendency during the Bush administrations to invoke a humanitarian rationale for self-interested military interventions, most notably in political rhetoric after the invasion of Iraq. This had the unfortunate general effect of undermining 'the idea of an impartial and neutral responsibility to protect'. This was a concept anyway which Washington was only lukewarm about.[119]

In this sense, when Western proponents of R2P decried the 2005–6 consensus as 'R2P lite', this outcome could not just be blamed on states overly protective of territorial sovereignty. The Darfur crisis confirmed a general lack of political will to shoulder the responsibility to protect, though the Russian and Chinese refusal to contemplate intervention there formed an immediate obstacle to action. Various states reluctant about such intervention found in this case that the language of responsibility to protect could be used to constrain rather than enable intervention, by arguing that this responsibility first lay with the states where human rights were threatened.[120] Overall, the consolidation of R2P as a norm or set of norms during 2005–10 was undermined by its indeterminacy, that is uncertainty about what was expected and disagreements about what ought to be expected.[121] Given this background, the decision of the Security Council to authorize military intervention in Libya in March 2011 (see chapter 8) after the use of R2P language, was remarkable and significant.

CONCLUSION: RUSSIA AND THE LEGACY OF THE KOSOVO CRISIS

NATO's campaign in the FRY was interpreted across most of the Russian political spectrum as a strategically determined case of intervention, masquerading as a humanitarian operation and undertaken in violation of international rules. In the Russian political narrative, this was confirmed during the following months and years by continued instability and human rights violations in and around Kosovo, together with separatist tendencies supported by Western states and organizations, eventually leading to confrontation over the recognition of Kosovo as a state in 2008.[122] The course of events on the ground, therefore, supported some of the heightened official rhetoric in Russia over Kosovo during March–April 1999, and helped entrench a Russian sense of grievance over this exercise of NATO, especially American power, in Europe.

With this adverse example in mind, Western humanitarian justifications for forceful measures overriding state sovereignty had scant credibility in Moscow during the decade after OAF. This might seem surprising since before OAF the Security Council, including Russia, had authorized or endorsed a number of forcible interventions which were partly, if not wholly, for humanitarian purposes, in Bosnia, Somalia, Rwanda, Haiti, and Sierra Leone. To be sure, these were each treated as *sui generis* rather than applying in principle some new norm or customary right of humanitarian intervention; they were case-by-case reactions. But they help explain why much of the international community effectively 'excused' the violation of law over Kosovo, though Russia did not.[123]

Russia represented OAF instead as a threat to international order and the UN Charter framework. This high-flown language was driven by two central preoccupations. First, Moscow feared that its authority as a Security Council member and its veto rights were under serious threat, alongside the erosion of the Council's function of collective legitimization among states. Secondly, Russian leaders agonized over the decline in their practical influence on European security, worries compounded by palpable Russian economic weakness. All this shook Russian confidence in its status and position in the power ranking of states and contributed to genuine, if overblown, fears about possible further NATO operations unconstrained by the UN Charter framework.

During 1999–2005 the Russian position evolved to accept in principle the legitimacy of military intervention based on human-focused conceptions of sovereignty in an extreme crisis, subject to Security Council authorization. This allowed Russia to retain a veto over action. As long as this element of the UN Charter system seemed intact (despite the clash over OAF and the rather different controversy in the UN over the Iraq War), Moscow neither set itself against nor was in denial over the evidence of evolving norms since the end of the Cold War concerning humanitarian protection in international society. Russia was quite aware of claims, especially in the UN and in the foreign policies of strong Western states, that security should not be viewed as existing internationally without human rights protections.

By the mid-2000s, despite evidence of increased solidarism in international society about the military protection of human beings, Russia still regarded itself as comfortably in the mainstream of states over the salience it attached to sovereignty. This was well illustrated by the qualifications to the R2P concept reflected in the 2005 General Assembly outcome document. Whereas developing countries were more concerned about the implications of R2P for territorial sovereignty, a number of more powerful developed states, including the US, had concerns about decision-making sovereignty, despite the general impetus behind R2P from other Western states.[124] As for Russia, its pluralist outlook embraced both sets of concerns.

In the wider context, it was the American focus on decision-making sovereignty that alarmed Russian leaders. The launch of the Iraq War without Security Council endorsement (accompanied later by some humanitarian rhetoric from the lead states in this intervention), left Russian leaders with the sense as in 1999 that the ground was slipping beneath their feet. Moscow's position at the centre of international rule-making seemed to be eclipsed by preponderant US power. Putin's growing denunciation of American hegemonic policies from 2006 emerged from this sense of grievance, as well as a belief that Western states led by the US were increasingly ready to intervene in the CIS regional order, at least politically, to promote liberal agendas. For the rest of the decade this political and strategic outlook left little scope for convergence between the normative outlook of Russia and major Western states over justified intervention based on humanitarian necessity.

4

Afghanistan and the 'Global War on Terror': A New Basis for Consensus?

The Russian–Western clash over Kosovo was a spectacular contrast to the collaboration achieved in the UN Security Council almost a decade previously, which resulted in the formal authorization of the Gulf War. At the time of OAF neither side could have expected that a new basis for international solidarity would present itself by the end of 2001, underwritten at least initially by Security Council cooperation. The primary theatre for cooperation, Afghanistan, was familiar to Russia as a source of non-traditional regional security threats. However, after the al-Qaeda attacks on American targets on 11 September 2001, the impressive scale of US-led resistance to transnational terrorism, beyond initial operations in Afghanistan, transformed earlier piecemeal counter-terrorist efforts into a global campaign.

This created opportunities for Russia to reinstate and burnish its image as a key contributor to wider international order. But the question was whether Russia, and other states with pluralist world views, would be ready to subscribe to Western, especially American definitions of the parameters of the new 'war on terror', which could challenge existing rules on the application of force. Or would Moscow insist that these definitions be collaboratively devised with Russia?

In autumn 2001 President Putin in fact presented himself quite quickly as at least a willing co-belligerent alongside Western states in this new offensive against terrorism, though this was not the automatic response of most of the Russian security elite. The UN Security Council reached a consensus over the need to take all necessary steps against those harbouring terrorism. Russia like other major states did not contest the American justification of its offensive against the Taliban on the grounds of self-defence. Moscow also appeared to accept common formulations over the legitimate use of force beyond Afghanistan.

From the outset, however, this discursive solidarity masked substantial differences in priorities and definitions of the wider terrorist challenge between Moscow and Washington. Russia remained focused essentially on a threat to domestic state order with limited regional spillover—Chechnya. Moscow consistently sought to mesh this into the core of global counter-terrorist operations and to justify the means it used to prevail in that specific conflict. During and after the campaign in Afghanistan Russia claimed a crucial link existed between the conflicts in Chechnya and Afghanistan.

Indeed it is striking how exceptional and short-lived the consensus over the campaign in Afghanistan proved to be in the unfolding American strategy for the 'war on terror'. By early 2002 controversy was already developing over potential intervention in Iraq. Russia's preoccupation with Chechnya was a weak point of connection with the shifting geographic and functional focus of American counter-terrorist strategy in the years after the 9/11 attacks. Indeed, Russian leaders increasingly regarded the extension of American terrorist-related military commitments, within and beyond CIS states, in competitive geostrategic terms as displacing Russian primacy in the CIS regional order.

As regards customary law and norms, the 9/11 attacks resulted in pressure to reinterpret established principles regulating the use of force. This paralleled the ongoing debate over responsibility to protect, discussed in the last chapter. The first phase of the military campaign in Afghanistan, which began in October 2001, had a rather clear legal or normative basis, after UN Security Council members accepted the American military response to the 9/11 attacks as a form of self-defence, even if this implied some revision of customary international law. This contrasted with growing controversy from 2002 over efforts to justify the *pre-emptive use of force*, or even preventive war against states, as examined in the next chapter. The broad consensus over the legitimacy of intervention in Afghanistan was soon overtaken by this new challenge to traditional rules on the use of force.

INTERVENTION IN AFGHANISTAN

Russia's response to the intervention in Afghanistan in 2001 was difficult to predict because of the lingering trauma of the decade-long Soviet military intervention in Afghanistan and the regional proxy war around it. In the 1990s, when a new stage of civil conflict erupted in Afghanistan, Moscow limited itself to an indirect and deniable form of military engagement in the country. As Taliban control spread through Afghanistan, the country became the theatre for an externalized civil war between two loose coalitions. Russia and Iran, with some Central Asian state support, backed the Northern Alliance of Afghan militias, whereas Pakistan, Saudia Arabia, and Turkey offered clandestine support for the Taliban.[1] Given the risks of escalation, Moscow confined its involvement to the provision of arms and covert military assistance to the Northern Alliance.[2]

The existence of a containable Afghanistan 'threat' could also be advantageous for Russian policy. As the Taliban extended its control in Afghanistan during 1996–2001, Russia worked to establish itself as a bastion of regional security order in CIS Central Asia through promoting Russia-led collective security structures, which made much of the dangers of the Taliban. This political objective was accompanied by gradually rising Russian concerns over transnational terrorist links between Afghanistan and Chechnya or radical Islamic movements in Central Asia. This had some connection also with the persistent challenge of narco-trafficking from Afghanistan. Overall, Afghanistan was viewed by Moscow in the 1990s through a prism of regional-level security preoccupations.

Military strikes against terrorist camps

For Western states, however, it was the presence of transnational terrorist groups with wider, even global, agendas on the territory of Afghanistan in the 1990s that attracted attention and defined Afghanistan as an ongoing threat to international order. Once the Russian leadership launched its second campaign in Chechnya it dwelt more on this wider threat in an effort to enlist support for its policy in Chechnya. For example, at the July 2000 G8 summit in Okinawa Putin claimed that Chechen rebels were receiving active assistance from the Taliban and depicted an arc of terrorist instability from the Philippines to the province of Kosovo, with Afghanistan in the middle.[3]

With this threat imagery in mind, Russia agreed with leading states before the 9/11 attacks on the need for measures against terrorist camps located in Afghanistan. Sanctions against the Taliban adopted by the UN Security Council in Resolution 1267 of October 1999 were affirmed as binding for Russian organizations by Presidential Decree 786. The additional sanctions of Resolution 1333, adopted in December 2000, reinforced this collective position.[4] The diplomatic efforts of the UN-sponsored Six plus Two Group of states (Afghanistan's neighbours, Iran, China, Pakistan, Tajikistan, Turkmenistan, Uzbekistan, plus the United States and Russia) represented a wide international consensus. None of this changed the Taliban's readiness to host terrorist camps.

One option was to go beyond diplomatic efforts and take military action against terrorist targets in Afghanistan. The Yeltsin leadership had been cautious about agreeing to direct military strikes against such camps, partly for fear that strikes could provoke retaliatory steps by the Taliban on Central Asian borders. However, such retaliation did not occur after American cruise missile strikes at terrorist training camps around Khowst in Afghanistan and at Sudan in August 1998. These strikes followed claims by US intelligence sources that Osama bin Laden's al-Qaeda network had been responsible for attacks on US embassies in Kenya and Tanzania.

There was a dilemma over the legality of such strikes. Washington justified its action on the grounds of self-defence, although the attacks had the character of a reprisal, which was unacceptable under customary international law. The US claimed the strikes conformed with Article 51 of the UN Charter as they were directed at putting an end to a sequence of terrorist attacks and preventing their recurrence. Very few states protested against the action.[5] British, German, and French leaders concurred on this occasion with an apparent blurring of the limits of Article 51. In contrast, President Yeltsin rejected the US legal justification and condemned the attacks. He had condemned US strikes against Iraq in September 1996 and later criticized US and UK missiles strikes against Iraq in December 1998. This was no doubt influenced partly by the looming possibility of NATO action in another theatre—against Kosovo.

However, the Russian view of limited strikes began to evolve from this 'principled' opposition, as a new security policy leadership emerged under Yeltsin's successor, Vladimir Putin. In the case of Afghanistan, Moscow seemed more disturbed by the American use of force close to CIS borders, with uncertain implications for regional order, than by legal principles or debate around the notion of anticipatory self-defence per se. Once Russia committed its own forces in 1999 to large-scale military operations in Chechnya, against what it defined as terrorism, it began to finesse the legal niceties of striking terrorist groups abroad with supposed transnational links to Chechnya.

Russia, now led by Vladimir Putin, even aired its own strike option. In May 2000 an aide to President Putin, after accusing the Taliban of training militants fighting Russian troops in Chechnya, claimed there was a real prospect that Russia would carry out 'preventive strikes' against the Taliban in Afghanistan if the interests of Russia or its Central Asian allies were threatened. Foreign Minister Igor Ivanov confirmed that this option was available 'if a potential or possible threat emerges in a given situation'. The secretary of the Russian Security Council, Sergei Ivanov, agreed, noting that 'Russia's hands must not be tied.'[6] This marked the beginning of growing convergence between Russian and American thinking on military pre-emption, when applied to 'terrorist' threats, as described in the next chapter.

Russia's threats in spring 2000 were rhetorical, however, since it lacked reliable capabilities to conduct air strikes, especially without access to Uzbek airfields.[7] Such strikes would also have risked an international backlash. Uzbekistan and Turkmenistan seemed opposed to drawing the ire of the Taliban in this way, while the Chinese President Jiang Zemin insisted that 'the regulation of the Afghan question with the use of force is not a solution', and that it should be decided 'without external intervention'.[8] This made it all the more difficult to conceive of joint US–Russian strikes or joint special operations against the Taliban, as unconfirmed reports suggested were proposed by Washington in autumn 2000 and spring 2001.[9]

International law, justifications, and intervention in Afghanistan

Russia, like other permanent members of the Security Council, consented to the legal case Washington offered for military intervention in Afghanistan after the 9/11 atrocities. However, this case was less clear than the collective self-defence claim that supported a consensus among the permanent five at the time of the Gulf War. For decades the UN had rejected self-defence claims related to military measures against alleged terrorists. Moreover, in autumn 2001, states could not be sure of the implications of agreeing with the US claim over Afghanistan for the potential justification of future military actions in the expanding 'war on terror'.[10]

The American right to self-defence in response to the al-Qaeda attacks was spelt out in the wording of Security Council Resolution 1368, rapidly issued on 12 September 2001, and Resolution 1373 issued on 28 September, which reaffirmed the inherent right of states to individual or collective self-defence in the context of the attacks.[11] Solidarity for the US among Western states was reinforced by the invocation of the collective self-defence provisions of the 1949 North Atlantic Treaty and the 1947 Inter-American Treaty of Reciprocal Assistance, while the Organization of American States specified the 9/11 events as an 'armed attack'.

Nevertheless, Washington could have resorted to other legal justifications. It might have sought explicit authorization for military action from the Security Council, it might have argued that it was responding to an invitation by the Northern Alliance, or possibly it could have claimed a right of humanitarian intervention. The reasons for not citing these other justifications, which we consider in turn below, reflect concerns about wider implications of efforts to adapt legal rules governing the use of force, including the position that could be adopted by a Security Council member like Russia.

Security Council Resolution 1368 expressed the Council's 'readiness to take all necessary steps' to respond to the 9/11 attacks, while Resolution 1373 decided that under Chapter VII all states shall 'take the necessary steps to prevent the commission of terrorist acts'. This could have provided the US with an arguable case whenever and wherever it decides that force is necessary to prevent such terrorist acts. However, this would have risked setting a far-reaching precedent; a state like Russia or China could then invoke Resolution 1373 in support of their own politically defined counter-terrorist measures. Such UN Security Council members could also block any attempt to clarify or rescind such Resolution 1373 authorization for military action through their veto powers.[12]

Alternatively, the US might have claimed that its intervention in Afghanistan was at the invitation of the Northern Alliance. But it was unclear whether the Alliance could be viewed as the legitimate government of Afghanistan, and this approach would have empowered the Alliance with the possible effect of obstructing a broad-based political transformation in Afghanistan. In terms of regional politics this claim could have fuelled Russian involvement (through its Northern Alliance connections) and alienated Pakistan. For different reasons Washington probably ruled out the (dubious) legal justification of unilateral humanitarian intervention at an early stage: this could limit it ability to use force, and anyway it hardly seemed appropriate to present a humanitarian argument in response to terrorist acts. Moreover, such a claim would hardly have been welcome in Moscow, for reasons discussed in the previous chapter.

In developing its self-defence justification the US had to overcome the widely held view that terrorist attacks in themselves do not constitute 'armed attacks' that validate military responses against sovereign states. As noted above, Washington gained broad support for its right to self-defence in the context of the 9/11 attacks. It proceeded to widen this claim to include the state of Afghanistan, on the grounds that the Taliban had provided refuge to Bin Laden and Al-Qaeda and refused to hand him over, and so had directly endorsed and assisted his acts. Secondly, it was argued, the continuation of the Taliban as the *de facto* government of Afghanistan in itself represented a threat of further terrorism.

The implicit consent of the Security Council to this approach, it has been claimed, had the important outcome of broadening the right of self-defence to include military responses against states which openly support or willingly harbour terrorist groups who have already attacked the respondent.[13] Despite US–Russian disputes over the use of force in other circumstances in following years, the Russian Foreign Ministry accepted that the 'modern understanding of the right for self-defence reflected in article 51 of the UN Charter includes the rights of states for self-defence in case of a large-scale terrorist attack on them from outside on the part of non-state subjects'.[14] Russia conceded that not only terrorist groups, but also states could then be subjected to military responses, in circumstances expressly defined and qualified by the Afghanistan case.

However, the justificatory approach chosen by the US for intervention in Afghanistan had deeper implications and a disturbing ambiguity, since it could be invoked again (by the US and potentially other countries), even in less serious cases or where the responsibility of the targeted state is less clear. It is persuasive that in part this seemed to represent 'a strategic decision directed at loosening the legal constraints on the use of force to the *ongoing* advantage of the US'.[15] This is clear on considering the issue of who should decide that sufficient evidence exists of state complicity in supporting or harbouring terrorists to justify the use of military forces. With the new single-minded US determination to prosecute a 'war on terror' it seemed likely that such an expanded right of self-defence would also foreshadow a diminution of the relevance and authority of the United Nations on matters related to the use of military force.

If Russian leaders feared such an outcome in autumn 2001, they avoided expressing their concerns publicly, despite their post-OAF sensitivities. They did not publicly encourage a US-led attack in response to 9/11, but their language reinforced unambiguously the core American claims justifying this intervention. At the outset of military operations in Afghanistan the Russian Foreign Ministry deplored Afghanistan as 'a world centre of international terrorism and extremism'. It affirmed the Taliban's specific responsibility for harbouring al-Qaeda and the continued threat represented by the Taliban.[16] Russia privately reinforced this point. Meeting NATO officials, Russian Defence Minister Sergei Ivanov described Bin Laden and the Taliban as effectively the same thing. In his metaphor, Bin Laden was the 'Inspector General of the Afghan Armed Forces'.[17] This replicated President Bush's description of the Taliban regime and al-Qaeda as 'virtually indistinguishable', together promoting terror abroad and imposing a reign of terror on Afghan people. The British government presented a similar view of a symbiotic Taliban–al-Qaeda relationship.[18]

Russia assented, therefore, to the claim that seemed to have gained general acceptance post 9/11 that force could be used as self-defence after a specific terrorist attack, if the attack is part of a planned hostile strategy and reliable evidence exists that further attacks are imminent. In legal terms, Russian jurists came to accept that the UN Security Council had determined that Article 51 self-defence measures 'can be triggered by an attack by a non-state-actor, when the actual attack has ceased but there are grounds to believe that it could be followed by new attacks'. The Security Council had not determined whether the US could strike against a state or non-state actor in this context. But Russian officials acceded to the interpretation of Western states that in principle a state sponsoring terrorism in the manner of Afghanistan under the Taliban could become the object of the exercise of the rights of self-defence.[19]

Moscow qualified this by arguing that Article 51 does not apply to an attack by terrorist groups with no connection to any state, 'because armed response would inevitably affect a state, which has nothing to do with an attack'. Then resort should be to bilateral and multilateral cooperative efforts to capture and punish the perpetrators and prevent future attacks. The exception would be when a country's government is unable to control part of its territory and cannot prevent terrorist activities against another state. Then the territory under the effective control of some armed group, which performs the functions of government, it was argued, might be viewed as a *de facto* state entity, and 'as an active sponsor of terrorism, can in principle become a target of the exercise of the right of self-defense'.[20]

In any event, the assent of the Security Council permanent members to the American position on self-defence in autumn 2001 set the stage not just for attacks against the Taliban, but the overthrow of Taliban rule, an important outcome for any analysis of the politics of military intervention. Given the controversy that grew over 'regime change' in subsequent debate about the expanding war on terror, it is striking how the US-led action that resulted in the deposition of the Taliban was not criticized from the legal standpoint of *proportionality* in the United Nations, either during the debates before the Security Council or in the plenary session of the General Assembly.[21] The argument that removing the Taliban regime could not be separated from the fight against al-Qaeda overcame concerns about the proportionality of the military measures undertaken in this case so that they could be defined as a lawful exercise of the right of self-defence.[22]

However, a new US political momentum was attached to these legal consequences. In legal terms the example of regime change in Afghanistan was *sui generis*, and American practice since Afghanistan suggests indeed that it has sought to avoid challenging the rules on the use of force on the grounds of terrorist attacks. Despite rhetoric about Iraqi support for terrorism in the build-up to the 2003 invasion of Iraq, for example, as noted in the following chapter, Washington only used this as a background political not legal justification for intervention in this case.[23] However, it is in *political* terms that the ousting of the Taliban might be regarded as exemplary—as fulfilment of Bush's promise that any 'nation that continues to harbor or support terrorism will be regarded by the United States as a hostile regime'.[24] This sounded draconian but in fact provided an opportunity for Russia.

The Russian political response to intervention in Afghanistan

Russia quickly positioned itself in the international mainstream after the 9/11 attacks, both through its direct expressions of support to the US and through rapid agreement in Security Council Resolution 1368 that the sponsors of the attacks would be held accountable and that all necessary steps should be taken to respond to the attacks. Russian leaders did not doubt that America was intent on decisive military action, whatever the legal basis Washington relied on for its response.

President Bush's proclamation 'you are with us or you are with the terrorists' represented a challenge for all states to cooperate with the looming US-led campaign. The initial inclination of the Russian security elite at large was to hedge rather than actively contribute to an American-led military campaign. This was expressed in Defence Minister Sergei Ivanov's forthright assertion on 14 September that 'I don't see any basis for even the hypothetical possibility of a NATO military operation on the territory of Central Asian states that belong to the Commonwealth of Independent States.'[25] This chimed with Russian public opinion, which was not only against such a campaign, but also a large majority was ready to 'condemn' any US attack against countries harbouring terrorists.[26]

Despite this, Russia had already aligned itself diplomatically alongside the US and other Security Council permanent members over the threat at hand, through previous Security Council resolutions in October 1999 (Resolution 1267) and December 2000 (Resolution 1333). These demanded that the Taliban cease to provide sanctuary and training for international terrorists and relinquish Osama Bin Laden. Given this record of Security Council agreement, Putin initially hoped that the United States might be persuaded to conduct the looming 'anti-terrorist operation' in Afghanistan within a UN framework; ideally the Security Council should assume the leading role. But this hope was quickly dashed, especially as it became apparent that the 'war on terror' declared by the US would not be confined to Afghanistan, though Afghanistan was the first priority and the object of the initial US-led offensive in October 2001.

In this rapidly evolving security environment, in which other states could be targeted by Washington, it appears that Putin began to focus on approaches to constrain the American use of force, to mitigate its wider unilateral impulse. Russia had little leverage, but Putin considered that this difficult task could be advanced to some extent if Russian cooperation brought it *within* the emerging anti-terrorist coalition.

At the same time, in offering support Putin angled for political *quid pro quos*, in specific fields of Russian–Western relations and in Russia's campaign in Chechnya. Listing Russian cooperative steps on 24 September, Putin offered only indirect military assistance to Washington, but held the door open for a bargain. He observed that 'other more extensive forms of cooperation' would depend on 'the general level and quality of Russia's relations with the states in question and mutual understanding in the sphere of combating international terrorism'. He then insisted that 'Chechen developments ought not to be understood outside the context of the struggle against international terrorism.'[27] In a closed presentation to NATO next day, Defence Minister Sergei Ivanov specified that 'the door had been opened for military cooperation on the ground', and Russia was waiting for Western proposals. At the same time he called for a 'legal proportionate response' of a counter-terrorist operation in Afghanistan.[28]

When US-led operations began some weeks later their eventual scale was uncertain and it was clear Russia had very limited influence over the prosecution of the campaign. The Russian elite were not sure whether Russia could or should take part in some way and nervous over possible spillover effects beyond Afghanistan. This was expressed in an anxious statement of the Russian State Duma on 9 November. It noted that 'forms of Russian participation in the international efforts should be determined based on the national interests of the Russian Federation', that actions should be coordinated in the UN to ensure 'the collective adoption of decisions', and these actions should 'be based on the principles and rules of international law'. The statement forecast that large-scale civilian casualties would destabilize the Central Asian region and 'inevitably lead to an escalation of tensions in the world'—a harbinger of later accusations over Iraq.[29]

Such worries were not unreasonable and help explain the reluctance of the Russian leadership to shift from legal to direct and substantive military alignment with the American use of force in Afghanistan, and especially to offer Russian military assets (whether or not these would have been accepted). In talks with NATO officials in late September, Defence Minister Ivanov had not precluded this option.[30] There was speculation and some alarm in the Russian press over possible options as the military campaign in Afghanistan unfolded. According to one report, for example, Moscow and Washington planned a joint ground operation into Afghanistan in March 2002 from north and south. They had concluded supposedly a secret pact to divide Afghanistan in a 'Yugoslavia scenario' along ethnic borders (a pro-American Pushtun state in the south and a pro-Moscow Tajik–Uzbek regime in the north). Another report claimed that Russian General Staff sources had heard of an American proposal to fund a corps of some 10,000 foreign volunteers for its anti-Taliban operation. Russians, it was suggested, would be the first to subscribe to this force.[31]

In reality Russian leaders did not seem eager to engage in combat, although watching the crumbling of Taliban defences they did not rule out some Russian commitment to peacekeeping in Afghanistan after major combat operations. Putin may have considered this option as a means to earn influence over the political outcome of the campaign in Afghanistan, as well as to maintain Russia's role as the principal 'security guarantor' for Central Asian states in light of the rapid conclusion of new American agreements on military access to Central Asian states. It was exactly this kind of Russian geopolitical approach, however, as well as practical issues of coordination and the contentious image of the Soviet military presence in Afghanistan in the 1980s, which probably dissuaded American planners from considering Russian contingents in joint operations or from encouraging Moscow to contribute to subsequent peacekeeping activities in Afghanistan.

In November 2001, however, the Russian position was hesitant. When Sergei Ivanov was asked if there were proposals 'to send the Russian army to Afghanistan under the UN aegis', he claimed 'there are attempts to push us into involvement in the hostilities in Afghanistan, but we refuse to be pushed'. He denied that Russia planned to participate in 'peacekeeping operations' in Afghanistan.[32] But a few weeks later he spoke of the need to study the status and purpose of peacekeepers in Afghanistan. The media even reported that the Russian General Staff had drawn up plans for about a thousand military personnel to join such a UN-supported force.

Russia finally issued firm official denials of such plans or intentions a week before UN Security Council Resolution 1386 on 20 December.[33] This authorized the formation of the International Security Assistance Force (ISAF) in Afghanistan and called on contributions to the force to assist the Afghan Interim Authority maintain security in and around Kabul.[34] After this, although it had no troop presence in ISAF, Russia was committed to the ongoing stabilization effort in Kabul. One influence on Russia's previous equivocal position over peacekeeping may have been speculation, as reported in the Russian press, over whether Afghanistan might be divided into 'some zones of responsibility'.[35] A comparison may be made with Kosovo, where Russia had tried hard, but unsuccessfully to obtain its own peacekeeping zone. The possibility of such a Russian zone in northern Afghanistan would have been geopolitically tempting for Russian leaders, especially if achieved easily with low military risk in the aftermath of US military operations deposing the Taliban.

Such an option of direct UN-sanctioned Russian presence in Afghanistan was clearly ruled out by the end of 2001. This left the temptation for Moscow to revive its shadowy military and political dealings with former Northern Alliance contacts. This was reflected in some Western concerns, after Taliban rule collapsed, that the arrival of an early contingent of Russian personnel from the 'Emergency Situations Ministry' to Kabul (including military intelligence representatives) might be part of a power play. Such troops might form the kernel of an expanding Russian contingent of ostensibly 'technical specialists', outside the emerging UN peacekeeping process. Ultimately, however, Russia kept its efforts at political manoeuvring in early post-Taliban Kabul in check and accepted the authority of the UN, which offered Russia at least some influence, as the body coordinating the political transition in Afghanistan.

In seeking influence over the campaign against the Taliban regime in autumn 2001 Russian leaders were especially frustrated in failing to rally behind them the CIS Central Asian states, let alone a wider set of CIS states. When Defence Minister Sergei Ivanov set himself against any possible NATO military operations against Afghanistan from the territory of Central Asian CIS states, he prefaced the statement he made just after the 9/11 attacks with the claim that 'Central Asia is within the zone of competence of the CIS Collective Security Treaty.'[36] This was a call for a Russia-led collective regional response. It ignored the fact that Uzbekistan and Turkmenistan were not members of the CIS Collective Security Treaty and showed scant regard in general for sovereign decision-making by Central Asian states.

In fact Putin soon had to put a brave face on 'approving' substantial support offered by these states to the campaign in Afghanistan. This support seemed poorly if at all coordinated with Russia. Offers to the US and NATO of access to airfields and other facilities, which were made by Kyrgyzstan, Tajikistan, and Uzbekistan, went further than Moscow expected or wished.[37] Since Russian troops were not included in ISAF, Moscow is also unlikely to have encouraged the Kazakh decision early in 2002 to provide a contingent of peacekeeping troops for the stabilization of Afghanistan.

Russia did not try to speak out on behalf of Central Asian or other CIS states about the kind of campaign that should be conducted in Afghanistan, and views about this in Central Asian capitals varied. Some Central Asian leaders initially hesitated over the prospect of the US waging war to depose the Taliban regime itself. This reflected fears of Taliban responses or the risk of large refugee flows northwards from Afghanistan. Turkmenistan, referring to its 'principles of neutrality and non-intervention', offered to mediate and ambitiously to host a UN centre to negotiate an acceptable solution over Afghanistan. In contrast, President Karimov of Uzbekistan was an ardent supporter of military strikes, once it became clear that the target list for these would include camps of the Islamic Movement of Uzbekistan (opposed to the Karimov regime) located in Afghanistan.[38]

Central Asian leaders did not reflect publicly on the legal rationale for intervention in Afghanistan. They preferred to approve the terminology of simple retaliation against terrorist attacks, since this could underwrite possible military strikes of their own against those they might designate as terrorists. Here they had common ground with Russia and China. This common view is revealed in the Kazakh Foreign Minister's summary of a statement pledging support for possible US military action in Afghanistan, issued after a meeting of the Shanghai Cooperation Organization on 17 September 2001: 'Support will be given to a rightful retaliation against the groups which support, sponsor, and carry out terrorist acts throughout the world.'[39] This prefigured the related debate on military pre-emption which flared up the following year, though the SCO focused on terrorist groups rather than states or state sponsors of terrorism.

Protracted war and new justifications

The rapid collapse of Taliban rule in autumn 2001, followed by the failure to capture Osama Bin Laden, prompted a shift in the rationale of the continuing military intervention. It changed from the core legal ground of self-defence, with its pluralist roots, gradually towards a more solidarist narrative of humanitarian objectives and political sustainability. This has both drawn from and fed back into evolving debates on the legitimate use of force. What had been an international conflict came to be defined as an internal conflict in Afghanistan. The justifications for foreign commitments to this conflict changed in ways that reflected the wider normative concerns of the many state contributors to the country's stabilization and state-building efforts. In the early 2000s Russia was uneasy about these shifts, since it was unhappy to endorse a model of seemingly open-ended Western influence in Afghanistan. But it accepted the need to bolster the fragile rule of the new post-Taliban Afghan administration.

At the outset the war was explicitly not presented as a humanitarian intervention.[40] But in promoting the goal of state-building and in resisting the Taliban, American policy-makers in particular came 'to embrace the language and rhetoric of a humanitarian cause'. This discourse gradually became more widespread despite neglect in actually addressing past and present violations and abuses of human rights or in promoting accountability in Afghanistan.[41] It seemed paradoxical in the context of the unfolding US-driven war on terror, which in the years after 2001 acted to displace humanitarian concerns in the wider discussion on legitimate intervention.

Indeed, in Afghanistan as well, humanitarian priorities have remained at odds with the logic of counter-terrorism. Counter-terrorist operations, which increasingly merged into a more standard counter-insurgency campaign, by their nature increased risks of violating international humanitarian law. Mounting civilian deaths at the hands of coalition forces, even if outside the category of war crimes, fuelled the resistance, threatened to make the conflict self-perpetuating, and placed in question the humanitarian commitment to Afghanistan professed by states involved in Operation Enduring Freedom.

Moreover, the longer this campaign continued, the more detached it became from its initial legal basis in self-defence. As a Western legal specialist observed, 'there is room for doubt as to whether it should still be seen as self-defence against terrorism or whether the authority for the operation now comes from the consent of the new regime in Afghanistan and the fight has become one to secure the stability of the government'.[42] Russia supported Security Council Resolution 1386 which established ISAF, but considered the annual UNSC renewal of ISAF's mandate as justified principally by the original core requirement to eliminate terrorist groups and suppress the Taliban. It viewed the stability of the Afghan government as necessary instrumentally for this security purpose.

As the extension of the ISAF mandate was subject to annual Security Council approval and hence to a notional Russian veto, Moscow found no reason to oppose the practical arguments to transfer ISAF under NATO command in April 2003. Yet for Russia this ongoing NATO role was only indirectly about Afghan political stability. Russia approved UNSC language calling for the creation of 'a strong democratic society and effective institutions of power' in Afghanistan. Yet Moscow has not regarded Afghanistan in any sense as suitable terrain for transplanting Western-defined political values or a liberal social agenda. Nor has Russia really regarded Afghanistan in terms of human security. To the extent that Moscow draws attention to UNSC text calling on forces in Afghanistan to increase 'their responsibility in protecting civilians', this reflects a focus on the outcome of the insurgency.[43] Russia considers the humanitarian issue of civilian deaths in Afghanistan primarily as a problem undermining counter-insurgency efforts.

Moscow's scepticism about ambitious goals for a pluralistic Afghan political process reflects the wider suspicions it developed about efforts at democracy building in the context of the war on terror. But for Russia, efforts to improve governance in the case of Afghanistan also have a particular resonance. Political goals for the state elaborated since 2001 remind Russian leaders of their own earlier decade-long and ultimately futile effort at political and social engineering in Afghanistan (albeit an effort imposed through coercion and wide-scale violence with only a façade of local political legitimacy).

Even in relation to ISAF's military mission the Russian stance has appeared as one of default pessimism. Partly this reflects the military stalemate and ultimate failure of the previous Soviet intervention. Russian generals, still influenced by that humiliation, warned in autumn 2001 about the intractability of Afghanistan as a military theatre. They were surely surprised by the speedy collapse of the Taliban regime, but perhaps not by the spread of insurrection in later years.[44]

By the late 2000s the Russian high command compared the precarious security situation in Afghanistan to the failed Soviet effort to support an Afghan administration that could not retain power on its own against an Islamist and ethnic insurgency. Speaking on the thirtieth anniversary of the Soviet invasion of Afghanistan, a senior Russian general insisted that coalition forces were making the same mistakes as Soviet troops had in the early 1980s, including the incitement of growing resistance as civilian casualties mounted.[45] In June 2010 Deputy Prime Minister Sergei Ivanov reinforced this sombre interpretation. 'Never again would a Russian soldier enter Afghanistan', he insisted, 'it's like asking the United States whether they will send troops to Vietnam... it's totally impossible.'[46] However, this left strategic uncertainty about the future.

The strategic context to the Afghanistan campaign

It is striking that, although Russia has benefited in security terms from the struggle to suppress the Taliban more obviously than in other theatres of the 'war on terror', the use of force in Afghanistan has hardly advanced principles of a 'cooperative security' relationship between Russia and Western forces. Russia has continued to view the Western engagement in Afghanistan instead largely through a geopolitical prism and in terms of competition.

This was reflected in Russia's temptation initially to engage in manoeuvring in post-Taliban Afghanistan and its lukewarm endorsement of the reform agenda for the country advanced by Western states. The Russian security elite has been focused overall on the impact of the Afghanistan campaign on the CIS regional order, especially on Russian strategic primacy in Central Asia

In particular, Moscow has resented the continued Western use of military facilities in Central Asian states, primarily in Uzbekistan (until 2005), Tajikistan, and Kyrgyzstan, and new Western security relationships with these states, for the protracted operations to stabilize Afghanistan. After the Taliban was overthrown, the desirability of this unprecedented American military presence in Central Asia was vigorously debated among Russian military and political commentators.[47] Traditional zero-sum geopolitical thinking was widespread. Some anticipated an inevitable extension of US control over military facilities in Kazakhstan and perhaps Georgia and Azerbaijan.[48]

As differences grew between Russia and the United States over the campaign against terrorism, US access to military facilities in Central Asia began to be analysed in Moscow in the context of the future of American global basing strategy. A variety of practical military-strategic and military-economic problems for Russia began to be associated with the US military presence in Central Asia.[49]

The official Russian position, presented by Moscow in the Russia–US Working Group on Afghanistan in 2002, was that the period of stationing of 'non-regional armed forces' in Central Asia would be 'limited to the period of the counter-terrorist operation in Afghanistan'.[50] However, to Moscow's frustration this period became open-ended, and at the same time it was clear that Washington was unprepared to accept the idea of some formal division of roles whereby the US-led coalition took responsibility for the security of Afghanistan, while Russian-led CIS forces assumed responsibility for the security of Central Asia. The paradox was that for Moscow a Western disengagement from Central Asian facilities and from Afghanistan itself, in the absence of effective stabilization of that country, was still viewed with considerable alarm. Russia has regarded the restoration of any form of Taliban dominance in Afghanistan as anathema.

A further reason why the Afghanistan regional campaign has failed to establish the basis for a wider Russian–Western cooperative security agenda has been Russian rivalry with NATO at the systemic level and continued Russian sensitivity to the NATO role in Afghanistan. After NATO headquarters assumed control of ISAF in 2003, there was a rather distant relationship for the rest of the decade between Moscow and the enlarging NATO operation.

For all their deep anxieties over the reinvigoration of the Taliban, after 2003 Russian officials remained equivocal about the prospect of an effective

'NATO success' in Afghanistan. After all, as the insurgency spread in Afghanistan, Russia–NATO differences were growing in the European theatre, and in the 2000s Russian leaders were increasingly perturbed by NATO's declared global remit (prefigured by the post-OAF debate). The Russian security elite, with their Soviet experience, also appreciated the historical irony of NATO forces, in their first major combat mission outside Europe, trapped in a commitment to a beleaguered government in Kabul. For Moscow this offered the positive strategic result of constraining NATO's ambitions in other geographic theatres.

Russia sought to influence the political outcome in Afghanistan. However, Russian officials became doubtful whether their reliance on UN diplomacy and insistence that the ISAF mission should remain until its Security Council mandate is fulfilled would be sufficient for this. Some openly questioned whether the large number of nations that support NATO's operations in Afghanistan mean 'NATO is turning into a "democratic" alternative to the UN'.[51] After the NATO HQ assumed control of ISAF, Russia noted that NATO no longer coordinated its operations in Afghanistan with the UN but simply notified it about them. Viewing this development, Moscow could not be certain whether NATO's motivation to intervene in conflicts in the future would be dampened by the whole experience of Afghanistan or perhaps liberated by an inclination to circumvent the UN.

By 2010 NATO policy in Afghanistan entered a period of strategic flux, as the staged withdrawal of NATO troops from the country in 2014 began to loom. Russia saw opportunities for influence in exploring military cooperation with NATO, through selling helicopters, through helping to train Afghan national security forces, and even through participating in counter-narcotics raids in Afghanistan.[52] This was reinforced by the offer of transit and supply routes for NATO forces through Russian territory towards Afghanistan, as well as the use of Russian territory for the staged withdrawal of NATO forces from Afghanistan.

Looking ahead Russia seems to anticipate a much reduced but only temporary NATO/US presence in Afghanistan, offset partly by an expanded political role in the country for Russia and other CIS states. Lavrov has called for 'restoration of the neutral status of Afghanistan' in the period 'after the completion of international stabilization efforts'.[53] This outcome is not implied, however, by the conclusion of a new long-term US–Afghan strategic partnership treaty, which enables Washington to retain bases in Afghanistan. President Karzai has assured that his country would never provide its territory for bases that could launch aggression against neighbouring countries.[54] This is unlikely, however, to change Moscow's perception of Afghanistan, over a decade after the initial US intervention, as posing an ongoing geopolitical challenge for Russia and not just a terrorist threat.

WANING SOLIDARITY OVER THE 'GLOBAL WAR ON TERROR'

The fragile security consensus around the Afghanistan campaign between Russia and major Western states formed a central pillar in the wider, diffuse, and more controversial unfolding 'global war on terror' driven by the United States. However, the initial Russian–American *discursive solidarity* about global counter-terrorism began to fragment quite quickly behind the scenes into tensions about the nature of the challenge. The international legal regulation of counter-terrorism, including the role of the United Nations in this effort, was also disputed.[55] In terms of evolving norms around the use of force, as we shall see more clearly in the next chapter, Moscow located itself awkwardly between the US and leading Western states sceptical of military-dominated counter-terrorism, especially France and Germany.

State targets of the 'war on terror'

The foundation for effective cooperation in the 'war on terror' had to be a considerable measure of agreement over the nature of the threat and the identity of the states contributing to it. But in Russian–US relations such agreement has been shallow at best. Speaking publicly to an American audience on 19 September 2001, in the traumatic days following 9/11, Russian Foreign Minister Igor Ivanov sounded a high note of optimism. He called for the creation of a global system of countering terrorism, arguing that the main thing was 'that we should be guided by the same principles in the same direction'. 'We are now united into a single front', he declaimed. 'I believe there will be no competition between us who will play the leading role.'[56]

But already some days later, in a closed session with NATO officials, Defence Minister Sergei Ivanov confirmed the problem of such a 'single front' image by listing states related to *Russia's* particular terrorist concerns. He referred to the presence of terrorists on ungoverned territories in Afghanistan, the Philippines, Chechnya, and Georgia. He also raised the danger of uncontrolled nuclear weapons if Pakistan were to collapse. But he also seemed to reach out to American concerns by specifying the problem of terrorists gaining hold of weapons of mass destruction, a scenario that would strongly influence Washington's emerging counter-proliferation policies.[57]

The different states at the centre of Russian and American concerns became explicit in President George Bush's State of the Union speech in January 2002. This shifted the focus of American counter-terrorist efforts from Afghanistan to the three countries which Bush labelled an 'axis of evil'—Iran, Iraq, and North Korea. But it also indicated, significantly, that Washington was ending a phase of the war in which it had worked in alignment with Russia (among other powers), and moving on to target a set of countries with which Moscow happened to have close ties.

Putin quickly objected to any 'drawing up of blacklists'. But during a visit to Europe in February Sergei Ivanov revealed Russia's own list of countries threatening the world with terrorism, one differing to the US list. He talked of 'propagators of extremist trends of Islam trained in Moslem educational institutions of Saudi Arabia, Pakistan and Egypt'—that is the sources of radical Sunni movements (all incidentally located in Western-aligned states), which could infiltrate foreign states.[58] Ivanov also reaffirmed his concern about regions where terrorists have filled a power vacuum, defined as the Middle East, the Balkans, Somalia, a number of Asian countries, and the North Caucasus, as well as Georgia.

Hence for Russia the problem beyond Afghanistan was not defined as one of active state *sponsorship* of terrorists, or even of hosting terrorists (as in Afghanistan); rather it was one of failed or failing states. This created serious ambiguities about the legal and practical responsibilities of regimes in such states. Ivanov warned against any expansion of the US 'war on terror' to other nations without absolute proof of their involvement in terrorist activities and without UN Security Council approval.[59]

Russia's warning expressed rising concern that Iraq, and perhaps Syria, was being positioned into the American line of fire. Soon after Bush's Axis of Evil speech Putin castigated the notion of rogue regimes used by the US as a pretext to launch a future war on Iraq.[60] Iraq was hardly an obvious sponsor of terrorism, since Saddam had harshly dealt with Islamist forces within Iraq. Nor—to meet the Russian criteria for a state of concern—was it a weak state with ungoverned regions used by terrorists (unless we accept the Turkish interpretation of Kurdish militias in the north of Iraq as terrorists).

It is from this point in time that Russian officials lost their inhibitions in publicly ascribing hidden geopolitical policy motivations behind the steadily expanding list of state 'sponsors' of terrorism drawn up by the US administration. This list soon included Cuba, Iran, Iraq, Libya, North Korea, Syria, and Sudan; all states except Sudan with which Russia happened to have fair to good relations. Russian–American solidarity, as we note at the end of this chapter, eventually fractured in response to the growing diversity of 'states of concern' under the US conception of the war on terror, as American counter-terrorism, counter-proliferation, and regime change motivations overlapped and reinforced each other.

Russia and the international regulation of force in counter-terrorism

The Russian leadership was aware that it could exercise little leverage by itself over America's definition of the international and transnational terrorist threat, or the states involved, or indeed over possible interventions in such states. However, some constraints on US activism might be achieved by campaigning for global agreements on definitions and the regulation of the terrorist challenge, and by seeking to place the whole agenda before the United Nations, despite the inchoate and multifaceted nature of the unfolding US-led campaign.

On one level Russia could appeal for the regulation of force in counter-terrorism, beyond the specific case of the Afghanistan intervention (despite the potential effect of this case on international law). It was essential, an officer argued in the Russian General Staff journal, 'to establish the international legal limits of the use of armed forces for the conduct of anti-terrorist measures beyond national borders'. This depended on agreement of two kinds: first, an international legal definition of terrorism accepted by all states in the United Nations, since 'the normative base of the struggle with terrorism does not correspond with contemporary realities'. Secondly, agreement should be achieved on the 'international legal regulation of the choice of means and the defined level of the use of force against terrorism'. Such regulation was all the more important, it was argued, because of the risks of escalation: terrorist threats could catalyse conflict or war between neighbour states, and instability created by terrorism within states may also result in armed confrontation between political forces, ethnic and religious groups.[61]

These proposals required agreement between major powers over the *process* of defining when counter-terrorist operations should be initiated. The question again was one of 'who sets the rules'. For the Russian civilian security studies specialist Alexei Arbatov, the way forward could be a new international convention or treaty on combating terrorism. Setting the bar high, he argued at the end of 2001 that this should include a 'precise and narrow' definition of international terrorism so that 'weaker powers should not be afraid that world powers might decide to broaden the definition for political considerations'. The treaty would also need articles on 'international mechanisms of making decisions concerning sanctions and the use of force against organisations of international terrorism and countries supporting them'.[62]

This kind of proposal could be seen as building on the injunction of UN Security Council Resolution 1373, which had obligated member states to take necessary measures to stop international terrorist activity. But the challenge of constraining the self-interested policies of powerful states (read as the US in Russian proposals) and reaching a definition of international terrorism was daunting. Moreover, the notion of defining the use of force under an international convention was complicated by the need for global interaction between a very wide range of counter-terrorist and law-enforcement agencies, which had different approaches to the role of force within states as well as beyond state borders. Arbatov recognized the issue in arguing that his convention should take into account the cooperation of secret services and the use of special counter-terrorist units and military contingents.[63]

Russian officials approved the wider international regulation of force in counter-terrorism, at least in principle. Already in October 2001 the Russian Federal Security Service head, Nikolai Patrushev, speaking alongside other CIS security service chiefs, called for all countries to coordinate their security services and law-enforcement agencies, based on UN decisions and principles, to create a global international security system against international terrorism and extremism.[64] The influential former Russian Interior Minister Anatoly Kulikov went further to argue for the creation of a single international structure to combat both international terrorism and transnational crime, which he regarded as interconnected phenomena. This kind of anti-terrorist centre, in his view, could be based in a reorganized Interpol, which should acquire rapid-reaction forces.[65]

There were two core problems. First, the multilateral constraints of such Russian ideas seemed directly aimed at and ran counter to the impulses of the expanding US response to the 9/11 attacks. In September 2002, addressing the 57th United Nations General Assembly, Russian Foreign Minister Igor Ivanov urged the transformation of the anti-terrorist coalition 'into a support structure of an effective security and cooperation system of the new millennium'.[66] But this high-flown discourse of multilateralism contrasted with growing acrimony over the scope of the US-driven 'war on terror'. Secondly, as we consider below, Moscow made clear that it had no intention of placing its own 'counter-terrorist war' in Chechnya under any multilateral regulation.

In practice during 2002–5 there was little progress in developing new UN-wide regulation of the extra-territorial employment of force by states for counter-terrorism, beyond the case of Afghanistan. Russia urged that the UN Counterterrorism Committee, a body created after UN Security Council Resolution 1373, should be strengthened and granted additional powers to report violations by states of their obligations to deal with terrorist threats to the UN Security Council. However, the committee continued to act as a sounding board and a channel for some information exchanges, while masking different approaches by states to counter-terrorism.[67] This difference in state practice was a major obstacle to efforts to draft a UN Comprehensive Convention against International Terrorism. Negotiations on this convention failed to reach a universal definition of terrorism.[68] The UN General Assembly eventually adopted an International Convention for the Suppression of Acts of Nuclear Terrorism in April 2005, without a vote. But this Russian-sponsored convention lacked UN Security Council authority, and had no significant effect on the approach of major powers to the use of force in counter-terrorism.

Chechnya and Russian 'war on terror' discourse

The Russian approach to regulating the international use of force for counter-terrorism cannot be understood properly outside the context of Moscow's fixation on restoring state control over Chechnya. From the beginning of the second Russian Chechnya campaign in October 1999, Russia defined its role in this (internationally accepted Russian) territory unequivocally as countering terrorism rather than combating efforts at separatism or secession.[69] The metaphors and concerns of the post-9/11 war on terrorism certainly have occupied a central place in Russian foreign policy *discourse*, especially in the UN, in relations with the United States and countries of the CIS. In practice, however, even when Russian officials have spoken in abstract or global terms about terrorism, Russian policies have linked the phenomenon narrowly to Chechnya and the North Caucasus and, to a much lesser degree, to Central Asia, including Afghanistan.

As Russian operations in Chechnya proceeded in July 2000, Putin warned about 'the creation of an extremist international in the so-called arc of instability beginning in the Philippines and ending in Kosovo'. He referred to an 'International Islamic Front' headed by Osama Bin Laden, which aimed to create an Islamic caliphate, including 'part of the contemporary territory of the Russian Federation'.[70] So Chechnya came to be categorized in Moscow as a key transnational terrorist-inspired conflict, even as the first stage in plans to create a global caliphate. Once American action against Afghanistan commenced in October 2001 Russia argued that, as one of the first states to combat foreign-sponsored terrorism, it considered itself justified in regarding the Afghanistan operations as 'a continuation of the anti-terrorist operation in Chechnya'.[71] Even well after the overthrow of the Taliban, Russia's UN envoy insisted on the unsubstantiated claim that there were 'large numbers of foreign mercenaries, particularly Chechens, among the terrorists still active in the country'.[72]

According to this discourse, the Russian state has been under attack from the outside rather than the inside. The responsibility for the mass violence in Chechnya then lies with the activities of small numbers of foreign fighters and radicals who entered Chechnya and are orchestrated from outside. An analogy is made with the American response to the 9/11 attacks, though in the case of Russian military action in Chechnya 'self-defence' was a political term rather than a legal requirement since the republic was recognized internationally as part of Russia. Putin referred further to the small incursion by Islamist groups from Chechnya into the Russian republic of Dagestan in August 1999, which preceded Russia's second campaign in Chechnya. 'International terrorism decided to go further and take away the Caucasus', he declaimed, 'which is why they went into Dagestan.' Those behind 'the attack on Dagestan', he warned, would have gone 'to the Volga areas and to Bashkortostan' (Muslim territories further in the Russian Federation).[73]

This alarmist image hints at, but diverts attention from, the deeper Russian concern, which was not terrorist infiltration as such but the breakdown and growing radicalization of Russia's Muslim communities by foreign Islamic influences. Indeed, the paradox of Russia's persistent invocation of 'war on terror' imagery since 9/11 is that there is little evidence that Moscow has held a serious interest in transnational terrorism of the global variant recognized by the US. In reality al-Qaeda as such has not been considered as Russia's direct enemy. Insofar as Russian leaders have been concerned about al-Qaeda and its affiliates, it has been to the quite limited extent they are believed to have financed the Chechen resistance and other Islamic organizations active in the North Caucasus and Central Asia.[74] Nor, without obvious links to these regional preoccupations, has Russia been much concerned about the challenge of states further afield placed in the American category of sponsors of terrorism. Moscow drew up its own list of problematic regions that terrorists could exploit, but Russian leaders only seemed to take seriously such regions located in Russia's own neighbourhood.

The key insight here is that Russia's use of 'war on terror discourse' was driven instrumentally by a much narrower agenda than similar language by the US and other major Western states. This expediency had several foreign policy and diplomatic dimensions, but overall was intended to attract international legitimacy for Russian state policy in Chechnya, especially from the United States. The objective for Russia was to retain the freedom to conduct domestic counter-terrorism unhindered, without international scrutiny, not only for security goals but also significantly for domestic political purposes—the supposed needs of counter-terrorism offered Russian leaders a principal justification for the progressive securitization of the Russian state.[75]

Analytically, Russia's claim that the Chechnya campaign launched in 1999 should be defined *essentially* in terms of combating terrorism, rather than as an insurgency or separatism, is certainly problematic. Spectacular outrages, such as the 2004 Beslan school hostage-taking, do not alter the fact that attacks on civilians and non-combatants by the Chechen resistance in the 2000s were not systematic and were 'peripheral to its main use of political violence'. This was directed against the Russian state's military, security, political, and economic assets.[76]

In terms of international politics, however, Putin's effort to legitimize his Chechnya policy was shrewd. Soon after 9/11 President Bush came to accept rather unequivocally that the Chechnya conflict should be interpreted as an exercise in counter-terrorism. It is true that even in the heyday of solidarity over the overthrow of the Taliban the US State Department was still ready to rebuke Moscow about Russian troops resorting to 'overwhelming force against civilian targets' and committing human rights violations.[77] But Russia could easily shrug this off, once the US publicly claimed that al-Qaeda was aiding terrorists in Chechnya.[78] This carried more weight for Moscow than the fact that the European Union failed to subscribe to the view that the war in Chechnya was an integral part of the 'global war on terror'. In fact, with more knowledge of possible links between al-Qaeda and the Chechen rebels after 9/11, major European states more readily accepted the characterization of the conflict as one of counter-terrorism and the EU reduced and softened its criticisms of Russian actions in Chechnya.[79]

Russia's persistent claim that the Chechnya 'counter-terrorist operation' was internationally inspired and a part of the 'global war on terror' was ironic since it has been accompanied by Moscow's insistence that Western states should have no direct role in the solution of the conflict. Far from the territory of Chechnya becoming a theatre for joint Russian–Western cooperative policy or normative convergence post-9/11, it remained a first-order Russian priority to keep a high bar against any extra-territorial presence, read by Moscow as intervention, in Chechnya by other states or international organizations. This was justified on the basis of a restrictive interpretation of state sovereignty.

This response may partly be explained by Moscow's lingering neuralgia, as previously described, about the risks of Kosovo-style humanitarian intervention in Chechnya. The main Russian impulse, however, seemed to be a determination to exclude restrictions on the Russian campaign in Chechnya that could follow international scrutiny of Russian operations, and to avert the insistent demands by states for Russian compliance with international humanitarian law, the body of regulation under *jus in bello*.[80] Russia's obdurate resistance to international concerns about possible war crimes committed in Chechnya confirmed that Moscow did not view the goal of interstate political solidarity over transnational terrorism as expressing or promising any deeper solidarism over the humanitarian context to military operations.

In fact, Russia remained defiantly pluralistic. In prosecuting its own 'war on terror', Russia had no intention of lowering the threshold of Russian sovereignty. It tried to keep Chechnya inaccessible to the world outside, yet simultaneously called for an international endorsement of its policy there, despite the extreme coercion and violations of international humanitarian law involved. Moscow claimed a sovereign right to employ force as it saw fit within the Russian state, but at the same time argued that the measures used were further justified since the Chechnya operation was part of the wider 'war on terror'. Russia's local experience in Chechnya was even purported to be relevant for combating terrorism within other international conflict zones.

However, Russian security experts struggled ineffectively to develop a 'concept (doctrine) of an anti-terrorist war' which 'goes beyond the framework of usual rules of using military force', but which still relies principally on military structures.[81] It was confusing and unrealistic for Russia to try to generalize from its own specific intra-state conflict to other transnational conflict zones. The Russian form of counter-terrorism in Chechnya emphasized suppressing resistance with harsh military means and permitted extensive ad hoc violence by state bodies. Although federal troops were supposedly conducting a counter-terrorist operation, Russian analysts pointed out at the time that, 'there are no operational or legal documents on that score'; as a result 'each individual commander on every level interprets the campaign as he finds it most convenient'.[82]

In reality these operations reflected scant regard for *jus in bello* or broader international norms on the application of force emerging among Western states, especially those regarding the treatment of civilian populations.[83] Given widespread humanitarian concerns over Chechnya, Moscow could hardly expect any 'model' of operations in Chechnya or claims about the demands of counter-terrorism to strike a chord among EU states. Nor was Washington interested in learning from or adapting to Russian local experience in Chechnya as it sought to expand the scope of counter-terrorist operations beyond Afghanistan (though in autumn 2001 the US had shown some interest in reviewing lessons of the very different Soviet campaign in Afghanistan in the 1980s). Ultimately there was little in Russia's Chechnya campaign that proved to be generalizable for the increasingly diffuse 'global war on terror'.

CONCLUSION: THE COLLAPSE OF CONSENSUS

In a broader sense Chechnya (albeit in a domestic state context) demonstrated the Russian readiness to use military power. This was constrained by Russia's limited capabilities for power projection beyond its immediate neighbourhood. Yet this focus on hard power brought Russia into closer company with the US than with major European states (except perhaps the UK) in the aftermath of 9/11. It was also reflected, as shown in the next chapter, in similar Russian–American views over pre-emptive military operations against terrorist groups in foreign states. In this respect Russia seemed ready to follow the US lead in self-interested efforts to revise the international regulation of the use of force.

This common language between Moscow and Washington on pre-emption was overwhelmed, however, by the weight of differences that developed between the two states over the nature and targets of global counter-terrorism, as the US merged this with its counter-proliferation agenda and linked it with the legitimacy of specific regimes. President Bush's State of the Union speech in January 2002 shifted the American focus to target a set of countries, or 'rogue regimes', with which Moscow happened to have close ties. If Moscow identified the existence of any wider terrorist threats beyond Chechnya and perhaps Central Asia, it considered risks to arise from failed or failing states. For Russia they did not originate from active state sponsors of terrorism, ones with ostensible interests in nuclear arms, as now claimed by the Bush administration.

These differences polarized over reactions towards Iraqi non-compliance with the international monitoring of its arms programmes. Russia adamantly resisted American efforts to conflate Iraqi policy with global terrorism. Saddam Hussein's Iraq could have nothing to do with terrorism, Defence Minister Sergei Ivanov proclaimed in autumn 2002, confirming the Russian fixation on Chechnya, since no Iraqis had been identified among the fighters from thirty to forty states on the side of the Chechen separatists.[84] Leaving aside Chechnya, Deputy Foreign Minister Vyacheslav Trubnikov insisted that 'the fight against terrorism and the situation around Iraq are absolutely different things'.[85] The deep controversy that developed over Iraq is examined in the following chapter.

For Russia the shift of emphasis in the US-dominated global 'war on terror' towards targeted counter-proliferation and demonizing 'axis of evil' states signalled the abandonment of its original consensual focus on Afghanistan. Moscow claimed this axis was bogus and driven by ulterior political, and in the case of Iraq also economic, objectives. At the same time Russia tended to downplay, though not dismiss, the nuclear ambitions of these states. Early in 2003 the Russian Nuclear Energy Minister, Alexander Rumyantsev, even claimed that 'all secret services agree that nuclear weapons have never been sold or bought' and that not one of the 'axis of evil' countries 'possesses the capacities that may lead to manufacture of nuclear weapons'.[86] This proved to be a blasé judgement in the case of North Korea at least. But it indicated the difficulty of agreeing on an intelligence file to build a case for a forceful international response to the nuclear ambitions and capabilities of states in breach of non-proliferation commitments.

A further problem was that 'axis of evil' rhetoric, with its implication that regime change was the ultimate objective, could in itself deepen the proliferation conundrum, as could military action against Iraq. This risk was acknowledged by the Russian politician, former senior defence official, and nuclear specialist Andrei Kokoshin, who claimed that a process of nuclearization could be triggered precisely by American action against the 'axis of evil' in the form of an attack on Iraq, since this could prompt other states to try to acquire the means to avoid Iraq's fate. For Kokoshin any such process would be a major concern for Russia. He speculated about the formation of a 'nuclear arc' along the perimeter of Russia: Japan, North Korea, China, India, Pakistan, Iran, and Israel.[87]

Among these states, the case of Pakistan illustrates well the divergent American and Russian official, public perspectives of proliferation, linked to the 'war on terror'. The 2002 US National Security Strategy exempted Pakistan, as well as India and Israel, from criticism of the 'axis of evil' variety, let alone the threat of US military intervention. The US approach to non-proliferation was selective—the American priority being to keep Pakistan on board after it had been persuaded 'to join' the 'war on terror', rather than to highlight the nuclear challenge it posed. This was done despite nuclear Pakistan's many years of support for the Taliban, Indian claims that it had been sponsoring terrorism in Kashmir, and reports that it had leaked nuclear know-how to other states.

In contrast, already shortly after the 9/11 attacks, Moscow identified Pakistan specifically as a risk for wider nuclear proliferation. Who would control the nuclear weapons were Pakistan to collapse? Defence Minister Sergei Ivanov asked NATO officials rhetorically.[88] Over the next few years Russia regularly emphasized the danger of the proliferation of nuclear materials or components of nuclear weapons from Pakistan.[89] For Russia, the insecure state of Pakistan has continued to pose more risk of extremist access to nuclear weapons or materials (already in place) than does the rather strong centralized state in Iran or than Saddam's state in Iraq had done.[90]

The irony here is that for many years Western intelligence agencies and proliferation specialists themselves have quietly shared a belief in the appreciable risk of nuclear terrorism linked to Pakistan. They have perceived conditions in Pakistan as enabling an intersection of proliferation and terrorism.[91] However, this perception seems to have been overridden by other political imperatives in the decisions by American leaders to threaten or use force against states under aegis of the 'global war on terror'.

The different proclaimed rankings in Moscow and Washington or other Western capitals of states of proliferation concern, overshadowed a more fundamental difference that had a powerful political effect on the readiness of the US to engage in not just pre-emptive but clearly preventive intervention: the Russian and American leaderships differed in essence about the overall likelihood of the possible use by terrorists of some form of weapons of mass destruction (WMD). For Russian leaders this simply seemed a lesser existential threat. Despite some general worries about Pakistani nuclear assets, their concern about the targeting of the Russian state or its cities was mainly associated with conventional if large-scale terrorist attacks, specifically ones sourced to Chechnya.

The situation was different for American leaders, ever mindful of the bolt-from-the-blue shock of 9/11. For them the low but real risk of the US being subject to a WMD attack was judged to be unacceptable and to be countered as a top priority. From this strategic consideration, magnified by political factors including a belief in the inherent hostility of the leadership of some states, came a determination to loosen earlier constraints on the possible need to employ force abroad. This set in motion a growing challenge to the legal and normative regulation of the use of force of a kind more fundamental than anything experienced before by the international community in the post-Cold War years.

5

Pre-emption, the Iraq War, and the Spectre of Unconstrained Force

The Iraq War in 2003 sharply divided the leading world powers and remains in many ways a touchstone for opinion on the legitimacy of military intervention in contemporary times. In terms of developing norms, the importance of this intervention was magnified by its implications for the increasingly controversial American commitment to the pre-emptive use of force to avert threats in cases where traditional self-defence norms do not seem to apply. As this chapter reveals, Russia's position in these debates came close to that of America on pre-emption, but this did not prevent Moscow's sharp opposition to the Iraq War on grounds of principle and expediency.

In autumn 2001 the most powerful states in the international system agreed to a modified interpretation of self-defence to sanction Operation Enduring Freedom in Afghanistan. But this rare consensus was soon in flux and overshadowed by the rising political momentum in Washington in 2002 for loosening constraints on the use of force more generally. The example of regime change in Afghanistan was presented as *sui generis* in legal terms, but for many in Washington the removal of the Taliban was regarded as exemplary in *political* terms and the norms around this spectacular intervention remained in flux.

What was agreed in autumn 2001 could be transformative. On the face of it the UN Security Council had acceded to new and indeterminate general norms that applied to the 'war on terror'. These were first the reconfiguration of certain types of terrorist violence as an 'armed attack for the purposes of the UN Charter Article 51 rights of self-defence'; second, the harbouring of terrorists, as a justification for the use of military force against a state; and third, that the use of force against a state harbouring terrorists does not necessarily 'become impermissible retaliation or illegal anticipatory self-defence, or exceed the rules of proportionality'.[1] In short this suggested that the groundwork to vindicate the *pre-emptive use of force* was emerging.

Western international lawyers qualified these changes, however, by claiming that 'harbouring' terrorists should only be a reason to invoke self-defence if there is proof of direct support or at least tacit approval of terrorist attacks by a state, except perhaps in cases of 'state failure'. Even in the case of states without any effective government, arguably only a carefully targeted armed response would be justified. Lawyers could point out further that these revisions to the framework of self-defence were conditional on certain criteria, the fulfilment of which should be agreed by the UN Security Council itself.[2]

Beyond strict legal positions, however, the *politics* of international law was crucial in the highly charged post 9/11 period, as expressed by a number of rhetorical questions. What if the US independently chose to define when the criteria for the use of force against terrorist attacks were present beyond the case of Afghanistan and to react regardless of UN authorization? What if the US shifted the justification for the use of force from terrorist presence as such, to the actions or even intentions of (the political category of) 'state sponsors of terrorism'? Could force be justified further by the risk of terrorist access to WMD or more generally by serious counter-proliferation challenges? Such questions were increasingly debated in Washington as the US administration contemplated a more expansive basis for justifying military action than that offered in autumn 2001, one supporting the validity of pre-emptive or even preventive military operations.

During 2001–3, as assessed below, Russia initially conceded the broad logic of the emerging US position on military pre-emption. However, as the military scope of American foreign policy activism grew, Moscow began to revert to its traditional pluralist sovereignty-focused mindset. In general Russia did not define pre-emptive self-defence as illegitimate, even if Russia and the US had in mind different threat scenarios and potential targets of pre-emptive force. As with its support for the 'war on terror' at large, the Russian discourse on pre-emption was driven by regional order goals, which initially distracted Russian leaders from the risks and implications of an American policy of pre-emption extending into broad doctrinal approval for preventive war.

PRE-EMPTION AND PREVENTIVE WAR

The American promotion of a doctrine of pre-emption before and after the Iraq War formed a major challenge to existing norms and risked an extended impasse between major powers over their interpretation of the core right of self-defence. Pre-emption reflects the idea that attacks may be prevented by disabling a threatening enemy. It can take the form of anticipatory self-defence—military action against an absolutely imminent threat. In the classic legal rendering this expresses 'a necessity of self-defence, instant, overwhelming, leaving no choice of means or no moment for deliberation'.[3] This leaves necessity and proportionality as precautionary criteria. More controversially, pre-emption could entail preventive military action to counter a future threat before it has matured. It is this that potentially challenged the UN Charter framework itself and raised the spectre of the exercise of unconstrained force by the dominant power in the international system.[4]

For most of the post-1945 era both versions of pre-emption had been resisted by US governments and the broader international community. Washington and Moscow were acutely conscious of the danger of conceding a right of pre-emptive self-defence during the Cold War when their states each maintained nuclear second-strike capabilities, other than in the narrow sense of a right to launch their missiles on receiving warning of an incoming enemy missile. A concern about the pre-emptive use of nuclear weapons has not evaporated from US–Russian relations. But this concern steadily subsided in Washington with the change in political climate since the Cold War.

The challenge of the 'Bush Doctrine'

There were elements of pre-emption in the policies of previous US administrations on the use of force. As we have noted, the American 1998 military strikes against targets in Afghanistan and Sudan prompted debate.[5] But it was only in June 2002 that President Bush proclaimed outright an expansive policy of pre-emptive military action, which moved towards the preventive or even precautionary use of force, as a response to the threat of weapons of mass destruction associated with international terrorism. 'We must take the battle to the enemy', Bush urged, and even if threats are not imminent 'if we wait for threats to have fully materialized, we will have waited too long'. This policy, widely described as the 'Bush Doctrine', was notable in removing the customary international law requirement of a palpable and imminent threat, on which basis anticipatory self-defence could be undertaken.[6] Indeed, it implied further the need to use force in response to rather open-ended and subjectively defined threats.

Bush's reformulation was extended in the US National Security Strategy, an annual report by the president to Congress, released in September 2002. In the relevant passages the document based itself on the pre-1945 customary right of self-defence. It failed to mention the UN Charter and reaffirmed the need to 'adapt the concept of imminent threat to the capabilities and objectives of today's adversaries'. This provided the basis for unilateral responses to more distant and uncertain challenges.[7] In November 2002 the State Department legal adviser offered an interpretation of the legal basis for pre-emptive military action that tried to place it more explicitly within the parameters of anticipatory self-defence.[8] However, the boundaries of the doctrine articulated by Bush and other senior US administration officials exceeded this. The focus seemed to be on the issue of 'rogue states' attempting to acquire WMD. But the circumstances in which Washington envisioned taking military action remained open-ended.[9]

A potential major international political outcome of this new rendering of pre-emptive self-defence would be to privilege the powerful. The factual assessment of whether the criterion of imminence was fulfilled, or could even be dispensed with in the face of what the National Security Strategy described as the danger of 'rogue states and terrorists' relying on 'acts of terror and potentially, the use of weapons of mass destruction', would depend considerably on the ability of powerful states or groups of states to influence these assessments, as well as their more extended intelligence assets (or their claims to have convincing intelligence sources). Taking this evaluation further, it could even imply that 'the law on self-defence would remain generally applicable—available as a diplomatic tool to be deployed against weak states—while the most powerful of countries would gain freedom to act as it chose'.[10]

Meanwhile, the international legal effect of the Bush administration's new formulation was one of confusion. The previous understanding that anticipatory self-defence must be assessed against the criteria of necessity and proportionality had imposed external measures of evaluation. In contrast the notion of 'threat pre-emption' (with all the subjective content this implies) did not form 'the expansion by analogy of an existing category'; rather it represented 'the launching of a new concept, one that cannot provide any effective normative guidance'. So what on the surface might appear as a legal norm, two legal specialists have argued, 'is actually no norm at all'. Significantly therefore, threat pre-emption, since it has lacked reasonable normative clarity and coherence, has been unable to discharge the justificatory function expected of legal categories in the international community at large.[11]

Returning to the international political context, it was evident that the revised relationship between unilateralism and the use of force implicit in the new American rendering of pre-emption could profoundly influence an international order still significantly defined by its pluralist currents. In such an international system an act of pre-emptive self-defence, based on a state's self-perceived good faith conviction, could appear 'like a serious or hysterical misjudgement to some other actors and like either cynical or self-deluded naked aggression to others'.[12] Many states did not believe it sufficient to rely on American good intentions as the unilateral thrust of American policy on the use of force unfolded. However, Russia was notable in choosing initially to complement rather than contest the US discourse on military pre-emption.

Russian discourse on pre-emption

One might expect Russia to have felt wrong-footed by the Bush Doctrine. It required a belief in the good faith of US convictions about developing WMD and terrorist threats. Moscow should also have identified the looming challenge it posed to the exclusive authority of the UN Security Council (and to Russian veto rights within it, with the international standing this brought) to respond to situations threatening international peace and security. On the other hand, to the extent the US stance on pre-emption sought to loosen legal constraints on the use of force by powerful states, it offered temptations for Russia (still wedded to a definition of itself as a 'great power' internationally with co-equal rights to the US) to advance its interests in its own neighbourhood, the CIS regional order. This helps explain Russia's own discourse on a form of pre-emption and reluctance to criticize Bush's new policy on pre-emption.

This potential strategic and conceptual 'spillover' was not confined just to Russia. The US National Security Strategy warned nations not to 'use pre-emption as a pretext for aggression'. However, it not surprising that the Security Strategy encouraged other states to rethink how they could advance their own national objectives by force. A leading legal specialist questioned whether the Strategy appeared as 'a green light for states wishing to suppress independence movements, to invite outside help for that purpose and to take cross-border action?'[13]

Russia's interpretation of pre-emption can be understood in this context. It largely reflected regional foreign policy concerns and instruments, mixed with its preoccupation with Chechnya. This was expressed in coercive policies, including threats of cross-border operations towards the Western-leaning neighbour state of Georgia.[14]

This becomes clear from a Russian letter to the UN Security Council on the first anniversary of the 9/11 attacks. In a clear reference to shifting norms since autumn 2001, the letter pointed to the dangers of 'territorial enclaves outside the control of national governments... unable or unwilling to counteract the terrorist threat'. It asserted Russia's right to self-defence against Chechen attacks and threatened unilateral action against supposed 'terrorist bases' in the lawless Pankisi Gorge in northern Georgia (adjacent to Chechnya) without Georgia's permission.[15] Moscow claimed that international terrorists were regularly coming from Georgian territory to carry out 'criminal actions on the territory of Russia'. Putin reaffirmed the threat of possible strikes and special operations were Georgia to fail to put an end to such 'guerrilla incursions'.[16]

If such claims were intended to test the international waters before a Russian military foray into Georgia, little headway was achieved. The US and EU states rejected Russia's right to invoke self-defence against terrorism in this case and remained critical of any Russian intervention in Georgia. Washington deplored violations of Georgian sovereignty and referred to bombings by Russian aircraft '*under the guise of* antiterrorist operations'[17]—an apparent reference to several 'deniable' cross-border raids since 1999 by unmarked planes and helicopters from Russian territory.[18] This exchange confirmed that Russia could not hope for any 'Georgia-for-Iraq' deal with the US—accepting each other's right to intervene in their 'state of concern'. America eventually dispatched some of its troops to Georgia, in agreement with Tbilisi, to train the Georgian military for anti-terrorism activities, which hollowed out Russian claims about 'terrorism' in the Pankisi Gorge.

Despite this setback over Georgia, Russian military and diplomatic spokesmen embraced the option of pre-emption and more specifically preventive strikes, especially in their neighbourhood. In October 2003 a high-level defence 'White Paper' (known as the Ivanov Doctrine after Defence Minister Sergei Ivanov) pointedly envisaged the *preventive* ('*preventivny*') use of military means. Ivanov interpreted the document in language similar to the US 2002 National Security Strategy and asserted Russia's right to use preventive military force in cases where a threat is growing and 'is visible, clear and unavoidable', including threats among CIS countries. But he extended the scope of preventive military action further. Force could be used 'if there is an attempt to limit Russia's access to regions that are essential to its survival, or those that are important from an economic or financial point of view'.[19] Indeed Ivanov did not preclude Russian preventive strikes more widely beyond the CIS region 'in various regions of the world', if this were dictated 'by the interests of Russia or by commitments to our allies'.[20]

This far exceeded the criteria for anticipatory self-defence. Russia's own hegemonic and open-ended language drew on and played back the preventive element in Bush's expansive notion of pre-emption.[21] Moscow even had to clarify to worried Western officials that the Ivanov Doctrine did not sanction preventive *nuclear* strikes (which would pose a wider challenge for the international system).[22]

In 2004 Russia suffered a wave of terrorist attacks. These rather clearly had domestic roots in Chechnya, but were categorized by Russian officials as international terrorism and were used to reaffirm a Russian policy of pre-emption. The new chief of the General Staff, Yuri Baluyevsky, claimed rhetorically that Russia could deliver preventive strikes on terrorist bases anywhere in the world. But even if 'terrorist camps' could be reliably located, Russia had limited technical capacities to carry out precise strikes at distance, such as with long-range aviation, certainly compared to the US. The retired Russian general Leonid Ivashov remarked bluntly that 'we have no means of applying either strategic or operational pressure on terrorists'.[23]

Obviously Russia would also risk interstate conflict by inflicting unilateral strikes based on its subjective evaluation of terrorism. Ivashov, a hawkish officer in other respects, recognized the risks of relativizing the sovereignty of states in this way: 'if we arrogate to ourselves the right to deliver strikes on other state's territory, we thereby implicitly consent to their right to hit our land' wherever terrorists are perceived to be.[24] Moreover, military strikes were no remedy for what the Russian political leadership perceived as a core component of foreign states' relationship to terrorism in Russia—the funding of 'terrorist' activities. Just before Baluyevsky's declaration, Putin admitted to a group of foreign specialists that 'there is no effective option of unleashing hostilities' against countries which host foundations funding such activities; he referred to Russia's long-established and stable relations with Arab countries in this context.[25]

The impression is left that the leadership of the Russian military and security services at least seized on the language of 'preventive strikes' without considering the possible regional backlash (the claims of neighbouring states for reciprocal rights) or the wider implications for Russia's pluralist discourse on sovereignty. The Russian military envied and wished to match the American ability to strike and militarily engage in remote theatres. They felt that 'equality' demanded a similar right for Russian forces (regardless of Russia's actual capabilities for power projection) to undertake swift, decisive, if limited operations, framed within the 'global war on terror'.

As for scenarios for such military action, it was hardly likely that Russia was considering participation in this period in joint operations with the US in Iraq, even after the overthrow of the Baath regime. Nor for the reasons mentioned were other operations distant from Russia practicable. But certain 'rights' of pre-emption in the putative context of counter-terrorism could offer Russia some cover in the event the need arose to implement contingency plans that may have been developed for more transparent strikes against targets in Georgia or possibly other CIS neighbour states.

Pre-emption possibly could provide also the justification for an operation elsewhere in the CIS region under the multilateral aegis of the fledgling Russia-led Collective Security Treaty Organization (CSTO). Moscow might wish to present an operation by the more capable Russian elements of the CSTO's planned rapid deployment forces as a preventive 'regional anti-terrorist engagement' (as discussed in chapter 6), even if Moscow's first recourse probably would be to cite 'collective self-defence' for any such operation. It is true that later in the decade CSTO officials denied that the organization would be used to deliver pre-emptive strikes against facilities or targets outside the CSTO member states.[26] Nevertheless, it seems that Moscow has sought to retain the hypothetical option of 'first strike' operations in its neighbourhood, despite the failure to achieve international consent for Russian action in Georgia's Pankisi Gorge.

As for the normative implications, Moscow anticipated that pre-emption, even its preventive variant, may acquire greater international acceptance. In November 2003 Putin hedged his bets, noting that Russia would adhere to the 'clear criteria for possible use of force' established by modern international law, but 'if the principle of preventive use of force is established in international practice, then Russia will have the right to act in a similar way to protect its national interests'.[27] By implication if such a new norm were to emerge Russia would welcome it and regard it as legitimate.

Some Russian international lawyers and officials, like many of their West European counterparts, remained loath to confer status on a doctrine of pre-emption.[28] One argued, for example, that to accept preventive self-defence, really a 'doctrine of preventive war', would be 'so destructive to the legal order based on the UN Charter that it would simply crumble away'.[29] Yet by the end of 2004 top leaders were nonchalant on the issue. Defence Minister Ivanov noted that Russia observed that in practice 'preventive strikes' are conducted 'in Afghanistan, in Iraq, in other regions of the world... It exists, it is already a norm of life.'[30] Deputy Russian Foreign Minister Yuri Fedorov confirmed that the Russian Foreign Ministry's position was that as a result of Article 51 'pre-emptive strikes at terrorist bases do not collide with international law'.[31]

At face value this position was curious. Russia was out of step with most countries and was strongly opposed to the war against Iraq which appeared to be motivated politically, and for the US partly justified legally, by the logic of pre-emption. However, a key issue is that Russia has avoided official language claiming the right to attack another *state* pre-emptively (thereby dissociating itself from the targeting of 'rogue states'), although it consented to the quite specific argument justifying intervention in Afghanistan in autumn 2001. Like a number of other states claiming rights of pre-emptive self-defence, Moscow justified 'a right to use force in a pre-emptive fashion against non-state entities employing what have come to be called "terrorist" methods'.[32]

In dealing with non-state entities, the Russian military leadership went beyond support for anticipatory self-defence, towards the preventive end of the pre-emption continuum. Sergei Ivanov confirmed this early in 2006: 'we define pre-emption not only as a capability to deliver strikes on terrorist groups but as other measures designed to prevent a threat from emerging long before there is a need to confront it'.[33] An emphasis on prevention is also implicit in Putin's assumption of presidential powers to deploy special forces and secret services in counter-terrorist operations abroad.[34] Russia sought flexibility in its choice of approaches to forestall putative developing threats. This also gave options to exercise pressure indirectly on a neighbour state like Georgia.

Ultimately Russia did not relinquish its pluralist focus on state sovereignty. This meant a high threshold for justifying the use of force against states as political entities. The suggestion in the 2003 'Ivanov Doctrine' that Russia could expand its preventive operations was anomalous. It may have reflected a military establishment struggling to raise its image at that time.[35] In fact Russia distanced itself from the kind of claim for pre-emptive self-defence made by the US, France, and Australia—a presumed right to strike pre-emptively against *states* when there is a risk of terrorists acquiring weapons of mass destruction from a 'rogue state'.[36] With Germany, Spain, and most developing countries, Russia viewed this claim to target states as dangerously open-ended and liable to abuse. This belief, coupled with concern over the marginalization of Russia's Security Council veto, as well as shock over Russia's collapsing influence in Iraq overall, explain Moscow's vigorous opposition to the US-led intervention in Iraq and rejection of any pre-emptive logic in this case.

INTERVENTION IN IRAQ

The Iraq War fractured the international community, exposing underlying fault lines over the global 'war on terror'. These divisions had formed as the US merged counter-terrorist, counter-proliferation, and other political objectives. Moscow was not alone in decrying the expanding American blacklist of state 'sponsors' of terrorism. China, for example, condemned this as the logic of the powerful, relying mainly on 'subjective judgements'. For Beijing such a rationale could be 'very easily abused and used as a pretext for war'.[37] In March 2003 France and Germany seemed to concur on this point. So Russia was far from isolated in the Security Council in renouncing such a major use of force unsanctioned by the UN. At the time Moscow tried to manoeuvre between states in a divided Western community, rather than to defy that community (as over Kosovo in 1999) or cooperate with it (as over Afghanistan in 2001).

The attack on Iraq forms an important case for analysis of evolving norms over the use of force and the challenges of pre-emption. It is a rare example in modern times of a major power (the US, as overwhelmingly dominant in this military intervention) committing itself to combat operations against another state, and recruiting allies for *preventive* reasons, albeit rhetorically dressed up in the language of pre-emption. The three Western military partners, the US, UK, and Australia, as we chart below, eventually chose a different legal justification for 'Operation Iraqi Freedom' on technical, procedural grounds. However, setting aside the legal claims, the principal political justifications for the US decision to resort to force were cast in terms of threat prevention.[38]

All this should be separated from the *motivations* of the US administration and its allies in attacking Iraq under Saddam Hussein in 2003, as well as the motivations of states including Russia in resisting that outcome. These motivations, which we do not need to resolve in charting normative evolution, were certainly mixed and reflected self-interested political, economic, and domestic policy objectives and issues of status, in addition to wider concerns for international order or universalist agendas.

The 2003 war and the Russian response were influenced by the recent history of antagonistic Western relations with Iraq and earlier military strikes against this state. The rationale for Operation Iraqi Freedom for the Western allies involved was rooted in the collectively imposed restrictions on Iraq since the time of the 1991 Gulf War ceasefire agreement. These were mandated and legitimized by the UN. However, in the second half of the 1990s the US, with some UK support, engaged in coercive actions against Iraq in the name of ensuring Iraqi compliance with UN resolutions and sanctions. This kind of enforcement tested the reactions of Russia and other states.

Even before this kind of punitive action on behalf of the UN, the US struck Baghdad with cruise missiles in June 1993, in reaction to intelligence reports that the Iraqi state had been behind a plot to assassinate the former US president George Bush. This unusual case occurred during Russia's brief distinctively pro-Western foreign policy orientation. Moscow did not categorize the attack as a reprisal, illegal under international law, 'not a question of crime and punishment', but noted mildly it was 'an action that the US views as the exercise of the state's inalienable right to self-defence'.[39]

In contrast, in the second half of the 1990s Russia opposed the use of military force against Iraq without an explicit UN Security Council authorization. It emphasized the need instead to use all possible diplomatic means to ensure Iraqi compliance with UN resolutions. In September 1996 America launched cruise missiles against military targets in southern Iraq, justifying this as a necessary response to Iraq's failure to comply fully with the needs of UN weapons inspectors in Iraq, as upholding the authority of the UN. For Moscow, however, such a response was 'disproportionate and unacceptable'.

Yeltsin condemned Operation Desert Fox, the American and British bombings of strategic Iraqi targets in December 1998, even more harshly, for having 'crudely violated the UN Charter and generally accepted principles of international law and the norms and rules of responsible behaviour of states'.[40] These examples, which occurred during a more assertive phase in Yeltsin's foreign policy, show Russia and the US appealing to the UN framework, but separated by clear blue water in the conclusions they reached. In the build-up to the 2003 Iraq War it was uncertain if the effort to cooperate after the 9/11 attacks and the Russian attraction to pre-emptive strikes under Putin had done more than paper over the political and normative divisions between Moscow and Washington over the appropriateness of employing force against Iraq.

International law, justifications, and intervention in Iraq

It is sometimes difficult to distinguish between the political, normative, and legal justifications advanced by the Bush administration for the military campaign against Iraq in 2003. It was a changing discourse and one addressed to different audiences, but this American discourse needs particular scrutiny since Washington drove the political and then military offensive, with compliant allies.

The US initially tried to convince the Security Council to mandate military action on the grounds of Iraqi links to terrorism and weapons of mass destruction. At times American statements leading up to March 2003 were cast in terms of pre-emptive attack against an imminent threat and at other times as preventive war to stop a future threat. These arguments were advanced alongside background claims by Bush administration officials that military force was justified to change a regime repressing the Iraqi people.

All these claims can be regarded as political rather than legal justifications, since Washington accepted eventually that a claim of self-defence against state (Iraqi) support to terrorism was unlikely to prove convincing (without a Security Council or more widely), although self-defence had always been the preferred legal justification by states for military action without Security Council mandate.[41] Consequently in the end the US and Britain chose to justify the war legally as an enforcement of previous UN resolutions, particularly those related to biological, chemical, and nuclear disarmament, which side-stepped the controversy around pre-emption.[42]

This technical legal approach had potential implications of its own for customary law. However, the international political rhetoric around the war and its consequences for the UN Charter system at large links Operation Iraqi Freedom very much with our previous examination of pre-emption. In essence, the pre-emptive, indeed preventive, thinking of American, British, and Australian leaders underlay the rationales used to make the case for war to their legislatures and public opinion. So it is important to examine those claims, as well as the reception they received in Russia and other states, even if the legality of the war does not stand or fall on them. They are revealing about the normative climate, about the persuasiveness of argumentation, and also the instrumental forms it took.

The justification for military intervention in Iraq as *pre-emptive self-defence against terrorist threats* conveniently dovetailed with the wider American discourse on the use of force in the 'war on terror'. The 2002 US National Security Strategy argued that 'when certain regimes with a history of aggression and support for terrorism pursue weapons of mass destruction, thereby endangering the international community, they jeopardise their sovereign immunity from intervention'.[43] At various times senior figures in the American leadership made loose allegations of links between al-Qaeda and Saddam Hussein. These claims were included in a briefing by Secretary of State Colin Powell for the UN Security Council in February 2003, when Washington tried and failed to secure a resolution for the use of force against Iraq.[44] After military operations began, the US continued to call for the destruction of Iraq's 'terrorist infrastructure'.[45]

Russia argued that such claims undermined the common front over counter-terrorism. A former head of the Russian Foreign Intelligence Service complained about 'a surprising mix of notions', since 'the fight against terrorism and the situation around Iraq are absolutely different things'.[46] When Operation Iraqi Freedom began, Putin insisted that Russia had never had any information on Iraq supporting international terrorism.[47]

Russian diplomats pointed out later the irony that it was only once security deteriorated in autumn 2003 in post-Saddam Iraq that a real threat arose of the country spawning a centre for international terrorism, one attractive to various external extremist and terrorist organizations.[48] It became quite widely accepted internationally that the attack on Iraq in itself turned the designation of the state as a terrorist haven into a self-fulfilling prophecy, and the claims that Iraq had sponsored terrorism before March 2003 were largely discredited later.[49]

The justification of *pre-emptive self-defence against the threat of Iraq's weapons of mass destruction*, against the threat of an attack on the US and others arising from Iraq's possession and development of WMD, was widely discussed but ultimately held in reserve by Washington as a supplementary legal argument.[50] US officials presented this alongside the primary legal charge of Iraqi non-compliance with the ceasefire regime binding on Iraq under Resolution 687 of 1991 and subsequent resolutions. However, it was not a part of the formal legal case offered by the UK and Australia for the invasion of Iraq (as opposed to the UK's well-publicized and instrumental political rhetoric over Saddam's WMD threats). This confirmed the doubt of these two states over the doctrine of pre-emptive action.[51]

This pre-emptive justification was directly contested by Russia, but also by Germany, France, and China in the Security Council, all of whom sought to continue the UN weapons inspections in Iraq established by Resolution 687 and reintroduced in 2002 under Resolution 1441. They did not accept that an imminent threat existed as portrayed by Washington and London. Just before the US-led attack commenced, Russian Foreign Minster Igor Ivanov explained that were he to have indisputable facts demonstrating a direct threat to US security from Iraqi territory 'then Russia, without any hesitation would be prepared to use all the means available under the United Nations Charter to eliminate such a threat'. Without such facts Russia called for a political settlement relying on the activities of the UN weapons inspection regime and the International Atomic Energy Agency, which in Ivanov's opinion 'enjoyed the complete trust of the international community'.[52]

The political claim that the invasion was justified by the imperatives for *regime change* was equally controversial, especially for Russia, whether this was in response to Saddam Hussein's domestic repression ('ending tyranny') or to realize the wider political vision of the Bush administration for the Middle East. The political impetus for this claim had been encouraged by the relatively easy overthrow of the Taliban. This previous case of regime change could be conceived by the US administration as a political precedent, one that had resulted in no real objections by other states observing the intervention, even if most states understood it as *sui generis* in a legal sense.

Regime change in Iraq, first called for by Bush soon after 9/11, was above all a political rallying cry. Before March 2003, the US administration did not try to package this as some kind of independent legal justification for military action in Iraq. Britain was explicit that regime change legally should not be an aim of any use of force against Iraq (even if it would be welcomed as a consequence of any such action). Neither Washington nor London presented threats of military action as based on some kind of militarized humanitarianism. However, after the invasion American politicians used the discourse of humanitarian intervention '*ex post facto* to reinforce other rhetorical claims, notably to extend the concept of "threat prevention"'.[53] As with the Afghanistan intervention, a humanitarian rationale was brought into service by politicians seeking to broaden the appeal of military action among domestic legislatures and public opinion.

This devalued evolving norms on humanitarian intervention, as analysed in chapter 3, since the intellectual as well as the legal arguments for characterizing the Iraq intervention as humanitarian have faced powerful challenges, whether we consider American motivations, the options available to stop Iraqi human rights atrocities, or the conduct of the war with respect to international humanitarian law, not to mention the grave humanitarian outcome of the war arising from the devastation of Iraqi economic infrastructure and eventual country-wide insurgency.[54]

For Russia, however, the real challenge perceived in American regime change discourse was its underlying transformative agenda, its relationship to a strategy or doctrinal commitment to spreading democracy and liberal reforms in the Middle East and beyond. As explored in the next chapter, this nexus of regime legitimacy, democracy promotion, and the use of force in American grand strategy was regarded by the Russian leadership as potentially threatening Russian sovereignty and (increasingly authoritarian) domestic state order as well as a gauntlet thrown down to those committed to a pluralist global order.

Putin's immediate response to the assault on Iraq was to reject any justification for it based on 'the desire to change the political regime in that country' as 'in direct contradiction to international law'.[55] Russian UN representative Lavrov condemned it as directly contrary to UN Charter basic principles.[56] He pointed out later that the argument that a war against Iraq 'was supposedly needed to start a process of democratic change throughout the Islamic world' could not have been recognized as legitimate by the global community or have received Security Council approval.[57] Putin interpreted this as a case of values advanced at sword point, arguing when questioned about Iraq, 'we cannot engage in exporting a capitalist, democratic revolution', else the world would embark 'on a very slippery slope of unending sequences of military conflicts'.[58]

This prefigured his trenchant critique of American 'unipolar' interventionism in later years.

This leaves the legal rationale actually offered for the Iraq campaign by its Western participants. As we have noted, Washington's initial, weaker line of defence was that of self-defence against a supposedly quasi-imminent danger posed to the US by the Iraqi regime as a result of its pursuit of WMD programmes (and less convincingly its links to terrorist organizations like al-Qaeda). However, besides serious doubts about the imminence of the Iraqi threat, this ran into all the problems of justifying pre-emption we have discussed.[59] So a second line of justification offered, supplanting the issue of individual defence, was that of collective defence. The Iraqi regime, it was claimed, threatened international peace and security at large by failing to observe the terms of the ceasefire concluded at the end of the 1991 Gulf War.

American and UK officials accused Iraq of violating UN Security Council Resolution 687 (1991), which required Iraq to destroy weapons of mass destruction, not to acquire or develop nuclear weapons, and to cooperate fully with the UN Special Commission. The interpretation of UN Security Council Resolution 1441 (November 2002) became a focus of controversy. This recognized that Iraq was in 'material breach' of the 1991 ceasefire, threatened it with 'serious consequences', but did not explicitly authorize (or taking account of earlier resolutions, we could say re-authorize) the use of force to redress the situation. As they lacked a mandate for force in Resolution 1441, the Western partners seeking action against Iraq chose to resort jointly to the controversial and procedural claim of *implied authorization* by the Security Council. In brief, relying on earlier post-Gulf War Security Council resolutions, they argued that Iraq's 'material breach of obligations removed the basis of the [Gulf War] ceasefire and authorized the use of force' to ensure Iraqi compliance with the ceasefire terms.[60]

A core issue in the legal debate around this has been whether 'the current views of the Council, which in March 2003, were, for the most part, against the use of force, trump its past authorisations?'[61] Yet even if statesmen could be persuaded of the continuing, or revived, validity of past resolutions (in the absence of a new resolution repudiating earlier positions), the use of this particular argument in this crisis was clearly difficult, as Adam Roberts observes, 'because of the doubtful quality of the evidence that Iraq still possessed weapons of mass destruction in significant quantities'.[62] Ultimately, the majority of the Security Council membership and most of the international community considered that the disarmament of Iraq could still be achieved through measures not involving the use of force. The military option was not ruled out but regarded as premature.[63]

For its part the Russian leadership claimed Baghdad had fulfilled virtually all the conditions set by the inspectors. Moscow was adamant that Resolution 1441 only authorized peaceful disarmament, 'excludes automatism in the use of force', and that no UN resolutions had authorized 'the violent overthrow of the leadership of a sovereign state'. The core Russian contention was that 'the Security Council alone had the right to evaluate the degree of cooperation by Iraq with the international inspectors and to adopt a decision on further steps to resolve the crisis'.[64] Russia was especially agitated by the apparent erosion of its Security Council veto, even as strong Western states claimed that their contemporary use of force was rooted in the system of Security Council resolutions. Foreign Minister Lavrov complained later about a trend whereby placing divisive issues on the Security Council's agenda meant that their consideration by the Security Council 'is seen as all but a carte blanche for the unilateral use of force purportedly in the interest of ensuring the implementation of UN Security Council resolutions'.[65]

The Russian political response to intervention in Iraq

During the mounting crisis over Iraqi compliance with the UN on-site weapons inspection regime, which was established to eradicate any Iraqi WMD programmes, Russia pursued various political objectives. Moscow publicly sought to prevent the outbreak of war and to terminate it as quickly as possible once it had occurred and bring the crisis back under the remit of UN and international decision-making. Russia's underlying goals were to assert itself as a key player in the international arena, to minimize harm to Russian relations with the United States, and to protect substantial Russian economic interests in Iraq. President Putin also took account of the need to sustain his domestic political standing in the approach to the State Duma elections in December 2003 and presidential elections scheduled for March 2004.[66]

Such varied objectives were difficult to integrate effectively and were best promoted by tactical manoeuvring rather than international confrontation, especially since Russia proved to have limited leverage in resisting the march to war. During 2002–3 Putin's approach was measured rather than militant. Russian diplomats were careful, for example, not to suggest that the Russian state had any obligation to honour the 1972 Soviet–Iraqi Treaty of Friendship and Cooperation, or to emphasize any other special ties of solidarity between Russia and Iraq.[67]

Putin also refrained from publicly calling for any *quid pro quos* to meet Russian regional goals in formulating its response to the Iraq crisis. In autumn 2002 there was some discussion among Russian politicians, which was possibly reflected in Russian UN diplomacy, about a geopolitical bargain: Russia would not object to American treatment of Iraq if America in exchange did not obstruct Russian handling of Georgia.[68] But this made no headway and was not hinted at later in official statements. In February 2003 rumours circulated about an alternative deal: Russian support for a new UN Security

Council resolution authorizing force against Iraq traded for more explicit US support for Russian military actions in Chechnya. This followed a speech by US Secretary of State Colin Powell, in which he specifically mentioned Iraqi support for al-Qaeda elements aiding Chechen rebels. But Russian leaders denied that this kind of horse-trading had been attempted.[69]

In terms of the politics of the UN Security Council, Putin also was careful not to act on domestic nationalist demands for Russia to try to invigorate some general anti-American coalition with China and France or Germany against the US. This would have been rejected by at least Paris or Berlin anyway. Instead Russian diplomats presented these countries as being united in agreeing that they could legitimately form their own evaluations of how to respond appropriately in the crisis over Iraq.

This is how Moscow justified the joint plan for Iraqi disarmament submitted by Russia, France, and Germany to the UN Security Council on 24 February 2003. However, this démarche had no deadline or automatic sanction for Iraqi non-compliance and it failed to obtain American support. By 5 March, Russia, France, and Germany were determined to try to prevent the adoption of a resolution authorizing the use of force. Five days later Russian Foreign Minister Igor Ivanov confirmed that if a new draft resolution on Iraq in the form of an ultimatum (tabled in the Security Council by the UK, the US, and Spain) were to be put to a vote, 'then Russia will vote against this resolution'.[70] President Jacques Chirac stated forcefully that France would also veto the draft. Ultimately Russia and France did not need to exercise their veto. Washington chose to forgo a Security Council vote since it could predict the outcome. It attacked Iraq with its partners on 19 March upon the expiry of a 48-hour ultimatum, which had been set by these states rather than by the UN.[71]

Putin rejected all the justifications for this war, as assessed above. However, he seems to have coolly accepted the reality of the war as a *fait accompli*. A major goal of Russian policy became the termination of the war within the UN framework and the re-engagement of the UN after the cessation of major hostilities. Russia also called on the activation of the UN to alleviate the humanitarian situation in Iraq and noted the potential for wider destabilization as this suffering extended to neighbouring countries. Russia's UN Representative Lavrov appealed for 'the right of the Iraqi people to decide their own political future and exercise control over their natural resources'.[72] This hinted at Russia's considerable commercial interests in the Iraqi energy sector.

Russia's dilemma was that it sought UN re-engagement in Iraq yet did not wish the UN to validate the US-led intervention. In Lavrov's words, 'we will continue to oppose attempts directly or indirectly to legitimize the actions of force against Iraq or to shift the responsibility for them on to the world community as represented by the UN'.[73] Yet the danger was, as a Russian specialist observed in May 2003, that 'making the UN an instrument of struggle with Washington, Moscow is but playing into the hands of the forces intent on doing away with the UN altogether'.[74]

Indeed UN Security Council Resolution 1483, adopted unanimously later that month, began the process of co-opting, of bringing under the UN umbrella, the outcome of this Western intervention.[75] Whichever way you looked at it, a prominent Russian analyst argued, the gist of Resolution 1483 was that the UN had legitimized, indeed had legalized, retrospectively the US/British occupation regime in Iraq and therefore the military action in Iraq per se. He argued that contrary to the gloss put on it by Russian Foreign Minister Igor Ivanov that 'the problem of Iraq has been brought back to the jurisdiction of the UN', and so UN Security Council unity had been restored, in fact 'the UN through the efforts of its Security Council members was brought back into the US foreign and military policy field'.[76]

In fact the UN Security Council scrupulously refrained from retrospectively legitimizing the invasion, as had happened implicitly in the case of Kosovo; it neither condoned nor condemned it. Resolution 1483 was about managing its consequences. Still, Russia swallowed its pride over the way this resolution *might* be viewed and focused on the benefits of being part of a UN process of oversight of the legacy of the intervention. In October 2003 Moscow assented to UN Security Council Resolution 1511 which authorized 'a multinational force under unified command to take all necessary measures to contribute to the maintenance of security and stability in Iraq'.[77] Putin talked thereafter of the need 'to achieve final unity of the international community on regulating Iraq' through further steps so that the UN 'has more capabilities of directly regulating the political situation there'.[78] After some haggling, with Russia and France seeking more specific endorsement of the sovereignty of the Iraqi government in military affairs,[79] in June 2004 the UN Security Council voted unanimously in favour of a resolution, sponsored by the US and the UK, providing an international imprimatur to the US-led coalition's handover of sovereignty to an interim Iraqi government.[80]

By the time the Russian, French, and German leaders met in Sochi at the end of August 2004, which followed three meetings of the trio in 2003, they hardly hinted at criticism of American policies and reaffirmed their commitment to Euro-Atlantic values.[81] This seemed a conscious effort to lay to rest previous media speculation about a trilateral 'anti-US axis' forged in opposition to Operation Iraqi Freedom. In fact the political goals of the three states' leaders in opposing the Iraq War had varied all along. For example, German Chancellor Gerhard Schroeder was driven primarily by domestic electoral needs. These differences, as well as Russia's own ambivalent view on pre-emption, meant that the three states were in no position to coordinate some norm-based challenge to the evolving US approach to force.

This is not to say that Russia had no hopes for this short-lived trilateralism. Writing in May 2003, an influential Russian specialist argued that the

Iraqi crisis had revealed the deeply rooted differences between the US and Western Europe 'in political culture, attitude towards international politics and towards the role of raw strength in international affairs'. He predicted this would lead to a 'competition for Russia'.[82] In fact, despite evidence of some transatlantic differences on how force should be employed, this greatly overstated the attractiveness of Russia as a partner, as well as the readiness of Moscow, Paris, and Berlin to bandwagon, at least beyond March 2003, in explicit opposition to Washington.

It seems that domestic nationalist forces in Russia, including military leaders, anticipated and hoped for an anti-American alignment, forged on the basis of international opposition to the Iraq War. There is some evidence also that Russia's pre-war position was influenced by erroneous military forecasts that the Iraqi military forces would offer protracted resistance, prolonging the war. With this in mind, the Russian press reported as early as January 2003 that there were plans to dispatch a few Russian naval vessels to the Persian Gulf. There was even some unrealistic speculation about a possible Russian intervention in the conflict, through a landing operation that would enable Russia to participate in the post-war reorganization of Iraq, presumably with access to oilfields in mind.[83] In the event Moscow kept well clear of the conflict militarily. The Russian high command was shocked by the ineffectiveness of the largely Russian-armed Iraqi armed forces, by the rapid occupation of Baghdad, and the overall technological prowess of the US military in spring 2003.[84]

Once war commenced Putin was careful to downplay Russia's previous close relationship with Iraq. Some weeks after the start of combat operations, as American forces made rapid progress, he observed that 'for political and economic reasons Russia does not have an interest in a US defeat in Iraq'.[85] This formulation still left Russia options over its policy. Should Russia adopt a position of not actively harming the American cause, but leaving it to extricate itself, as the war was not 'our war'? Or alternatively should Moscow increase its support of Washington and its partners in Iraq in the UN Security Council with the hope in exchange of retrieving some support for Russian commercial interests in Iraq? As we have shown, Russian policy eventually leaned towards the latter.

The further step of Russian military support for US-led stabilization of Iraq, of becoming in a sense a party to the intervention, was more controversial in Moscow. It would represent a volte-face for Russian policy. However, by September 2003 Putin first noted that 'theoretically' he did not exclude 'the participation of our military in the normalization of the situation' in Iraq, even under US command, if this were decided in the Security Council.[86] Later that year he raised the prospect of Russian armed forces in a multinational UN peacekeeping operation in Iraq, if the conditions for this were established. Without such an operation, Igor Ivanov qualified, Russian troops would not become an adjunct to 'occupation forces' in the country.[87]

The terms for such Russian involvement would have been difficult to negotiate. By autumn 2004 Putin signalled a shift in thinking, observing that to date 'Russia is not prepared to cooperate over law-enforcement and military cooperation' in Iraq, though it was ready to cooperate in training personnel, with the assistance of the Russian Ministry of Emergency Situations.[88] In fact a training mission for the Iraqi armed forces was developed under NATO, and Russia remained thereafter largely disengaged from post-intervention military stabilization efforts in Iraq.[89]

Finally, we should note Russia's pronounced failure to reflect or guide the response of the CIS states as a regional group in its policies and discourse on military intervention in Iraq. The reactions of other CIS states on the crisis varied considerably, and mostly they did not look to Russia for a lead over this use of force outside their region. Moscow hoped otherwise. On the eve of the war the deputy secretary of the Russian Security Council, Oleg Chernov, pronounced that 'all CIS states' faced 'an important task of elaborating a unified position in relation to the possible hostilities in the Persian Gulf'.[90] The Security Councils (a low-level body) of the *subset* of CIS states in the Russia-led Collective Security Treaty structure did indeed agree to issue a statement criticizing the military action as 'counter to the principles and rules of international law'.[91] Nonetheless, Moscow's wishful thinking about a broad support base for the Russian position over Iraq among CIS states was quickly exposed.

Georgia, Azerbaijan, Kazakhstan, and Uzbekistan clearly favoured the US-led operation, offering its participants the use of their air space or even airfields.[92] When the die was cast, the major CIS states gravitated towards American power regardless of Russian exhortations. For example, Kazakhstan had shadowed Russian views over the Iraq crisis, opposing military action without explicit UN authorization. Yet on the outbreak of war Kazakh statements shifted to emphasize the high value Kazakhstan attached to strategic partnership with the US and the US-led anti-terrorist coalition.[93] Russian chagrin over the war failed to prevent Ukraine, Georgia, and Azerbaijan from participating in peacekeeping activities in Iraq once they were invited to do this by Washington in May 2003. Moscow had to watch on the sidelines as these states earned their credentials as military partners in the US-led coalition.

CONCLUSION: INTERNATIONAL SOCIETY FRACTURED

The doctrine of threat pre-emption has been an especially controversial aspect of normative and legal claims over military intervention since at least 2002. It came to a head with the US-led campaign in Iraq, which fractured international society more deeply than any other post-Cold War military intervention.

Russia's position has fluctuated in this debate, but Moscow certainly has not been at odds with most leading Western states over the notion of pre-emption as such, as over humanitarian intervention. Instead Russia has found itself in company with Washington and various other states in exploring the potential for pre-emption or even preventive strikes beyond anticipatory self-defence, at least against non-state entities. Yet Russia joined a major line-up of states in opposing the US-led campaign in Iraq and in rejecting any pre-emptive or preventive justification for this war.

The general doctrine of pre-emption has divided the international community. On one side are states supporting pre-emption to varying degrees. Besides the US and Russia, these have included the UK and Australia (though these two did not present it as a legal justification for their participation in the attack on Iraq), as well as Israel, Italy, and to a lesser degree Japan and Taiwan. States publicly opposing pre-emption have included France, Germany, China, the Non-aligned group, the Islamic Conference of Foreign Ministers, and many lesser states.[94] Overall, pre-emption does not seem to have become more consolidated normatively or in customary law, in the sense of a combination of state practice and the belief that the practice is based on legal obligation. This is true whether we refer to the right to attack another state pre-emptively, or the right to use force pre-emptively against non-state entities employing what may be termed 'terrorist' methods.

The dominant view has remained that only the UN can authorize military action in the absence of a prior armed attack. In September 2003 UN Secretary-General Kofi Annan warned the General Assembly bluntly that the adoption of a doctrine on pre-emption 'could set precedents' resulting in 'a proliferation of the unilateral and lawless use of force, with or without justification'.[95] The Security Council has neither explicitly endorsed nor disapproved of pre-emptive self-defence. But that simply reflects the veto rights of Security Council powers.

By the mid-2000s the most that could be conceived of was the possibility of limited change or clarification in customary law for the case of a truly imminent attack. This was mooted in late 2004 by the UN Secretary-General's High Level Panel on Threats, Challenges and Change. The Panel argued that military action by a threatened state could be potentially lawful if 'the threatened attack is imminent, no other means would deflect it and the action is proportionate'.[96] But no normative shift in favour of pre-emption in any other sense, let alone preventive military action, can be deduced from general state discourse or practice before or since the Iraq War. The Bush administration itself toned down the expansive claims of 2002 in the 2006 National Security Strategy. The new document stressed considerably more the alternatives to military pre-emption and placed more reliance on multilateral solutions.[97]

For Russia, however, the challenge of the Iraq War and its aftermath was not centred on the dangers of pre-emption per se. Before this operation the dangers of preventive war had been highlighted earlier and more keenly by France and Germany than by Russia. Moscow allowed itself to be shielded to an extent by these two powers, which were even more forthright in opposing military action against Iraq, and tried to present itself as occupying the normative mainstream. This was important for Putin also to retrieve a semblance of still being engaged in the US-led wider 'war on terror'. He did not wish to appear adversarial to the US over Iraq and did not lobby to form a new anti-American coalition with Paris and Berlin. Moreover, beyond the relationship with the US, a primary Russian objective was to preserve its status and influence as a Security Council P5 member. With this in mind Moscow scaled down its rhetoric soon after the military campaign in Iraq commenced and sought to integrate the *fait accompli* of the intervention within a UN framework. At the regional level simultaneously Russia sought to safeguard its material interests in Iraq and prevent an extension of the military operation to other states such as Syria.

Although Russia engaged in this diplomatic manoeuvring, it was shocked by the way UN authorization of military action in Iraq was bypassed, neutering Russian veto rights and undermining Russian institutional power in that most exclusive of clubs, the Security Council. This replayed the humiliation and sense of grievance Moscow felt four years earlier during the otherwise different case of intervention over Kosovo. As the attack on Iraq loomed in autumn 2002 and early spring 2003, Moscow mounted a rearguard action with France and Germany to preserve the Security Council as the fount of procedural legitimacy for the use of force. But for Moscow and Paris at least, the issue was more broadly also about defending the authority of Security Council decision-making.

In this sense the justifications presented in the political and legal wrangling over intervention in Iraq were not just indicative of the normative interplay, but overlay issues of fundamental importance for international order: the role of powerful states in rule-making and the extent to which power disparities can be accommodated within multilateral rules and the UN Charter system itself. Only against the background of these considerations is it possible to understand the divisive impact of the Iraq intervention on international order and more specifically on the Russian leadership.

In spring 2003, few nations accepted that credible evidence could be shown of either WMDs in Iraq or an operational link between al-Qaeda and the regime in Baghdad. But the core issue as it transpired was not 'who was right and who was wrong but *who gets to decide what to do*'. In this sense the challenge the UN system faced was 'not one of devising new rules but of reaching agreement on who gets to apply them'.[98] This could never be just a procedural question; it was one of structural power and politics in the international system. As described in chapter 8, it motivated Russia's challenge to what its leadership came to condemn as a 'hegemonic' international order.

The dilemma for relatively weaker states like Russia in 2003 was expressed well in the challenging response of an American international lawyer to the division over Iraq in the Security Council: 'the world now requires decision-making processes more frankly hierarchical, less sensitive to the claims of sovereignty, and, as a likely consequence, more decisive and expeditious than has been the norm within the United Nations framework'.[99] This was implicit in the thinking of some senior officials in the Bush administration before and after the Iraq intervention, even if it was not proclaimed explicitly as a policy objective by the American leadership.

Russia for its part bridled at the implied challenge to pluralist principles. Putin protested over the attack on Iraq that 'the principle of immutable sovereignty of a state' would be thrown into question 'if we allow international law to be replaced by "the law of the fist" whereby the strong is always right and has the right to do anything and in choosing methods to achieve his goals is not constrained by anything'.[100] This repudiation of special influence for the most powerful states in rule-making (notably at a time of relative Russian weakness in the international system) was developed later in a Russian discourse that rejected the 'oligarchic model' in international affairs, by which rights and responsibilities are determined by financial-economic and military strength.[101]

In reality, however, Russia was not a principled multilateralist. In the crisis diplomacy of spring 2003 it perceived multilateral rules, like France, primarily as a means to constrain American 'hyperpower' and Washington's discretion in deploying its military capabilities. This is not to say that Russian leaders did not accept the wider benefits of an international society influenced by norms and customary law, even if like American leaders they might occasionally circumvent such constraints to pursue particularist interests. Overall, the Iraq War left the Russian leadership alarmed that the foundational non-intervention norm, beyond the debate on pre-emption, was rapidly losing its constraining influence on the regulation of force in a US-dominated system and that Russia's post-Cold War trump card of UN P5 membership had been significantly diminished.

6

Contested Norms in the CIS Regional Order

This chapter turns to the regional dimension of the normative interplay between Russia, other CIS states, and major Western states. So far, our analysis of military interventions has focused on norms and customary law as evolving and often contested *global* standards of conduct, and we will return to this in chapter 8. However, we discussed how norms may interact between the global and regional levels in the introduction to this volume and at various points in our examination of major interventions so far. This requires fuller investigation.

The domain of a norm, if it is weak, may be confined to a region, or it may be promoted, defined, and interpreted for that region by a regionally preponderant or hegemonic power. Russia has sought particular influence over the region comprised of much of the former territory of the Soviet Union and this directs attention to the *CIS regional order*. This leads to two questions. First, how far has Russia's commitment to global standards been influenced by standards of conduct defined within and for its neighbourhood, the CIS region, or for the Russian state itself? Conversely, how far has that regional order been shaped by normative evolution in the global order?

Chapters 6 and 7 offer the region-level analysis to explore these questions. This chapter analyses Russian efforts to shape regional norms to legitimize its military interventions in the early 1990s. It also investigates Russian resistance a decade later to what it branded as Western political intervention in the CIS region. We argue that this behaviour was strongly influenced by Russian political interests, the hierarchical structure of power in the CIS region, and Russian views on state order. Russia has tended to be selective in interpreting how global order norms on the use of force should be applied at the CIS regional level where it identifies core national interests. But it has avoided doing this too flagrantly or frequently for fear of undermining the wider regulation of force in an international system where it has limited leverage.

A flurry of Russian military interventions in CIS conflicts occurred during the early 1990s. After this the next major use of Russian forces in the region was the short, high-intensity war with Georgia in 2008 (assessed in chapter 7). Russian officials described the early military operations as peacekeeping (or in more literal translation 'peace-creating') missions. As analysed in a large literature, however, the circumstances of these operations, especially at their inception, mean they cannot properly be defined as regional peacekeeping and enforcement action, as governed by Chapter VIII of the UN Charter.[1] Therefore we study them as regional interventions, although Russia has tried to legitimize them as peacekeeping operations under CIS or other international mandates.

These early interventions transformed the emerging CIS regional order into a theatre for contested norms and interpretations of sovereignty, non-intervention, and the use of force. Russia struggled to achieve collective understandings with CIS states over these basic principles. Moscow's declaration of its 'special responsibility' in its 'near abroad' signalled a more competitive dynamic in the region with Western states. A consensus began to form within the Russian political elite from 1993 about the need to avert Western intrusion in this zone of proclaimed Russian interests.

This chapter first examines Russian definitions of the CIS regional order in the early 1990s. It assesses Russian efforts to legitimize its interventions under the guise of peacekeeping and the response of other states. It evaluates the debate on the mandating authority for these operations and whether a regional understanding emerged on the acceptability of mandates provided by the CIS organization. The analysis then advances a decade to examine a different kind of debate on the normative underpinning of the CIS regional order: the controversy over *political* interventions accompanying the 2003–5 'coloured revolutions' in CIS states. As these events did not involve the use of force they did not involve *jus ad bellum* justifications. But this contentious debate illustrates an important theme of this study, the entrenchment of Russia's pluralist perspective on international order. Russia branded these upheavals in CIS states as Western-inspired, value-based political interventions challenging state order. Finally, we assess the role of the primary regional structure promoted by Russia in the 2000s, the Collective Security Treaty Organization (CSTO). This body has promoted a Russia-led political solidarity around pluralist norms. But it has also revived debate about the option of a regional mandate for the use of force, and since the end of the decade has raised the prospect of Russia-led interventions in crises within the states of the region.

RUSSIA ASSERTS PRIMACY IN THE NEW CIS REGIONAL ORDER

The rapid dissolution of the Soviet Union at the end of 1991 made the management of order among and within the new successor states a top priority of Moscow's new leaders. This steadily displaced the universalist and solidarist currents of Gorbachev's 'New Thinking'. Indeed most of the leadership and political elite of the new Russian state found it difficult to accept that the other post-Soviet states, the erstwhile union republics of the USSR, could exercise more than a contingent and qualified sovereignty. This was expressed in the favoured term, the 'near abroad'. The sovereign equality of the new states was formally acknowledged in founding documents of the Commonwealth of Independent States, as well as the Collective Security Treaty signed in Tashkent in May 1992. But in practice Moscow did not conceive of itself as conducting real 'foreign policy' with its CIS partners in the first post-Soviet years.

The close functional interdependence between Russia and most of these new states reinforced this attitude. For Russian leaders Moscow's relationships with CIS states were legitimately hierarchical; Russian leadership was assumed, as was renewed regional integration, centred around the gravitational pull of Moscow. These assumptions were an unsurprising legacy of over seventy years of Soviet statehood, driven by decisions in Moscow, and found expression in the post-1991 political category of the 'post-Soviet space'. On the first anniversary of the CIS founding agreement Foreign Minister Kozyrev praised the CIS in this vein for helping to preserve 'some sort of single space'.[2]

Russian primacy in the CIS regional order also reflected the new Russian state's insistence on its rights as a great power in the wider international system. The consensus emerged within the Russian leadership that Russia's status as a great power granted it rights and responsibilities in its quasi-dependent CIS neighbouring states. As proclaimed by Yeltsin early in 1994, this meant Russia should be 'first among equals' among the former Soviet republics.[3] For the Russian leadership, it was natural, therefore, that Russia should play the main role in defining the normative framework for relations with these states, including how to determine the appropriate use of military force.

These root assumptions only solidified after a broad debate in Russia about the role of force in the near-abroad. This was stimulated by a flurry of Russian interventions in different forms, driven largely by events on the ground, in Moldova in May 1992, in South Ossetia in July 1992, in Tajikistan in September 1992, and in Abkhazia during 1992–4. A major challenge was that in each of these military involvements Moscow was left with seemingly open-ended commitments, from which it would be difficult to extract its forces. Russia also began to over-extend the forces it had available for such operations.

There were three broad competing schools of thought in Moscow during 1992–4 about the use of force in CIS states, which may be defined loosely as Liberals, moderate nationalists, and radical nationalists. Liberals were reluctant to use such force. If this proved essential to end bloodshed and disorder, however, they believed it should be done through legitimate international organizations such as the UN, the CSCE/OSCE, as well as, in their opinion, the CIS. Effective peacekeeping would show Russian commitment to principles of international law and order. This standpoint dominated the Russian discourse and policy process until spring 1992.

For the next two years, however, this perspective competed with that of pragmatists or moderate nationalists. The latter argued that Russia had a special role and responsibility to act against threats within and outside the CIS region. They believed this validated the Russian use of force as a last resort, even unilaterally, although to acquire legitimacy and share the burden this would better be done through international organizations. As the military leadership became more of a policy actor in its own right in the CIS, the Russian foreign ministry's Liberal discourse jarred with the assertive conduct of Russian military units on the ground in the local conflicts.[4] By mid to late 1993 a consensus solidified around the moderate nationalist perspective, as President Boris Yeltsin and Foreign Minister Andrei Kozyrev veered towards this centre ground. This contrasted with the views of the third body of thinking, expressed by more radical nationalists and communists. These maintained that force could be used to establish Russian dominance throughout the former Soviet Union. To avoid multilateral constraints this preferably would be done unilaterally.[5]

After 1993 it was a key premise of the moderate nationalist consensus that Russia occupied a uniquely influential and legitimate role in managing security and stabilizing conflicts in the CIS region. This expressed a hierarchical and exceptionalist position in relation to other CIS states. It was reaffirmed during 1991–3 by many influential Russian politicians and enshrined in Russia's foreign policy 'concept' of December 1992. Yeltsin confirmed it in a renowned speech in February 1993, when he claimed that international organizations, including the UN, should 'grant Russia special powers as a guarantor of peace and stability in former regions of the USSR'.[6] For Kozyrev this role of guarantor was driven by the location of the former Soviet republics in a 'zone of interest and special responsibility' for Russia. Therefore it would be an 'unwarranted loss' for Russia 'to pull out completely from the zones of traditional influence which evolved or...were won over centuries'.[7] Locally based Russian forces would hold the line and ensure Moscow's special role in the region.

These assertions were widely received in Western states as tantamount to a Russian Monroe Doctrine. They reverberated through Russian policy for the next fifteen years and were revived in 2008 by President Medvedev's call to acknowledge Russian 'privileged interests' in its neighbourhood. By arguing that Russian 'responsibilities' justified a continued Russian military presence in CIS conflict zones, Moscow claimed to represent the collective interests of CIS states and the wider community of states, not just Russia's national interests. A senior military spokesman asserted in 1994 in this way, that the world community should recognize Russia as a guarantor in the CIS region 'against the expansion of local conflicts into regional wars'.[8] Interventions and peacekeeping Russian-style supposedly would prevent conflicts spilling over from one CIS state to another or even to non-CIS states.

In practice what emerged was a concept of forward defence in a post-Soviet 'strategic space' that very much reflected Russian national priorities and pursuit of regional primacy.[9] It was expressed in a decision by the Russian Security Council in autumn 1993 not to seek to construct border defences on Russian borders but to maintain large parts of the old Soviet borders, which had become the outer CIS borders, especially in Central Asia and perhaps the South Caucasus.[10] In this vein the commander of Russian border troops justified his troops' presence in Tajikistan out of the need to defend CIS security as a whole and Russia's own 'geopolitical interests on these borderlines'.[11]

The notion of the CIS region as a Russian forward security zone was also expressed in an ambitious plan approved by Yeltsin to establish twenty-eight Russian military bases outside Russia on the territory of former Soviet states.[12] This plan failed to materialize. However, the Russian aspiration for a forward defence zone within former Soviet territory remained. This relativized the sovereignty of other CIS states and validated the continued presence of Russian forces where they had localized conflicts or imposed ceasefire agreements.

The counterpart to Moscow's assertion of its role as a regional security guarantor was its claim that NATO and the US had no legitimate role in CIS conflict zones. A NATO role was all the more unwelcome for Moscow in the early 1990s when Russia was struggling to rally post-Soviet states under the new multilateral CIS framework and to legitimize its local military presence on the basis of 'CIS mandates' (see below).

Russian military officers were nervous about NATO's intentions. In summer 1992 a senior officer warned that the intensification of military conflicts between former Soviet republics could lead to direct intervention by NATO forces, perhaps under the pretext of guaranteeing 'international control' over the nuclear potential of the former Soviet arsenal.[13] Marshal Shaposhnikov, the CIS Joint Forces Commander-in-Chief, revisited this scenario at the end of the year. He denied that NATO could acquire any rights, within the CSCE framework, to use its armed forces to settle local conflicts on the external border of the CIS.[14]

Russia also rejected any UN or CSCE devolution of peacekeeping in CIS conflicts to regional powers such as Turkey in place of Russia. In autumn 1993 Kozyrev declared flatly that 'the transfer of peacekeeping functions to regional powers is absolutely unacceptable' in the former USSR, as a 'zone of Russian interests'. If Russia were to leave these areas, he predicted, the 'resultant vacuum will immediately be filled by other forces... maybe even hostile to Russian interests'.[15] This zero-sum mentality had been expressed even more starkly during the hostilities in Nagorno-Karabakh in spring 1992, when Shaposhnikov had warned Turkey that foreign intervention in the conflict would place states on the brink of a third world war.[16]

As nationalist currents spread in domestic politics, Moscow was increasingly sensitive to any potential US military involvement in CIS conflict zones. Russian military commentators played back the debate over Russian policy by warning about the Pentagon's new readiness 'to engage in decisive intervention under the guise of "peacekeeping" for settling regional conflicts'. Such interventions would be coordinated supposedly with the military operations of the UN and other international organizations such as NATO and the CSCE.[17]

Such concerns were not helped by a leaked US State Department 'non-paper' (Presidential Review Directive 13), circulated in August 1993. This draft policy directive rejected a greater Russian role in peacekeeping in the former Soviet Union and declared that the US should be prepared to support UN peacekeeping operations in the region even if these opposed Russian interests.[18] This quickly received a blunt Russian response that the US would not be permitted to become involved in peacekeeping in the area.[19] A senior American official then clarified that Washington claimed no formal role for itself in such operations.[20]

This spat shows that Washington had developed some interest at least in mediation in regional disputes on former Soviet territory. There is no evidence, however, that the US seriously considered becoming more fully involved militarily in post-Soviet conflicts in the early 1990s. NATO similarly had no wish to risk a dangerous confrontation with Russia through a military intervention in the South Caucasus or Central Asia, especially without any compelling strategic rationale for such operations. Nor could NATO justify any such action to public opinion in its member states.

Nevertheless, the US, in its national capacity and as the dominant state in post-Cold War NATO, still rejected Russian primacy in or hegemonic security management of the emerging CIS regional order. In February 1994 the US Defence Secretary, William Perry, spoke out against Russian 'thoughts of creating spheres of influence or interest' and warned that 'if Russian forces operate beyond Russia's borders, they must do so in accord with international law'.[21] US officials publicly disagreed with 'a special role for Russia in the Caucasus'.[22] In essence they resisted Russia's deployment of forces in ostensible peacekeeping roles which appeared 'as part of a co-ordinated strategy of pursuing influence by limiting the sovereignty of other CIS states'.[23]

The lines were drawn at the UN General Assembly in September 1994, when President Yeltsin lashed back, warning Western states against attempts themselves to 'exploit conflicts' between CIS countries. He described Russia's ties with CIS states as a blood relationship and claimed that Russian 'peacekeeping' had brought settlements closer in virtually all the armed conflicts in former Soviet states.[24]

Despite this difference in principle over Russia's role in the CIS regional order, there was speculation by commentators that the great powers might be ready to strike a bargain that they would play by the rules but still police their backyards. Such 'spheres of influence peacekeeping', it was suggested, lay behind the adoption of a UN Security Council resolution which authorized an American-led invasion of Haiti on 31 July 1994. Russian support was gained supposedly by Washington's agreement to a parallel UN resolution which endorsed the Russian 'peacekeeping mission' in Abkhazia. Both powers then agreed to the UN observing their operations.[25] However, even if there was a specific trade-off of this kind in the backroom politics of the Security Council, there is no evidence to suggest that 'spheres of influence peacekeeping' became more broadly accepted.

This leaves the question of whether certain 'regional norms' over military engagement in local conflicts could form under conditions of hierarchy within the CIS security order. In a region of nascent, self-conscious sovereign states Russia could not expect to develop stable, predictable relationships by relying just on spheres of influence logic or the assertion of Russian 'special responsibilities'. As confirmed below, however, it was difficult for Russian leaders to change their cognitive paradigm to enable regional norms to cohere on matters so sensitive to the sovereignty of other CIS states.

RUSSIAN-STYLE 'PEACEKEEPING' IN THE CIS

In reality, Russia struggled to formulate justifications for its military interventions during 1991–3 that would be acceptable widely to CIS regional partners. This reflected the different circumstances in each theatre and differing Russian motivations from case to case. Russian operations on the ground were tailored to local requirements and possibilities, combining overt and covert actions. Even so, prompted by Russia, these operations and the entrenchment of 'frozen conflicts' after ceasefires have been the basis of attempts to develop some legal and normative regulation specific to the CIS region. The extent to which it has been internalized by other CIS states and expressed in interstate relations has varied from state to state and over time. A dominant category in Russian discourse on these military involvements has been that of peacekeeping.

Before examining Russian-style peacekeeping, we should distinguish a related but distinct controversy—Moscow's assertion of its right to protect the rights and interests of the Russian diaspora or of Russian citizens scattered throughout post-Soviet states and its effort to gain the acquiescence of other CIS state leaders for such claims.

The call to protect the Russian ethnic diaspora was heard in the context of various Russian interventions in the early 1990s. It was primarily a rallying cry in Russian domestic politics and the Russian leadership (as opposed to radical nationalist politicians) was cautious generally not to justify its military actions specifically on such ethnically divisive grounds. It was rather obvious that an effort to present the protection of a state's national diaspora as justified risked regional conflict. For example, this could justify Uzbekistan's protection of its own diaspora in other Central Asian states.

A Russian claim to defend its *citizens* abroad was not much less divisive within the post-Soviet region, given the uncertain status of Russian citizenship in the early 1990s. A draft Russian military doctrine published in May 1992 showed how the issue could encourage intervention. It defined one of the basic tasks of the military as defence of 'the rights and interests of citizens of Russia and people linked with it ethnically and culturally abroad'.[26] Although the final text of the military doctrine in November 1993 toned this down, it still defined 'the suppression of the rights, freedoms and lawful interests of Russian citizens in foreign states' as a source of military danger.[27]

In his 1994 New Year broadcast, Yeltsin pledged to Russians in neighbour states that 'on the basis of law and solidarity, we defend and will defend you and our common interests'.[28] Russian military intervention to protect its citizens in sovereign CIS states, without their consent, could not be defined as self-defence under international law. But Russian officials were inclined to disparage the sovereignty of CIS states in crises endangering Russian citizens. For example, a Russian official referring to the crisis in the Transdniester region in Moldova in 1992, argued 'a regime that kills people merely for trying to defend their human dignity cannot rely on sovereignty to protect it... Russia will stop the killers, since there is no one else to do it.'[29]

One Russian approach in the early 1990s and periodically after that was to repackage the defence of Russian citizens as a human rights issue. By linking it to the promotion of universal values this might appeal to an international audience also beyond the CIS region. Speaking to the UN General Assembly in autumn 1993, Kozyrev claimed that 'peacekeeping and the protection of human rights, particularly that of national minorities' had become the Russian foreign policy priority, above all in the former Soviet territory.[30] However, this co-option of solidarist language was not convincing. Russian protection of ethnic Russians or Russian citizens, rather than all those whose human rights were imperilled in the region, did not come across as driven by human rights concerns rather than standard national interests. This controversy was replayed fifteen years later at the time of the Russia–Georgia war.

Russian intervention justified as 'peacekeeping'

In intervening in the CIS conflicts of the early 1990s Russia relied mainly on its locally deployed forces and those which it brought under its own jurisdiction, rather than on projecting additional troops from Russia. Secessionist forces were armed from Russian local arms stockpiles. Russia later claimed that such arms transfers as occurred resulted from the lack of central political control over its local commanders, but this is not wholly convincing. Other forms of covert Russian support occurred. For example, in Abkhazia Moscow turned a blind eye to the mobilization of militias from the North Caucasus in support of Abkhaz leaders and apparently planned and assisted the counter-offensive against Georgian troops in 1993. In other cases Russian troops were more directly and visibly involved.

Russian leaders resorted to different categories of justifications for their interventions in Abkhazia, Moldova, South Ossetia, and Tajikistan. Initially they hoped these could be integrated within the framework of a common defence or collective security system. The Tashkent Treaty on Collective Security, signed by six former Soviet republics in May 1992 (and joined by Azerbaijan, Georgia, and Belarus in 1993), specified the common task of fighting local wars and stopping armed conflicts. But its principal focus was defence against external aggression and this failed to offer a legitimate basis for intervening in conflicts within CIS states.[31]

Secondly, Russia made some effort to justify these interventions on the basis of bilateral military agreements with the government of the country involved. This was the case, for example, with the increasingly overt Russian support for the government of President Emomali Rakhmonov in Tajikistan during 1992–3. This obscured the reality that state to state agreements followed Russia's chaotic initial interventions.

At the first stage of the civil war in Tajikistan the locally based Russian forces took sides and supported the pro-communist Popular Front. It was only in September 1992, in response to an initial request by the Tajik government, that Moscow ordered its 201st division to assist in such matters as separating the opponents, protecting refugees, and protecting communications sites. The role of this division was formalized later in bilateral agreements.[32] However, Russia was unconvincing when it denied any interference 'in the internal political affairs of sovereign Tajikistan'. It claimed that it acted as an impartial third party mediator in the conflict rather than 'on the side of Tajikistan's government forces'.[33]

It was still less convincing for Russia to legitimize its interventions through bilateral agreements in conditions elsewhere in the CIS region where the local governments doubted Russian intentions and sought to avoid dependence on Moscow, or where chaotic local conditions made it difficult to reach agreement with any government. It was anyway difficult to justify intervention in terms of customary international law where this privileged one party in a clear civil conflict, especially where this party could be viewed as a separatist entity within a recognized state. This was the case in Georgia (the conflicts in South Ossetia and Abkhazia, although these regions had lacked any experience of control by the new Georgian state) and Moldova (the conflict around Transdniester).

The difficulties in resorting to standard collective defence arguments help explain why official Russian discourse shifted to emphasize the legitimacy of Russian interventions as an exercise in *international peacekeeping*. In autumn 2003 Kozyrev claimed that 'in all cases without exception, Russia's peacemaking efforts in the former USSR have been made with the consent of and at the request of the parties to the conflict, and its peacekeeping contingents have been sent into the conflict zones on the basis of appropriate agreements'.[34] However, Russia's initial interventions were not convincingly legitimized by agreements that were signed *after* Russian forces had enforced ceasefires and changed the balance of military advantage on the ground, even setting aside the problem of Russian coercive action in reaching those agreements.[35]

Nor in such cases were the agreements Russia reached 'appropriate', using Kozyrev's term, in relation to wider international norms and standards on peacekeeping. During 2003–4 Kozyrev advocated Russian-style alternatives to 'classical' UN standards for peacekeeping operations. He accepted that Russia was 'subordinate to universal legal rules' as part of the global system of international relations. But he appealed to the international community to recognize the effectiveness of 'new approaches' to peacekeeping in Transdniester and South Ossetia. This meant the inclusion of the parties to the conflict as well as a 'neighbouring country' (Russia in these cases) in peacekeeping operations, so-called 'third party peacekeeping', rather than just neutral states.[36] Moscow tried to include this language in relevant UN and CSCE/OSCE resolutions. The Russian military command claimed that Russian experience 'enriches the world experience of peacekeeping'. This was linked to the state's Security Council responsibility for maintaining international peace and security.[37] So Moscow sought to adjust global principles of UN peacekeeping to accommodate Russian practice in regional CIS conflicts.

Western states rejected such Russian-style peacekeeping principles as 'peacekeeping' in terms of global UN standards. For example, a US State Department draft policy directive in 1993 reflected the general view in insisting that all peacekeeping efforts in the former Soviet Union should comply fully with the CSCE rules laid down in the July 1992 Helsinki summit—that is they should only act with the consent of involved parties and observe neutrality. This document also stipulated that such operations should respect all borders, preserve democratic politics, be of finite duration, and remain under strict political control by UN officials in New York.[38]

Undeterred by this clash in perspective with Western states, Kozyrev called for a UN mandate for the Russian-led efforts. This could be done through a formal devolution by the UN of its peacekeeping responsibilities to the CIS as a 'regional organization', as defined by Chapter VIII of the UN Charter.[39] UN or CSCE observers, in his view, could then be involved after the achievement of ceasefire agreements. Effectively these observers would support Russian troops as a third force.

UN Secretary-General Boutros Boutros-Ghali yielded little ground in response. By spring 1994 he accepted the theoretical option of including Russian forces in a broader international peacekeeping contingent in the CIS region under a UN aegis. But in his view Russian forces could compose no more than 20–30 per cent of the total number in such a contingent, which should also be under sole UN command. Boutros-Ghali was adamant that the structure of Russian-style peacekeeping could not simply be transformed into a UN force.[40]

On a practical level the mandate controversy reflected Moscow's hope that UN funding could be extracted for Russia-led operations in CIS conflicts. Yet at heart the controversy was a struggle over the wider legitimacy of these operations. As previously shown, post-Cold War Russia has relied heavily on the discursive power of the Security Council as a conveyor of legitimacy in the wider international system. It was a blow for Moscow, but hardly surprising, that the UN was unprepared simply to whitewash Russian self-interested and partial interventions as UN operations. With a realization of this, by February 1994 Moscow shifted ground and claimed that its peacekeeping deployments were anyway fully legal and did not need a UN mandate to authorize them or legitimize their operations.[41]

Even so, the Russian leadership recognized the benefit of limited UN monitoring missions in providing some legitimacy for these operations in the wider international community. Russia acceded to a Security Council resolution to form a UN mission in Abkhazia, UNOMIG (Resolution 937, 21 July 1994). This was followed in December 1994 by the Security Council resolving to establish a mission in Tajikistan to monitor implementation of the local ceasefire agreement, UNMOT.[42] Over time these missions acted to some degree as conveyors of UN norms and regulations on peacekeeping and thereby moderated the Russian partiality on the ground that accompanied the initial ceasefire arrangements in Abkhazia and Tajikistan.

CIS multilateralism as a source of legitimacy

Russia failed to achieve the gold standard of a UN mandate for Russian-style peacekeeping operations (a standard acknowledged more readily by Russian politicians with Liberal tendencies than by more nationalist ones). In seeking legitimacy, therefore, Moscow fell back on the image of regional multilateralism, to CIS collective mandates, to justify the operations it led and the prolongation of the peacekeeping arrangements it established. CIS multilateralism was the principle on offer to endorse interventions *ex post facto*, to entrench Russian forces in CIS conflicts and peacekeeping structures, or even to sanction new 'collective' operations. Russia also had some hopes that a CIS umbrella could spread the financial and military burden of such operations.

Russian discourse might be considered to reflect the deepening political and normative, rather than strategic character of post-Cold War multilateralism, 'shaped by shared notions about when the use of force is legitimate and appropriate'.[43] However, the previous discussion on the CIS regional order confirms that strategic considerations were also significantly at play; CIS multilateralism operated under conditions of Russian regional primacy. Indeed the evolving CIS structure could be manipulated strategically to promote Russian interests. These considerations of hierarchy and power raise serious doubts about the potential for CIS multilateralism to reflect or induce shared understandings about the appropriate use of force in the CIS region.

It was conceivable, as will be explored in the last section of this chapter, that norms around CIS multilateralism and the use of force, which were coercively promoted by Russia in the early 1990s, could be internalized and more consensually accepted by at least a subgroup of CIS states in later years. However, when the early interventions were launched Russia lacked a credible multilateral CIS cover. The decisions on interventions were made on an *ad hoc* basis after Russian involvement had been initiated by local Russian forces in the field and the 'peacekeeping' formats followed later.[44]

A brief survey confirms this. In the case of South Ossetia there was no pretence of CIS multilateralism in sponsoring such peacekeeping. Russia reacted on the basis of an agreement it had mediated between the parties. In Abkhazia Russian 'peacekeepers' were deployed late in 1993 by decision of the Russian government. At this time they lacked a CIS mandate, which was only adopted in a proper form in October 1994. Moreover, it only really existed on paper, since Russia remained the only CIS state contributing any soldiers or funds to the regional peacekeeping force.[45] In the case of Tajikistan, the CIS decision to dispatch peacekeeping forces was not made before September 1993 and was signed just by Russia, Kazakhstan, Uzbekistan, and Kyrgyzstan.[46] A mandate for the joint forces in Tajikistan was not adopted until April 1994.

Among these diverse operations, the mandate agreed for the 'collective peacekeeping forces' in Tajikistan was the only one which held some promise as an expression of multilateral thinking on regional intervention, at least for a subgroup of CIS states. The collective aspect reflected the concerns by the Central Asian states at the time about the deployment of Russian-only peacekeeping forces in troubled former Soviet republics.[47] Yet despite the multilateral principle, Kazakhstan, Uzbekistan, and Kyrgyzstan were reluctant to offer their own troops to the collective force in Tajikistan. Fifty per cent of the total was earmarked to come from these local states, but they only provided small contingents and the core remained forces of Russia's locally deployed 201st division. Even so, these Central Asian states had agreed with Russia on the need to intervene if fighting continued in Tajikistan and they called on the UN Security Council to give political support to CIS joint peacekeeping forces.[48]

It has been suggested that a deal was agreed behind the scenes between Russia and Central Asian states, offering the CIS framework as legal cover for Russia: 'Russia would continue to carry the burden in Tajikistan and the Central Asian states would secure for Moscow carte blanche for any intervention in the Caucasus.'[49] However, even if this was the case, it reflected no CIS-wide consensus. Indeed suspicion and mistrust of Russian troops were such that most CIS member states rejected Russian proposals to form permanent, joint peacekeeping mechanisms for CIS territory. Most of the states refused to send their own national troops to conflict zones (the exceptions were the small contributions to the Tajikistan operation).[50]

Essentially, from the early days of the CIS as a multilateral forum, the majority of states of the region were unwilling to legitimize the Russian exercise of force by placing it under collective CIS cover. When the CIS was founded in December 1991, the heads of the new states aired the notion of CIS international armed forces tasked to mediate in conflicts. The CIS Charter anticipated in Article 11 that groups of military observers and collective peacekeeping forces could promote regional security.[51] It took until a summit in March 1992 for nearly all the CIS member states to agree on the terms of these units. By this agreement any intervention by such forces before a ceasefire or without a request by all the conflicting sides was forbidden, as was the use of these forces in combat actions.[52] This was consistent with international norms, but was clearly contrary to the actual Russian practice in CIS conflicts.

Russia chose not to apply the terms of the March 1992 agreement or to formally refer to it in documents on the conflicts in Tajikistan or Abkhazia. The other CIS states in turn offered Russia only lip service in support of 'CIS peacekeeping' in the Georgian-Abkhaz conflict zone in 1994.[53] This CIS fig leaf then became an entrenched feature of the Russian presence in that conflict.

In the first half of the 1990s the CIS states struggled to consolidate their sovereignty, to contain interstate disputes, and to manage various challenges to domestic state order. They were sensitive to possible interventionist policies, not only by Russia but also other CIS neighbours. Efforts at CIS multilateralism could not ignore these concerns. They were reflected, for example, in a memorandum the CIS heads of state adopted in 1995 on 'maintaining peace and stability' in the CIS.

This document set on record the determination of CIS states not to tolerate or support separatism, and it was sponsored by Kazakhstan, a state which had concerns about irredentism among ethnic Russians in its northern regions.[54] Yet this resistance to separatism jarred with Russian policies in the regions of South Ossetia, Abkhazia, and Transdniester. Russia had declared its official support for the territorial integrity of Georgia and Moldova (and was unrelenting in resisting separatism in Chechnya). But it had supported the separatist side in their internal conflicts and remained entrenched in the separatist regions. These contradictions over separatism were an enduring source of tension with pluralist norms on sovereignty in the CIS regional order.

In January 1996 Moscow secured the approval of eight CIS states for a detailed conceptual document on the settlement of conflicts in the CIS. However, it was not signed by four major CIS states, Belarus, Ukraine, Kazakhstan, and Azerbaijan. The accompanying document, 'Statutes of CIS Collective Peacekeeping Forces', was signed by only six CIS states.[55] This shows Russia failed to achieve common understandings on peacekeeping or interventions in conflicts with important CIS states sensitive about their sovereignty. A sticking point in the Russia-sponsored documents was their claim that the CIS organization has the responsibility and authority to decide on the use of military force to maintain peace in CIS territory, except in cases where consent from the government or parties involved in the conflict is absent.[56] The latter cases, described as 'peace enforcement' in the documents, would require a Security Council mandate.

In the second half of the 1990s most CIS states shifted further from accepting a 'CIS mandate' for anything that Russia might define as peacekeeping in the region and came to adopt the straightforward position that only the UN can authorize the deployment of collective military forces in a conflict. The national peacekeeping units, which several CIS states began to form, could only be deployed therefore under a UN mandate. This applied to Ukrainian, Georgian, Kazakh, Kyrgyz, and Uzbek peacekeeping units.[57] At the close of the 1990s, this confirmed the absence of anything like a CIS-wide consensus supporting and legitimizing emerging regional norms for the use of force.

THE CIS REGIONAL ORDER AND 'COLOURED REVOLUTIONS'

No new military conflicts flared up in the CIS region in the late 1990s (except in Chechnya) or the first years of the next decade, and Russian forces, presented as peacekeeping units, remained entrenched in Abkhazia, South Ossetia, and Transdniester. However, Russian regional primacy in Central Asia was eroded during 2001–3 as the US established new pragmatic security relationships with local states in connection with the operations in Afghanistan. This was followed by what Moscow perceived as a more fundamental challenge to its role and influence in the CIS region, the so-called 'coloured revolutions'.

The Rose Revolution in Tbilisi in November 2003 ousted President Eduard Shevardnadze, the Orange Revolution in Kiev in November–December 2004 confirmed the removal of President Leonid Kuchma, and the Tulip Revolution in Bishkek in March 2005 swept President Askar Akayev from power. In Georgia and Ukraine this resulted in unambiguously Western-oriented leaderships.

The 'revolutions' followed competition around election processes,[58] which Moscow interpreted as part of a CIS-wide strategic contest, in which Western states sought to shift local foreign and security policy alignments in their favour by replacing incumbent leaders.

These political upheavals were neither enabled by nor did they trigger military interventions of any kind. No foreign military forces, Russian or Western, were deployed at the time to shape the domestic political arrangements or electoral outcomes in Georgia, Ukraine, or Kyrgyzstan. So the coloured revolutions did not prompt legal or normative justifications on the use of military force as examined in previous chapters. However, they link to our analysis in several other respects.

First, the Russian reaction confirmed that Moscow viewed the CIS region as a theatre increasingly locked into a wider systemic competition with Western states. Russia viewed the revolutions through a strategic prism. Its official rhetoric portrayed them as a softer form of Western interventionism, which was just more blatant in other regions of the world. Secondly, these upheavals reinforced political differentiation between and within states in the CIS regional order and so changed the political landscape. In normative terms this was reflected now more clearly in a contest between solidarist and pluralist outlooks on justice and order. Appeals by reformist leaders and Western states to respect universal values were countered by the primacy attached by incumbent leaders in Tbilisi, Kiev, and Bishkek, as well as Russian officials, to preserving domestic 'constitutional order'.

Russian leaders reacted bitterly to the unexpected overthrow of political leaders in the three CIS states, claiming this was orchestrated by the hidden and not so hidden hand of Western politicians driven by *Realpolitik* interests. In the most simplistic terms, one official characterized the revolutions as 'a combination of peaceful and violent methods designed to topple regimes disagreeable to the United States'. 'Washington maintains', he affirmed, that such revolutions 'cost less than the toppling of regimes through military intervention'.[59] In this strategic logic, mass protests against fraudulent elections in Kiev were engineered abroad and similar in impulse to US efforts at regime change with the use of force in cases outside the CIS region, such as in Iraq.

Ironically, Russia itself may have contemplated some form of military intervention in Georgia as events led to the Rose Revolution. In October 2003 Defence Minister Sergei Ivanov described a new threat to Russia as 'intervention in internal affairs by foreign states or by organisations supported by foreign states'. Elaborating on his controversial views on pre-emption (assessed in the previous chapter), he warned that Moscow might use military force within the CIS if a complex, unstable situation develops, or if there is a direct threat to Russian citizens or ethnic Russians.[60] In the event, Moscow did not act on this warning, which had revived the early 1990s discourse of protecting Russian citizens. Nor was such language used during the Orange Revolution, when the geopolitical stakes were much higher and many more Russian citizens were involved, including in the territorial flashpoint of Crimea.

The Russian leadership was surely aware of the serious international repercussions and probable dangerous instability within these CIS states that any new and undeniable Russian military intrusion into them would pose, not to mention the active nationalist resistance such action could provoke. Perhaps only in Kyrgyzstan did a military incursion offer tolerable risks. After President Akayev had been ousted Sergei Ivanov admitted that Russia had been prepared during the uprising to airlift troops to Bishkek, supposedly to protect Russian citizens.[61]

Moscow would have found it especially difficult to present legal and normative grounds for deploying forces to sustain the incumbent presidents in power, given its insistence on the illegality of previous Western military interventions, and the sensitivity of CIS states over their formal sovereignty. At the same time the basic logic of Russia's Monroe Doctrine had not been renounced. Early in 2006 Ivanov wrote that Russia's top concern was the internal situation in certain CIS states and that Russia and its military should be prepared to thwart: a 'political or military-political conflict or process that has a potential to pose a direct threat to Russia's security or to change the geopolitical reality in a region of Russia's strategic interest'.[62]

In the event, the struggle around the coloured revolutions was confined to political channels. Russia accused Western states and Western-supported organizations and NGOs of illegitimate intervention in the political processes of these countries for *Realpolitik*, strategic ends. It described such 'exported revolutions' as fuelled by Western financial contributions and 'political technologies' and claimed that Western states had promoted violations of state and constitutional order in the CIS states. In direct contrast, Western states and organizations deplored Russian recognition of rigged election results and made much of the need to uphold universal principles and norms of democratic governance and civil liberties in CIS states in the face of oppressive state policies.[63]

Moscow focused on ostensible Western strategic designs, especially US and EU efforts, to wrest CIS states from their natural gravitation towards Russia. It denied outright that either the interests of Western politicians in the coloured revolutions or the reformist movements in Georgia and Ukraine were driven by any normative, universalist agenda. Russian spokesmen dismissed the relevance of such an agenda in the election debates. This reflected a general tendency by Russian officials during the Putin administrations to claim that strategic designs lay behind Western normative language on foreign policy matters.[64]

On the other hand, the Russian response to efforts at political transformation in CIS states was normative in itself. Moscow encouraged CIS leaderships to adhere to the increasingly statist governance norms which characterized the Russian state and its security institutions. In this sense, by the mid-2000s the regional political terrain of the CIS states had become one of contested norms around governance and domestic state order. This was reflected in and reinforced the solidarist–pluralist dichotomy we have discussed at the international systemic level.

In broad terms the coloured revolutions in Georgia and Ukraine represented an alternative normative trajectory to that associated with Russia and Russian primacy. Of course the clarity of choice between these alternatives could be idealized by nationalist leaders as well as Western observers. It was not surprising also that some politicians in Tbilisi, Kiev, and Bishkek used the language of principles for instrumental reasons, to advance local political positions. Nonetheless, the programmes of Mikheil Saakashvili in Georgia and Viktor Yushchenko in Ukraine expressed a distinct normative trajectory.

On one level this expressed broad international, especially Western, norms on democratization and civil liberties. On another level it built on specific European Union expectations about the diffusion of norms in its CIS 'shared neighbourhood' with Russia. This stoked Russian fears about losing primacy in the CIS region, as it saw the region transformed into a battleground between alternative conceptions of legitimate political authority as well as security relationships.

One outcome during Putin's second presidency was the challenge Russia mounted to the Western 'hegemonic' international order, in terms of norms as well as power, as analysed in chapter 8. However, from the mid-2000s Russian officials also built on earlier ideas to develop a statist quasi-ideology, summarized in the concept of Russia as a 'sovereign democracy', which formed a strong domestic state foundation to Moscow's pluralist conception of order. It was also calculated to appeal to authoritarian leaderships in CIS states thrown on the defensive by the coloured revolutions and 'external' agendas for governance and civil rights. 'Sovereign democracy' as concept or slogan, in essence, meant a political system that is protected from external pressures.[65]

This concept reflected an exaggerated belief among Russian policy circles in the role of the West in fomenting and guiding especially the Orange Revolution in Ukraine. There was distinct alarm that this might be followed by foreign attempts to undermine the legitimacy of the Russian political system and even to foster a popular revolt in Moscow, with the strategic goal of subordinating Russia to the West.[66] During Putin's second administration this nervousness about the vulnerability of Russian domestic state order, particularly the highly centralized polity dominated by Putin and his entourage, strongly motivated the Kremlin to sustain pluralist regional norms, prioritizing order over justice.

Moscow was energetic in seeking to insulate itself from 'Orange processes'. Ambrosio describes this as a process of authoritarian resistance to regional democratic trends, which has included bolstering the political status quo in neighbouring CIS states which escaped coloured revolutions, working to reverse the impetus of the coloured revolutions themselves in Ukraine and Georgia, and mobilizing domestic support to counter an array of supposed threats to Russian sovereignty from external forces which in common challenged the legitimacy of Russian domestic political arrangements.[67]

It cannot be proved that these measures stemmed some advancing wave of democratic diffusion in the CIS region during 2005–10, since the circumstances of political change in Georgia, Ukraine, and Kyrgyzstan varied considerably, and they also varied greatly with other CIS states, for example in the extent to which they could be grounded in a vibrant civil society. But there is little doubt that in Russian thinking the normative and strategic challenges it faced were merged and the Russian policy elite regarded it as of first rate importance to sustain the region, as defined already in the early 1990s, as a zone of 'special responsibility' for Russia by preventing any more falling dominoes in the form of coloured revolutions.

An example was Tajikistan. In a secret US diplomatic cable in November 2005 the American ambassador in Tajikistan, Richard E. Hoagland, claimed that 'Moscow is determined to do everything possible to prevent a "colour revolution" in Tajikistan' and truly feared this possibility. He put the case of Tajikistan in a wider normative context, as understood by senior US diplomats, in asserting that 'Russia still requires clear-eyed scrutiny for the havoc it can play with the [US] President's democracy agenda and larger goals for transformational diplomacy in the former Soviet republics.'[68]

It is reasonable to conclude that Moscow's support and its ability to find common cause with leaders in the Central Asian states, as well as at least Belarus and Azerbaijan, in resisting the democratization and governance agendas of the US and other Western states, played a major role in quelling challenges to disputed elections in these states.

However, the Russian leadership also drew lessons from its noisy and ultimately ineffectual role in opposing the Orange Revolution. During the following years it sought to build ties to a broader spectrum of political forces in CIS states than had been done in Ukraine in 2004–5. This extended the options Moscow had to influence the outcome of possible future power struggles confronting its authoritarian CIS partners.

The results of this approach were demonstrated in April 2010 when the Kyrgyz president, Kurmanbek Bakiyev (who had replaced Akayev in 2005), was overthrown by chaotic and seemingly spontaneous demonstrations. Russian relations with Bakiyev had deteriorated in previous months (after he reneged on a promise to close the US airbase at Manas), and there were reports of Russian officials cooperating closely with opposition leaders before Bakiyev was ousted. The new provisional Kyrgyz government was quickly recognized by Russia before any other state. Russia offered emergency financial aid and established good relations with it.[69]

In this case Moscow's response was calibrated to influence events but to avoid evidence of overt intervention in the crisis. It was accompanied by a staged military demonstration. Some 150 Russian paratroopers were dispatched to reinforce the Kant air base outside Bishkek, which was operationally under Russian control. The Russian Chief of General Staff described their task merely as providing 'security for our families, our garrisons and the equipment and armaments there'. 'Nobody has appealed to us for help yet', he observed.[70] This reinforcement was probably covered by the agreements in force on the Kant base. Yet these forces, together with others at Kant, might have responded to a request for assistance from the fragile provisional government (initially unrecognized by other states) during the power transition, although in the event this did not occur.

This case of regime change showed that the discourse under Medvedev's presidency avoided the crude Russian view of 'exported revolutions' of 2003–5, although Moscow's falling out with Bakiyev played a part in this verbal shift. During 2005–10 Russia was still inclined to shore up established regimes in the CIS regional order. But it became apparent that the challenge to 'constitutional order' was not just associated with liberal Western-oriented movements, NGOs and organizations, and the agendas they promoted. In the Central Asian republics opposition by radical Islamist groups was also at the forefront of Russian concerns. An important ambiguity remained: whether the political solidarity Russia offered its partners could spill over into unwanted intervention, given the potent mix of sensitivities over sovereignty, power disparities, and Russia's insistence on 'special responsibilities' in its CIS neighbourhood.

REGIONAL STRUCTURES: SOLIDARITY AND INTERVENTION?

During the first and second Putin presidencies regional multilateral structures served as an important instrument for Russia to consolidate a coalition of like-minded CIS states. This was an essential part of Russia's persistent claim that it represents the core of an integrated region, and that the weight of this region should be expressed in Russian and CIS 'external' negotiations at the systemic level with other powers and international bodies. In terms of comparative regionalism, Russia sought recognition for what could be defined as a managerial or order-producing role in the CIS region. This role might be compared to other 'second-tier' powers seeking to enhance their global standing through the shadow they cast in a particular region.[71]

In practice, however, Russia's effort to sustain its primacy and to 'represent' the region internationally compromised the sovereignty of its weaker

CIS partners. Their readiness to accede to Moscow's assumption of the role of regional 'security manager' varied considerably. In the 1990s most CIS states had drawn the line at consenting to an open-ended 'CIS mandate' for what essentially would be Russian-defined peacekeeping operations. During the following decade, as Russian hopes for pan-CIS arrangements in various fields faded, Moscow was more successful in championing regional structures formed of smaller CIS state 'coalitions of the willing'.

The principal function of these regional structures has been political. This was boosted by the shock of the coloured revolutions for conservative CIS regimes. Regional coordination reinforced political solidarity and a common normative discourse between the Russian elite and those of authoritarian regimes, especially in Central Asia and Belarus. The leaders of these states privileged domestic state order and resisted 'external' normative agendas that questioned their legitimacy. This common understanding gave a particular purpose to regional structures—one of 'protective integration' in upholding regime security. Therefore such structures embodied a virtual rather than substantive regionalism.[72] Formal agreements on economic, trade, or security cooperation often were not implemented, but the function of political solidarity still gave purpose to the dialogue and formal statements of such meetings. This applied to the most prominent regional structure of this kind, the Collective Security Treaty Organization.

A major uncertainty has been whether and how political bonding for purposes of regime security could be reinforced by Russian military means. The Russian military apparatus has remained overwhelmingly the strongest among CSTO states. Collective decision-making in the CSTO implied that there should be no 'intervention' in member states. Yet in the second half of the 2000s ambiguities developed about whether and how force might be used in scenarios other than the prime stated purpose of the CSTO, collective defence against an external attack. During intra-state conflicts or periods of political destabilization in CIS states might the CSTO be activated in ways that would express not so much solidarity and mutual consent but intervention? Might even the Shanghai Cooperation Organization (SCO), the other broad macro-regional Eurasian organization, have some role in crises of domestic order within member states?

The prospect of intra-state conflict

In May 2002 Russia joined Armenia, Kazakhstan, Kyrgyzstan, Tajikistan, and Uzbekistan in establishing the Collective Security Organization. This was launched next year as the Collective Security Treaty Organization (CSTO). It envisaged coordination of 'foreign policy positions regarding international and regional security problems' and a collective security system.[73] But it was soon clear that problems in developing a common 'CSTO foreign policy thinking' showed the wariness of CSTO member states about Russian efforts to rein in their sovereignty. Agreement was reached on the desirability of some cooperation over counter-terrorism. But the other member states seemed doubtful about Moscow's capacity for effective and impartial counter-terrorist military intervention in Central Asia or elsewhere.[74]

As the spectre of 'coloured revolutions' loomed, however, status quo-oriented authoritarian leaders appeared to revise their view of the function and purposes of the CSTO. They viewed it increasingly as an instrument to enlist Russian support for regime security, as a vehicle to bandwagon with Russia in forging a kind of Eurasian political club that only selectively promotes and applies Euro-Atlantic political principles and values (or openly resists them).[75] The CSTO offered a form of normative bandwagoning, or 'protective integration', to bolster the political legitimacy of CSTO presidents on the international stage. This legitimacy had come under question in the OSCE, the EU, and Western-oriented international organizations.

Yet there was also a potential military dimension to Russian support for regime security in CSTO states. Russian forces locally deployed in Central Asia, Belarus, or perhaps Armenia, under the guise of CSTO mutual support and reinforced by bilateral agreements, in principle could offer limited military assistance to shore up beleaguered local regimes faced by domestic revolts. As previously noted, Russia was prepared to airlift troops to Bishkek after President Akayev was ousted in 2005, and reinforcements actually were sent to the Kant base in May 2010 when Bakiyev was overthrown.[76]

One specialist notes that the CSTO counter-terrorist exercises scheduled for March 2005 in Kyrgyzstan, 'were urgently moved to Tajikistan in order to avoid the impression of a possible intervention in the revolutionary chaos'.[77] Yet the scenario the exercises rehearsed was telling: one side used public discontent with election results to attempt to overthrow the government, while the other side practised the use of collective security forces to protect the sovereignty and territorial integrity of Tajikistan. Further annual CSTO exercises similarly appeared 'to legitimize collective actions to repel attempts of regime change by connecting domestic oppositions to foreign aggressors and terrorists'.[78] As the Arab Spring reverberated, one goal of the 'Tsentr-2011' CSTO exercises, involving over 12,000 troops, according to the Russian Chief of General Staff Army-General Nikolai Makarov, was specifically to prepare member states to respond to mass unrest similar to that seen in Libya and Syria.[79]

Such exercises were linked to a persistent Russian strategic objective, the development of CSTO Collective Rapid Reaction Forces (CRRF). It was eventually agreed that such forces should be formed of earmarked national contingents from CSTO member states, which would work together in a crisis, most likely in Central Asia. They were assigned the formal role of collective defence against 'external' attacks. However, the scenarios for CSTO 'military assistance', as well as the distinction between CSTO assistance and a Russian national deployment, were not transparent.

Could this assistance be provided, for example, in response to a power struggle with high stakes in the key Central Asian state of Uzbekistan? The basis for a separate Russian military deployment to Uzbekistan, with Tashkent's approval, in the event of a national crisis, was laid out in principle in a bilateral Russian–Uzbek treaty of November 2005. However, Tashkent, a regional competitor of Russia in Central Asia, has been cautious since then to avoid the further step of consenting to even a small permanent Russian military presence on its territory, even under a supposed CSTO aegis. Since 2005 President Karimov has striven instead for Russian political backing and solidarity. Indeed the 2005 bilateral treaty had been agreed after Russia supported Karimov's military suppression of demonstrators in the town of Andijan—in a brutal imposition of domestic 'state order'. The CSTO expressed its 'protective integration' function in refraining from any criticism of Uzbekistan in that severe crisis. In August 2006 Uzbekistan was re-admitted to the CSTO, which it had left in 2003. In June 2012 it suspended its membership.

After the coloured revolutions the Russian leadership must have acknowledged the risks of any military intervention in political turmoil within Central Asian states, especially in the absence of a clear exit strategy. This had been an object lesson of the Russian military deployment in the 1990s in the civil war in Tajikistan. In 2006 the (Russian) CSTO Secretary-General, Nikolai Bordyuzha, claimed that the option of using military force in internal conflicts had not been discussed in the CSTO at any level. Yet with nervousness about coloured revolutions still gripping Russian leaders, Bordyuzha described 'the potential of the CSTO' as available 'for the prevention of armed conflict, bloodshed and mass unrest on the part of warring political groups striving for power in this or that country'.[80]

This scenario of a CSTO role in a local intra-state power struggle has been contentious for various reasons. First, it is difficult to equate with the founding documents of the organization. These focus on security challenges and threats external to CSTO states, in which case a CSTO state could appeal to the right to collective defence. In contrast, the legality of supporting one or other party in such an intra-state conflict and the way their consent to such an intervention could be determined have been questionable. It would be difficult to justify such action convincingly in regional or wider international terms, which would be problematic for Russia given its criticism of Western interventions in other regions.

Secondly, the interest of the other CSTO state leaders in Russian military support for regime security in the region has been double-edged. They would probably only welcome such a Russian role, as opposed to political or intelligence support, as a last resort, if their regime were in serious jeopardy.

Russia's CSTO partners have been aware of the long-term effects of previous Russian military interventions in the early 1990s in Tajikistan, Georgia, and Moldova—including the lasting deployment of Russian troops in those states in one format or another.

Authoritarian leaders are unlikely to trust that Moscow will necessarily take their side in major political crises in their states, rather than balance strategically between favoured local political candidates or even support pro-Russian opposition figures (despite all the promise of protective integration). After its clumsy tactics during the Orange Revolution in Ukraine, Moscow has been more ready to develop discreet contacts with a variety of secular political groupings in Central Asia or Belarus. These contacts could be used in bargaining between Moscow and local leaders, if the latter became reliant on political support from their powerful northern neighbour during power struggles in their states.

The prospect of a military-security role for the Shanghai Cooperation Organization in intra-state crises has been even more problematic, given the strong Chinese presence in this body (it includes Russia, China, Kazakhstan, Uzbekistan, Tajikistan, and Kyrgyzstan). The SCO like the CSTO has sustained pluralist political solidarity between its member states, but this has not spread to bonding over new regional principles on the appropriate use of force. As China is a member the SCO has not operated in hierarchical terms favourable to Moscow in any consistent way. China's presence also heightens sensitivities over sovereignty, for historical and cultural reasons.

The SCO has expressed its protective integration function though resisting externally 'imposed' norms in the form of democratic processes and good governance. Central Asian leaders, presiding over illiberal states alongside Russia and China, have promoted SCO principles which represent norms contrary to those promoted globally by the US and like-minded powers.[81] At the same time, the strong sovereignty-orientation of the so-called SCO 'Shanghai spirit' has reinforced the foundational principle of non-interference in the domestic affairs of member states. The option of an SCO mandate to authorize regional military deployments has not been aired. Claims in 2005 that Moscow was interested, to avert coloured revolutions, in an SCO stamp of approval for possible invited operations by Russian forces in Central Asia have not been substantiated.[82] Indeed the SCO prohibition against interventions in domestic state order is considered to extend to intra-regional relations as well as to conduct in the wider global order.

The SCO has been cautious, therefore, about its potential role in conflict prevention, beyond sustaining peaceful dialogue between its members.[83] The 2007 Bishkek SCO summit raised the goal of a regional conflict prevention mechanism within the SCO framework.[84] This idea remained on the drawing board until revived by President Nazarbayev at the Astana SCO summit in June 2011, when he proposed a council for resolving territorial and regional conflicts in the 'SCO's area of responsibility'.[85] Yet it is unlikely that the label of conflict prevention, under an SCO aegis, will be used to provide cover for an invited military operation by one or more SCO states in a future internal conflict in another member state. For Russia this role is better earmarked, if at all, for the CSTO, as we explore below, and the possible use of Chinese troops in such a scenario remains too geopolitically and culturally sensitive for any Central Asian state or indeed Russia to contemplate.

New crises and the CSTO response

The controversy over a potential CSTO role in intra-state conflicts was fuelled by two quite different crises. The first was the serious civil conflict in Kyrgyzstan in June 2010, a significant threat to stability in Central Asia. The second was the onset of the Arab Spring in spring 2011, which for Russian and other CSTO leaders revived the insecurities prompted by the coloured revolutions half a decade earlier.

By the time of the inter-ethnic crisis in Kyrgyzstan the CSTO supposedly had available its own peacekeeping force, formed of national units of CSTO states (except Uzbekistan which had opted out of this plan), which were separate to larger CSTO collective rapid reaction forces (CRRF). However, despite the repeated appeals during the crisis for the involvement of 'third party force' by Roza Otunbayeva, the leader of the Kyrgyz provisional government (after the ouster of President Bakiyev), there was no deployment of CSTO units. The inaction of the CSTO (chaired by Russia at the time) in the crisis may be explained formally by restrictions in the CSTO Charter. But it also exposed deep divisions and distrust in the organization over any precedent for the use of force in an internal conflict in a partner state, especially when responding to an appeal by a provisional government was tantamount to supporting one side in a sectarian conflict.[86] Kyrgyzstan's large neighbours Kazakhstan and Uzbekistan in particular seemed to question the need for such intervention.[87]

In discussing the June 2010 crisis, Russian military and political leaders themselves also showed no enthusiasm for inserting their forces, whether under a CSTO flag or independently. This exposed Moscow's longstanding insistence on its security responsibilities in the CIS region as a discourse that was primarily intended to delineate *politically* a zone of Russian interests. In the complex emergency of June 2010, which eventually displaced some 400,000 people, it was uncertain whether Russia either had the trained forces for such messy inter-ethnic strife, which potentially could spread further in the Ferghana Valley across state borders, or the political will and funding to embark on a possibly open-ended commitment. Russian officials notably refrained from any rhetoric on the need to 'protect our citizens', although Russian citizens residing in Kyrgyzstan anyway did not seem in peril.

The Kyrgyz crisis prompted some rethinking, however, over the potential for a CSTO military response in such an emergency. The CSTO was proceeding, Bordyuzha claimed in 2011, to take measures to 'localise attempts to repeat the events of last year'.[88] He mooted CSTO intervention when the national authorities of member countries 'are unable to protect the constitutional order, the lives and safety of citizens are threatened, violent mass disorders are under way'.[89] From 2011 Russian officials encouraged a debate over CSTO reform, including possible criteria to invoke the organization's assistance provisions during an internal upheaval within member states.[90]

This followed a CSTO meeting at the end of 2010, when most CSTO states were persuaded for the first time to consider such assistance, although the principle of host government consent for any intervention remained in place. Even so, a full normative, legal, or indeed political consensus has not emerged among CSTO leaders to enable an effective response in such a domestic upheaval. In particular Uzbekistan resisted shifting the orientation of the CSTO from external defence to intra-state crises.[91] It seems to matter little whether the scenario involves deploying CSTO peacekeeping forces, which might appear appropriate as a stabilizing force for such crises, or deploying the organization's collective rapid reaction forces, which were developed supposedly for defence against 'external' threats. Both options have been hamstrung by underlying suspicions between CSTO states, such as tense relations between Uzbekistan and Tajikistan, as well as 'the distrust of the ruling elites of the region's countries in Moscow's true intentions'.[92]

The problem has been reflected in differences over the mandate for the CRRF, which has replayed the 'CIS mandate' controversy of the 1990s. Russia has sought agreement that future CSTO troop deployments and operations could be authorized by decisions of the CSTO's Collective Security Council (its top political authority) and that CRRF forces could be dispatched to member states' territories during high security threats with or without a UN mandate.[93] However, Uzbekistan in particular (but not alone among CSTO states) has been alive to the risk of Moscow using the CSTO simply to validate its own self-interested military actions in the region.

Tashkent has insisted not only that CRRF should not be used to resolve disputes that may arise between CIS and CSTO states, but that any decision on the deployment of CSTO forces should be by consensus (as established by Article 12 of the CSTO Charter), not activated by some 'automatic' trigger or by a simple majority of CSTO member states.[94] Consensus decision-making has offered each state a veto that could pre-empt any unwanted Russia intervention under a nominal CSTO flag, for example, in a crisis of authority in Uzbekistan's Central Asian 'backyard' (as perceived by Tashkent) or in Tashkent itself.

Dissent by Uzbekistan, geographically the key Central Asian CIS state, has hollowed out the 'collective' nature of the CRRF. It has also deterred Russia from using the CSTO label as cover to go beyond the role of 'protective integration' to enforce a *Realpolitik* interpretation of its 'special responsibilities' in the region. Uzbekistan suspended its CSTO membership in June 2012. As a result, Tashkent may lose its veto in the CSTO. But this means that the practical options of CSTO flagged military involvement in an intra-state crisis in Central Asia become still more difficult.

Uzbekistan reportedly has feared that if CRRF forces were used in response to a domestic crisis in a CSTO state 'these forces may be used in the interests of the enemies of the ruling regime'.[95] Such suspicions could only be reinforced by the apparent Russian approval for the overthrow of President Bakiyev in Kyrgyzstan in 2010, which could be read as a geopolitical gambit in Uzbekistan's 'near abroad'. At the CSTO summit in December that year, President Karimov bluntly insisted that the organization should focus on countering external threats and that any CSTO intervention to quell violence inside member states should be excluded.[96]

This fractious background made the CSTO response to the 'Arab Spring' all the more sensitive. At a CSTO discussion on this phenomenon in August 2011 Bordyuzha jumped at the opportunity for reinvigorated political bonding between member states. For him the toppling of authoritarian leaders in Egypt and Tunisia, mass demonstrations in Bahrain, Yemen, and Syria, and chaotic resistance in Libya all represented a challenge to state order not a democratic opportunity He even implied that the Western hand Russia had identified behind the earlier coloured revolutions was again at work. Transnational financial and political structures, he warned, would 'be striving to provoke various disturbances... for the purposes of countries' internal destabilisation'.[97]

This perspective was shared by several other CSTO state leaders, who condemned the 'destructive role' played by social networks in the Arab Spring protests. Kazakh president Nazarbayev spoke of the views the leaders exchanged on 'global and regional risks to the security and stability of the CSTO member states connected with recent events in the world'. In short the Arab Spring was viewed as an extra-regional challenge to CIS regional and domestic order. The reaction it evoked confirmed the CSTO's role of protective integration. Bordyuzha talked of the 'great attention' CSTO leaders now paid 'to the issues of raising solidarity and mutual support in the organisation's work, particularly in the sphere of foreign policy'.[98] This expressed a solid dose of wishful thinking by Russian staff of the CSTO, yet more intelligence and political coordination between CSTO regimes could be expected. The CSTO states also agreed to create a unified preventive strategy for cyberspace, to regulate regional 'information space'.[99]

Overall, CSTO leaders felt vulnerable to the spread of revolutionary contagion from the Middle East and North Africa, but a number of them remained cautious about bonding around Russia-led principles on how and when force might be applied in their region. These leaders, particularly Uzbek president Karimov, also suspected that Russia viewed the CSTO through a wider geopolitical lens. This broader focus is suggested by Bordyuzha's description of the new CSTO peacekeeping forces in April 2011, as ready to carry out tasks not only in the 'CSTO's area of responsibility' (for which he sought no UN mandate) but also elsewhere under a UN Security Council mandate.[100] A declaration he signed with the UN Secretary-General on behalf of the CSTO was trumpeted as 'recognition of our organization's authority, its ability to contribute to ensuring security on the global scale'.[101]

The image of CSTO peacekeeping is one promoted less to stabilize local crises than to legitimize on the wider international stage an exclusive Russia-led CSTO zone of regional responsibility (displacing, for example, the NATO Partnership for Peace framework). Moscow does not regard CSTO operations in this zone as dependent on a devolved UN mandate. However, to earn recognition for this special regional role, there is an effort to deploy a token presence of CSTO-flagged troops further afield, in genuine UN peacekeeping operations. Moscow hopes this will cultivate the impression in the wider international community that the CSTO operates as a real collective undertaking on security, with cooperative military procedures, in tune with international norms on peacekeeping, rather than as an instrument for Russian regional policy.

Western states have remained suspicions, however, that the CSTO acts as a Russian project to insert itself between Western and CSTO countries and stake out an exclusive CSTO region. They have noted that officials from Russia, but not other CIS states, have tended to talk in exclusive terms about the 'CSTO space', and that these other CIS states have wished also to interact, for example, with the Euro-Atlantic Partnership Council and NATO structures, in discussing their regional security or options for peacekeeping. Kazakhstan, for example, prides itself on the preparedness of its Kazbat peacekeeping battalion, which was formed with US assistance, conducts exercises with Western states, and is earmarked for UN authorized operations, independent of the CSTO.[102]

On the other hand Russia extracted an agreement from its fellow CSTO states (except Uzbekistan) in December 2011, whereby individual member states would need the consent of all other CSTO states in the future to host a foreign military base on their territory.[103] This followed soon after a reported Russian effort to reach agreement at a CSTO foreign ministers meeting at the UN General Assembly to the formulation of a common position over a list of security and foreign policy issues.[104] Uzbekistan's frustration with such Russian attempts to railroad collective CSTO positions helps explain Tashkent's decision to suspend its CSTO membership in June 2012.

In conclusion, the CSTO's political solidarity role has failed to 'spill over' into understandings about appropriate military responses to internal conflicts in CIS states. New crises have exposed the dysfunctional nature of the CSTO's security apparatus, the significant limitations of its founding documents, focused on external threats or terrorism, and the unwillingness of at least Uzbekistan to revise that focus. By 2010, arguably it was 'precisely the sudden collapse of apparently outwardly stable authoritarian orders that constitutes the main threat to regional peace and security' in Eurasia.[105]

Russia has no solution to this quandary, but for years has striven to block effective Western security engagement in the CIS region, not just in the form of NATO but also the OSCE (with its peacekeeping mandate). This has left the CIS regional order, especially its Central Asian flank, fractured and tense. The Arab Spring has made regional leaders more defensive about their domestic political legitimacy and cohesion as well as their standing in the wider international community. At the same time, insecure CIS states remain sensitive to possible regional encroachments on their sovereignty if their grip on power weakens, whether that might be undertaken by their immediate neighbours, by Moscow, or (especially for Uzbekistan) by a Russia-led structure like the CSTO.

CONCLUSION: A FRACTURED REGIONAL ORDER

This chapter confirms that regional norms that serve to legitimize Russian or Russia-led military interventions among CIS states as peacekeeping have been aired in Russian discourse but have failed to become embedded. Most CIS state leaders did not consent to Russian proposals to confirm a CIS mandate (in the 1990s) or CSTO mandate (in the 2000s) for the use of force, without UN authorization, especially in conditions of intra-state conflict. This resistance only began to waver in 2010 as some leaders came to view the challenge of the Arab Spring as offsetting the risks of appealing to Russia to support the stability of their regimes. But no CIS state has acquiesced to Russian claims for exclusive rights to protect its citizens abroad by force of arms.

The Russian leadership has been more successful, especially since the 2003–5 coloured revolutions, in rallying regional political solidarity among a subset of CIS states against what they have branded a form of Western political intervention in their domestic state affairs. This solidarity has reflected a determination to bolster regime security in the face of new demands for representative governance, a determination boosted by new fears about political contagion from the Arab Spring.

The contrast between these two sets of responses is explained by the nexus of sovereignty and regime security in the mindset of CIS leaders, especially those nervous about the influence of 'external' Western solidarist principles. After the dissolution of the USSR, as the dependence of CIS state leaders on

Moscow declined, in varying degrees they developed a core commitment to national sovereignty as a means of enhancing their domestic legitimacy. They sought to widen their options for autonomous decision-making in foreign and security policies. Consequently their acceptance of Russian discourse about CIS 'integration' and their participation in various macro-regional structures was not aimed at pooling sovereignty.

This commitment to substantiating their sovereignty meant that the other CIS leaders resisted to the extent they could the consolidation of a new hierarchical regulation of the post-Soviet order under Russian tutelage, even if aspects of Russian security assistance were still desirable. Moscow could not assume the general compliance of CIS partner states with its security preferences, even if states like Belarus sometimes appeared close to mapping their security policies onto those of Russia. Indeed, for these smaller CIS states, the pluralist approach they tended to display in the wider international system has been intended to form a protective barrier also against intrusive influences or demands within their own region.

The intention was not only to fend off the overbearing policies of Russian politicians with a sense of entitlement among former Soviet territories. It was viewed as necessary equally by smaller states in the CIS region, especially in Central Asia, to fend off the domineering policies of other neighbours. Mutual suspicions and antagonisms between adjacent authoritarian states ran high, despite their common rejection of 'external' normative agendas. The South Caucasus region also remained deeply divided. Therefore CIS leaders tried to insist on the letter of declarations that CIS states including Russia signed in various regional settings on mutual equality and non-interference, as well as resistance to separatism and secession.

On the other hand, since the collapse of the USSR, with the brief exception of 1991–3, leading Russian politicians rather consistently assumed the existence of Russian primacy in what has been termed variously the 'near abroad', the 'post-Soviet space', or 'the CSTO zone of responsibility'. Another incarnation of this since 2008 has been Russia's 'sphere of privileged interests'. These spatial images have expressed an effort, to greater or lesser extent, to enclose other CIS states in a Russia-led hierarchical regional order, which limits their opportunities for wider international commitments, especially in matters of military security. For Moscow it has been natural to relativize and qualify the sovereignty of smaller and at various times dependent former Soviet republics, despite all the formal discourse about sovereign equality.

This has also been expressed in a selective Russian application of traditional norms of the global order and the UN Charter system, including basic principles governing the use of force and the prohibition of support for separatism, in a region where Moscow has continued to identity central and exclusive Russian national interests. This approach often has clashed with the core interests of smaller CIS states. It has been inconsistent also with the pluralist principles Russia itself espoused in wider international forums, especially during the Putin presidencies in the 2000s. These contradictions were brought to the fore by Russian intervention in Georgia in August 2008 and the tortuous justifications offered for that major military operation.

7

Russian Intervention in Georgia 2008

In August 2008 Russia conducted a five-day, high-intensity war with Georgia. This was exceptional since it developed into the first Russian military offensive against a foreign state, as opposed to participation just within a civil conflict, since the end of the Cold War. It was a military intervention which profoundly challenged Georgian state integrity and for some weeks threatened the overthrow of the Georgian government and leadership. However, the Russian leadership denied it had this political objective or even that it had been at war with Georgia.

The crucible of conflict was South Ossetia, a secessionist region which had existed outside Georgian political control throughout Georgia's post-Cold War independent statehood, but had been recognized as part of Georgia *de jure* by all states, including Russia. Moscow claimed that a Georgian military attack on South Ossetia precipitated an unavoidable Russian peacekeeping response. Russia presented its military offensive, hardly convincingly, as peacekeeping enforcement (or coercing Georgia to peace) and bolstered this claim with a variety of other legal and normative justifications. Georgia deplored the Russian invasion of Georgian territory both in South Ossetia and deeper into Georgia.

Differences between Russia and Georgia in defining the conflict reflected sharply contested narratives about the onset of war.[1] Controversy flared over Russia's *jus ad bellum* justifications for its military action, in particular whether Moscow could appeal to self-defence, as well as over Russian political and normative claims for the use of force against Georgia. On close examination the arguments Moscow used quickly reveal weaknesses and contradictions. This is what might be expected of legal and normative claims enlisted hastily in the service of an intervention motivated by strategic or political ends. As we reveal, neither established principles of international law nor emerging norms on the use of force proved to be strong constraints on Russian action in this case.

On the other hand, Russian discourse, the diplomatic campaign it conducted alongside its military campaign, was cast very much in terms of legal principles and norms (especially focused on the weakness of Georgian claims about their strikes against the town of Tskhinvali in South Ossetia at the outset of the conflict), and the detail of this is important for our wider study. In this chapter we assess the legal and normative contest over the August 2008 conflict. The intention is not so much to 'prove' Russian military operations as illegal and illegitimate, as to consider what Russian justifications reveal about its responsiveness to international norms and law and whether Russian claims had a specific application to conduct at the CIS regional level.

The previous chapter's discussion of Russian policy in the CIS region raises the question of how far Russian conduct in the conflict with Georgia was defined more by a Moscow-centred hierarchy, and perhaps the implicit propagation of Russian-defined regional norms, than by the application of broader international norms or established legal principles. If this kind of regional exceptionalism was at play, then Russia did not want to make it explicit at a time when it was seeking to assume the mantle of global 'responsibilities' in its wider foreign policy. But it remained difficult for Moscow to square its Georgia operation with its vigorous diplomatic campaign in international forums over the previous few years (see next chapter) against the American use of force in foreign interventions. The Russian discourse over the August 2008 war, as examined below, is challenging in its legal *jus ad bellum* justifications, interesting in its (mis)use of humanitarian claims, and unsettling in its support for political secession.

INTERNATIONAL LAW AND RUSSIAN JUSTIFICATIONS FOR INTERVENTION IN GEORGIA

Russian leaders and officials advanced a variety of legal arguments to validate their military incursion into South Ossetia and by extension their wider campaign deeper into Georgia. Without a UN Security Council mandate, or any UNSC debate on the campaign, Russia based its claims essentially on self-defence. This was consistent with the wider Russian legal focus on UN Charter principles.

In Moscow's initial declaration about the Georgian attack on the South Ossetian city of Tskhinvali, President Medvedev accused Georgian troops of committing 'what amounts to an act of aggression against Russian peacekeepers located there and the civilian population in South Ossetia', the majority of whom were 'citizens of the Russian Federation'.[2] However, in the August 2008 conflict self-defence claims could not apply to the defence of Russian territory, and were weak or abusive when applied to the defence of Russian military personnel and citizens located in South Ossetia, as we proceed to argue.

We should first consider the claim that Georgian 'aggression' against South Ossetia was an 'attack on Russia', or as the Russian Foreign Ministry argued, Georgia's 'illegal use of force against the Russian Federation' forced Russia to use its 'right to self-defence under Article 51 of the UN Charter'.[3] Russia has unyieldingly kept to the 'we were attacked first' claim and in this context referred to the definition of an act of aggression in UN General Assembly Resolution 3314 of 1974.[4]

As a result, in August 2008 Moscow did not resort to legal or even political claims based on pre-emption or the need for the preventive use of force in South Ossetia, despite its interest in this controversial rationale for military action with a specific focus on Georgia earlier in the decade (especially the Pankisi Gorge dispute). Moscow claimed that Georgia had formulated detailed plans for aggression against Abkhazia—an accusation hotly denied by Tbilisi. Nevertheless, Russian officials did not cite the need to pre-empt these plans as legal grounds for the entry of Russian troops into Abkhazia, which formed part of its wider offensive against Georgia in August 2008.

The 'attack on Russia' rationale on one level focused rather simply on which of the three parties—Georgian forces, South Ossetian forces, or Russian forces—*initiated hostilities*, in the sense of military action in South Ossetia on 7 August 2008. Framing it in these terms tends to discount the fact that there had been skirmishes between Georgian forces and South Ossetian militia groups for months before the final collapse of the ceasefire. The issue was muddied by circumstantial but quite compelling evidence of some unauthorized Russian military presence in the conflict zone already before the crisis became acute on 7 August 2008.[5] To add to the confusion, some hundreds of 'volunteer' irregular forces from North Ossetia in the Russian Federation arrived in South Ossetia, a little before the Georgian strikes on Tskhinvali, and these were integrated into the South Ossetian Interior Ministry forces.[6] Russia frequently had assisted the transit of armed irregulars to the region from North Ossetia.[7]

Russia's general claim of Georgian 'aggression' against South Ossetia could offer no legal basis, however, for Russia's offensive or other forms of combat against Georgia, since Russian territory itself was not under attack. The separate legal discussion about whether Georgia's attack against Tskhinvali constituted aggression (even in the absence of persuasive evidence of a prior 'invasion' of Georgian territory by regular Russian forces), does not alter this point of law.[8] The political reasonableness of the Georgian offensive, in a region that had not experienced rule by post-Soviet Georgia, might be challenged, but this offers no legal vindication for the Russian campaign in Georgia.

Nor could Russia justify its military activities on the grounds of 'collective self-defence' under international law, since the South Ossetian authorities could not validly invite Russian military support. The International

Criminal Court has found that in contemporary international law there is no general right of intervention in support of an opposition within another state. South Ossetia, even as an entity short of statehood, could rely on unilateral self-defence in order to repel Georgian attacks, but collective self-defence in unison with Russia was not permitted.[9] Russia had the legal position of a third-party state in relation to the South Ossetia secessionist entity before August 2008, despite all its previous involvement with the region, including the pervasive presence of its security personnel in the South Ossetian administration, and despite the fact that South Ossetia borders the Russian Federation.[10]

A stronger Russian case for self-defence arose from the claim that Georgian military action (in the course of its operation in Tskhinvali) against the Russian peacekeeping contingent deployed in South Ossetia could be construed as an armed attack on Russia.[11] Ten Russian peacekeepers eventually lost their lives in South Ossetia, although only some of these were killed during Georgia's initial assault on Tskhinvali. Differences remain about the exchange of fire and one could point to extensive collusion between the Russian contingent and South Ossetian irregular forces.[12] Regardless of this, however, Moscow's self-defence rationale is heavily undermined by the sweeping Russian military action that followed the initial clash.[13]

Russia could possibly claim there were grounds for emergency assistance or evacuation of its peacekeepers in South Ossetia from foreign soil—a rapid and limited surgical operation, proportionate to urgent needs.[14] But the need for this could not justify the scale of the actual Russian response, its extension to undisputed Georgian territory far beyond the conflict zone in Western Georgia and towards Tbilisi, or the open-ended seemingly punitive use of force. Russia could not dismiss the well-established customary international law requirements of necessity (military action taken as a last resort) and proportionality (action proportional to the established defensive need) in claiming self-defence. Moscow's assertion that its use of force was 'strictly proportional to the scale of the [Georgian] attack' and the need to prevent future military attacks,[15] which required Russia to 'neutralize' the military infrastructure of the Georgian 'aggressor', was rejected by all major Western states and widely dismissed internationally.[16]

This leaves the Russian self-defence claim with the widest foreign policy reverberations beyond the conflict with Georgia, which evokes earlier political claims by Russian officials about CIS conflict zones, *the defence of Russian citizens*. The solemn refrain of Russian officials was that the 'life and dignity of our citizens, wherever they are, will be protected in accordance with the Constitution of the Russian Federation'. The assertion of Russia's right to defend by force its 'citizens' outside its borders in South Ossetia and beyond and 'not to allow the death of its compatriots to go unpunished', appeared quite open-ended and punitive.[17]

As with similar declarations in the 1990s these were essentially political statements. In legal terms it is more than doubtful that an attack on Russian passport holders could be represented as an attack on Russia itself.[18] There exists no specific customary law right to protect or rescue one's own nationals abroad and diplomatic protection can only be exercised by peaceful means. Indeed, the forceful protection of nationals abroad has served often just as a pretext for interventions which have been viewed as unlawful. Admittedly, despite this legal position, it has widely been held in the international community, based on state practice, that an attack on a state's nationals might justify a response in the form of a strictly localized and proportionate rescue operation. However, the extensive and punitive Russian campaign in Georgia went far beyond this low threshold for the use of force. So it could not be characterized as such a rescue operation with a political rationale derived from the practice of other states.[19]

States may have an interest in the human rights and well-being of groups of peoples with whom they share ties of kinship or citizenship. This is not a right under international law, however, regardless of how Russia chooses to define its constitutional responsibilities.[20] But since Russia proclaimed so forcefully its political determination to defend its citizens abroad, the *way* South Ossetians acquired 'Russian citizenship' has attracted considerable attention. This has relevance for a legal analysis since a UN Charter Article 51 'self-defence' justification is even less convincing when a country first confers its citizenship on a large number of people outside its borders over a quite short period of time (in this case in South Osssetia), without the consent of the legal state within which these people are located (Georgia), as Russia did, and then claims it is entitled to intervene coercively to protect them.

The issue is clearest with respect to those citizens who more recently acquired Russian citizenship, through a broad Russian policy to confer Russian nationality in simplified procedures. As regards this group, the EU fact-finding mission on the conflict concludes trenchantly, 'it seems abusive to rely on their need for protection as a reason for intervention, because Russia itself has created this reason for intervention through its own policy'.[21] In other words, the widespread distribution of Russian passports in the 2000s to people living in South Ossetia and Abkhazia, who are mostly not even co-ethnic Russians, has offered what could well be regarded as a fig leaf for this Russian assertion of its 'right to protect'—a right which lacks legal foundation.[22]

In the South Ossetia case it is the nature of the South Ossetian *political* project that makes Russian claims about intervention based on the citizenship issue appear so self-serving. In terms of political intentionality it is relevant to distinguish between two cases. First a state (here Russia) seeking to protect the 'lives and dignity' of its citizens who are merely living in another country. Secondly, a government defending citizens abroad who are engaged in creating their own independent state (an effort pursued for many years in South

Ossetia before Russia formally recognized this independence) on the territory of another country. Notably this was also happening under the umbrella of the troops of the peacekeeping force sent by the same state that provided the separatists with foreign passports.[23]

In addition to this raft of justifications related to self-defence, Medvedev sought to present the Russian operations against Georgia as under some kind of international legal authorization by depicting Georgia's assault on Tskhinvali as a 'gross violation of the mandates that the international community gave Russia in the peace process' in South Ossetia.[24] Russia characterized the large-scale deployment of troops of its 58th Army and other units to South Ossetia as a 'reinforced Russian peacekeeping contingent'. In this sense Moscow described itself not as a party to the conflict in August 2008, but as fulfilling the peacekeeping function assumed in the Sochi (Dagomys) agreement of June 1992, which regulated the 1991–2 conflict around South Ossetia.[25] As its offensive expanded, Russia presented not only South Ossetia, but also a security 'buffer zone' in undisputed Georgian territory and beyond, as under the temporary custody of (Russian) troops operating under an internationally approved mandate.[26]

These claims were widely rejected internationally. Western states were blunt that unilateral support for one of the conflicting parties in South Ossetia could not be justified as a peacekeeping mission.[27] Nor did other states accept that certain unspecific terms in the texts of earlier agreements on conflict regulation in South Ossetia, about taking the measures necessary to preserve peace and order, could represent *carte blanche* rights on the use of force to achieve this end. Since August 2008 Russian officials have tried to argue this. As a legal point, Article 103 of the UN Charter precludes states from creating broader rights to use force than those provided for in the Charter, regardless of how Russia chose to interpret documents on the role of the joint peacekeeping forces in South Ossetia.[28]

In brief, Russia had no legal grounds to define its action against Georgia unilaterally as international peacekeeping. Indeed, Moscow's presentation of this action as 'coercing Georgia to peace' or 'enforcing peace' on Georgia, flatly contradicted the statement in Russia's own Foreign Policy Concept of July 2008, immediately before the conflict, that Russia 'firmly proceeds from the premise that only the UN Security Council has the authority to sanction the use of force for the purpose of coercion to peace'.[29]

Western leaders did not reject these various Russian legal arguments systematically as in the analysis above. This was partly because of some confusion over the actual course of events at the start of the conflict in South Ossetia and the imperative need, fronted by the EU, to apply diplomacy to limit and then reverse the Russian offensive. But Western leaders firmly argued that, regardless of what happened when Tskhinvali came under fire, the Russian military action which followed was egregious, disproportionate for self-defence, and therefore for some states could be defined as aggression.[30] The EU's special commission on the conflict, as we have shown, rejected most of the Russian claims and all of its legal justifications for the extension of its campaign deep into Georgia.

RUSSIAN HUMANITARIAN CLAIMS FOR INTERVENTION IN GEORGIA

Russian justifications for the war with Georgia went beyond these legal claims and co-opted humanitarian language in a graphic contrast to their response to previous Western interventions. Moscow stridently deplored the 'humanitarian catastrophe' inflicted on South Ossetia by Georgia. One explanation for such Russian claims based on solidarist language is that Moscow believed that the Georgian attack on Tskhinvali provided an arguable basis to persuade at least some foreign states of the legitimacy of the large-scale Russian operations which ensued. Secondly, Russian leaders may have hoped to mobilize broad public support within Russia itself for strong action beyond Russian borders by defining the object of Russian 'humanitarianism' in South Ossetia as Russian 'citizens', whom Russia had to defend against 'aggression'.

The analysis below argues that political instrumentality did indeed shape Russian humanitarian claims. However, we should also consider whether these claims reflected a deeper recognition and acceptance by the Russian leadership by 2008 that the legitimacy of contemporary interventions is significantly enhanced if they can credibly be presented as in response to humanitarian emergencies. Such an understanding could have encouraged Russian officials to present their intervention in these terms, even if there was no agreement in international society that the existence of a humanitarian emergency was a sufficient condition for military action and controversy continued over the concept of R2P.

From the outset of the campaign the Russian leadership levelled an exceptionally serious accusation against their Georgian counterparts: they explicitly twinned Georgian 'aggression' in Tskhinvali with 'genocide'. After Putin's introduction of this term early in the crisis it was simply reiterated by Russian officials and politicians.[31] They argued that the Russian mission aimed to prevent an unfolding humanitarian disaster and secondly to save those for whom Russia is responsible.[32] Moscow accused Georgia of a catalogue of violations of international humanitarian laws, duplicating the rationale for interventions in the Balkans in the 1990s.[33]

An extreme accusation, which was disseminated instantly through Russian state-controlled media, was that Georgia's attack on Tskhinvali on its own resulted in over two thousand deaths, mostly Ossetians and a majority of them

Russian citizens. This was pure incendiary rhetoric. It was never explained how this figure was derived and by December 2009 the official documented Russian figure of South Ossetian civilians killed in the conflict had been reduced to 162[34]—fewer civilian deaths than the approximately 228 who died on the Georgian side.[35] However, the Head of the Investigations Committee of the Russian prosecutor's office continued to claim that he had full proof of genocide by the Georgian authorities, by which he meant the extermination of an ethnic group or a nation on the grounds of ethnicity or nationality.[36]

The genocide accusations soon acquired a political function. They were central to Russian justifications for its decision to permanently recognize South Ossetia and Abkhazia as separate states. These charges also formed the core of a political campaign to vilify President Saakashvili as a 'war criminal' and hence place him beyond the political pale. This position contrasted with Russia's strong criticism of the decision by the ICC prosecutor to indict the Sudanese president Omer al-Bashir on genocide charges.

In fact Russian claims of genocide and ethnic cleansing by Georgia contrasted with undeniable evidence, including satellite images, of the destruction of Georgian villages and the forced displacement of thousands of ethnic Georgians by the South Ossetian militia, both in South Ossetia in the wake of the Russian military advance and for a period even deeper in Georgia.[37] The Ossetian leadership used the claims of genocide committed by Georgia to help justify their actions in driving the Georgian civilian population out of South Ossetia. A detailed Amnesty International Report concluded that both Georgia and Russia had seriously violated international humanitarian law during their war.[38]

Even disregarding Russian genocide claims, Moscow's presentation of its campaign in Georgia as some kind of humanitarian intervention is unconvincing on a number of grounds. First, even if we regard Russia as simply reacting to the Georgian assault on Tskhinvali, the scale of the Russian operation was clearly disproportionate as a militarized humanitarian response, especially once Russian forces penetrated deeper into Georgia. Secondly, Russian operations lacked a Security Council mandate, which Russia had previously insisted on for Western interventions. Third, there has been little to show that Russia has actually held serious humanitarian concerns in South Ossetia at any time in the post-Soviet period. Russian leaders had displayed tenuous interest in the physical well-being of the ethnic Ossetian population in South Ossetia in past years, as opposed to their political project. Nor did Russia's Chechnya campaigns suggest Russian commitment in the wider region to the principles of proportionality and discrimination in war or acceptance of the obligation to protect non-combatants.[39]

Given these considerations it is surprising that Russia explicitly invoked a normative justification for its August 2008 campaign, based on Responsibility to Protect (R2P), a concept for which Russia had shown little prior enthusiasm (see chapter 3). The unfolding humanitarian disaster in South Ossetia, Lavrov claimed, was such that the Russian Constitution and Russian laws made it 'unavoidable for us to exercise responsibility to protect'.[40] Russia later found itself in an angry exchange with Georgia, at the 63rd Session of the UN General Assembly in July 2009, over its claim that the concept applied to its operations in South Ossetia. Georgia bluntly criticized the 'ingenious—even cynical—misapplication of the R2P principle', its abuse when 'a State... began to invoke quasi-legalistic justifications for unilateral military action'. The Russian delegate did not debate the content of R2P but simply responded that 'Russians had saved South Ossetians and Abkhazians from destruction.'[41]

Russian officials have spoken in a similar vein of Russia's rights 'as an effective guarantor of peace and humanitarian security' in the conflict with Georgia.[42] Therefore Russia invoked an unambiguous solidarist discourse in affirming some variant of R2P norms and the needs of human security. However, closer scrutiny shows that Russia was hardly driven by R2P imperatives, at least those that have reasonably been inferred by states since the 2005 UN World Summit.

First, we need to consider the seriousness of the threats in South Ossetia and the proportionality of Russia's response. Despite Russian claims, there was no good evidence of mass atrocity crimes in the region or an imminent or actual threat of them (a reasonable precautionary criterion for R2P). Moreover, Russia's intervention did not seem tailored to ensure the physical protection of the population; it went far beyond the scope of what would be necessary for that end. Admittedly this requirement of proportionality for R2P to apply was not set out explicitly in the 2005 Outcome Document, but it is consistent with international humanitarian law.[43]

Second, the Russian intervention in South Ossetia was not really about the protection of civilians at large as expected by the R2P concept, but the protection of [Russian] nationals. Lavrov adapted R2P language, arguing that 'sovereignty... presupposes responsibility', meaning 'first and foremost, responsibility to one's own citizens'.[44] 'The life and dignity of our citizens, wherever they are, will be protected' he promised.[45] Russia's NATO envoy was even blunter: 'the issue of using military force to protect our citizens is a matter of principle', albeit 'within the framework of the humanitarian aim of saving peoples'.[46] Russian officials blurred the distinction between the responsibility of a state to protect its population inside its borders, and the responsibilities a state maintains for populations *outside* its borders.

As noted in chapter 3, it was already generally understood that the 'the R2P norm concerns the responsibility of a state to protect populations within its *own* borders, the measures the international community must take to assist that state in protecting its populations', and only after that the international community's potential responsibility to take action, through the United Nations, 'when the state in whose borders the populations are found manifestly fails to protect them'. Notably it does not confer authority on an individual country to take direct action to protect its nationals located outside its own borders.[47] As one of the architects of the R2P initiative observed, the defence of nationals 'has been the basis for all kinds of interventions in the past that were not humanitarian'.[48]

Finally, and crucially, as Russia itself had previously insisted, there is no legal authority for a R2P-based military intervention without UN Security Council approval, and Russia lacked this when it sent its troops into South Ossetia and then other regions of Georgia. This is all the more salient given the continued significance attached by Russian leaders to formal UNSC authorization in all proposals to deploy military personnel to uphold peace and security. It is reasonable to conclude, as most states have done, that the Russian reference to R2P to validate its military action in Georgia has been abusive and unhelpful for efforts to consolidate R2P principles in international society at large.

SOVEREIGNTY AND SECESSION AS CONTESTED CONCEPTS IN THE CIS REGION

Russian justifications for intervention in Georgia in August 2008 were not only flawed on legal and normative grounds, but also seemed to reflect an abiding hierarchical view of order in the CIS region. At root this has meant a tendency by Russia to relativize the core principles of the wider international system, sovereignty and territorial integrity, in its relations with neighbouring CIS states. This has been particularly pronounced where Moscow has maintained special relationships with secessionist regions within CIS states (Georgia, Moldova).[49] As previously argued, Russian leaders have tried to foster certain region-level norms, such as assent to 'CIS mandates' for the use of force, and have made some efforts to reinterpret general legal principles and norms for application in the CIS region, for example in asserting the right to protect Russian citizens abroad.

Russia's qualified view of sovereignty and territorial integrity in the 'near abroad', or the 'CIS space', has been most apparent in relations with Georgia. It became explicit after the August 2008 war and culminated in Russia's formal recognition of South Ossetia and Abkhazia as separate states late that month. However, even before the conflict, Russia did little to disprove Georgian claims that it was pursuing a process of *de facto* absorption of South Ossetia and Abkhazia.[50] This was reflected in the pervasive presence of Russian security personnel in the South Ossetian administration, in the Russian supply of arms and military equipment to separatists in South Ossetia and Abkhazia, and in the Russian tendency to turn a blind eye to the periodic flow of armed and unarmed 'volunteers' from North Ossetia to South Osssetia during periods of tension.[51] A Russian presidential decree in April 2008 went so far as to establish direct official Russian relations with the South Ossetian and Abkhazian authorities.

When most Western states formally recognized Kosovo in early 2008 Putin lambasted such 'unilateral' action as immoral and illegal, as an act that 'breaks the entire system of international relations', and noted that 'nobody was talking about the recognition of Abkhazia or South Ossetia'.[52] However, this is exactly what Medvedev proceeded to do on 26 August 2008 after the campaign in Georgia.

The rationale for recognizing these regions as states is based on a particular understanding of sovereignty. Russian officials argued first that Georgia's proclamation of independence in 1991 had violated the right of South Ossetia and Abkhazia to self-determination, as prescribed in April 1990 by the Soviet Law on Secession of Union Republics from the USSR. Secondly, they presented the 'will of the people' inhabiting these regions as an overriding principle. Defined in this way, the will of ethnic sub-state groups in South Ossetia and Abkhazia eclipsed the collective will of all the people of the state of Georgia. In the case of Kosovo, Western states had claimed that their recognition of the region should be viewed as *sui generis* rather than as a precedent. In contrast, in the cases of South Ossetia and Abkhazia, Russia explicitly privileged a minority interpretation of the right to self-determination over territorial integrity. In so doing Moscow cast a shadow over the sovereignty of other CIS states.[53]

Moscow appealed to the so-called 'Friendly Relations Declaration', adopted at the 25th Session of the UN General Assembly in October 1970, to claim that 'sovereignty presupposes the duty of a state to refrain from any forcible action which deprives people living on its territory of their right to self-determination, freedom and independence'. On this basis Russia argued that Georgia had undermined its own territorial integrity by attacking Tskhinvali and had compelled Russia to recognize the secessionist regions.[54]

The legal case here is not compelling. Under international law, ethnic peoples, groups, or minorities may invoke the so-called internal (defensive) right to self-determination (which affects the organization of state order). However, there has been a consensus in principle that these groups are not entitled to an external (offensive) right to self-determination that is primarily geared towards constructing an independent state of one's own, namely secession, which would infringe the territorial integrity of the mother state. This distinction reflects state practice in general, despite the controversial case of Kosovo, which outside the colonial context has been extremely reluctant to accept unilateral secession of parts of independent states.[55]

This prevailing view admittedly has been opposed by a minority view in international legal scholarship, which envisages the possibility of 'remedial secession'. This holds that ethnic groups should be entitled to a right of separation in extreme, exceptional cases involving massive human rights violations, where 'the state apparatus would need to be exposed as a torturous regime of terror and a tyrannical system'.[56] However, first this cannot be proven of the Georgian state, despite the harrowing experiences of many South Ossetians and Abkhaz early in the 1990s and the narrative of oppression they present.[57] Secondly, while the idea of secession as a last resort for ending the oppression of a people arguably might influence the recognition policies of states, in fact there exists no case of non-colonial new state creation in the UN Charter era that acts as a clear example of remedial secession.[58]

Medvedev resorted, however, to just such a remedial secession argument. He claimed that 'sovereignty as the will of the people' justified the right of South Ossetia and Abkhazia to express their choice for secession as a political act. This was a more explicit statement of occasional earlier Russian claims about separatist regions, denoting a form of qualified sovereignty for Russia's CIS neighbours.[59] Thus sovereignty should be subject to the 'will of the people' within their states, however that should be defined. The 'will of the people' claim represented a political challenge to a variety of CIS states with autonomous regions, breakaway regions, or simply compact minority ethnic groups. As for Georgia, it was contrary to numerous UN Security Council resolutions that had emphasized its territorial integrity. Moreover, it could be viewed as a challenge by Russia's major neighbours with concerns about domestic separatism, Turkey, Iran, and China. Indeed, Medvedev's formulation contravenes Russia's own policy towards Chechnya and arguably some other North Caucasus autonomous republics.

If Russia was testing international reactions through its definition of sovereignty in Georgia as 'the will of the people', it made little headway among Western states. On meeting Medvedev in July 2009, President Obama emphasized that 'state sovereignty must be a cornerstone of international order... we must apply this principle to all nations—and that includes nations like Georgia and Ukraine'.[60] This admonition was certainly shared by EU states and seemed intended in particular to rein in Russian efforts to reinterpret Georgian as well as Ukrainian sovereignty.

Obama's statement repudiated another controversial Russian formulation, issued as Russia consolidated its control over South Ossetia and Abkhazia. Medvedev proclaimed that 'there are regions in which Russia has privileged interests', regions that 'are home to countries with which we share special historical relations'.[61] This assertion of Russia's privileges, implicitly, unlike other powers, hierarchically over and above other post-Soviet states, resulted in further unease among CIS and Western states. Lavrov eventually glossed over the dispute, conceding that these inter-CIS relations are 'mutually privileged', that Russia's closest neighbours ostensibly 'have the same privileged interests in Russia'.[62]

This soothing restatement of Medvedev's dictum left uncertain at the time whether a more self-confident Russia, bolstered by rising material capabilities, was seeking to expand the scope of its 'privileged' interests. One way this might be expressed was a Russian assertion of its own definitions of rules and norms in the CIS regional order, including those related to the self-determination of peoples, the protection of Russian citizens, or the security policy choices of CIS states.

THE AFTERMATH OF CONFLICT

Before the intervention in Georgia the Russian leadership regarded itself as in a deepening normative contest with Western states, both regionally and globally, during a period of transition in Russia's favour in the wider international political system. However, after the clash with Georgia, which Russian leaders chose to present to their domestic audience as a regional proxy war with the United States, there is little evidence of a strategic effort by Moscow to entrench new Russian-defined rules and norms in CIS interstate relations. Russia still hoped, as shown in the previous chapter, to use the CSTO (although uninvolved in the August 2008 conflict) to shape the terms under which force could be employed in the region. On the other hand, Russia found itself almost completely isolated internationally over the recognition of South Ossetia and Abkhazia, it became absorbed by the unexpectedly harsh effects of the global financial crisis on Russia, and it responded to the amelioration of Russian–American relations during the Obama administration.

As a result, the regional spillover of Russia's recognition of South Ossetia and Abkhazia was limited. Initially Moscow kept its options open about whether such recognition represented a 'precedent' in relation to other CIS states or whether it regards these cases as 'exclusive'.[63] This ambiguity was both a source of encouragement to the separatist Nagorno-Karabakh and Transdniester regions and of tension with Azerbaijan and Moldova.[64] It also fuelled the hopes of Russian nationalists who believe that, by a loose analogy, the Crimean region in Ukraine deserves at least greater autonomy. However, Russian leaders must have been aware that encouraging the formal secession of these regions would not only create a deep rift between Russia and more CIS states, but could also fan separatist sentiments in Russia's own North Caucasus republics. In practice after August 2008 Moscow did not encourage the remaining separatist regions in the CIS to expect Russian recognition of their statehood at some future date.

The implications of Moscow's claims to protect its citizens militarily, wherever they are located, were more ambiguous. In November 2008 Medvedev boasted to deputies of the Russian Federal Assembly that the 'August crisis' had forced a moment of truth on Russia and 'we really proved...that we are able to protect our citizens'.[65] This might be read to imply that Russia could resort again to such claims, if it had to justify forceful action in another conflict with a CIS state. These claims could be conflated with the 'will of the people' argument, whereas the rationale of protecting Russian peacekeepers, which were only left in Transdniester in the CIS region, would be more difficult to revive. On the other hand, on the most volatile potential front, the borders of South Ossetia and Abkhazia, Moscow no longer needed to enlist such dubious justifications in the event of renewed conflict. After August 2008 Russia made clear that here it could resort to a simple self-defence argument. This would be based on the presence of Russian combat personnel, which replaced the Russian forces previously designated as 'peacekeepers' and were assigned to guard the borders of the new 'states', under the terms of bilateral agreements signed with Moscow.

During 2008–9 there was particular nervousness in Ukraine over the implications of the increasing proportion of Russian citizens in Crimea (although dual citizenship is prohibited under Ukrainian law). Kiev tried to rein in the distribution of Russian passports by the Russian consulate in Simferopol. An underlying fear of the Ukrainian leadership was that these citizens (whose total number is unknown) could conceivably offer Russia a pretext to come to their 'protection' in a future crisis, perhaps one engineered calculatedly. The intention might have been, for example, to stall the withdrawal of the Russian Black Sea Fleet from its principal base in Sevastopol. Alternatively, how would Russia react if Ukraine used force against a demonstration by ethnic Russians in Sevastopol against a draft law on Ukraine's accession to NATO?[66]

These concerns mounted when Russian–Ukrainian relations plunged in autumn 2008. Russia directly implicated Ukraine in the Russia–Georgia conflict, almost as if deliberately seeking a *casus belli* (at least for rhetorical purposes). For example, it accused regular military units of the Ukrainian Defence Ministry of participating in that conflict.[67] Putin accused Ukraine of the 'crime' of supplying Georgia with hardware and arms during the conflict.[68] This was worrying in light of the thinking about Russian involvement in future conflicts sketched out by Russian military chiefs. The likelihood of localized wars unfolding was judged to be 'quite probable', as the result of the intensification of the 'territorial aspirations of states'. It was predicted that there might also be 'internal state armed conflicts with national and national-ethnic roots'.[69] This gloomy outlook was reinforced in Russia's 2009 National Security Strategy document.

In reality, however, there has been no close parallel between the relatively quiescent Crimea and the protracted, bitter contest over South Ossetia. Ukraine has not had an undeclared state within its state, staffed by Russian security officials, like Georgia confronted in South Ossetia. The only indigenous ethnic group in Crimea, the Crimean Tatars, has remained loyal to

Kiev.[70] Moscow also has a variety of means to influence Ukraine's security and foreign policy through formal and informal political relationships. This has been more effective than a policy based on high risk coercive diplomacy or even military brinksmanship using the citizenship of Russian passport holders to foment opposition in Crimea.

By spring 2010 Russia anyway had achieved its primary strategic objectives in Ukraine. In April the symbol of the Orange Revolution, Viktor Yushchenko, was replaced as Ukrainian president by Viktor Yanukovych. He quickly agreed to extend the lease of the Sevastopol naval base to Russia for twenty-five years, plus an automatic prolongation of five years. He also rejected NATO membership as a Ukrainian strategic goal. As official Russian–Ukrainian relations improved, concerns about the citizenship issue abated. Ukraine and other CIS states noted that the new Russian Military Doctrine of February 2010 declared it 'legitimate' for Russia to use its armed forces 'to protect its citizens outside Russia, in accordance with generally recognized principles and norms of international law'.[71] But this could be read as just another expression of a traditional mantra that could be traced back to the early 1990s.

The difficulty for Russia to advance norms for the CIS regional order on the back of the conflict with Georgia had been signalled by the equivocal responses of CIS states to Russia's demonstration of force in autumn 2008. Ukraine had been solidly critical of Russian action, but all CIS states were disturbed. Notably Russia failed to obtain an endorsement of its justifications to intervene in Georgia, let alone recognize South Ossetia and Abkhazia, at a summit of the Shanghai Cooperation Organization at the end of August 2008. Four Central Asian CIS states took cover from Russian lobbying behind China and the summit's final declaration was studiously neutral over Moscow's military action in Georgia. It even reaffirmed the SCO states' commitment to 'efforts aimed at preserving the unity of a state and its territorial integrity', a phrase which could be applied to Georgia's struggle with its breakaway regions.[72]

During autumn 2008, after bilateral meetings with Russian leaders (and lacking the supportive role of China, in the SCO), Central Asian and other CIS states offered Russia placatory forms of verbal support for its military drive in Georgia.[73] In September 2008 the CSTO foreign ministers went further to condemn the Georgian government's 'aggression' and approved Russia's 'peacekeeping efforts' in the campaign in Georgia.[74] Moscow later praised its CSTO partners for 'consistently supporting us in countering anti-Russian attacks in connection with events in the South Caucasus at multilateral forums and international platforms'.[75] This exaggerated the case, but clearly Russia valued any and all ways CIS leaders could be presented as endorsing Russian justifications for intervention in Georgia.

This support was seriously compromised, however, by the outright rejection by all CIS states, including Russia's inner CSTO partners, of formal recognition for South Ossetia and Abkhazia. President Nazarbayev expressed a general view in bluntly stating that 'Kazakhstan's position on the territorial integrity of states and the unacceptability of separatism remain constant.'[76] CIS states were shocked both by the Russian empowerment of separatism and its redrawing of CIS state borders. By recognizing South Ossetia and Abkhazia, Russia overturned a foundational CIS-wide regional norm. This was that the only territories of the former Soviet Union that merited recognition would be those that corresponded to first-level administrative subdivisions of the old Soviet state—the Union republics—which became the new post-Soviet states.

Notably the Russian-led CSTO played no role at all in the active phase of the Georgia crisis, even to camouflage Russian operations, although previous CSTO documents had defined the Caucasus as a 'CSTO collective security region' and had undertaken to establish CSTO peacekeepers. Against this background, and given the sensitivity of secession as well as of Russia's call to protect its citizens among CIS states, it is not surprising that there is little evidence that Russia's justifications for its Georgia operation have acquired normative traction in discourse in the CSTO setting or other Russia-led regional frameworks. CIS states have remained wedded to their territorial sovereignty and remain unsettled by Russian arguments which relativize Georgian sovereignty.

As we explore further below and in the conclusion to this volume, this regional discourse on the use of force was influenced by and connected to the wider international 'legal and normative battlefield', as viewed by Moscow. In this contested environment Russian leaders sought to increase policy options for the future as well as reduce damage to its international reputation and image. It is notable that even in the case of intervention in Georgia, when in practice Russia was not much constrained by established law, Moscow showed a relentless effort to present its action as in conformity with (its own interpretation of) international law and even emerging normative standards.

In contrast, Russian leaders were much less concerned about justifying their actions in terms of domestic legal process. In August 2008 Russia lacked any domestic legal right to send its forces into Georgia, since its territorial integrity was not under threat and it had no defence treaties with the then unrecognized South Ossetia or Abkhazia. According to the Russian Constitution the Federation Council should have been convened to authorize the use of Russian military forces outside Russian borders and this was not done. A Federation Council resolution was needed even for the introduction of Russian 'peacekeeping' units into South Ossetia.[77]

As an afterthought, however, the Russian leadership showed some interest in establishing their domestic legal case for future interventions. A year after the campaign in Georgia Medvedev introduced amendments to the Federal Law on Defence. These permit use of Russian military force abroad to 'prevent an aggression' against other 'countries' (a vague formulation, which in the Russian definition would also apply to the 'states' of South Ossetia and

Abkhazia), to defend Russian units deployed abroad (widely dispersed among CIS states, such as in Sevastopol in Crimea), as well as to protect Russian citizens.[78] Taken together these could be applied to a wide range of interventionary scenarios. In practice, however, in any such scenario Russian state law could not override international legal prohibitions on the use of force.

CONCLUSION: THE CIS REGIONAL ORDER IN DISARRAY

International alarm over the Russian operation in Georgia largely reflected uncertainty whether this was an exceptional violent outcome of local catalysts of conflict, or whether it represented a more strategic and premeditated use of force by Moscow which could foreshadow other interventions in post-Soviet conflict zones. This chapter has not sought to identity underlying Russian motivations, but it can reasonably be argued that Moscow's intervention expressed its strategic interests in relation to Georgia at least, if not the wider CIS region.[79] Yet it is probable that Russia was also opportunistic in its decision-making around the conflict. A Western official in a confidential high-level assessment summed up Russian recognition of South Ossetia and Abkhazia in this vein as '"tactical adhocery", perhaps regretted given the lack of support for recognition even from Russia's close friends'.[80]

This chapter gives rise to parallel questions about Russia's legal and normative justifications for the war with Georgia. The Russian discourse appears especially instrumental. As a leading Russian specialist pointed out, 'Russia came up with its own interpretation of what constitutes, in this particular case, genocide, humanitarian intervention and the responsibility to protect...Moscow took international law in its own hands, where its interests were directly affected.'[81] But was this intended to advance strategic or tactical objectives? Beyond such instrumentality, moreover, did the use of humanitarian claims in itself reflect some normative shift in Moscow?

If Russian justifications were instrumental but tactical this implies they were devised, perhaps rather hastily, just to justify an exceptional use of force against a CIS state. They sought to vindicate Russian military action simultaneously to domestic Russian, CIS regional, and wider international audiences. The result was a scattershot approach as Moscow resorted to a variety of legal and normative/humanitarian justifications. These claims then were intended to convey at least a surface plausibility to one or more of these audiences. They relied on a dextrous use of selective legal references and normative language, centred around Russia's imperative need for self-defence and a dramatic exaggeration of the human costs of Georgia's own dubious operation against Tskhinvali.

For Moscow the overall success of this discursive campaign in international forums and the media (the latter for Russian and CIS audiences) would depend first on the strength of domestic and CIS regional support for Russian actions, and secondly on whether broader international criticism could be deflected, or at least limited to secondary accusations, such as the lack of proportionality of Russian military actions deeper into Georgia beyond South Ossetia.

In its discourse directed as Western states, beyond a foundational self-defence claim, Moscow could try to play back the 'lessons' of Western interventions, such as an emphasis on the defence of oppressed minorities, the practice of humanitarian intervention, or even a doctrine of military pre-emption (though the latter generally was avoided).[82] References to R2P also fell into this category. The political intention of such discourse was to create sufficient ambivalence about the nature of the Russia–South Ossetia–Georgia conflict, at least for major European powers (especially Germany and France) and important developing states (such as Russia's BRICS partners), for these states to limit their response to the Russian intervention (an outcome which was also expedient for these states in terms of their economic relations with Russia).

A strategic rather than tactical use of Russia's legal and normative claims in August 2008 would be more challenging for other states in the region and for the wider international community. This could take several forms. One such use was specifically to constrain Georgian security policy options by creating ambivalence among major NATO states over where responsibility for the conflict around South Ossetia lay. The aim was to alter thinking among major NATO states about the advisability of drawing Georgia into NATO. In practice, in autumn 2008 Germany and France did indeed rule out Georgian entry into NATO for at least the medium term. This Russian strategic objective seems confirmed by Medvedev's admission two years after the conflict that 'if we had faltered in 2008, geopolitical arrangements would be different now and a number of countries... would have probably been in NATO'.[83]

We should also consider if Russian discourse in August 2008 had a more ambitious strategic objective. Moscow may have been exploring the latitude to reshape customary international law on the use of force and the preconditions of sovereignty, at least as applied to states in the CIS region (and to Georgia, which left the CIS). Russia may have been testing international responses and seeking international acquiescence for Russia-defined regional rules and norms, that is tacit acceptance if not formal acknowledgement of Russian exceptionalism in its zone of 'privileged interests'.

To be sure Russian officials could not unilaterally modify the legal goalposts on self-defence and self-determination or redefine emerging R2P principles. However, they may have believed that their claims about the protection of citizens (bolstered by their passport policy), or less likely about sovereignty as the 'will of the people' could gain some traction internationally, if not clearly repudiated, so that they might be deployed again as a diplomatic resource to consolidate their regional influence or to respond to future crises with post-Soviet neighbour states.

To the extent that such thinking was present, it reflected a conviction that Russia had developed the material capabilities to be heard internationally and had opportunities in its neighbourhood. Russia would appeal to rules and norms to make more usable a hard power complement to other instruments aimed at asserting its global status and its predominance in the CIS region. Russian exceptionalist claims then expressed a confidence that Russia could exert growing structural influence as an independent 'pole' of power in the international system at large.

This analysis of instrumentalist Russian policy leaves some ambiguity over Moscow's forceful use of Russian humanitarian claims: the description of Russia as 'a guarantor of humanitarian security', the call on R2P, the focus on supposed genocide. In the next chapter we analyse evidence during the Medvedev presidency, at least in the case of intervention in Libya, of some Russian accommodation of solidarist arguments for the use of force, although these remain conditional on a Security Council mandate.

In conclusion, Russian state practice in the years since August 2008 does not provide clear evidence to confirm that its justifications for intervention in Georgia were devised strategically, to lay the legal or normative groundwork for a more interventionary policy in general in Russia's region of 'privileged interests', rather than concocted *ad hoc* and hastily. Of course these justifications may have had an initial strategic purpose in the CIS region, but after testing them in August 2008 Russia decided not to extend the 'legal battlefield' or its normative claims in the face of the quite widespread international repudiation of most of the Russian rationale for its campaign in Georgia (though Russia continued righteously to assert it had responded defensively to Georgian aggression). Just as with US claims over military pre-emption earlier in the decade, the international reaction to Russian intervention in Georgia helped to reaffirm customary international law on the matters affected, and discouraged its further abuse, although Russian claims have contributed to the erosion of the proportionality criterion in self-defence.[84]

In a future crisis in its neighbourhood, however, Moscow could possibly revive and exploit once again the claim of protecting its citizens abroad. This option is made easier by the more flexible interpretations in this area which have come to be favoured by a number of states faced by the threat of transnational terrorism. However, since 2008 Russian leaders have refrained from privileging external self-determination, the secession of regions, in other CIS regions beyond Georgia. Moscow has been alive to the risk of further alienating CIS and other important partners over this incendiary issue.

In many respects Russian recognition of South Ossetia and Abkhazia, and the effort to construct a legal rationale around this provocative act, has been an own goal in Russian policy. It has posed also the risk of a discursive and policy 'entrapment' if secessionist impulses were to grow in other CIS states or republics in Russia's Northern Caucasus. Russia's formal recognition of separatism in a sovereign neighbour state (Georgia) as the result of a war justified on dubious grounds has had a specific outcome: it means Moscow has no realistic prospect of challenging Western states in solidarity with some CIS or Eurasian group of states over the law and norms regulating the legitimate use of force.

8

Russian Global Perspectives and Contemporary Military Intervention

The Russian response to Western-led military interventions reflects a wider context of global diplomacy and discourse. This wider context reveals similar underlying sources of tension between Russia and Western powers to those previously discussed: the normative basis of international order, legality, constitutionality—the controversy over 'who makes the rules' and how such rules are applied—as well as how these relate to structural power. The first half of this chapter studies several major Russian campaigns and strategies to assert itself as a global actor or to constrain Western global policies, especially during Putin's first two presidencies, which illustrate this wider context: Putin's vociferous campaign against Western 'hegemony', Moscow's efforts to project itself within a concert of great powers, and Russian resistance to NATO 'going global'.

Against this background the second half of the chapter provides a focused analysis of two major contemporary controversies over military intervention: the threat of intervention in Iran and the remarkable UN mandated intervention in Libya in 2011. We assess whether these cases confirm persistent themes identified in previous chapters.

Russian global diplomacy and discourse in the 2000s reveal the importance Moscow attaches to shifts and disparities of power between top ranked states in the international system. Yet a symbiotic relationship exists between norms and power in international society. The assessments states make about their relative power shape the interpretation, evolution, and diffusion of norms. In this respect a significant feature of Russian thinking on contemporary rule-making and understanding of norms since the Yeltsin leadership has been its revisionist impulse. According to a widely held belief in Moscow, during the first post-Cold War decade Western powers exploited Russia's relative weakness in the international system decade to consolidate their structural and normative 'hegemony'. Nevertheless, despite this geopolitical judgement, our analysis traces evidence of normative and legal traction, as expected in an evolving society of states rather than a simple constellation of power relations.

This chapter initially analyses the nature of the challenge Russia mounted to Western, especially American, 'hegemony' and US unilateralism in international security policy. In the second half of the 2000s Russian leaders accused Washington with renewed fervour of riding roughshod over law and norms regulating the use of force. They revived their earlier condemnation of US 'regime change' rhetoric and practice as fundamentally illegitimate. American global policies, as well as NATO's developing global aspirations, were perceived as stoking competition *inter alia* over the CIS regional order.

This reflected Putin's growing confidence by his second presidency that Russia could compete seriously at the global as well as regional level with Western powers and should do so more assertively. This confidence was buoyed up by an optimistic judgement about Russia's prospects in the global ranking of powers, based on its rapid energy-fuelled growth, at least until 2008. But it also rested on a shrewd belief that the wider Western solidarist agenda remained vulnerable. Putin seemed to believe this agenda could be tarred with the unilateralist thrust of US policies, which had triggered international alarm, even among European powers. For Russia, international strategic rivalry was closely related to tension over evolving international norms.

From the mid-2000s the discourse of Russian leaders envisioned a multi-normative global environment, but one still subject to the UN Charter legal framework. This environment was one shaped by a quite limited core of universalist principles. It was state-centred and an environment in which Russian leaders insisted they could compete in pluralist terms to advance their vision of appropriate international behaviour. In brief it could be characterized as a thin international society, overseen by a system of great power management and regulation, in which Russia features prominently. Moscow asserted its right to participate fully with other major states in defining the rules of this system and in revising the norms of global governance.

The core elements of this international vision were sustained when Dmitri Medvedev replaced Putin as president in 2008. Medvedev was more inclined than Putin to talk of international principles in universalist rather than relativist terms. He projected less confidence about the trajectory of Russian material power than his predecessor. Yet Russia's less impressive economic performance during the Medvedev presidency (2008–12) failed to change the conviction in the leadership that a reordering of the international power hierarchy in favour of Russia was inevitable (that Russia in GDP terms would join the world's top five economies in the medium term). The premise remains in Moscow that the Western 'hegemonic' order will progressively be displaced, undermining the promotion of solidarist norms—the normative dimension of 'hegemony'.

Has this belief in the decline of the 'hegemonic' order made Russia more confident in challenging the rationale and legitimacy of contemporary

Western-led military interventions? How does this depend on Russian views on the requirements of collective decision-making and rule-making? We examine the controversies over Iran and Libya to show that, as with the cases previously studied, the Russian response has been determined by how norms, legality, and constitutionality interact with power and security policy concerns at global, regional, and domestic state levels.

The case of Iran threatens to revive the dispute over military pre-emption that preceded the Iraq War in 2003 and it engages significant Russian interests. Russia has defined the threat of military action against Iran, especially by Washington, as a graphic expression of the 'hegemonic' power structure. On the other hand, Moscow has worked diplomatically alongside other major powers to constrain Iranian nuclear ambitions. This case is distinctive since normative and legal arguments against the use of force have been muted among the leaders of the major Western states, which have focused instead on the supposed Iranian violation of non-proliferation norms.

In contrast, in spring 2011 the UN Security Council rapidly agreed to authorize military action in Libya in response to a humanitarian emergency. The operation was assisted rather than controlled by the dominant power in the system, the United States, and Russia only had secondary material interests involved. The Russian response in this case raises intriguing questions about a possible normative turn in Moscow towards international justice and the consolidation of R2P as a global policy imperative. Yet in refrains familiar to the past, Russia soon accused Western powers of exceeding the authority of the Security Council in implementing the UN mandate in Libya, of using humanitarian justifications to conceal strategic interests and the illegitimate goal of regime change. Moscow worried that a new axis of NATO influence in North Africa could follow the Libya operation, but it also feared the implications of the Libya 'model' of power transition for regime security closer to home. All this made it doubtful that Russia would permit Security Council authorization of further enforcement actions in the context of popular revolts in Syria or elsewhere in the Middle East.

THE RUSSIAN CAMPAIGN AGAINST WESTERN 'HEGEMONY'

Many of the themes of Moscow's campaign against Western 'hegemony' during the second Putin administration had been aired previously around the time of the attack on Iraq in 2003.[1] Indeed Russia had condemned American unilateralism often in the 1990s and found support for this stance in the UN General Assembly, in the regional organizations of developing states, and in Chinese statements.[2] However, Russia's more forthright rejection of Western dominance in global power relations and rule-making came later and was signalled most publicly by Putin in his speech at the Munich conference on security policy in February 2007.

This speech set the contours of a critique which challenged the legality, constitutionality, and ultimately legitimacy of the US predisposition to use force.[3]

Putin initially rejected the 'pernicious' notion of a unipolar world, connoting 'one centre of authority, one centre of force, one centre of decision-making... one sovereign'. His alternative vision was a world with many centres of influence, regulated multilaterally. He proceeded to condemn the 'almost uncontained hyper use of force—military force—in international affairs, force that is plunging the world into an abyss of permanent conflicts'. He claimed this was accompanied by increasing 'disdain for the basic principles of international law', while legal norms were approximating to the legal system of one state, the US. Putin was adamant that the use of force, as well as UN Charter peacekeeping operations, could only be legitimized by the Security Council and that the decisions of neither NATO nor the EU could substitute for this.

Foreign Minister Lavrov fleshed out this critique. He attacked the 'virtual reality of a unipolar world', on practical, pluralist grounds as unable to meet global challenges, as alien to the 'cultural and civilizational diversity' of the world, and as beyond the capabilities of any one country or coalition to impose on the rest. Lavrov evoked instead a vision of constitutionality, by which Russia was positioned in 'an emerging collective leadership of the major states of the world'. Russia was ready to 'play in team' and 'according to the rules', as long as these were rules elaborated jointly with direct Russian participation.[4] In other words Russia would defend its corner and outlook in a process of collective rule.

For Moscow multilateral global governance of this kind would be infused by competition. During Putin's second term Moscow described the emergent multilateralism as enabled by greater Russian foreign policy independence, alongside the rise of other states in Asia, especially China and India—an autonomy which rested on their increased material capabilities compared to the 1990s. As a result, 'a real competitive environment has emerged on the market of ideas for the future world order'.[5] This order, Russian leaders insisted, whatever its outcome, would increasingly be influenced by Russia, together with other states located outside the core Western political community. As globalization goes beyond Western civilization, Lavrov asserted, 'the West is losing its monopoly to establish the rules of the game, the standards'.[6]

If Moscow considered these rules of the game as negotiable, however, it described this negotiation as conducted in the framework of irreducible legal principles. In autumn 2007 Lavrov described 'a real threat... to the existing international legal order', were this to materialize, as a 'red line' for Russia.[7]

Russia would vigorously seek to shape and constrain evolving norms, understood as unconsolidated standards of international conduct. But it would hold fast to traditional, pluralist legal precepts.

This search for refuge in legality was enshrined in Russia's new Foreign Policy Concept issued in July 2008. The Concept upbraided the 'arbitrary and politically motivated interpretation by certain countries of fundamental international legal norms and principles such as non-use of force or threat of force... respect for sovereignty'. It scorned 'attempts to portray violations of international law as its "creative" application'. The Concept insisted that UN Charter Article 51 remained an adequate legal basis for the use of force in self-defence, including in response to international terrorism and the proliferation of weapons of mass destruction.[8]

This represented a retreat from a more fluid and relativist Russian approach to these legal principles earlier in the decade. In June 2003 Russian Deputy Foreign Minister Yuri Fedotov talked of 'the progressive evolution of customary and conventional international law alike' in the collective fight against terrorism.[9] Putin agreed in addressing the UN General Assembly in September 2003. He described international law as 'a changing category as not inflexible'.[10] Russia began discussions to form a working group with American political scientists and lawmakers to 'formulate the philosophy behind new international laws, the mechanisms for the use or non-use of force and involvement or non-involvement in regional conflicts'.[11]

For a period in the early 2000s such flexibility was accompanied by a definite solidarist tone in some Russian pronouncements. Fedotov recognized 'the strengthening of human rights protection and in general the governance by international norms of the relations involving individuals' as an important aspect of the evolution of international law. He claimed also in practice that Russia was 'consistently expanding its participation in international mechanisms for the protection of human rights'.[12] In line with this the Russian Supreme Court noted that according to the Russian Constitution 'international norms and principles are part of the Russian legal system'. New recommendations were drafted for lower Russian courts to use these norms and principles, including the precedents of the European court, within Russia's domestic jurisdiction.[13]

Five years later, the whole Russian emphasis had shifted from the flexible evolution of law back to a more rigid focus on foundational legal principles and a more essentialist view of sovereignty. In a major policy speech, seeking to cast a veil over recent Russian military action against Georgia, Medvedev tried to take the high ground, criticizing 'force divorced from law... as happened in Iraq' and 'any selective application of the basic principles of international law', since 'legality cannot be "selective"'.[14] In fact this sought to deflect creative legal evolution. After 2003 Russia steadily strengthened its defensive screen in the CIS regional order against the perceived challenge of the coloured revolutions (as analysed in chapter 6). It also reinforced its pluralist defences at the global level against challenges to the legitimacy of its domestic political arrangements.[15]

As for multilateralism, Russia viewed this as a means of framing the developing competition over future global order, over the international rules of the game, which it claimed had been unfairly stacked against it in a period of relative Russian weakness. As the power disparities of the earlier post-Cold War period between Russia and Western states narrowed, Moscow expected these rules to be reviewed or even revised. However, as we have argued, this was not a call for creative thinking about customary international law at large, let alone that related to the principle of sovereignty or *jus ad bellum*. Instead, multilateralism, in contrast to leadership or hegemony under unipolarity, should be realized in some kind of 'concert' of the leading nations.

RUSSIA IN A CONCERT OF GREAT POWERS

This kind of concert, as conceived by Russian leaders, would regulate the competition of the major powers through affirming common rules and the special responsibility of these powers to govern at the global level. Crucially the process would be interest-driven and not require bonding around any set of core values, as with the EU concept of multilateralism.[16] Further, since the concert concept presupposes the inclusion of Russia, Moscow regards the multilateral decision-making of Western regional organizations such as NATO and the EU as lacking legitimacy beyond their territorial remit.

The multilateral diplomacy Russia propagates is intended to underpin and reflect a new distribution of power in what is viewed as an emerging multipolar world. This multilateralism should reach beyond the Western powers and in addition to Russia should embrace especially the rising powers of China, India, and Brazil, with whom Moscow has sought to coordinate foreign policy positions in the BRICs grouping.

This was apparent in the Russian approach to the first summit of G8 states held in Russia, in St Petersburg in 2006, when China, India, South Africa, Brazil, and Mexico were involved in the preparations for the summit. A well-connected Russian specialist expansively described this as a serious step towards 'bringing together the great powers—a "concert of nations" for the 21st century'. He proposed that 'the powerful and responsible powers should unite and form an organization on a par with the UN, a controlling body, which will sometimes impose definite standards of conduct on the world community'. Not only should it be able to enforce certain rules of conduct, but decisions should be made on the principle of a qualified majority (which could leave Western member states outvoted).[17]

However, Russia has never officially called for the creation of such a body as its preferred expression of multipolarity. It has been unrealistic to expect Western powers to subject their decision-making authority to this kind of forum, and the structure of the UN Security Council anyway already fits Russian discursive criteria for multilateralism. In principle the permanent five could be characterized already as an embryonic collective leadership. However, Russia has complained that the composition of the Security Council does not sufficiently reflect the power distribution of states that qualify for global management in the emerging multipolar order. Russian officials loftily propose that the UN 'should serve as a framework for a new global regulation structure, based on a diversity of global and regional players'.[18]

For all this rhetoric, the Security Council cannot serve as an embodiment of collective security and Russia has put little real effort behind Security Council reform. Collective security is unsustainable when the permanent five clash in this forum, given their veto rights, a right which Russia prizes highly. Moscow has been explicit that in 'all scenarios for the enlargement of the Council's composition, the status of the current SC permanent Member States, including the veto power, should remain unchanged'.[19] Moreover, since Yeltsin's leadership Russia consistently has been reluctant to transfer key international security issues, particularly those relevant to international peace and security, to the Security Council, except when the issue has been one of engaging the UN after a Western-led intervention. This continued through Putin's second presidential term as Russia gave pride of place to sovereignty and insisted that Moscow could act as an independent pole of power in global affairs.

Moscow's views on transferring core international security issues to the Security Council have expressed both the importance it attaches to the status of its permanent five membership and its anxiety over US unilateralism. After Russia failed to prevent air strikes in Iraq in 1998 and NATO intervention in Kosovo in 1999 by threatening to veto resolutions of the Council, it appeared to draw the lesson that 'failure to reach agreement within the Security Council could easily lead to a decline in the prestige of the latter, as well as in the privileges Russia enjoys as a permanent member'.[20] Subsequently Russia tried to avoid bringing controversies to the Council that might force it to the dilemma of either endorsing a US/Western action, at least tacitly (through abstaining over a vote), or vetoing it which could further reduce the Council's importance.

As illustrated in chapter 5, this approach to the UN unravelled in February 2003. Russia then came close to the need to veto the US co-sponsored resolution which would have paved the way to coercive action in Iraq. In the event the US bypassed the Security Council and attacked Iraq without seeking Council authorization for military action. Russia soon tried to re-engage the UN in

Iraq as a means to constrain unfettered US power, to bind it into a broader consensus, but worried that Washington might now bypass the Security Council habitually. This kind of response—rhetorical insistence on the procedural legitimacy of Security Council resolutions, yet nervousness that the US in pursuit of international primacy might be prepared to break out of the UN Charter framework altogether—continued through the 2000s.

Russia's preference for great power concert over real multilateralism is also shown in the way it has prized G8 membership. Putin called for recognition of Russia's global status in chairing the G8 in 2006.[21] However, Moscow has not regarded the G8 in any respect as a substitute for the UN Security Council, with its protective mechanism of the veto.[22] The G8 has made no effort to displace UN authority over the use of force and has focused on international economics far more than security issues. Moreover, the political solidarity the G8 seeks to project as a grouping of the *democratic* great powers has offered no support for Russia's wider normative campaign—quite the reverse. So within the primarily Western G8 Russia has used membership defensively as a means to mitigate the effects of the normative hegemony it complains about in other forums.

Russia initially saw the evolution of the G8 into the wider G20 forum as an opportunity for diluting the influence of Western powers. In this sense the G20, as anticipated by a prominent specialist, could work as 'a new Concert of Nations... of the most powerful and responsible states capable of assuming responsibility for global governance'.[23] In a document issued before the April 2009 G20 summit in London, Moscow claimed that collective decision-making could only be efficient if 'legitimated' through representing the interests of a wide range of participants. The document also called optimistically for replacing the 'obsolescent unipolar world economic order' by 'a system based on the interaction of several major centres'.[24]

In reality, Russia itself has appeared economically too weak to be taken seriously as the core of such a centre (which for Russia would be a grouping of integrated CIS states). It has been taken aback to find itself with rather little geoeconomic or geopolitical leverage in the G20 setting. The membership of the G20 allows the dilution of Western dominance in the G8, but as a forum it has shied away from Russian 'anti-hegemony' rhetoric.

This kind of grandstanding had a more appreciative, if still cautious, reception in joint meetings of the BRIC (Brazil, Russia, India, and China) nations, which began in earnest in 2006. BRIC heads of states' summits have been held since 2009 and South Africa joined the group at the end of 2010 (forming BRICS).[25] In the Russian narrative this loose gathering is a natural association of 'rising powers', which has the collective weight to moderate if not displace the global institutional and normative dominance of Western powers. With this comes an idealistic portrayal of coordination between the BRIC nations (including its role as a bloc in the G20), as a new mechanism 'of network diplomacy and collective leadership of major world powers'. The BRICs have been described as 'united by the identity or similarity of their approaches towards key international issues'.[26]

This is the rhetoric of public diplomacy. The BRIC nations in common certainly have tended to express a pluralist focus on sovereignty and share the Russian expectation that global power is shifting steadily in their favour. But their diversity in many other respects has prevented them from cohering around any distinct, collectively promoted set of global principles.[27] As early as a 'troika' meeting of Russian, Indian, and Chinese foreign ministers in June 2005, Russian Foreign Minister Lavrov talked of their joint approaches to global issues 'based on principles of international law and multipolarity'.[28] But the commitment to a similar mantra in the wider BRICs format has failed to reveal how far each state has internalized emerging global norms, or the extent to which each has been ready to confront the US over understandings of global order.

Russia's key partner for any substantive global concert to champion a pluralist order would need to be China. But this is problematic since it has been far from clear that China has wished to adopt this role, let alone develop it into an explicit axis with Russia against US-led hegemony.

It is true that in the 2000s the two powers displayed considerable normative congruence in their international postures. For both Russia and China the UN has served, among other functions, as an instrument to constrain US unilateralism, with the Security Council as the fount of procedural legitimacy (in which both hold veto rights). They clearly prioritize order rather than justice as the goal of state action and have tended to invoke sovereignty in defence of their domestic jurisdiction, as a means to avert intrusion in their internal affairs (including for China in Taiwan, as for Russia in Chechnya). In the regional setting in Eurasia they agree that externally 'imposed' norms (such as on governance) by 'non-regional' powers should be resisted and have tended to relativize democracy and civil rights. This acts as a basis for solidarity, alongside other member states, in the Shanghai Cooperation Organization.[29]

This is accompanied by complementary official Russian and Chinese attitudes to the use of force, centred conservatively on the UN Charter system. This was on display during the Kosovo crisis in 1999. By summer 2001 the Chinese and Russian leaders still jointly condemned 'attempts at subversion of the fundamental norms of international law by means of such concepts of humanitarian intervention and limited sovereignty'.[30] Their discourse in the UN Security Council was framed in similar terms in rejecting not only OAF in 1999, but also the US-led attack on Iraq in 2003. Since then Moscow and Beijing have continued to reject regime change as any rationale for intervention (despite acceding to the overthrow of the Taliban in 2001). They have positioned themselves together also at the conservative end of the continuum of state responses to R2P, emphasizing in the first place the responsibility of states for the protection of their citizens.[31]

Despite this congruence in outlook China has consistently been averse to an explicit alignment with Russia to balance against US unipolarity or a US-led hegemonic order, rather than a loose 'strategic partnership'. Beijing has not been prepared to risk the onset of adversarial relations with Washington through such a strategy. This has limited the consolidation of the Sino-Russian core of a concert of entrenched pluralist powers. This remains an unlikely prospect anyway so long as there remain significant differences between the wider normative preferences of Moscow and Beijing, including over international economic governance.[32]

The vision of an eventual Sino-American G2 relationship has emerged as a tempting alternative for China to Russia's notion of a multipolar concert. This becomes only more likely as the disparity in material capabilities between Russia and China, helped by reduced Russian economic growth since 2008, works ever more in Beijing's favour. This in turn may reinforce persistent underlying perceptions in Moscow that China represents a serious medium-term threat to Russian control over Siberia and the Russian Far East, a source of nervousness which tempers any deeper affinity between the two powers' elites and publics. On a more practical level, China is aware that, despite efforts by the BRICs states to consult as a group in the UN, and for all Russian leaders' talk of multilateralism, Russia has been prone to independent action in Security Council diplomacy (such as bypassing China to mend fences with Western states over OAF in May–June 1999). Indeed Putin has prized the Russian capacity to act as an 'independent pole of power'.

The Russian notion of a multilateral 'concert', therefore, has had two variants. One involves defending Russian interests robustly within the clubs of the big players, quintessentially the UN Security Council and below that the G8 and G20. However, a second variant represents an effort to create counter-hegemonic balancing structures of normatively like-minded major states, as through BRICs, or bilaterally through an axis with China. This has a regional expression also in the form of the CSTO (plus other CIS groupings) and to a degree the SCO (though hierarchy clearly plays more of a role for the smaller states in these regional forums). For Moscow the second variant of concert ideally might offer Russia its own coalition to counteract coalitions of Western states bound together by their own norms and security interests, especially NATO. The Russian search for its own coalition is likely to continue as long as it has limited influence over the agendas of Western organizations and views them as seeking extra-regional, even global responsibilities eclipsing Russia's own global aspirations.

RUSSIA'S REPUDIATION OF NATO'S GLOBAL ROLE

For Moscow, NATO embodies Russian exclusion from the 'hegemonic' international order. Russia seeks to develop its 'concerts' and greatly values its Security Council membership, but has no comparable club to NATO. Remaining outside the core decision-making of NATO, despite limited consultations in the NATO–Russia Council since May 1992, Moscow has been especially alert to any sign of Alliance interest in global order tasks and to arguments aimed to justify such an extension of NATO's remit. After 2001 this required more careful assessments about how far Washington is ready to work through NATO for potential operations, rather than rely on 'coalitions of the willing' or just on American capabilities.

In a similar way Russia has denied that the European Union (the other main Western club) can independently provide a legitimate mandate for the use of force under its European Security and Defence Policy (ESDP). Moscow insists this would need to be sanctioned by the OSCE and the UN Security Council, where of course a Russian veto could be deployed. However, the EU has not been in the crosshairs of Russian criticism over the authorization or justifications for the use of force for a number of reasons.

There was a debate in Moscow in the early 2000s about whether ESDP might develop to some extent autonomously from NATO. Since then, however, Russian leaders have better understood that even after the EU has fully developed its rapid reaction corps and arrived at a unified decision, it would remain up to the NATO allies to approve the use of these means for EU-initiated actions. Even for more limited crisis management the EU may have to borrow NATO assets and capabilities, as the two institutions agreed at the end of 2002. Therefore Moscow feels its concerns over ESDP are better addressed in the general context of Russia–NATO relations.[33]

Russia has certainly been wary of any possibility that EU crisis management in the future could focus on what the EU defines as its security neighbourhood, on long-standing frozen conflicts in CIS states. But little of this kind has been achieved so far.[34] Moreover, Moscow could take heart from the way the EU involvement in the 2008 Russia–Georgia crisis did not counteract Russian core objectives in that crisis, let alone involve any sabre rattling. Overall, for various reasons Russia doubts that potential EU crisis management or peacekeeping operations could take the form of military intervention (as defined in the introduction to this study).

It should be noted, although this is only tangentially related to the use of force debate, the EU represents a different kind of challenge for Moscow. Since at least the early 2000s Russian leaders have been nervous and critical about the influence the EU seeks broadly as a regional normative power in CIS neighbour states. Much of the Russian political elite has tended to interpret this wider normative effort unsophisticatedly in terms of EU–Russia geopolitical rivalry.[35]

In contrast to the functionally and so far regionally limited ESDP, the scope of potential NATO operations has been a persistent Russian concern. Chapter 3 of this study assessed Russian criticism of NATO's new Strategic Concept in April 1999, which anticipated crisis response operations by the Allies in theatres beyond those which traditionally preoccupied NATO. Russia protested that the Balkan region had been chosen to test a 'NATO-centrist' concept of world order. Moving on to chapter 4 we noted that in April 2003 Russia assented to the transfer of ISAF to NATO command in Afghanistan, and the Alliance decided the following year to expand the ISAF mission to the whole of Afghanistan. However, Russian rivalry with NATO in the wider international context left Moscow sensitive to the NATO role in Afghanistan and equivocal about any outcome defined as 'success' for NATO. One growing concern, as expressed by a senior Russian official, was that with so many nations actively supporting NATO operations in Afghanistan 'NATO is turning into a "democratic" alternative to the UN.'[36]

Russian leaders could nurture the hope that NATO's growing commitment in Afghanistan would constrain its ambitions in other geographic theatres. They also noted for better or worse that Washington had bypassed NATO in planning its attack on Iraq in 2003. Yet Moscow expressed growing distrust of NATO's transformation objectives, after the Alliance expressed its determination at its 2004 Istanbul summit 'to address effectively the threats our territory, forces and populations face from wherever they may come'.[37] Observing the NATO summit in Riga in November 2006, Russia was clearly apprehensive over the potential expansion of NATO security responsibilities globally to face global threats, assisted by global partnerships with non-NATO states.[38]

In spring 2008 Putin bluntly voiced his distrust of NATO 'aspirations to play a global role in the area of security' and its extension into areas such as energy security, cyber security, etc. He claimed 'the criteria for the use of military force by NATO remain unclear, as does its relationship with the United Nations Security Council'.[39] This criticism continued with Russian officials under the Medvedev presidency, as NATO proceeded to discuss a new strategic concept, to replace the version issued in 1999 (which was adopted in November 2010).[40]

Lavrov rejected NATO's description of the UN 'as a partner to be consulted with', since 'when it comes to the use of force, consultations are not a format to be applied to the UN'. He accused NATO documents of ignoring UN Charter terms on the use of force, which 'could tempt us to say, if NATO can do it, why can't we?' NATO's neglect of international law in this context, he warned, 'will trigger a chain reaction'.[41]

Such allusions to Moscow's readiness itself perhaps to 'break out' of legal constraints on the use of force (as it did in the 2008 Russia–Georgia war) are absent from key public documents on Russian security. Yet the danger of NATO expanding its power and 'global functions' tops the list of military dangers (defined as situations that could lead to a military threat) in Russia's new Military Doctrine of February 2010.[42]

Russian trepidation over NATO 'going global' during Putin's second presidential term accompanied a harsher assessment of US global force deployments, and how these might be reflected in NATO, than earlier in the decade.[43] After 2006 Russia was much less ready to accept that these deployments were influenced heavily by common goals in the 'war on terror' and ratcheted up its critique of Western hegemony.

In 2004 Russian Defence Minister Sergei Ivanov had been relaxed about the shift in the US global force posture. He admitted that 'we know about the Americans' plans for reconfiguring their forces and we understand them...I see nothing alarming in those plans.'[44] Former Defence Minister Pavel Grachev explained that American bases naturally would lie near Russian borders, since they would largely be concentrated along the 'arc of instability' extending through the Near and Middle East.[45] The major redeployment of US bases and armed forces abroad announced in August 2004, a Russian specialist noted, was also done with an eye towards the growing power of China. 'The strategy is ceasing to be anti-Russian in the traditional sense', he admitted, and considered this also applied to the growing US presence in CIS states.[46]

In the second half of the decade this sanguine analysis was increasingly displaced by simpler and more alarmist interpretations, especially among senior officials of the politically influential security elite in Moscow. An article typifying such approaches in 2006 described US redeployments as leading towards a 'new military empire', involving 'the textbook geopolitical manoeuvre: put Russia in a ring so as to constrain it and deter its geopolitical aspirations'. The US presence in the Black Sea, the Caspian region, and Central Asia feature prominently in this revived zero-sum perspective.[47]

With it came the growing conviction in the Russian security policy elite that NATO was more or less locked into US planning as a single constellation of power, that Washington had 'meticulously planned measures designed to pass global functions to the NATO force potential, despite existing international law norms and regulations'. As NATO interests were globalized, this would squeeze Russia 'to the margins' in international security decision-making.[48]

For the Russian security establishment this was happening in a world in which competition between leading world powers (including Russia) will intensify and in which new sources of conflict are emerging. The 2009 Russian National Security Strategy (NSS) portrays a volatile international security landscape threatened by just such competition and conflicts, primarily over scarce energy resources of the Middle East, parts of the Arctic region, the Caspian Basin, and Central Asia. A competitive struggle for resources is envisaged, 'that might be resolved by a decision to use military power'—seemingly implying new military interventions influenced by energy needs.[49]

In the next phrase the NSS even warns that 'the existing balance of forces on the borders of the Russian Federation and its allies can be changed'.[50] Of course the Russian military command evaluates a variety of scenarios of conflict near Russian borders unrelated to the danger of 'resource wars' and only some of these scenarios are related to Western powers. It is striking, however, that two and a half years after the presentation of the NSS, the Chief of General Staff, Army-General Nikolai Makarov, estimated that the potential for armed conflict along the entire Russian periphery had grown dramatically over the previous twenty years.[51]

The NSS defines Russia's main military threats as Western, the US and NATO. But it judges that the world will be ever less oriented to the West as other power centres emerge. In this and other evaluations the Russian leadership projects the optimistic belief that Russia, despite the post-2008 weakening of its economy, will insert itself more prominently into the intensifying global competition. It has been an article of faith that Russia remains on a trajectory to global power (at least to be counted among the top five economies), while both the material and normative foundations of Western dominance are weakening. The assertion of alternative non-Western values (as represented by the Chinese or Russian social models), meanwhile is perceived in itself as a potential source of interstate conflict. The overall conclusion of the NSS is that force will become more, not less, likely in the future.[52]

The Russian leadership's apprehensions about the future security environment and the repercussions of this for CIS regional and domestic order have made Moscow all the more insistent on being centrally involved in any debate by major powers on the legal and normative regulation of force. Russia's engagement in this debate, in the cases analysed below, in fact shows more nuance than Putin's vociferous campaign against the 'hegemonic' power structure might lead one to expect. This partly reflected the 'reset'—efforts to moderate diplomatic tensions during the period of overlap between the new US administration under Barack Obama (from early 2009) and the presidency of Dmitri Medvevev (2008–12, during which Putin as prime minister remained the *éminence grise* and power broker). However, the Medvedev interregnum, before Putin returned to formal leadership of the Russian state, failed to displace deep-seated differences about the justifiable use of force between Moscow and Washington.

THE THREAT OF INTERVENTION IN IRAN

The implied or explicit threat of military action against Iran by the US, Israel, and some European powers hangs over diplomatic efforts to avert the militarization of Iran's nuclear programme. Some form of military intervention, at least in the form of limited strikes against Iranian nuclear facilities, has been urged as a policy of last resort, principally by certain Israeli and US politicians. This shows that the logic of preventive use of force for counter-proliferation remains alive in the US body politic and in the leadership of some other states.

In essence, a select few Western powers may be ready again, as in 2003 (though this time with perhaps the passive consent of a wider group of states, including Gulf states), to claim that Iranian compliance with non-proliferation norms and Security Council demands can and should be enforced by military means, failing diplomatic efforts, even in the absence of an explicit Security Council mandate.

This sets the stage for another strenuously contested intervention, since Russia (as well as China in the Security Council) has consistently rejected the legitimacy of any forceful action against Iran, even in response to Tehran's clear defiance of the Security Council. This position reflects Russian state interests and threat evaluations. It also seems to reflect a belief that the military options mooted do not reflect a commitment to uphold non-proliferation norms so much as reflect other hegemonic goals, aligned with the state of Israel. These considerations of power politics appear to be mixed in with some real concern in Moscow over the erosion of core principles on the use of force.

International law, justifications, and intervention in Iran

The US has reduced its emphasis on military pre-emption as a strategic option since the Iraq War. This makes it doubtful that Washington would try to present a legal, rather than political, case for preventive military action against Iran (which had not even been done in 2003). In January 2002 President George W. Bush had bundled Iran together with Iraq and North Korea as part of his 'axis of evil'. The 2002 US National Security Strategy had accused these states of posing similar threats through their links to terrorist groups and their illicit efforts to develop a military nuclear programme. The NSS made expansive claims about military pre-emption. However, by 2006 the NSS paid considerably more attention to the alternatives to military pre-emption and placed more reliance on multilateral solutions.[53]

The Obama administration reinforced this stance. As a presidential candidate in 2008, Obama warned the American Society of International Law that 'the preventive use of force may be necessary, but rarely'.[54] As a former lawyer, however, he had to be aware of the legal weakness of such preventive logic. In his initial discourse on Iran as president Obama emphasized international law and norms, rather than military options. By mid-2009 this language shifted towards Iran's international 'obligations'.[55] Still, the Obama administration continued to emphasize the need for a multilateral diplomatic resolution of the Iranian nuclear challenge over the contemplation of military action. The NSS of May 2010 downplayed prevention and pre-emption in general.

Where does this leave justifications for intervention in Iran? Even with the stalling of multilateral diplomacy over Iran, US and West European officials have avoided specifying in advance legal arguments to justify potential military action against Iran.[56] Western leaders have skirted around the whole issue of the legality of such action in their speeches on the dispute. For example, in a major speech in March 2012 Obama told that his efforts to prevent Iran from obtaining a nuclear weapon include the option of 'a military effort to be prepared for any contingency'. He then promised that 'I will not hesitate to use force when it is necessary to defend the United States and its interests.'[57] This could imply a scenario of self-defence. In principle self-defence could be triggered if Iran were rash enough to attack American forces or assets in the Gulf region in an escalating crisis. But Washington cannot count on such a scenario.

Some American jurists and academics have claimed that both the US and Israel could invoke the right of pre-emptive self-defence, that Iranian rhetoric against Israel poses an 'imminent' threat. Others seem on firmer legal ground in arguing that 'the idea that the United States is under imminent threat from Iran is preposterous', while for Israel the threat is not preposterous but 'it just isn't imminent'.[58]

Any legal justifications that Western or Israeli leaders may offer for their future actions over Iran will be part of a process of political persuasion on the international stage, as with previous interventions. However, a feature of the Western discussion of the possible use of force against Iran is the assumption that any such action will need to circumvent a probable Russian and Chinese Security Council veto. Indeed, during years of controversy over Iranian nuclear policy Russian leaders seem to have taken seriously the scenario of an American military operation against Iran without a separate and explicit UN Security Council mandate.[59]

Moscow remembers well the legal case offered by the US and UK for attacking Iraq in 2003—implied authority to use force based on previous Security Council resolutions. To limit the recurrence of similar logic, Russia with some European and other states has done its best to avoid offering the US any legal pretext through the Security Council for the use of force against Iran. During 2002–6 Moscow attempted to prevent the Iran case from even being turned over to the Security Council. It first approved the diplomatic efforts of EU nations and then exerted much effort itself seeking, and failing, to obtain full Iranian cooperation with the International Atomic Energy Agency (IAEA).

When the Security Council became more deeply involved in the Iranian case Russia was especially cautious about acceding to any language that might allow the US to claim implied authority to use force.[60] This is evident in Security Council Resolutions 1737 (2006) and 1747 (2007), which imposed sanctions after the IAEA reported that Iran had not taken the required steps.[61] More recently, Resolution 1929 (2010), which tightened these sanctions, specified that nothing in it 'compels states to take measures or actions exceeding the scope of this resolution, including the use of force or the threat of force'. When Moscow approved the resolution it recorded its conviction 'that there is no alternative to a peaceful diplomatic settlement of the Iranian nuclear issue' and that this postulate is 'reflected in the text of the resolution'.[62]

As a second line of defence to counter calls for military action against Iran, Russia has insisted on robust evidence that Iran has been pursuing a nuclear bomb and claims it has received no such documentary proof. It has made a disparaging analogy with the abuse of intelligence claims in spring 2003. Lavrov appealed in June 2008 for 'real facts' 'each time when a unilateral or any other action is planned on the pretext of carrying out decisions of the IAEA or UN Security Council'.[63] Moscow has set a high threshold of proof and in January 2011 Medvedev denied outright that there was evidence of Iran seeking a bomb. A detailed IAEA report, released that November with damning conclusions on the Iranian nuclear programme, was ridiculed by the Russian government as 'a compilation of known facts to which a politicized ring is deliberately given'.[64] Russia then set itself against imposing further sanctions on Iran.

Russian political and security responses in the controversy over Iran

In its international diplomacy there are limits, however, to Russian readiness to shield Iran. Moscow certainly has the means to deploy its Security Council veto to protect Tehran from further sanctions or coercive language in UN resolutions. Russia could avoid isolation in this action if it receives continued Chinese support in the Security Council. Yet this stance replays the dilemma exposed since the US-led attack on Iraq in 2003: the US ultimately may bypass the UN, while it remains a Russian priority to ensure the UN retains a central role in resolving international security conflicts.

This UN role also requires a strong response to Iran's clear defiance of previous Security Council resolutions and IAEA demands. Otherwise this top body, and Russia as one of its custodians, 'could lose their credibility as globally legitimate arbiters'.[65] Moscow risks its cherished role in the global 'concert of great powers' if it persists in unyielding diplomatic protection of Iran in the UN (since the controversy engages deeper Western and regional interests in the Middle East than the post-2011 conflict in Syria). Russia also has specific normative and instrumental reasons to uphold the integrity of the nuclear non-proliferation regime.

Given these considerations, Russian intransigence over Iran is unlikely just to reflect a general resistance to the hegemonic exercise of force by the US. Arguably it is rooted in apprehensions about a wider war and its regional security consequences. Moscow seems to fear the uncontained escalation of an operation against Iran. Russian officials conjecture that even limited strikes against Iran could evolve into a major campaign aiming to overturn the Iranian regime. This scenario partly reflects practical counter-proliferation objectives. Air and missile strikes alone on Iran's nuclear infrastructure would most probably set back but not terminate the country's supposed military nuclear programme, whether these were to be conducted by the US, by Israel, or through a combination of their efforts. The reliable military destruction of that programme would require a much larger military operation.

Such an operation could then mutate into a US-driven 'preventive war', with the goal of regime change to eradicate a variety of supposed threats from Iran, despite American experiences in Iraq and Afghanistan. The previous US discourse on regime change subsided under President Obama. Yet Tehran could interpret the use of air power and targeted missile strikes at key Iranian facilities, perhaps even if initiated by Israel, as the beginning of a regime-toppling war and retaliate against US interests worldwide.[66]

The Arab Spring in 2011 also revived some hope in Washington that a political transformation in Iran might be possible as a side benefit of a military campaign, or that this could even be promoted by punitive sanctions against Tehran.[67] In autumn 2011 a US congressional hearing was told that the Pentagon had a series of contingency plans for military action, ranging from all-out war to limited operations against Iran, which Obama had signed off on. The UK might well join American strikes against Iran.[68]

Russian analysts have speculated extensively about the severe security consequences of a more extensive military campaign against Iran.[69] On the one hand, a successful US-led operation of this kind, resulting finally in a pro-Western government, is viewed as inimical to Russian interests. On the other hand, a chaotic outcome, fuelled by insurgency as in Iraq after 2003, and accompanied by instability and extremism near Russian southern borders, would also be highly undesirable for Moscow.[70]

A particular Russian concern has been the possible fracturing of the Iranian state along ethnic lines, with ethnic Azeris in Iran heading to the territory of Azerbaijan, resulting in a 'humanitarian catastrophe'. Alternatively, Russian officials have warned that forceful actions against Iran would unify the Iranians, provoke discontent in the Arab world, activate Hamas and Hezbollah in Palestine, and exacerbate the situation in the whole of the Middle East and Central Asia.[71] If the Russian leadership is persuaded at all by these scenarios, it has reason to oppose even limited strikes against Iranian nuclear facilities, since the risks involved would much outweigh the benefits for the Russian state and economy of an ensuing rise in oil and gas prices.

Russia not only fears such risks of a major war with Iran. It also has traditional commercial and geopolitical interests at stake. Moscow has developed a substantial economic and trade relationship with Iran, including in civilian nuclear technology and conventional arms. In pursuing this trade Russia does not recognize American unilateral sanctions on Iran as binding under international law. Secondly, Russia has relied on a solid partnership with the current Iranian authorities for leverage in its wider foreign policy in the Middle East and to enable trade-offs in bilateral relations with the US. As a matter of foreign policy strategy, Moscow may have favoured prolonging relations of *controlled tension* between Iran and Western states. This allows Russia to present itself as indispensable to any putative 'solution' to the Iranian nuclear conundrum, raising Russian status and its international leverage, especially in relation to the US.

A *Realpolitik* strategy of this kind can be pursued since most Russian officials have been rather dismissive of the concerns of the US and other major Western countries like France about Iran as a threatening, destabilizing power. The risks and threat evaluation arising from such concerns are central to Washington's preventive thinking, premised as it is on the need to act against dangers before they gather. At root, Russia assesses the risks of an Iranian military nuclear programme differently.[72] Its assessment is shared by some other CIS states. Kazakhstan (a state with nuclear weapons formerly on its own territory), for example, questions why the debate on Iran's nuclear programme does not involve discussion of the cases of Pakistan or Israel, which have avoided international sanctions over their nuclear weapons.[73]

The difference between Moscow and Western capitals arises not over the desirability of an Iranian nuclear weapons capability. The Russian leadership clearly opposes this. It does not view Iran as a stable ally and has to factor in a possible deterioration of future Russian–Iranian relations. Like Western powers, Moscow does not wish other states to follow the Iranian example of secretive nuclear policy and it seeks to uphold the non-proliferation norm.[74] Yet Moscow seems to consider that ultimately, if all non-military efforts to prevent this fail, it could coexist with a nuclear Iran, like a nuclear India and Pakistan, undesirable though this may be. Russian officials have become quite blunt that 'Russia regards a nuclear Iran as something unacceptable.'[75] But for the US, like Israel, this outcome seems more truly unacceptable, since they conflate counter-proliferation objectives with the war on terror and the vulnerability of Israel and this combination of threats is associated with the Iranian state.

Moreover, Russian officials have consistently been more doubtful than senior American leaders about the imminence of a *usable* Iranian military nuclear capability. The Russian military in particular has downplayed Iran's ability to develop longer-range ballistic delivery systems—Washington's justification for its planned missile-defence deployments. Moscow argued at the end of 2009 that Iran's missiles were very primitive, too short-range, and developed primarily for possible regional use.[76] US officials sought to counter this view the following year by sharing intelligence which indicated that North Korea had sent Iran missiles based on a Russian design that were capable of reaching Moscow.[77]

Given these different estimates and interests over Iran, Russia has called for the continuation of negotiations assisted by the IAEA to constrain Iran's nuclear programme. If this makes no effective progress then the prospect of a major division among world powers over the legitimacy of 'preventive' military measures against Iran is likely to loom large. The specific legal justifications or the *casus belli* that might be presented by a state or states for such an attack could vary. But they are unlikely to be accepted by either Russia or China or be embedded in any wider understandings about the acceptable use of force. The failure of diplomacy this represents would damage the standing of the Security Council, set back effort to forge consensus over norms between major powers, and create new risks for regional security.

INTERVENTION IN LIBYA

The rapid route to military intervention in Libya in spring 2011 contrasts sharply with the extended controversy between major powers over Iran. The Libyan operation was catalysed by an escalating crisis within the Libyan state: from street protests in mid-February 2011, to civil war within weeks, to attacks by the Libyan government on civilians and towns, which sparked widespread international condemnation. On 17 March the Security Council adopted Resolution 1973, authorizing a no-fly zone over Libya. This was remarkable since it was the first time the Council had mandated the use of military force for humanitarian purposes against the wishes of a functioning state. The resolution was carried since Russia, as well as four other sceptical Security Council members, abstained in the crucial vote.

In the crucial weeks before Resolution 1973 Russian official statements were consistent with the solidarist concerns of major Western powers. Moscow backed a Security Council statement on 22 February deploring 'the repression against peaceful demonstrators' and called on Tripoli 'to meet its responsibility to protect its civilians'.[78] A joint Russia–EU statement echoed these sentiments and a Russian presidential statement warned that such acts, if continued, would qualify as crimes under international law.[79] Moscow also accepted Security Council Resolution 1970, which reimposed the arms embargo on Libya, among other sanctions.[80]

The idea of imposing a no-fly zone on Libya, first mooted by France and the UK, was more controversial. Initially Moscow and others including China and the African Union opposed this idea, on principle and for practical reasons. However, the notion also divided EU governments and was regarded with uncertainty by the US administration. The tide of opinion shifted in the second week of March once the Gulf Cooperation Council (GCC) and the Organization of the Islamic Conference (OIC) urged the creation of a no-fly zone and as the threat of a massacre in the city of Benghazi loomed. Russia temporized and proposed that a possible no-fly zone be approved only once a ceasefire had been established and broken by Tripoli.[81] The UK and France rejected this and then the balance of opinion in the Security Council tipped towards Resolution 1973, despite the latitude in military action it provided.

International law, justifications, and intervention in Libya

In the debate prior to Resolution 1973 a prominent view was that a UN Chapter VII authorization would be essential to establish the legality of any military action in Libya. This principle was accepted not only by the traditionally sovereignty-focused states, but also by most major Western states. Western leaders did not try to circumvent the issue, for example by reviving the argument that previous UN resolutions offered implied authority to act forcibly. For example, the NATO Secretary-General Anders Fogh Rasmussen reiterated that the alliance would help protect civilians in Libya only if there was 'a demonstrable need, *clear legal basis*, and strong regional support' (my emphasis).[82] An emergency EU summit on 11 March issued the same formula to determine whether member states should examine 'all necessary options' to protect the Libyan civilian population.[83]

While there was still uncertainty whether a Chapter VII mandate could be achieved, French president Nicolas Sarkozy reportedly suggested, however, that France and the UK could agree on a bilateral operation, possibly carried out through NATO, if they could obtain the support of an Arab country. But the UK did not confirm this and significantly, contrary to the process towards intervention in Iraq in 2003 for example, Washington insisted instead on seeking UN legal authority for the military action under discussion. At least this was the case once Obama had been convinced that a toughly worded resolution for a no-fly zone would be militarily practicable by permitting air strikes against Libyan military targets on land and sea.[84]

Resolution 1973 explicitly justified its call for action on the grounds of extreme humanitarian need. It condemned the 'gross and systematic violation of human rights' in Libya and resolved that such attacks 'against the civilian population may amount to crimes against humanity'. This led to its authorization of UN members, under Chapter VII, to 'take all necessary measures... to protect civilians and civilian populated areas under threat of attack' in Libya, 'while excluding a foreign occupation force of any form on any part of Libyan territory'.[85] This unequivocally established a humanitarian rationale for a military response in Libya for those states ready to act.[86] Yet the resolution allowed participating states significant latitude to determine what would be militarily possible and this ambiguity may have been deliberate, to avoid a veto of the resolution.

The humanitarian justification was developed, explicitly and graphically, in the discourse of Western states justifying the ensuing military action in Libya. But these states mostly presented the UN-sanctioned defence of human rights as inseparable from the political rights of the Libyan people 'to determine their own destiny', in the context of the Arab Spring. This concern is not discussed in Resolution 1973. Obama raised this theme in a speech delivered early in the crisis.[87] It was restated in the Security Council debate on Resolution 1973 by the UK; France called democracy to prevail over dictatorship in Libya.[88] Some days later, the British Foreign Secretary explained the no-fly zone was being enforced 'to protect civilians against a government that has responded to legitimate demands for change with crushing military force'.[89] Such assertions show how Western powers tied the UN sanctioned defence of civilians with political transformation in Libya, an expectation which could easily shade into regime change. In this delicate terrain legal justifications spill over into political ones.

President Obama tried to walk a fine line on the issue in a major address to the nation on Libya on 28 March 2011.[90] The core justification for the action taken was described as the 'brutal repression and a looming humanitarian crisis' in Libya, 'to stop a massacre', and legal authorization came with Resolution 1973. He noted that further permissive conditions offered the US a 'unique ability' (note the effort to steer away from precedent) to stop the violence: 'a broad coalition prepared to join us, the support of Arab countries, and a plea for help from the Libyan people themselves'.

Yet Obama was cautious not to focus on American promotion of democracy in the crisis. He defined the US military mission as 'narrowly focused on saving lives'. He explicitly described it as a mistake to broaden it 'to include regime change', since this would be outside the UN mandate, would lead the coalition to splinter, and since 'we went down that road in Iraq' at great cost. Overthrowing Qaddafi would still be pursued, but through non-military means and it remained an American strategic interest, Obama claimed, to help prevent democratic impulses in the wider region from being eclipsed by dictatorship. This would happen, Obama predicted, if Qaddafi were to overrun those who opposed him.[91]

A difficulty from the outset was that the political expectation of Western states such as France, the UK, and the US that Qaddafi should be overthrown brought out legal ambiguities in the language of Resolution 1973, especially around partiality, that is taking sides in the conflict. On the one hand, it is arguable that partiality, in what soon appeared as a civil war on the ground in Libya, was built into the reference in the resolution not only to the 'protection of civilians' but also the 'protection of civilian populated areas'. With this mission the Security Council 'was effectively inserting itself into the ongoing struggle, putting certain cities out of bounds for Qaddafi and his forces'.[92]

Beyond this general point, however, it remained unclear first whether Muammar Qaddafi himself, as head of the Libyan military command structure, could be targeted to protect civilians. Secondly, could the earlier Security Council Resolution 1970, which had imposed an arms embargo on Libya, be overridden by the 'all necessary means' language of Resolution 1973, such that arms could be transferred to anti-Qaddafi rebels? Thirdly, in a further possible escalation, could even ground troops eventually be used by states enforcing the UN resolution so long as they did not form (in the words of Resolution 1973) 'a foreign occupation force'?

The contested interpretations triggered by such options, as the Libyan campaign developed, led to tension between Western powers on the one hand and Russia, as well as China and a number of other major states, on the other hand. In this case, therefore, the unusual passage of an enabling UN resolution did not foreclose debate on the legitimate use of force, including the legality of the measures taken. Rather the focus shifted to the permissible limits of the mandate agreed.[93] Therefore we analyse below Russian discourse in the weeks and months after the passage of Resolution 1972 and not just the Russian views around the time of the Security Council vote on 17 March 2011.

Russia and justifications for intervention in Libya

As we have noted, before Resolution 1973 official Russian statements accepted the seriousness of the threat to civilians in Libya, but were reticent about the appropriate response. After all by spring 2011 the Russian body politic seemed to have an ingrained aversion to Western-led interventions, Russian criticism of NATO going global was still running high, and the 'reset' in Russian relations with the Obama administration had not ended periodic Russian denunciations of US hegemony. It is hardly surprising, therefore, that in the Security Council debate on the text of Resolution 1973 Russia focused its criticism on the vagueness by Western states about how the broad mandate of the resolution would be implemented.

In this debate, however, the Russian representative, Vitaly Churkin, positioned Russia in the normative mainstream. He did not seek to privilege Libyan sovereignty over the need for potential forcible measures in the intensifying humanitarian crisis. Rather he claimed that 'we are firm and consistent advocates of the protection of the civilian population', that Moscow was 'guided by this basic principle as well as by common humanitarian values that we share with both the sponsors as well as other Council members'. This unusually specific solidarist stance also led to a line of criticism. Churkin speculated, probably with the analogy of Iraq in mind, about 'the inevitable humanitarian consequences of the excessive use of outside force in Libya'.[94]

Despite this ostensible normative congruence, Russia abstained in the vote. This reflected a situation, Churkin explained, in which Russia had not received answers to its 'concrete and legitimate' questions on 'how the no-fly zone would be enforced, what the rules of engagement would be and what limits on the use of force there would be'. He deplored provisions introduced into the text of Resolution 1973 that 'could potentially open the door to large-scale military intervention'.[95] Sergei Lavrov later would describe the 'all necessary means' term as 'a dimensionless formulation that allows one to legalistically interpret it in whatever way one desires'.[96]

This concern about the breadth of the mandate, it should be noted, was not confined to Russia or even Russia and China in the Security Council. Germany spoke of 'the danger of being drawn into a protracted military conflict that would affect the wider region', India noted there was no clarity about 'the details of enforcement measures', while Brazil in turn expressed concern that the resolution, in contemplating measures far beyond the initial no-fly zone concept, could result in more harm than good to civilians in Libya.[97] All these states abstained in the vote.

The Russian leadership appears to have been fully conscious of the escalatory potential of the resolution it chose not to veto. It was both persuaded of the need for action to protect the Libyan population and felt more comfortable in the group of BRICS countries abstaining (plus Germany) in this case than in isolating itself through the use of its veto (see below). In line with this, some days after the operation in Libya began, President Medvedev confirmed that 'overall' Resolution 1973 'reflects our understanding of events in Libya too, but not completely'. The consequences of Russia's 'qualified decision' not to use its veto were obvious, he noted, so 'it would be wrong for us to start flapping about now and say that we didn't know what we were doing'. At this point he only raised a mild reminder about the need for proportionality in the use of force.[98]

In establishing this official Russian response, Medvedev must have been aware that it was against the grain of more nationalist political opinion in Russia, including within its Foreign Ministry. Just a day before a Foreign Ministry spokesman had branded it 'unacceptable' to use the mandate of Resolution 1973, 'the adoption of which was quite an ambiguous step, in order to achieve goals that go far beyond its provisions'.[99] The Russian ambassador to Libya reportedly opposed Medvedev's line and lobbied on behalf of Qaddafi. He was dismissed and stripped of honours. A senior defence official, ignoring the role of the Security Council and Russian discourse within it, argued that the forces of the new coalition were 'forgetting that international law does not accept so-called bombing for humanitarian reasons'.[100] It seems such positions typified wider Russian opposition to the Libya operation.[101]

These critics found high-level support. A few days after the passage of Resolution 1973 Prime Minister Vladimir Putin described it as 'flawed and inadequate' since 'it authorises anyone to take any measures against a sovereign state'. He provocatively compared it to 'a medieval call to crusade'. He drew a direct line of comparison between American (note not European) interventions in Yugoslavia, Afghanistan, and Iraq, observing 'now its Libya's turn—and the pretext is the protection of the civilian population'.[102] Medvedev immediately rejected this reference to 'crusades', in a rare admonishment to Putin during their period of power in tandem. Yet a few days later Russian Defence Minister Anatoly Serdyukov accused the coalition of killing civilians and demanded an immediate end to its campaign, and the Russian State Duma adopted a statement that, while in other respects close to Medvedev's position, condemned the 'indiscriminate force' of the coalition forces.[103]

It is tempting to interpret this as a clash in normative vision between Medvedev's genuine acceptance of the humanitarian justification for the Libya operation and Putin's unreconstituted pluralist perspective and instinctive aversion to the Western use of force. Yet such a clear division between the two is unlikely. Given the domestic power play in Moscow it is very probable that Putin had approved, however grudgingly, the Russian abstention over Resolution 1973. After that decision it seems he chose to play to a certain domestic political audience, in trademark populist criticism of US policies, just as Medvedev had become quite effective in playing to international audiences.[104]

Regardless of how this Medvedev–Putin balancing act operated, however, the image of normative congruence with Western states over the case for action in Libya faded from late March as the overall Russian diplomatic stance became increasingly critical of the military *implementation* of the Security Council mandate, especially about what could be justified in terms of the core objective of protecting civilians.

Russian criticism mounted in particular once the coalition more clearly, if still not publicly, focused its campaign on overthrowing the Qaddafi regime and as the related possibility of a ground operation targeting the assets of that regime became more likely. Probably neither were a surprise to Medvedev, astute Russian diplomats, or military leaders from early in the campaign.[105] By late April Medvedev himself implied Qaddafi should step down and a month later after a G8 summit he conceded that G8 leaders had been unanimous that Qaddafi's regime 'has lost legitimacy and he must leave'.[106]

However, the notion of regime change still touched a raw nerve at the top of the centralized Russian state, since it expressed not only the judgement of Western states about the political legitimacy of a leadership, in an intervention backed by force, but also clear support for one side in a civil war, beyond the mandate agreed in the UN. Indeed it contradicted the position President Obama had adopted in his main speech justifying the intervention that 'our military mission is narrowly focused on saving lives', that 'broadening our military mission to include regime change would be a mistake'. Besides the issue of the UN mandate, Obama had judged in practical terms that this wider mission would splinter the coalition, require the US to use ground troops, or risk killing many civilians from the air.[107]

To call for regime change, Lavrov claimed, also made the insurgent side in Libya more intractable (unwilling to consider a ceasefire). But the greater danger, he argued repeatedly through spring and summer 2011, was the belief that 'the foreigners will help us' to overthrow the regime 'may be contagious and appear among the protesters in other countries of the region' hoping that the international community will assist them. This, he warned, would be 'an invitation to a whole array of civil wars'.[108] With such thinking, it took until 1 September 2011 for Russia officially to recognize the opposition National Transitional Council (NTC) as the sole legitimate power in Libya.

From spring 2011 Moscow accused coalition forces of a series of infringements of Resolution 1973, driven by efforts at regime change: the declaration of Qaddafi and his relatives as 'legitimate targets' (as well as the final bombing of Qaddafi's convoy as he tried to escape on 20 October), the 'disproportionate use of force' resulting in the death of civilians, and the targeting of Libyan state infrastructure and civilian sites.[109] Russia also prepared itself to resist challenges to the arms embargo for Libya, imposed by Resolution 1970. The notion of providing arms to the insurgents was controversial among the coalition states, and in the end was not properly put to the test. However, by the end of March US secretary of state Hilary Clinton at least was of the view that Resolution 1973 'amended or overrode the absolute prohibition on arms to anyone in Libya'. The UK also moved towards this interpretation.[110] In contrast Russia argued that the ban on delivering 'military assistance' to the territory of Libya should include the provision of military instructors.[111] Russia also decried the use of Western special forces, once this became public.

These Russian claims and arguments required political persuasion and lobbying within the Security Council and the wider international community. This discursive process was underpinned by various diplomatic and foreign policy strategies and interests. We turn now to this international political context.

The Russian political response to intervention in Libya

Russian material interests tied to the incumbent regime in Libya in spring 2011 were clearly secondary compared to such interests in Iran or Syria, or indeed those which had existed in Iraq in 2003.[112] Therefore, the international political context, interpreted through the categories analysed earlier in this chapter, weighed heavily in Russian decision-making over Resolution 1973 and the ensuring military campaign.

Firstly, this was not a potential intervention that was promoted according to Moscow's 'hegemonic' script. Russian leaders knew that it was France and Britain, rather than the US, which had initiated Security Council discussion on the no-fly zone, even if Washington proceeded to press for a broad mandate. Washington lobbied Russia actively before the key vote. Moscow was aware of Obama's efforts to avoid the impression of US 'ownership' of the planned operation. Even if the US did not retain in all respects a back seat role in the campaign that ensued, it was certainly part of a more balanced 'coalition of the willing' than during the 2003 Iraq War.

Moreover, when Obama described American strategic interests as part of his political rationale for contributing to (not leading) action in Libya (as he was obliged to do for his domestic audience), he phrased these interests in multilateralist rather than defensive unilateralist terms. His argument that inaction would have meant the writ of the Security Council would have appeared as empty words, 'crippling that institution's future credibility to uphold peace and security', dovetailed in principle with the importance Russia attached to preserving the authority of the Security Council.[113] On the other hand, once they had obtained their mandate the US and other Western powers were careful to prevent the Libya campaign from being brought before the Council for any further authorization during the course of operations.

Secondly, Russian diplomats, as those of other states, were impressed by the growing alarm over Libya of the regional Arab League, as well as the Organization of Islamic Conference, once these bodies supported a no-fly zone. Faced by this, a blunt Russian veto of Resolution 1973 would have isolated Moscow over the issue in the Middle East and even the larger Muslim world. It would have been awkward for Russia to be outflanked on the principle of non-intervention by bodies (despite the Arab Spring) of still essentially conservative, sovereignty-focused states (even if the African Union rejected any intervention in Libya). Security Council members of various continents, including the US, admitted they were influenced by the call for action in Libya by regional bodies—a sense of what we might call 'regional legitimacy'.[114]

Thirdly, in its Security Council diplomacy in mid-March 2011 Russia presented itself as in a bloc formed of BRICS nations plus Germany and therefore aligned with a broad cross-section of international opinion. Bandwagoning with other abstaining states, Russian diplomats could argue, enabled the UN to preserve its role in the crisis and offered Russia the possibility of constraining the scope of intervention in Libya. For a senior Russian parliamentarian, as part of the abstaining bloc Russia was 'in the position now to demand exact observance of provisions of Resolution 1973 from whoever voted for it—without sharing responsibility for its political consequences with them'.[115] This proved to be wishful thinking, however, given the latitude of that resolution.

Once the Libyan operation was underway Russia struggled to sustain the face-saving image of such bloc diplomacy. Criticizing coalition strikes, Lavrov tried to speak in these terms, proclaiming that 'in the opinion of Brazil, India, China, Russia and South Africa, the coalition's responses to the questions raised cannot satisfy us'.[116] Yet Moscow showed little readiness to coordinate with its BRICS partners when shifting its own policies on Libya, such as in deciding to reject the legitimacy of Qaddafi's regime (at a G8 summit), or in offering its services as a mediator in the conflict.

Russia made less effort than during previous Western-led interventions to rally other CIS states behind its perspectives on the Libya crisis. The awkwardness for Russia of squaring these views with its previous denigration of humanitarian intervention, as well as the preference of CIS states not to begin sniping politically at the coalition with little prospect of making a difference, could explain this. Even the Russian CSTO Secretary-General issued a non-committal statement.[117]

As it was, Russia found it difficult to leverage Resolution 1973 to constrain coalition operations. A problem from the outset was that Russia felt marginalized by the establishment in April of a new multilateral Contact Group for political guidance on operations in Libya. This included NATO members, several Arab League members, and a number of international organizations, but Moscow did not participate in it (Russia first attended a Contact Group session in September 2011). Lavrov complained, on reasonable procedural grounds, that 'from the viewpoint of international law this group has no legitimacy' in monitoring the implementation of UN resolutions on Libya, that this legitimacy rested solely with the Security Council.[118]

Moscow hoped in particular to use its membership of the Council to extract trade-offs in exchange for the UN sanctioning a possible ground military campaign in Libya. It deplored the prospect of such an escalation and denied that ground operations had been mandated by Resolution 1973. However, in April Lavrov noted that if such a mandate were sought it should be taken to the Council and 'we will discuss, try to understand what is planned'. This hinted that Russian approval for a ground operation might at least be negotiable. At the same time Moscow claimed Security Council authorization would be needed not only for such NATO plans, but even for limited EU plans to accompany humanitarian cargoes to Libya.[119]

Another approach, appealing to Russia's sense of its global status and its active role in a concert of great powers, was to offer itself as a mediator in the Libyan crisis. Medvedev found some support for this in talks held on the sidelines of the G8 summit at the end of May.[120] By June, however, Moscow conceded that the African Union was better placed to play the lead role in any such mediation.

Russia's chief mediator, Mikhail Margelov, even mooted the idea of deploying Russian peacekeeping forces in Libya under a UN mandate, following a ceasefire and the beginning of a 'national dialogue'. A senior Russian parliamentarian suggested alternatively that a Russian contingent under UN authorization be dispatched, without such conditions, simply 'after the completion of NATO's military operation there'.[121] However, nothing came of these ideas for a Russian peacekeeping role in Libya once the UN agreed to lift the no-fly zone over Libya at the end of October.

This led to NATO concluding coalition operations in Libya, which were brought under its command at the end of March. Overall, Russia had little success in limiting the escalation of these operations (though there was no real ground operation). Russia had argued that the Security Council should endorse the consistency of this NATO campaign with the implementation of the mandate in Resolution 1973, to provide legitimacy for the operations. But Moscow failed to establish this principle, which had the wider goal of constraining other potential NATO expeditionary tasks. However, similar Russian efforts are likely to continue. For example, at a meeting of the NATO–Russia Council in November 2011, Moscow circulated a draft statement on a legal framework for decisions on the use of force. The stated purpose was 'to return NATO to the legal framework' defined by the UN Security Council.[122]

As with the Western-dominated interventions previously examined, in this case Russia was keenly concerned about the implications for general NATO planning on the use of force. The Russian military command styled it as 'the first "field test" for NATO's new strategic concept'.[123] More specifically, the Libya campaign could be assessed as a model of modern NATO operations on the European periphery, in the emerging conflict environment portrayed by the 2009 Russian National Security Strategy. After a meeting of the NATO–Russia Council in December 2011 Lavrov complained that 'some of our partners suggest the so-called "Libyan model" as the prototype for the future'. He objected flatly to this.[124] He was referring only partly to the dispute over the UN mandate.

Russian leaders also seemed concerned about the possibility of NATO becoming emboldened by the success of this new military operation on its southern flank. Yet they knew that the campaign did not fit well their category of US hegemony. At the end of the campaign, only seven of twenty-eight NATO countries were participating in combat actions and the US remained 'supportive' rather than in command. This was an image of a more disaggregated alliance. An astute Russian analyst observed that it could suit the US if leading European states could resolve 'at least medium tasks in the zone directly adjacent to Europe'. In this way, he forecast, 'NATO, having made an unsuccessful sally into the global arena in the late nineties and early 2000's, is returning to a regional role.'[125] Regardless of this possibility, interpretations of the Libya case for the future use of force remain contested.

Implications beyond the Libya case

Among Security Council members Russia was especially vocal in expressing its dissatisfaction with the constitutionalism or procedural legitimacy underpinning the Libya intervention, despite the passage of Resolution 1973. This could be problematic for future UN authorizations for the use of force. However, there remains an intriguing ambiguity about the wider normative implications of the case.

In terms of process and rule-making, Russia's central complaint was that once Resolution 1973 was passed Western powers precluded any further debate in the Security Council over its implementation. The sense was that coalition forces, in referring to 'all necessary means', acted as if provided with a blank cheque. This was an old concern, which had arisen over implementation of the previous Chapter VII authorization for action against Iraq in the Gulf War. In spring 2011 Russia tried to argue that the Council and its members were endowed with some collective right to monitor the proper implementation of the mandate, as a continuing discursive process, preferably to be tested through further resolutions. Failing this, Lavrov warned, Moscow would examine 'any new proposals for the Security Council to authorize intervention in an internal conflict through a huge magnifying glass'.[126]

Russia specified that for 'authorization to use force to achieve a shared goal', any new resolution would have to specify 'who is going to use this authorization, what are the rules of engagement and what are the limits of the use of force'.[127] This 'explicit formulation' should include the arrangements for the command and control of operations. Russia presented such criteria for future UN authorizations as agreed jointly with China and other BRICS states.[128] This was not just an abstract effort to tighten UN mandates. It confirmed that a mandate for any follow-on intervention, especially in the escalating crisis in Syria, but possibly also for other potential offshoots of the Arab Spring, would be much more difficult to achieve than Resolution 1973.

In spring 2011 Lavrov described 'attempts to reproduce the Libyan experience in other countries and regions' such as Syria, Yemen, or Bahrain as 'very dangerous'.[129]

As noted previously, Moscow feared 'contagion' from the Libya case, spread by hopes among protesters in different countries that, in seeking regime change, 'foreigners will help us'. From May 2011 onward Russian officials claimed that the Syrian case differed to Libya, since regime opponents in Syria supposedly used violence from the beginning (a view not shared by Western states) and continued to do so. Moscow claimed such protesters then calculatedly sought condemnation of the regime by NATO and the Security Council to enrol their support.

Russia tried to limit Security Council involvement in the Syrian case from the outset. In June it claimed, in legally relevant language, that 'the situation does not present a threat to international peace and security'. Rather 'quite considerable consequences for the Middle East region' could result exactly from interference in Syrian internal affairs.[130] Moscow presented the approach taken to the political crisis in Yemen as an alternative model for Syria, 'where all the external players worked extremely patiently and persistently with all the sides, without ultimatums, encouraging them to compromise'.[131] Security Council Resolution 2014 in October 2011 codified the framework for a settlement in Yemen.

During summer 2011 President Medvedev signalled that, despite Russia's call for 'impartiality', there were limits to its readiness to shield the Syrian regime. As with the Libyan case, Russia took note of the Arab League's involvement, its condemnation of Assad's violent repression of protesters. Seeking not to be outflanked by this regional body, while (with China) blocking UN condemnation of the Syrian regime, Medvedev warned Syrian president Bashar al-Assad in August 2011 that unless he implemented reforms urgently and made peace with the opposition, he would 'face a sad fate and at the end of the day we will also have to take some kind of decision'.[132]

Unlike the Libya case, however, when the Arab League decided to impose sanctions on Syria and harshly criticized Assad's brutality, Russian leaders refused to follow mainstream Arab opinion. Moscow remained loath to endorse any path towards the replacement of Assad's regime, even indirectly through new strong UN sanctions. Russia worked with China and tried to coordinate with other BRICS states to avert any Security Council resolution on Syria that did not rule out external military intervention. In October 2011 Russia and China vetoed a resolution drafted by Western states which called for a Syrian-led political process and condemned 'grave and systematic human rights violation' in Syria. The BRICS states on the Council—Brazil, India, and South Africa—abstained.[133]

During UN debate early in 2012 Russia continued to reject any sanctions against Syria or the employment of the Council's instruments 'to justify any eventual foreign military interference'. Moscow denied the Council had the right to 'impose parameters for an internal political settlement' in Syria.[134] However, in February 2012 when Russia and China jointly vetoed a new strongly worded draft resolution (although this still refrained from any threat of or allusion to possible forcible UN action) they found all thirteen other Council members, including other BRICS states, ranged in support of the resolution. In a weak defence of its vote Russia repeated its call for impartiality and criticized other Council members for 'calling for regime change' in Syria and 'encouraging the opposition towards power... nurturing the armed struggle'.[135] This was a far cry from the language at the time Resolution 1973 was adopted.

Therefore Russia could stand back to back with China, but could no longer try to present its position on Syria as typifying pluralist sentiments among fellow BRICS states. Nor could Russia rely on solidarity with CIS states. Most CIS leaders were reticent or hedged in this new crisis. In autumn 2011 Kazakhstan stated cautiously that a Libyan type 'full intervention' was not acceptable in the case of Syria.[136] Azerbaijan, however, relishing its status as a new non-permanent member of the Security Council, voted in favour of the February 2012 resolution, although it observed that nothing in the draft authorized Chapter VII measures under Article 42 of the UN Charter.[137]

Turning to the normative implications of the Libya intervention, for all the confusion over Syria an important question is whether the Libya crisis appeared to draw Russia into a more consolidated understanding of the Responsibility to Protect as a norm of international society. The Security Council's authorization of the use of military force for human protection against the wishes of a functioning state was remarkable and has undoubtedly raised the profile of R2P in the international community. On the other hand, the insistent claims by Russia, China, and some other states that Resolution 1973 was implemented abusively, as well as sharp differences over the Syria crisis despite its grave humanitarian issues, indicate that views on R2P as an imperative for action, especially by the international community, remain seriously contested.

Arguably, very particular circumstances lay behind the Russian and Chinese abstentions on Resolution 1973, which allowed Security Council action to proceed. The support of regional organizations for a no-fly zone was influential in this case. For individual abstaining states it became important not to be perceived as an impediment to action (through a 'no' vote), which could enable atrocities to occur in Libya. The chance composition of the Security Council also allowed Moscow to present itself in a global bloc of abstaining BRICS states with similar doubts over Western actions, reinforced by Germany. Moreover, President Medvedev, who lacked Putin's history of animosity to Western-led interventions, possibly had more influence over Russian UN policy in spring 2011 than a year later as Putin approached his re-election as president.

Even so, R2P was certainly a reference point in discourse preceding the Libya operation. Libya's responsibility to protect *its population* was referred to in a Security Council press statement (22 February), in Resolution 1970 (26 February), and in Resolution 1973 itself. The fact that the latter did not refer to the responsibility of the *international community* confirms that R2P was not fully embraced by the Council, and suggests it was contested by some Council members 'as an appropriate rationale for military action'.[138] As we have noted, however, Russia placed itself in the normative mainstream by acknowledging the humanitarian crisis in Libya and accepting the need to protect endangered civilian populations. This implied a shift from previous Russian disparagement of Western 'humanitarian intervention'.

The problem for Russia was not just the dilution of the humanitarian focus of the Libya campaign the more it went on and hence the distortion of the UN mandate, but the way that R2P language was seized on by key Western leaders as determining not just a UN but in this case a NATO mission. NATO Secretary-General Anders Fogh Rasmussen described NATO in Libya as lying at the heart of a 'broad international effort' to turn R2P 'into reality', and claimed 'we all have a moral responsibility to be ready to respond to similar calls from the United Nations in the future'.[139] Russia accused NATO of interpreting its Libya operation 'as a model' for its future exercise of R2P, of appropriating R2P to legitimate its future missions.[140]

Russia could still veto future R2P-based action based on such a model. However, given uncertainty about the geographical scope of NATO planning, Russian leaders were unsettled by 'hints that NATO could be endowed with a right to use force under the concept of "responsibility to protect" without a proper Security Council mandate'. Some Western politicians, Moscow claimed, were circulating the thesis that this mandate would not be required 'for military intervention in case of threats to a civilian population in a country'. If this were to become part of NATO strategy and operational planning, Russia warned, in language similar to its rhetoric during the 1999 Kosovo crisis, it could undermine 'the very foundation of existing world order'.[141] Once again the Russian view of constitutionalism in the global system was focused on the collective legitimacy provided by the Security Council. Conveniently this also provides a mechanism to constrain the exercise of NATO and US power.

Moscow has also explicitly belittled the humanitarian basis of the Libya campaign. This began soon after the passage of Resolution 1973. Putin set the tone by complaining 'how easily decisions on the use of force are taken... against the backdrop of those concerns for human rights and humanism that are allegedly practiced in the modern civilized world'.[142] By October 2011 Moscow's derision was more fulsome. Lavrov described the Libya operation as a 'drama... which carried off tens of thousands of lives under the resonant slogans about the protection of civilians'. He promised that Russia would 'not allow anything like this to happen again in the future'.[143]

In brief, Russia made tentative solidarist overtures to the wider international community at the time of Resolution 1973. These were cast aside, however, later in the year as the Syrian crisis intensified and as the Russian political elite took stock of Putin's imminent and certain return as Russian president in spring 2012. When Russia and China alone vetoed a draft Security Council resolution in February 2012, which condemned graphic human rights violations in Syria, it was clear the Russian fixation on CIS regional and domestic order once again trumped its commitment to the human-focused imperatives of R2P.

CONCLUSION: THE CHALLENGE OF NEW CONFLICTS

Russia presented its challenge to American and wider Western 'hegemony' in the international system during Putin's second presidential term in terms of principle, legality, and compliance with the UN Charter system. Putin called for the democratization of interstate relations, which essentially amounted to a levelling down of hegemonic power.

This chapter confirms that beyond high-flown rhetoric, the Russian leadership was principally focused on constitutionalist procedures, of who determines and shapes the rules and principles states are called on to follow, and how such international regulation is modified. Rules and norms related to the use of force were understood to be of overriding importance. But this was not about any true equality of states in rule-making. Russia remained wedded to the notion of a concert of great powers, operating in various configurations, but always including Russia in a prominent role. The ultimate expression of this concert is in the Security Council, where permanent members could exercise their veto rights. For Moscow, the exclusive NATO format was incompatible with this notion of concert, so Russia vigorously resisted NATO's efforts to expand its military tasks globally. As in the past, Russia also flatly rejected NATO's authority to sidestep the Security Council and mandate the use of force.

From at least 2006 Putin's discourse revealed some confidence that Russia could position itself at the forefront of an international pluralist backlash to the excessive reliance on force by the first administration of George W. Bush. Moscow hoped to mobilize the growing weight of the BRICs group of states and others affronted by US unilateralist policies and searching for ways to move towards a more multipolar international system. In this sense the Russian campaign went beyond the use of force issue. Putin and his entourage hoped that the US and major Western states could be thrown on the defensive over aspects of their wider solidarist agenda. Moscow expected, for example, that the image of democratization could be tarnished with the legacy of regime change in Iraq.

Russian reliance on the concert formed by the Security Council reinforced a persistent dilemma—how to ensure that the Security Council would remain centre stage in new international crises that could lead to some form of military action. For all their financial clout and developing diplomatic influence, the emerging powers lacked military muscle for such crises. America had the military capability, yet Russia was not the only BRICs state that did not trust the US to use force in ways it supported. For years, therefore, Moscow had been reluctant to allow Security Council authorization for the American use of *any* level of force.

Arguably 'the underlying condition for the UN's willingness to lend legal and political legitimacy to the use of American power is Washington's willingness to exercise restraint in the use of that power'.[144] Russia, like China and some other emerging powers, has doubted US restraint in military operations, even during the presidency of Barack Obama, given the experience of previous US-led interventions. At the same time they have been loath to envisage the possible alternative scenario of new coalitions of the willing, which are prepared to use force and bypass the Security Council. This scenario threatens to devalue the international role and status of that top forum and to weaken the principles by which it operates.

For years Russia has anticipated new international crises and therefore has to expect these dilemmas of procedural legitimacy and rule-making to recur. Official Russian documents, released during the Medvedev presidency, foresee an increasingly conflictual international environment driven by geopolitical competition and access to resources. Beyond this gloomy prognosis the Russian leadership has been gripped by a new preoccupation—the upsurge of conflicts associated with the Arab Spring. A series of intra-state crises have toppled longstanding authoritarian regimes. This in turn has shaken the statist world view and confidence of Russian leaders. It has reinforced their determination to raise pluralist barriers against 'externally' instigated regime change.

This backdrop has also raised the stakes in the international debate over how best to respond to fears over the Iranian nuclear programme. The Iran controversy exposes well the Russian quandary over the role of the Security Council. Moscow has robustly opposed any UN language that might later be exploited to justify an attack on Iranian targets, while also searching for ways to avoid unilateral pre-emptive actions by the US and/or Israel wholly outside the UN framework.

This is not to say that in contemporary crises Russia is likely to block any UN mandate entrusting the use of force. Russia with other Security Council members agreed to Resolution 1975, at the end of March 2011, which gave full support to the distant UN operation in Côte d'Ivoire (UNOCI) 'to use all necessary means to carry out its mandate to protect civilians under imminent threat of physical violence'.[145] Notably, however, this did not underwrite an intervention in the terms we have previously defined. It empowered further action by a peacekeeping operation which had already received host country consent. With such consent Russia could dissociate what followed from what it regarded as coercive regime change. Russia probably also found it easier to approve this mandate since the ensuing military action in Côte d'Ivoire involved French rather than US forces and removed a leader who had already lost at the polls.

This leaves Resolution 1973 over Libya when Moscow by abstaining acceded to military action in a humanitarian emergency. This case is notable not only in examining the process and evolution of rule-making, but also potentially for charting our concern with changing norms over the use of force. Two different interpretations of the case may be offered. First, it revealed simply that bridges were being laid over previous normative divisions and that by 2011 R2P principles were more embedded in international society. Secondly, emphasis could be put on the exceptional nature of this intervention, of its permissive conditions and of the discourse that surrounded it. It could be noted that the group of Security Council members which abstained over Resolution 1973 included influential states that remain sceptical about the motivations and efficacy of Western-driven military interventions.

The UN vote over Libya and the accompanying discourse, including that of Russia, undoubtedly provided some support to R2P as a norm. Yet Russia's response to the implementation of Resolution 1973 and to the protracted crisis in Syria has to dampen expectations about a new era of normative congruence around R2P principles. Moscow could not credibly challenge the procedural legitimacy of the debate over and decision to intervene in Libya, in which the Security Council played its proper role. Nor could the Russian leadership reasonably argue that the road to war in Libya resembled their template of US-led hegemonic policy. Once operations in Libya commenced, however, Moscow soon accused Western powers of exceeding the Security Council's mandate and of abusing its authority in the pursuit of illegitimate goals. This reaction and Russia's vigorous resistance, as of early 2013, to any slide towards a parallel response in the crisis over Syria, makes the Libya intervention appear as *sui generis*, rather than as the precursor of further Security Council authorized military interventions with the passive compliance of Russian leaders.

9

Conclusion

This book integrates scholarship on military interventions and the use of force with an original evaluation of Russia's role in international society. It offers a comparative analysis of Russian normative, legal, and political responses to major interventions over a period of more than two decades. Russia has occupied an important role in the post-Cold War international system, assisted by its Security Council P5 membership. It has exercised significant influence on how military interventions have been perceived, authorized, and legitimized. The focus on a major power offers a channel to trace the wider process of evolving, contested norms and customary law related to the use of force, as well as the political context to interventions. The book assesses the justificatory discourse of Russia and Western powers at the outset of major military campaigns from the Gulf War in 1990 to the Libya intervention in 2011 to chart the struggle between these states to reach agreed standards of conduct.

This discursive process has been acutely political and shaped by disparities in power between states. We reveal this by analysing a variety of Russian responses to interventions, including UN Security Council diplomacy and the politics of international law. As argued in this conclusion, however, considerations of power are insufficient to account for the normative friction or occasional congruence over the use of force between Russia and Western states since the late 1980s. For this it is necessary to acknowledge the salience of underlying and quite persistent Russian perceptions about order. These perceptions influence policy as well as discourse at different levels: the international system (global diplomacy), region (CIS diplomacy), and state (domestic politics). However, they interact and ultimately are rooted within the Russian state. We conclude that Russia and Western states should entertain no illusions that their perspectives on intervention and the use of force are likely to merge in the medium term.

RUSSIA AND MILITARY INTERVENTION: PERSISTENT TRENDS

Since the late Gorbachev years there have been only brief periods of broad convergence between the policy of Russia and Western powers over the norms, law, and politics of major military interventions. This occurred, with some fluctuations, in debate around the Gulf War during 1990–1, during the initial period of Yeltsin's presidency during 1991–2, less evidently later that decade, and perhaps in a tentative and short-lived fashion at the beginning of the Libya crisis in March 2011. Overall, during the post-Cold War era, Russian congruence with major Western states over the coercive use of force (rather than peacekeeping) has been episodic. The research puzzle this presents is not so much to account for variation in or the pattern of Russian approaches to interventions. Rather it is to explain the *consistency* of Russian scepticism and resistance to Western-led interventions, as well as the controversy which its own regional interventions have aroused in Western states.

This puzzle is not resolved by relying on the conceptual framework of realism or neo-realism, as a brief survey of Russian–Western tensions indicates. The first major case studied was anomalous. Moscow and Western capitals achieved substantial legal and normative congruence over the use of force at the outset of the Gulf War. Realists argue that Russian alignment with Western states at the time was driven principally by Russia's need for cooperation at a time of palpable decline in its relative material capabilities, an influence that continued into the early Yeltsin years. In fact the Gulf crisis involved an unusually clear violation of state sovereignty and territorial integrity. However, besides this the *extent* of Gorbachev's alignment with Western powers, in the face of serious domestic opposition, when other options were available, still needs to be explained. Nor does realism convincingly account for the growing hostility of the Russian leadership and political elite to the Western use of force in the second half of the 1990s, culminating in the dramatic showdown over Kosovo in 1999. This was not long after a precipitous slump in the Russian economy triggered by the 1998 rouble devaluation. Russian defence spending, moreover, was close to rock bottom. Russia did not bandwagon with Western states. It decried Western policy, even if it did not have the means or political will to develop any effective balancing strategy against Western powers.

Realists offer a better case in arguing that the initial period of Russian–Western bonding over the 'war on terror', during 2001–3, especially support for intervention in Afghanistan, could be viewed as a case of bandwagoning, around the agenda of counter-terrorism. Russian approval for a form of military pre-emption in this period might be explained as instrumental and mimicking US conduct. But the question remains why antagonism over the use of force resurfaced over the Iraq War and mounted during Putin's second presidency.

It might be argued that Russia, with other major European powers, was alarmed by the expansion of the geographic scope of American military interventions, beyond the exceptional case of Afghanistan, to Iraq and potentially other states, especially under the first administration of George W. Bush. This reinforced Moscow's traditional inclination to take refuge in the UN Charter legal framework and to highlight its constraints on the use of force.[1]

A renewed Russian emphasis on legality in this period was instrumental in seeking to constrain US power. But it was also diplomatically shrewd. Russia embraced the discourse and rhetoric of international law just as the US began to withdraw from participating in international legal regimes or limited its role. Russia sought to present itself as a stabilizing power in a volatile international environment.

On the other hand, the assertion of American military power in itself does not explain adequately why Putin chose to project Russia increasingly and overtly as the shield against international 'legal nihilism', as the primary challenger to what he branded as the 'hegemonic' international order fronted by the US and NATO. It does not account for Russia's persistent reluctance to agree formally to broaden the UN category of threats to international peace and security to include humanitarian emergencies. This resistance was briefly replaced by a humanitarian discourse at the onset of the Libya crisis in 2011, but after that Moscow reverted to its conventional trenchant opposition to Western-led intervention.

The argument in this volume is that the persistence of tensions between Russia and Western states over intervention, especially the rift over the potential application of force in humanitarian emergencies and the acceptability of regime change as an outcome of intervention, arises from normative friction. Throughout the period studied, norms, as well as customary law, have served to constrain and enable the behaviour of states, yet serious differences have remained. Such normative friction does not simply express the calculations of relative power between major states. For Russian leaders and the political elite it has been rooted in understandings of regional and domestic order. It is undeniable that Russian apprehensions about force at the service of power have been important, especially in the European theatre and in the Russian analysis of NATO global strategy. Yet normative divergence has mattered and not just on a Russian–Western axis. The normative and legal basis of intervention in Iraq and the use of force more widely in the prosecution of the 'war on terror', at least during the first half of the 2000s, caused a deep rift in the transatlantic community and also among European powers.

An examination of norms is especially revealing for the 'outlier' case of Russian discourse and policy during the Gulf War. A synergy in diplomacy between Russia and Western powers was nourished by the universalistic thrust of Gorbachev's New Thinking on foreign and security policy, including its emphasis on all-human values. It enabled a brief period of normative congruence between Moscow and Western powers (lubricated by certain unilateral Soviet concessions). New Thinking failed, however, to sink deep roots in the Russian political elite or society at large. A focus on order within the state re-emerged as power was contested within Moscow, and as the new Russian state engaged in conflicts first on its periphery and then the North

Caucasus. Domestic political support for idealistic humanism in Russia's new foreign policy faded in the early 1990s.

In terms of the English School distinction between solidarist and pluralist international outlooks, Russia has appeared mainly as a qualified pluralist state since that period. This stance was consolidated in the later years of Yeltsin's presidency. Russian discourse was increasingly sceptical about the solidarist focus on individuals rather than states. It displayed lacklustre interest in efforts to 'thicken' the normative content of international society. More emphasis was given to the pluralist language of sovereignty and non-intervention. By the end of the 1990s Moscow led diplomatic resistance to the notion of developing criteria for humanitarian intervention.

However, Russian tension with Western powers over the use of force, especially since the Kosovo crisis, also has reflected more fundamental differences about who establishes the normative agenda in the first place.[2] This question of who makes the rules is one of constitutionalist procedures in the global system. It has been expressed in Moscow's assertion of rightful influence, most prominently by Putin, and the way Russia has prized its Security Council membership. Putin has tried to rally support for Russian positions from major emerging powers (the BRICS group), ones which promise a shift in global politics and the ability to constrain the previous capacity of the Western states to set global standards and rules of behaviour.[3] Alongside the BRICS and the non-aligned states, Russia has questioned whether the norms and legal claims cited to justify Western-led interventions have been representative of the will of the international community at large.[4]

Procedural rules in international society and how these are influenced by disparities in power provide an important context for understanding the normative tensions we have described. Russian self-consciousness about its power ranking helps to explain why Russia does not act as if fully signed up to non-Western pluralism. This is evident if we accept Ayoob's argument about tension between the Northern and Southern perspectives on order and justice in the international system. Ayoob claims that 'while the North is primarily interested in justice within states and order among them, the South is basically committed to order within states and justice among them'.[5] For Russia justice among states (regardless of how this had been regarded in the era of Soviet ideology) has been about its acceptance within a concert of major powers and not, for example, an expression of sovereign equality with its smaller CIS neighbours.

Nevertheless, the criticism of solidarist approaches to intervention found in official and academic Russian discourse has quite a lot in common with central concerns of Western pluralist scholars about humanitarian intervention: that sovereign states are not likely to agree as to what counts as injustice or oppression inside a state, and so are unlikely to agree when humanitarian intervention would be justified; that efforts to assert a consensus on human rights may undermine the fragile order existing in international society; indeed that humanitarian intervention in whatever guise may escalate into a wider more destabilizing conflict. For conflicts from Kosovo to Libya Russia has argued that 'ultimately only the people themselves can determine the fate of their countries and that outside military intervention in internal conflicts poses risks of spiralling confrontation in the respective parts of the world'.[6]

JUSTIFICATIONS, NORMATIVE CHANGE, AND INTERNATIONAL LAW IN REVIEW

This volume analyses justifications for intervention as an indicator of norms and normative change. Such justifications may be used to hide the often complex motives of states, but an important premise of the study is that justifications seek to connect actions to evolving standards of appropriate and acceptable behaviour. Norms may be violated by states, but once they become embedded in international organizations (such as the UN) and institutions, the process of norm institutionalization, such abuse happens less and at greater cost to the violating state. Studies of humanitarian intervention, for example, have revealed a shift historically towards the multilateral organization of such action, preferably under UN auspices or with explicit multilateral consent.[7]

A key question is how far the Kosovo intervention in 1999 and the reconfigured debate that followed about states' responsibility to protect their citizens precipitated a basic shift towards humanitarian norms in international society. Or was this a development just within a particular sphere of international society?

As we show, the weakness of normative and legal justifications by Western states for Operation Allied Force in 1999, the abusive appeal to humanitarianism by the US during the Iraq War, the controversy over bypassing Security Council authorization, as well as the cautious American approach in the emerging debate on R2P, all positioned Russia's continued repudiation of armed humanitarianism in the early 2000s rather more in the mainstream of international society than on its fringes. The pluralist charge that Western states were ready to promote a new standard of civilization, in the form of armed intervention justified by the defence of human rights, found some resonance beyond Russia among other sovereignty-oriented non-Western leaderships.

In the period after the 2005 UN World Summit conference the Russian position on R2P remained quite centrist. Overall, however, Moscow chose to cast itself as the most vocal major power and Security Council member in contesting Security Council involvement in humanitarian crises. By 2011, at the outset of the Libya crisis, Russia used solidarist language in what seemed a broader shift among states to institutionalize R2P norms. But Russia repudiated the ensuing Libya campaign and Putin presented obdurate resistance to Security Council approval for more decisive action to assist the civilian population as the Syria crisis degenerated into civil war.

In contrast, Russian discourse and policy conformed quite closely with Western powers over the one major intervention which was undertaken clearly in response to egregious acts of transnational terrorism and was justified on the grounds of self-defence. In the case of intervention in Afghanistan in 2001 and efforts at stabilization in that state, Moscow even acceded to modifications in customary law to underpin the action taken. An important influence at the time was Russia's effort to validate its own military campaign in Chechnya.

Moscow has been conservative over change in customary international law, aware of the tendency for dominant powers (hence America) to drive such change. Yet Russian leaders, considering military options in their neighbourhood, went beyond the rationale for the Afghanistan campaign to explore the acceptability of variants of pre-emptive self-defence in the early 2000s, mimicking the US. Later in the decade Russian international lawyers remained interested in the notion of pre-emptive strikes against terrorist groups, though not against sovereign states.[8] In 2011 Russia suggested that the United Nation's prior endorsement of the American right of self-defence in 2001 by extension justified the US operation which led to the death of Osama Bin Laden in Pakistan.[9]

Despite this position in response to terrorism, Russia has tended to hold fast to a form of international legal positivism in its broader stance on military intervention and the use of force. This is especially so when contesting solidarist claims for intervention. International legal positivists claim that only unilateral or collective self-defence and Security Council enforcement action under Chapter VII of the UN Charter can form exceptions to the Charter's general prohibition on the use of force.

Russia has yielded only some ground from this traditionalist interpretation to emerging norms on the use of force. Moscow has positioned itself far from a naturalist reading of international law, especially a human-rights approach that views individuals as the subjects of international law and the role of international law as the protection of human rights. This alternative perspective, which has particular currency in UN circles, has been anathema to Moscow under Putin, even if the Russian state formally accepts the binding quality of international humanitarian law.[10] From its predominantly pluralist stance, Russia has expected international law essentially to regulate the competition of states, to constrain Western power as well as to provide a discursive shield for the Russian state, rather than to protect human beings.

Russia legalistic discourse, emphasizing lawful conduct in terms of the international legal system, has often been used also as a yardstick of legitimacy. However, Moscow has conceived of international legitimacy particularly as conduct which complies with a legally structured constitutional order at the global level, as expressed through the UN Charter system. To legitimize military intervention this requires a focus on procedural rules, rather than basic values. As noted previously, the question of 'who makes the rules' has been of abiding concern to Russian leaders. This has also shaped their view of the appropriateness of international standards, of norms. The recognition of Russia's role in rule-making, and in defining the normative agenda itself, speaks directly to its international status and leverage. This suffered a steep decline during the 1990s. The Russian political elite struggled thereafter to restore some sense of international grandeur.

Consequently when Russia felt its Security Council veto had been eclipsed, over Kosovo in 1999 and Iraq in 2003, it shook Russian confidence and rankled deeply. It was this, as well as emerging concerns over the implications for CIS regional and domestic Russian state order (see below), rather than the infringement of legal principle, that drove Moscow's acrimonious rhetoric under Yeltsin and Putin about the dangers of a 'lawless world'. The Russian focus on constitutionality in the international system was also reflected in its acerbic response at different times to the planned extension of NATO's global role, to the prospect of NATO just consulting the UN but not submitting itself to Security Council authorization for the use of force. In summer 2010 Lavrov testily responded that 'this will provoke the temptation to say: if NATO can do it, why can't we?'[11]

Russia even described the application of force in Libya in 2011, despite the authorization provided by Resolution 1973, as a failure to legitimize collective actions. It argued that a group of Western states had seized the agenda over the application of military force, as with earlier interventions in Kosovo and Iraq.[12] Russia worries about this recurring in the form of action against Iran, where it has been difficult to envisage any Western or Israeli use of force achieving Security Council endorsement or conforming to UN Charter principles on the use of force. For Russia the dilemma has been how to avoid Security Council validation of military action against Iran without the serious risk that certain states will bypass the Security Council altogether in deciding on an intervention and so further erode Russia's rule-making influence and veto power.

Yet for all its insistence on international legality and procedural rules, Russia acknowledges that change in customary law is possible and that this occurs not just in response to state practice and *opinio juris*, but may also be influenced discursively through debates on the application of military force. Equally, Russian diplomats appear to acknowledge that normative justifications can be influential and gain traction in international society, if not contested. Russia invoked humanitarian claims at the time of its intervention in Georgia in 2008 and used humanitarian language before military action began in Libya in March 2011. However, these are troubling cases if we seek evidence of some shift towards solidarism in Russian diplomacy. Moscow's abusive use of such claims in the Georgian case, as analysed in chapter 7, and defence of the Syrian regime from Security Council censure during 2011–12 raise questions about the instrumental nature of normative discourse and about norm compliance.

This study has not sought to determine which factors best encourage norm compliance among states, but we can recognize a spectrum of reasons why a state may wish to legitimize its conduct by reference to a shared norm. First, there are instrumental decisions to avoid reputational or other costs; here a norm is not considered to have inherent value and therefore is not 'internalized'. Second, further along the spectrum there is 'mimicking', where compliance is driven more by generalized concern about social exclusion. In these two cases, states and other actors 'are likely to adopt the norm's language while persisting with established patterns of behaviour'. This is helped by the indeterminacy of a norm like R2P.[13] Such mimicking may form a route to the eventual internalization of a norm, but this process could also be reversed.[14] Russian justifications for its intervention in Georgia in 2008 seemed to combine instrumentalism and mimicking. If the Libya crisis initially suggested some Russian internalization of R2P, the case of Syria shows regression to a position consistent with entrenched Russian perspectives on regional and domestic state order.

NORMS, LAW, AND THE CIS REGIONAL ORDER

In the introduction to this volume it was suggested that the domain of a norm, if contested or weak, may be confined to a region, or it may be promoted, defined, and interpreted for that region by a regionally preponderant or hegemonic power. In chapter 6 we argue that the power structure within the CIS region has been hierarchical, in favour of Russia. This has been reflected in Russian interventionism in the regional order, most explicitly in the early 1990s. Our analysis confirms that Russian efforts to maintain this power structure in the CIS region qualify the sovereignty of smaller states. We raise the question whether there has been an effort in the region to develop certain norms as well as treaty principles, albeit ones mainly defined by Russia. Specifically, has it been possible for norms related to the use of force to emerge?

The concept of regional public orders offers insights. It suggests the possibility that Russia, as a would-be regional hegemon, has a particular conception of norms which it enforces, and seeks to socialize others into viewing as legitimate, within its sphere of influence.[15] As regards the use of force these could relate to mandates for peacekeeping, self-determination, the protection of Russian citizens abroad, etc. The consolidation of this kind of normative regionalism, its evolution into some kind of 'regional international society', depends, however, on the internalization of its constituent norms by states other than Russia. For this, as for international society at the global level, coerced compliance to regional rules and norms should be exceptional. Compliance should increasingly be motivated by considerations of self-interest and ultimately legitimacy, by which point the intrinsic value of the norm is acknowledged.[16]

Since at least the early 2000s there is evidence that a particular form of self-interested normative regionalism has emerged among authoritarian CIS leaderships (principally Russia, Belarus, and Central Asian states). They have bonded with Moscow through regional structures as a political act to fend off solidarist agendas promoted by Western states and organizations and to bolster their regime security. The concept of human security in contrast is almost absent in the discourse and security doctrines of these states.

However, such an 'authoritarian convergence' offers a poor prospect for the consolidation of a regional international society among even a subset of CIS states, while the much more demanding task of developing regional norms on matters related to the use of force has foundered on the rock of state sovereignty. CIS leaders of all political shades in practice have sought to retain their sovereign decision-making authority, for example, in approving peacekeeping in their neighbourhood (in the absence of a UN Security Council mandate). They have resisted providing Russia-dominated regional structures, the CIS in the 1990s or the CSTO since 2003, with broad mandates for the use of force. Nor have they codified any special rights for Russia to protect its citizens abroad (essentially in CIS conflicts). During 2010–12, with the outbreak of the popular revolts of the Arab Spring, most CSTO member states were persuaded to offer this body a potential military role in intra-state crises. But this was rejected by the strategically core Central Asian state, Uzbekistan, which suspended its CSTO membership in 2012.

In brief, CIS states have been wary of Russian power, knowing that Russia has traditionally regarded sovereignty as a capacity not a right. For Moscow sovereignty has implied self-sufficiency and sovereign power has been equated with Great Power. As a corollary, according to this thinking, besides Russia none of the other CIS states can be truly sovereign. This perception antagonizes even the non-Western oriented CIS leaders.

Russia considers the image it has adopted as a central player in the wider international system to support and validate its assumption of special security 'responsibilities' in its chosen regional theatre. Russia has presented itself as the security manager of what was termed the 'near abroad' in the 1990s, or in President Medvedev's phrase in 2008, 'regions in which Russia has privileged interests'. For Moscow, it has been a hallmark of a great, aspiring global, power to be able to shape if not control the political and security policy trajectory of a neighbouring regional order (this also provides the context to the 2008 Russia–Georgia war).

One aspect of this Russian ambition links the CIS region to global norms—Russia's hope that CIS states will join its discourse and policy stance in condemning Western-led interventions. However, we show that CIS state leaders have generally been reluctant to condemn outright NATO and American justifications for their military campaigns, or to be corralled into repeating Russian rhetoric about the threats posed the Western 'hegemonic order'. Russia has failed to solidify some kind of Eurasian pluralist front of CIS states or even Shanghai Cooperation Organization states against Western-led interventions to buttress its global diplomacy. This kind of grandstanding has had a little more success in the wider setting of the BRICS group, which Moscow expects to influence global rule-making more broadly.

Russia's defiant responses to Western-led interventions to some extent have reflected the fear that such use of force may cascade down to the CIS regional order. Moscow has sought to forestall any precedent of legitimizing Western interventions further afield, especially if this involves bypassing the Russian Security Council veto, in part with such regional implications in mind. Ever since the clash over Kosovo in 1999, Russian media commentators and even officials have popularized scenarios of Western involvement within conflicts in the CIS region, or sometimes the Russian Federation itself such as Chechnya. Such alarmist thinking has fluctuated and been influenced by calculations of the changing power balance in Europe and globally. This has reflected some anxiety about NATO 'out of area' strategic planning, as well as competition with Western states over the security policy trajectory of CIS countries.

It may seem unlikely that Russian leaders have seriously considered Western military intervention in a CIS conflict, let alone Chechnya, as a possibility. However, this would disregard traditional Russian fears of encirclement and concerns over ebbing Russian influence in many CIS states. Russia has appeared to bolster its pluralist defences in global diplomacy against Western 'intrusion' in this regional order. During Putin's first two presidential terms Russia contested emerging norms or changes in customary law, and resisted Security Council mandates, when it was feared these might later be used to justify international attention to humanitarian crises in the CIS and other regions where Russian interests were centred. The underlying concern was that normative or legal claims might be geographically redirected to validate externally assisted regime change in CIS states, especially after the US developed a focus on regime change in the Middle East.

The CIS coloured revolutions during 2003–5, which Putin characterized as 'state projects' by Western powers, strongly reinforced his determination to resist 'external intrusion' in general in Russia's neighbourhood. This impulse was reinvigorated in 2011, when the Arab Spring showed the vulnerability of longstanding authoritarian rulers and the Libya intervention confirmed how action for humanitarian objectives led by Western states could easily escalate into a determination to replace the local leadership.

Russia's major military intervention in Georgia in 2008 offers further evidence of how for Moscow norms and legal principles interact between global and regional levels. In justifying its campaign in Georgia Moscow appealed to the legal right of self-defence (not the contested notion of military pre-emption), rooted in the UN Charter's respect for sovereignty, and bolstered this with humanitarian claims drawn from global solidarist discourse. On the other hand, Russia's actual conduct in Georgia and the wider CIS region continued to display its belief in a firmly hierarchical order, with qualified sovereignty for smaller states, and was inconsistent with humanitarian norms, such as R2P.

The inconsistency of Russian diplomacy and official discourse with global standards, in this crisis and other periods of tension with CIS neighbours, reflects an effort to sustain a dual normative order, regional and global. One way of viewing this might be in terms of 'hybrid norms'; Russian officials have often interpreted norms differently when applied to the CIS regional setting. Moscow has exercised discretion in interpreting global principles of sovereignty and non-intervention in a region it which it asserts special entitlements. The same has applied to customary law in specific fields, such as the protection of (Russian) nationals abroad.

Such discretion, a pick and mix approach, in general has been unconvincing to other states. If expressed too frequently or blatantly it would undermine the normative and legal regulation on which Russia relies in the international system at large. However, a wider study may show it as hardly unique behaviour for major powers with ambitions to manage their neighbouring regions. This would require further research on the role of hegemons in different world regions and the possible emergence, as noted in chapter 1, of 'regional public orders'.

Be that as it may, in the 2008 crisis with Georgia Moscow probably also hoped that its battery of normative and legal claims might be persuasive by reverberating among different leaders, elites, and publics: within Western states and the international community at large, within the CIS region, and domestically within the Russian state. The targeting of different audiences with overlapping arguments may account for the 'scattershot' approach of Russian discourse in this crisis. However, Russia's subsequent recognition of South Ossetia and Azkhazia, by privileging separatism and secession over sovereignty, was an own goal for Russian policy with its CIS partners. Moscow's provocative recognition of new states in Georgia, after subjecting it to a major military offensive, with no efforts to explore alternative political arrangements, has also made it difficult to sustain a righteous legalistic posture on the wider international stage in criticizing Western-led interventions.

NORMS, LAW, AND RUSSIAN STATE ORDER

The introduction of this study posed a central hypothesis: that a crucial relationship exists between, on the one hand, Russian normative preferences and strategic priorities with respect to *international* order (both global and CIS regional), and on the other hand the Russian understanding of domestic *state* order. Moscow's conception of international society, it was suggested, has reflected a front rank priority to preserve its domestic structure of power. This domestic structure traditionally has been centralized and hierarchical, and has given primacy to order over justice. It is manifested in official Moscow's qualified pluralist emphasis on sovereignty on the international stage and its increasing resistance after the early 1990s (with some fluctuations) to efforts to transmit 'external' norms and values, read as Western values, to the Russian domestic order.

Our analysis confirms that the leadership and much of the political elite in Russia have perceived a close relationship between domestic and international order. This explains Russia's diplomatic stance and international behaviour in ways that cannot be done just by focusing on the country's relative power in the international system or on the differing mindsets of presidents Yeltsin (more open, flexible) and Putin (more closed, entrenched). Gorbachev, it is true, attempted to challenge the dominance of domestic state order, to gradually reform the traditional hierarchy of power within the state and to introduce the solidarist thinking of all-human values and the interdependence of states. To succeed this required a revolution in domestic political values and foreign policy thinking. However, this effort at norm transformation failed to establish roots in the Soviet and then Russian political establishment and society. The effort to reorder values was not widely recognized as of inherent worth and so was not internalized by elites.

Normative contestation in Russian domestic politics continued into the 1990s. Even towards the end of the Yeltsin presidency it was reflected in fierce debates within Moscow over the Western intervention in Kosovo. It was subdued, however, in the early 2000s as an emphasis on statist values progressively became the official political orthodoxy under Putin. The slogan of 'sovereign democracy' linked the defence of the hierarchical Russian domestic political order with autonomy in international affairs.

Moscow clashed with Western powers on the regional level over the legitimacy of the coloured revolutions in CIS states and on the wider international stage over support for regime change in the Middle East. Russia also resisted efforts more generally to advance human security at the expense of state sovereignty. These processes and agendas challenged the pluralist shell Putin sought to maintain around the Russian state and his underlying insistence that Russia alone should define what was acceptable in its process of state building and the preservation of domestic order (including over

Chechnya). Tension in Russian–Western relations mounted during Putin's second presidential term, as evidence accumulated that democratic values and procedures, as prized by Western states, were failing to consolidate either intellectually among the Russian elite or institutionally within the Russian state.

The authoritarian trajectory of Russian politics under Putin cannot simply be explained away or justified by referring to Russia's own national culture and traditions. Nonetheless, a focus on domestic order, hierarchy, and control has been strongly represented, even historically embedded, in Russian political culture.[17] This focus was increasingly present in the dominant political discourse under Putin. It began to reassert itself already during Yeltsin's leadership in the 1990s, despite the progress made in democratization in that period. 'In the case of norm innovation', Bellamy argued, 'states, most particularly the great powers, will be motivated to reproduce at the international level the values enshrined in their domestic political cultures.'[18] This nexus of values helps explain the persistence of normative tension between Russia and liberal Western powers over solidarist justifications for intervention in the domestic jurisdiction of states.

This conclusion requires some qualification and clarification. First, besides Russia many other pluralist-minded states have prioritized their domestic political structure and indeed regime security, China being only the most notable. Secondly, since 2001 the exigencies of the 'war on terror' have considerably complicated the relationship between the domestic political values of states and international norms. For example, the efforts of those who advocate a solidarist interpretation of R2P have often been undermined by the conduct of major Western states. Russian diplomats, among others, could also expose broader inconsistencies between Western normative/legal discourse and conduct. Thirdly, it is noteworthy that the salience of domestic political values has had particular influence on American compliance with various international norms in the period studied.[19]

After 2001 the 'war on terror', as defined principally by the US in a broader coalition, provided scope for more flexible interpretations of norms and international law and loosened their constraining influence on the use of force in general. Exceptionalism in the global policy outlook of the US, especially before Obama's election in 2008, was the source of substantial international friction over rules and rule-making. Russian discourse and policy displayed its own form of exceptionalism, but this was focused particularly on the CIS regional theatre. This made it easier for Russia to take refuge in legalistic claims in global diplomacy, especially since major European powers also sought to avoid the unravelling of established law.

By the time Putin returned to his third presidential term in spring 2012 the debate on intervention had shifted its focus from the 'war on terror' to the Arab Spring. Yet Putin's interpretation of the Libya intervention and crisis in

Syria remained defiantly at odds with that of Western powers. If we review the previous decade of Russian discourse it is Russia's fixation on traditional sovereignty which shines through. Russian leaders have drawn a line between the coloured revolutions in CIS states, US policies under George W. Bush for regime change, and to a considerable extent the uprisings of the Arab Spring. These phenomena have been presented similarly as externally inspired efforts to transform the domestic order of states for strategic ends, a process ultimately threatening Moscow itself. A report by the Russian Chief of General Staff in November 2011, for example, described the use of the coloured revolutions 'technique' by 'some countries' leaders' in removing regimes in the Middle East and North Africa. He suggested this technique may be applied later to Russia.[20]

The Russian leadership has displayed a deep aversion to validating efforts to change the structure of power and authority within foreign states by force of arms, with the exception of the overthrow of the Taliban and of course its own interventions in CIS conflicts. This is true even if such political change, whether in Kosovo, Iraq, or Libya, occurred only as an eventual outcome of interventions, for which diverse normative and legal justifications had previously been offered. However, Russian antipathy to linking the notion of regime legitimacy to any external enforcement action is a pluralist red line shared not only by many other states where regime security is prioritized over human security, but also by those who simply distrust the strong to impose justice as *they* understand it.[21]

The events in Libya in 2011 and Syria since that year show such pluralist resistance in international society has weakened in the face of egregious human rights abuses by states. The Russian leadership's response, however, betrays insecurities at both international and domestic levels of policy. Russia asserts its credentials as an aspirant global power and prizes its Security Council membership, yet remains preoccupied by disparities in global power. It wields its Security Council veto to influence international rule-making and talks of the rise of non-Western powers, yet still lacks confidence about its ability to shape international norms. Even so, Russian leaders accept that normative and legal constraints on the use of force may evolve and in various ways have evolved since the early 1990s, with implications for sovereignty. They accept that new understandings on these matters develop through a politically charged discursive exchange among states in which they must engage.

Nevertheless, despite Putin's re-election to his third presidential term in spring 2012, the current Russian leadership enjoys uncertain political legitimacy at home and abroad. It nurses fears of becoming the object of greater leverage by Western powers, especially the United States, if domestic tensions rise in Russia or the wider CIS region. This factor reinforces a traditional determination by Moscow to hold fast to its Security Council veto, to privilege sovereignty at the expense of humanitarian protection in international society, and to resist consolidation of a human-focused conception of international justice. Russia remains entrenched on the periphery of the Western community of states, seeking further inclusion yet unprepared in the pursuit of this goal to reconfigure its particular understanding of regional and domestic state order.

Notes

Chapter 1 Military Intervention, Norms, and the Case of Russia

1. Christian Reus-Smit, 'International Law', in John Baylis, Steve Smith, and Patricia Owens (eds.), *The Globalization of World Politics: An Introduction to International Relations* (New York: Oxford University Press, 2008), pp. 279–94 (p. 290). See also David Armstrong, Theo Farrell, and Hélène Lambert, *International Law and International Relations* (Cambridge: Cambridge University Press, 2007), pp. 95–106.
2. S. Neil MacFarlane, *Intervention in Contemporary World Politics* (Oxford: International Institute for Strategic Studies, 2002), Adelphi Paper 350, p. 14.
3. Martha Finnemore, 'Constructing Norms of Humanitarian Intervention', in Peter J. Katzenstein (ed.), *The Culture of National Security: Norms and Identity in World Politics* (New York: Columbia University Press, 1996), p. 154.
4. Until Resolution 1973, authorizing a no-fly zone over Libya in March 2011, the Security Council had never authorized the use of military force for humanitarian purposes against the wishes of a functioning state.
5. For an analysis of the normative frameworks governing targeted killings and related legal issues, see Nils Melzer, *Targeted Killing in International Law* (Oxford: Oxford University Press, 2008). See also Amitai Etzioni, 'The "Secret" Matrix', *The World Today*, 66/7 (July 2010), pp. 11–14.
6. For Chapter VII, see http://www.un.org/en/documents/charter/chapter7.shtml.
7. On this and associated literature see David Armstrong, 'Introduction', *International Studies*, 31, Special Issue, 'Force and Legitimacy in World Politics' (December 2005), pp. 9–11.
8. Martha Finnemore and Kathryn Sikkink, 'International Norm Dynamics and Political Change', *International Organization*, 52/4 (Autumn 1998), p. 916.
9. Finnemore and Sikkink, 'International Norm Dynamics and Political Change', p. 891.
10. Finnemore, 'Constructing Norms of Humanitarian Intervention', pp. 157–8.
11. Finnemore, 'Constructing Norms of Humanitarian Intervention', pp. 157–8. See also Friedrich V. Kratochwil, 'How Do Norms Matter?', in Michael Byers (ed.), *The Role of Law in International Politics* (Oxford: Oxford University Press, 2000), pp. 35–68.
12. MacFarlane, *Intervention in Contemporary World Politics*, p. 11.
13. Tim Dunne, 'The New Agenda', in Alex Bellamy (ed.), *International Society and its Critics* (Oxford: Oxford University Press, 2005), p. 69.
14. Finnemore and Sikkink, 'International Norm Dynamics and Political Change', p. 892.
15. Finnemore, 'Constructing Norms of Humanitarian Intervention', p. 159.

16. See Martha Finnemore, 'Changing Norms of Humanitarian Intervention', and 'Intervention and International Order', in Martha Finnemore, *The Purpose of Intervention: Changing Beliefs about the Use of Force* (Ithaca and London: Cornell University Press, 2003), chs. 3 and 4.
17. Ian Johnstone, 'Discursive Power in the UN Security Council', *Journal of International Law and International Relations*, 2/1 (Winter 2005), pp. 73, 87–8.
18. While political scientists have tended to slip into discussion of 'sovereignty' as if it were a norm, it is in fact a collection of norms and the mix of rules and practices that have structured it has varied significantly over time; Finnemore and Sikkink, 'International Norm Dynamics and Political Change', p. 891.
19. See, for example, Nicholas J. Wheeler, *Saving Strangers: Humanitarian Intervention in International Society* (Oxford: Oxford University Press, 2000); Nicholas Kerton-Johnson, *Justifying America's Wars: The Conduct and Practice of US Military Intervention* (London: Routledge, 2011).
20. In chapter 4 some more attention is paid to the practice of intervention in Afghanistan since this protracted campaign has been important for understanding the wider, politically malleable 'war on terror' and use of force debates around that.
21. Andrew Hurrell, 'Legitimacy and the Use of Force: Can the Circle be Squared?', *Review of International Studies*, 31, Special Issue, 'Force and Legitimacy in World Politics' (December 2005), pp. 16–17.
22. Theoretical approaches to the concept of legitimacy in international relations, with particular reference to intervention, are reviewed in Corneliu Bjola, *Legitimising the Use of Force in International Politics: Kosovo, Iraq and the Ethics of Intervention* (London and New York: Routledge, 2009), pp. 1–18. For a wider study on the sources of normative change and the process by which international society comes to accept certain principles and practices of legitimacy rather than others, see Ian Clark, *International Legitimacy and World Society* (Oxford: Oxford University Press, 2007).
23. Jens Steffek, 'Legitimacy in International Relations: From State Compliance to Citizen Consensus', in Achim Hurrelmann, Steffen Schneider, and Jens Steffek (eds.), *Legitimacy in an Age of Global Politics* (Basingstoke: Palgrave Macmillan, 2007), pp. 175–92.
24. Rosemary Foot and Andrew Walter, *China, the United States and Global Order* (Cambridge: Cambridge University Press, 2011), pp. 290–3.
25. These are explored in *Review of International Studies*, 31, Special Issue, 'Force and Legitimacy in World Politics' (December 2005).
26. Richard Falk, 'Legality and Legitimacy: The Quest for Principled Flexibility and Restraint', *Review of International Studies*, 31, Special Issue, 'Force and Legitimacy in World Politics' (December 2005), pp. 33–50.
27. Hurrell, 'Legitimacy and the Use of Force', p. 19.
28. Hurrell, 'Legitimacy and the Use of Force', p. 18.
29. Hurrell, 'Legitimacy and the Use of Force', pp. 24–5. Ian Clark, *Legitimacy in International Society* (Oxford: Oxford University Press, 2005), pp. 194–206.
30. Clark, *Legitimacy in International Society*, pp. 207–9, 216, 252–6.
31. John G. Ikenberry, *After Victory: Institutions, Strategic Restraint and the Rebuilding of Order after Major Wars* (Princeton, NJ: Princeton University Press, 2001), as cited in Clark, *Legitimacy in International Society*, p. 220.

32. Regarding CIS conflicts see Andrew Bennett, *Condemned to Repetition? The Rise, Fall and Reprise of Soviet-Russian Military Interventionism, 1973–1996* (Cambridge, MA: MIT Press, 1999), pp. 301–28.
33. For the role of such interpretative communities, see Bjola, *Legitimising the Use of Force in International Politics*, pp. 15–16.
34. For an assessment of Russian foreign and security policy decision-making as of 2005, including the input of the State Duma, see Stephen White, 'The Domestic Management of Russia's Foreign and Security Policy', in Roy Allison, Margot Light, and Stephen White, *Putin's Russia and the Enlarged Europe* (Oxford: Blackwell, 2006), pp. 30–41.
35. At the time of writing (July 2012), Prikhodko had been deputy head of the Presidential administration in charge of international affairs, as well as head of the Presidential Foreign Policy Directorate, since 1999.
36. During the controversy over intervention in Iraq in 2003, for example, Russian Deputy Foreign Minister Yuri Fedorov covered all UN business in the ministry, especially related to Security Council proceedings, and oversaw the ministry's International Organizations and Legal departments.
37. Roy Allison, 'Military Factors in Foreign Policy', in Neil Malcolm, Alex Pravda, Roy Allison, and Margot Light, *Internal Factors in Russian Foreign Policy* (Oxford: Oxford University Press, 1996), pp. 220–85.
38. Brandon M. Stewart and Yuri M. Zhukov, 'Use of Force and Civil–Military Relations in Russia: An Automated Content Analysis', in Paul B. Rich (ed.), *Crisis in the Caucasus: Russia, Georgia and the West* (London: Routledge, 2011), pp. 70, 86–7. The source base was 7,920 public statements. See also Allison, 'Military Factors in Foreign Policy'.
39. See Nicholas J. Wheeler, 'Pluralist and Solidarist Conceptions of International Society: Bull and Vincent on Humanitarian Intervention', *Millennium*, 21/3 (1992), pp. 463–87.
40. For an examination of the nature of plural and pluralist civilizations for the analysis of world politics see Peter J. Katzenstein (ed.), *Civilizations in World Politics: Plural and Pluralist Perspectives* (London: Routledge, 2009).
41. MacFarlane, 'Intervention in Contemporary World Politics', pp. 1–2. See Jennifer M. Welsh, 'A Normative Case for Pluralism: Reassessing Vincent's Views on Humanitarian Intervention', *International Affairs*, 87/5 (September 2011), pp. 1193–204; Mohammed Ayoob, 'Humanitarian Intervention and State Sovereignty', *The International Journal of Human Rights*, 6/1 (Spring 2001), pp. 81–102.
42. Martha Finnemore, 'Fights About Rules: The Role of Efficacy and Power in Changing Multilateralism', *Review of International Studies*, 31, Special Issue, 'Force and Legitimacy in World Politics' (December 2005), pp. 188–94.
43. Armstrong, 'Introduction', p. 10.
44. Barry Buzan, 'The Middle East through English School Theory', in Barry Buzan and Ana Gonzalez-Pelaez (eds.), *International Society and the Middle East: English School Theory at the Regional Level* (Basingstoke: Palgrave Macmillan, 2009), pp. 28–30.
45. Buzan, 'The Middle East through English School Theory', pp. 34–5.
46. Christopher J. Borgen, 'Whose Public, Whose Order? Imperium, Region, and Normative Friction', *Yale Journal of International Law*, 32 (2007), pp. 333–41.

47. S. Neil MacFarlane, 'Russian Perspectives on Order and Justice', in Rosemary Foot, John Gaddis, and Andrew Hurrell (eds.), *Order and Justice in International Relations* (Oxford: Oxford University Press, 2003), pp. 184–5, 206.

Chapter 2 The Soviet Union and Cold War Interventions

1. In the following analysis I draw on Martha Finnemore, *The Purpose of Intervention: Changing Beliefs about the Use of Force* (Ithaca and London: Cornell University Press, 2003), pp. 124–9.
2. For an empirical survey of types and patterns of Soviet intervention see Alex P. Schmid, *Soviet Military Interventions since 1945* (New Brunswick and Oxford: Transaction Books, 1985), pp. 143–59.
3. This global struggle is best presented by Odd Arne Westad, *The Global Cold War: Third World Interventions and the Making of Our Times* (Cambridge: Cambridge University Press, 2005). There are numerous Cold War era analyses of specific interventions in the Third World. For one overview see Karen A. Feste, *American and Soviet Intervention: Effects on World Stability* (New York: Crane Russak, 1990). A growing literature re-examines these interventions on the basis of more recently released primary source materials.
4. For an argument that in the Soviet discussion of intervention there existed a perceived relationship between the freedom of Soviet interventionist behaviour and the specific stage of the strategic balance (which during Brezhnev's leadership was believed to be moving in the Soviet favour), see Keith Payne, 'Are They Interested in Stability? The Soviet View of Intervention', *Comparative Strategy*, 3/1 (1983), pp. 1–24.
5. Alexander I. George, 'US–Soviet Global Rivalry: Norms of Competition', *Journal of Peace Research*, 23/3 (1986), pp. 244–62.
6. Such norms of competition are identified in Roy Allison and Phil Williams, 'Crisis Prevention: Patterns and Prospects', in Roy Allison and Phil Williams (eds.), *Superpower Competition and Crisis Prevention in the Third World* (Cambridge: Cambridge University Press, 1990), pp. 249–57.
7. Finnemore, *The Purpose of Intervention*, p. 135.
8. For a critique of the lawlessness of this intervention, see Francis A. Boyle et al., 'International Lawlessness in Grenada', *The American Journal of International Law*, 78 (1984), pp. 172–5. See also Christopher C. Joyner, 'The United States Action in Grenada: Reflections on the Lawfulness of Invasion', *The American Journal of International Law*, 78 (1984), pp. 131–44.
9. A careful examination of these claims by one international lawyer concluded that 'the U.S. action was in disregard of the pertinent norms and principles of international law on the use of force' and that 'the intervention was evidently dictated by political considerations'. Ved P. Nanda, 'The Validity of the United States Intervention in Panama under International Law', *The American Journal of International Law*, 84 (1990), p. 502.
10. Thomas Franck and Edward Weisband, *World Politics: Verbal Strategies among the Superpowers* (New York: Oxford University Press, 1971), especially pp. 96–113.
11. Boyle, 'International Lawlessness in Grenada', p. 174.

12. As cited in Rein Mullerson, 'Self-Defense in the Contemporary World', in Lori Fisler Damrosch and David J. Scheffer (eds.), *Law and Force in the New International Order* (Boulder: Westview Press, 1991), p. 16. For analysis of the *Nicaragua* case see Mullerson, 'Self-Defense in the Contemporary World', pp. 16–21 and, among many contemporary legal analyses, Christine Gray, *International Law and the Use of Force* (Cambridge: Cambridge University Press, 2008), pp. 15–16, 169–83.
13. Address before a Joint Session of the Congress on the State of the Union, 6 February 1985, as cited in Mullerson, 'Self-Defense in the Contemporary World', p. 15.
14. For a broad discussion of such factors in relation to foreign policies see Alfred J. Richter, 'How Persistent are Persistent Factors?', in Robert Legvold (ed.), *Russian Foreign Policy in the 21st Century and the Shadow of the Past* (New York: Columbia University Press, 2007), pp. 205–78.
15. S. Neil MacFarlane, 'Russian Perspectives on Order and Justice', in Rosemary Foot, John Gaddis, and Andrew Hurrell (eds.), *Order and Justice in International Relations* (Oxford: Oxford University Press, 2003), p. 188.
16. MacFarlane, 'Russian Perspectives on Order and Justice', p. 186.
17. John Quigley, 'Perestroika and International Law', *The American Journal of International Law*, 82/4 (October 1988), p. 795.
18. For the clash over international legal principles, understandings of sovereignty, and the application of law see, for example, M. M. Abakov (ed.), *Narusheniya SShA Norm Mezhdunarodnogo Prava* (Moscow: Mezhdunarodnye Otnosheniya, 1984).
19. See Julian Lider, *Correlation of Forces: An Analysis of Marxist-Leninist Concepts* (Aldershot: Gower, 1986); Julian Lider, 'The Correlation of World Forces: The Soviet Concept', *Journal of Peace Research*, 17/2 (1980), pp. 151–71.
20. MacFarlane, 'Russian Perspectives on Order and Justice', p. 187.
21. For general analyses of these Soviet claims see R. Vincent, 'Soviet Doctrine and Practice', in Raymond John Vincent, *Nonintervention and International Order* (Princeton, NJ: Princeton University Press, 1974), pp. 145–87; A. Cassese (ed.), *The Current Legal Regulation of the Use of Force* (Dordrecht: Martinus Nijhoff, 1986), pp. 433–77; Caroline Thomas, *New States, Sovereignty and Intervention* (Aldershot: Gower, 1985), pp. 52–63.
22. Robert A. Jones, *The Soviet Concept of Limited Sovereignty: From Lenin to Gorbachev* (Basingstoke: Macmillan, 1990), pp. 87–9.
23. Jones, *The Soviet Concept of Limited Sovereignty*, p. 90.
24. John Norton Moore and Robert F. Turner, *International Law and the Brezhnev Doctrine* (Lanham, MD: University Press of America, 1987), pp. 88–93.
25. This ideological justification was set out in 'The Defence of Socialism is a Supreme International Duty', *Pravda*, 22 August 1968, p. 3. See also Moore and Turner, *International Law and the Brezhnev Doctrine*, pp. 94–102. Soviet decision-making in this case is analysed in Jiri Valenta, *Soviet Intervention in Czechoslovavkia, 1968* (Baltimore: Johns Hopkins University Press, 1979) and Karen Dawisha, *The Kremlin and the Prague Spring* (Berkeley: University of California Press, 1984).
26. Speech by Gromyko on 3 October 1968; by Brezhnev on 12 November 1968, as cited in Moore and Turner, *International Law and the Brezhnev Doctrine*, p. 102.

27. Arguably this applied to the leaders of Yugoslavia (Tito), Albania (Hoxha), and Romania (Ceausescu). See Christopher D. Jones, 'Soviet Hegemony in Eastern Europe: The Dynamics of Political Autonomy and Military Intervention', *World Politics*, 29/2 (January 1977), pp. 216–41. For varying patterns of Soviet intervention in Eastern Europe see Jiri Valenta, 'Revolutionary Change, Soviet Intervention and "Normalization" in East-Central Europe', *Comparative Politics*, 16/2 (January 1984), pp. 133–40.
28. For internal Soviet decision-making on the intervention, based on released primary source material, see Artemy Kalinovsky, 'Decision-Making and the Soviet War in Afghanistan: From Intervention to Withdrawal', *Journal of Cold War Studies*, 11/4 (2009), pp. 46–73; Westad, *The Global Cold War*, pp. 316–26; Odd Arne Westad, 'Concerning the Situation in "A": New Russian Evidence on the Soviet Intervention in Afghanistan', *Cold War International History Project Bulletin*, 8–9 (Winter 1996/7), pp. 128–32. For a large tranche of primary Soviet documents used in these analyses see the virtual archive of the Cold War International History Project at http://wwics.si.edu. See also 'Kak prinimalos' reshenie', *Voenno-istoricheskiy zhurnal*, 7 (1991), pp. 40–52; A. O. Gokov, 'Vvod sovetskikh voysk v Afganistan v 1979 godu', *Voenno-istoricheskiy zhurnal*, 12 (2009), 43–4.
29. For an evaluation of motivations in the case of Afghanistan, see A. Z. Hilali, 'The Soviet Decision-Making for Intervention in Afghanistan and its Motives', *The Journal of Slavic Military Studies*, 16/2 (June 2003), pp. 113–45.
30. In a letter to Soviet Communist Party leader Leonid Brezhnev in early December 1979 the Soviet KGB head Yuri Andropov claimed that Amin's conduct had created 'a danger of losing the domestic achievements of the Afghan revolution', and that there was now no guarantee that Amin 'in order to secure his personal power, would not turn to the West', Westad, *The Global Cold War*, pp. 319–20. For a comparison of the Czech and Afghan interventions (although without the benefit of Soviet primary source material), see Jiri Valenta, 'From Prague to Kabul: The Soviet Style of Invasion', *International Security*, 5/2 (Fall 1980), pp. 114–41.
31. General Assembly, Sixth Emergency Special Session, ES-6/2, 14 January 1980, available at http://daccess-dds-ny.un.org/doc/RESOLUTION/GEN/NRO/209/43/IMG/NR020943.pdf. Cuba, however, which at the time chaired the Non-Aligned Movement, supported the Soviet position. We may note that the US invasion of Grenada a few years later received a roughly similar General Assembly negative vote.
32. Vernon Aspaturian, 'Soviet Global Power and the Correlation of Forces', *Problems of Communism*, 29 (May–June 1980), p. 17.
33. This case is made by Rafael Reuveny and Aseem Prakash, 'The Afghanistan War and the Breakdown of the Soviet Union', *Review of International Studies*, 25/4 (1999), pp. 693–708.
34. For decision-making on Soviet withdrawal from Afghanistan, see Kalinovsky, 'Decision-Making and the Soviet War in Afghanistan', pp. 59–73; Fred Halliday, 'Soviet Foreign Policymaking and the Afghanistan War: From "Second Mongolia" to "Bleeding Wound"', *Review of International Studies*, 25/4 (1999), pp. 679–91; Diego Cordovez and Selig Harrison, *Out of Afghanistan: The Inside Story of the Soviet Withdrawal* (Oxford: Oxford University Press, 1995). For an argument that

for several years Gorbachev applied a form of the Brezhnev Doctrine to the Third World, but 'modified it to exclude non-vital Third World Marxist allies, which can not be defended with comparatively moderate military assistance from the established socialist states', see Mark N. Katz, 'The Evolution of the Brezhnev Doctrine under Gorbachev', in Kurt M. Campbell and S. Neil MacFarlane (eds.), *Gorbachev's Third World Dilemmas* (London: Routledge, 1989), p. 57.

35. For an argument that realist and liberal explanations cannot adequately account for New Thinking's revolutionary character that made the transformation of superpower relations possible, see Robert G. Herman, 'Identity, Norms and National Security: The Soviet Foreign Policy Revolution and the End of the Cold War', in Peter J. Katzenstein (ed.), *The Culture of National Security: Norms and Identity in World Politics* (New York: Columbia University Press, 1996), pp. 271–36. Herman identifies a profound reconceptualization of Soviet state interests 'rooted in new collective understandings about casual relationships in international politics and in regulatory and constitutive norms', p. 310.
36. For the new potential for superpower cooperation over regional conflicts see Melvin A Goodman (ed.), *The End of Superpower Conflict in the Third World* (Boulder: Westview Press, 1992).
37. See Mikhail Gorbachev, *Perestroika: New Thinking for our Country and the* World (2nd edn.) (London: Fontana Collins, 1988). Among many Western studies see Stephen M. Meyer, 'The Sources and Prospects of Gorbachev's New Political Thinking on Security', *International Security*, 13 (Fall 1988), pp. 124–63; Roy Allison, 'New Thinking on Defence Policy in the Soviet Union', in Ken Booth (ed.), *New Thinking about Strategy and International Security* (London: Unwin Hyman, 1991), pp. 215–43; Elizabeth K. Valkenier, 'New Soviet Thinking about the Third World', *World Policy Journal*, 4/4 (Fall 1987), pp. 651–74; Robert Legvold, 'The Revolution in Soviet Foreign Policy', *Foreign Affairs*, 68/1 (1989), pp. 82–98.
38. Steven Kull, *Burying Lenin: The Revolution in Soviet Ideology and Foreign Policy* (Boulder: Westview Press, 1992), p. 165.
39. Rey Koslowski and Friedrich Kratochwil, 'Understanding Change in International Politics: The Soviet Empire's Demise and the International System', *International Organization*, 48/2 (Spring 1994), pp. 215–47.
40. As argued by Andrew Bennett, 'The Guns That Did Not Smoke: Ideas and the Soviet Non-Use of Force in 1989', *Journal of Cold War Studies*, 7/2 (Spring 2005), pp. 81–109.
41. Speech on 7 December 1988, *Pravda*, 8 December 1988, as cited in Kull, *Burying Lenin*, p. 166. See also John Quigley, 'Perestroika and International Law', pp. 788–97.
42. These Soviet proposals are analysed in Jonathan Haslam, 'The UN and the Soviet Union: New Thinking?', *International Affairs*, 65/4 (Autumn 1989), pp. 677–84; Thomas G. Weiss and Meryl A. Kessler, 'Moscow's U.N. Policy', *Foreign Affairs*, 79 (Summer 1990), pp. 94–112.
43. This process is recounted in Cordovez and Harrison, *Out of Afghanistan*.
44. For this retrenchment in Soviet Third World policy see Margot Light, 'Soviet Policy in the Third World', *International Affairs*, 67/2 (April 1991), pp. 263–80; 'Gorbachev's "New Thinking" and Third World Regional Conflicts Conceptualized',

Part 1 in Jiri Valenta and Frank Cibulka (eds.), *Gorbachev's New Thinking and Third World Conflicts* (New Brunswick and London: Transaction Publishers, 1990).

45. Although, as analysed in later chapters in this volume, a dominant power in the international system, such as the US, is well-placed to influence the adaptation of legal norms to conform with political objectives.
46. For analyses of legal justifications in the process leading to the Gulf War see Marc Weller, 'The United Nations and the *jus ad bellum*', in Peter Rowe (ed.), *The Gulf War 1990–91 in International and English Law* (London: Routledge, 1993), pp. 23–45; Paul W. Kahn, 'Lessons for International Law from the Gulf War', *Stanford Law Review*, 45/2 (January 1993), pp. 425–41; Ken Matthews, *The Gulf Conflict and International Relations* (London: Routledge, 1993), pp. 139–44.
47. Weller, 'The United Nations and the *jus ad bellum*', p. 25. Notably the rationale for this collective response in autumn 1990 remained the need to enforce Kuwait's sovereign rights rather than the requirement to protect Kuwaiti citizens.
48. Lawrence Freedman and Efraim Karsh, *The Gulf Conflict 1990–1991: Diplomacy and War in the New World Order* (Princeton, NJ: Princeton University Press, 1993), p. 73.
49. Freedman and Karsh, *The Gulf Conflict 1990–1991*, p. 212.
50. Kahn, 'Lessons for International Law from the Gulf War', p. 431.
51. Resolution 678, 29 November 1990, adopted by 12 votes to 2 (Cuba and Yemen) with 1 abstention (China), available at http://dacess-dds-ny.un.org/doc/RESOLUTION/GEN/NRO/575/IMG/NR057528.pdf.
52. Soviet statement on 9 September 1990, *The Guardian*, 10 September 1990.
53. Statement by Gorbachev on 31 August 1990, *The Guardian*, 1 September 1990; Gorbachev–Bush Joint Statement, 9 September 1990, Tass, 9 September 1990, in *BBC Summary of World Broadcasts. Soviet Union* (henceforth SU) 0866 C1/1, 11 September 1990.
54. Speech to UN General Assembly on 25 September 1990, *The Guardian*, 26 September 1990, p. 1.
55. Speech to UN General Assembly on 25 September 1990, *The Guardian*, 26 September 1990, p. 8.
56. Statement to emergency session of the USSR Supreme Soviet Presidium, Moscow central television, 17 January 1991, as cited in Benjamin J. Lambeth, *Desert Storm and its Meaning: The View from Moscow* (Santa Monica: RAND Report, 1992), p. 23.
57. Interview on Soviet Gostelradio, 26 January 1991, SU/0981 A1/3, 28 January 1991.
58. Weller, 'The United Nations and the *jus ad bellum*', pp. 35–6.
59. Freedman and Karsh, *The Gulf Conflict 1990–1991*, p. 376.
60. For example, interview with Marshal of the Soviet Union V. G. Kulikov, *Rabochaya Tribuna*, 19 February 1991, p. 1, in *Joint Publication Research Service* (henceforth JPRS) UMA-91-008, 18 March 1991. Kulikov also raised the issue of proportionality and the tension between the new thinking proclaimed by the world community and 'the massacre that was brought about in the Persian Gulf zone', which 'shows quite graphically how dubious such approaches become when the world community attempts to create a new order using an old instrument, by which I mean war'.

61. Interview for *L'Unita*, 28 February 1991, p. 6, in *Foreign Broadcast Information Service* (henceforth FBIS) SOV-91-042, 4 March 1991.
62. The Soviet ambassador to Turkey, Albert Chernyshev, interview on 28 January 1991, SU/0982 A4/4, 29 January 1991.
63. Interview for *L'Unita*, 28 February 1991, p. 6, FBIS-SOV-91-042, 4 March 1991.
64. Andrei S. Grachev (deputy head of the Central Committee's International Department and subsequently Gorbachev's personal spokesman), 'A War for Peace?', *Novoye vremya*, 17 (April 1991), pp. 20–2.
65. For a good analysis of these domestic debates, see Galia Golan, 'Gorbachev's Difficult Time in the Gulf', *Political Science Quarterly*, 107/2 (Summer 1992), pp. 213–30.
66. Edwin Bacon, 'Military Reform and Soviet Analysis of the 1991 Gulf War', *The Journal of Soviet Military Studies*, 5/2 (June 1992), p. 184. See also throughout Lambeth, *Desert Storm and its Meaning*.
67. For example, General Vladimir Lobov, Chief of Staff of the armed forces of the Warsaw Pact, noting the deployment of US and NATO troops and equipment to the Gulf, queried 'whether this kind of situation will lead to a significant expansion of NATO's southern flank', and asked 'How will all this affect the East–West strategic balance?' Moscow World Service, 19 September 1990, SU/0375 A4/1, 21 September 1990. For geopolitical analyses by military specialists, see V. A. Veselov, D. G. Yevstaf'ev, and P. P. Skorospelov, 'Geopoliticheskiy aspekt voyny v zone Persidskogo zaliva', *Voennaya mysl*, 3 (1993), pp. 20–7; Major-General A. Gushev, 'Voenno-politicheskie posledstviya voyny v zone Persidskogo zaliva', *Zarubezhnoe voennoe obozrenie*, 8 (1991), pp. 3–7.
68. Freedman and Karsh, *The Gulf Conflict 1990–1991*, p. 375.
69. For the convolutions of this policy see Freedman and Karsh, *The Gulf Conflict 1990–1991*, pp. 76–80, 125–7, 162–5, 175–9, 374–85; Graham E. Fuller, 'Moscow and the Gulf War', *Foreign Affairs*, 70/3 (Summer 1991), pp. 55–76.
70. Suzanne Crow, 'Primakov and the Soviet Peace Initiative', *Radio Free Europe/Radio Liberty Report on the USSR*,. 3/9, 1 March 1991, pp. 14–17.
71. Speech to UN General Assembly, 25 September 1990, *The Guardian*, 26 September 1990, p. 1.
72. Lambeth, *Desert Storm and its Meaning*, pp. 12–13.
73. Lambeth, *Desert Storm and its Meaning*, p. 19; Freedman and Karsh, *The Gulf Conflict 1990–1991*, pp. 126–7.
74. Text circulated by Shevardnadze to joint session of the chambers of the USSR Supreme Soviet, 12 December 1990, Tass, 12 December 1990, SU/0948 C1/1, 15 December 1990. Shevardnadze qualified his statement, however, in promising the use of force by the USSR, against Iraq by implication 'in cases where the life and security of Soviet citizens are threatened'.
75. Excerpts of speech on 20 December 1990, SU/0953 i, 21 December 1990. This was just after the deputy commander of the Soviet Indian Ocean fleet rejected outright the idea that any Soviet naval forces could be sent to the Gulf; Rear Admiral V. Boyarkin. 'A "Cyclone" is Brewing', *Sovetskaya Rossiya*, 19 December 1990.
76. Press conference by A. A. Besmertnykh, 28 February 1991, 'On the Eve of Talks', *Pravda*, 1 March 1991, p. 4.

77. Address to UN General Assembly, *New York Times*, 2 October 1990, p. A12; Address to the nation, 16 January 1991, both cited in Kull, *Burying Lenin*, p. 173.
78. *Pravda*, 1 March 1991, p. 4; *Washington Post*, 1 March 1991, p. 31.
79. Resolution 688, 5 April 1991, http://daccess-dds.un.org/doc/RESOLUTION/GEN/NRO/596/24/IMG/NR059624.pdf.
80. Weller, 'The United Nations and the *jus ad bellum*', p. 45.
81. Response to query from a group of RSFSR People's Deputies, *Krasnaya zvezda*, 8 June 1991, p. 2.
82. For the decline of the New Thinking in the new Russian state, see Celeste A. Wallander, 'Lost and Found: Gorbachev's "New Thinking"', *The Washington Quarterly*, 25/1 (Winter 2002), pp. 117–29.

Chapter 3 Humanitarian Intervention, Kosovo, and Beyond: Divergent Norms

1. In the large literature on the international dimensions of the Kosovo conflict see, for example, Alex Bellamy, *Kosovo and International Society* (Basingstoke: Palgrave Macmillan, 2002); Ken Booth (ed.), *The Kosovo Tragedy: The Human Rights Dimensions* (London: Frank Cass, 2001); Marc Weller, *Contested Statehood: Kosovo's Struggle for Independence* (Oxford: Oxford University Press, 2009); and for the views of the communications director at the time for US Deputy Secretary of State Strobe Talbott, John Norris, *Collision Course: NATO, Russia and Kosovo* (Westport, CT: Praeger, 2005). On the discussion of OAF as a humanitarian war, see especially Nicholas J. Wheeler, *Saving Strangers: Humanitarian Intervention in International Society* (Oxford: Oxford University Press, 2000), pp. 257–84.
2. For an analysis which emphasizes Russian accusations against NATO action around Kosovo, see Derek Averre, 'From Pristina to Tskhinvali: The Legacy of Operation Allied Force in Russia's Relations with the West', *International Affairs*, 85/3 (May 2009), pp. 575–87.
3. Weller, *Contested Statehood*, p. 157. German Foreign Minister Klaus Kinkel emphasized in particular that NATO had not created any new legal instrument, which could be the basis for a general licence for NATO to do interventions; Wheeler, *Saving Strangers*, p. 262.
4. Press conference, released on 25 March 1999, in Heike Krieger (ed.), *The Kosovo Conflict and International Law: An Analytical Documentation 1974–1999* (Cambridge: Cambridge University Press, 2001), p. 419.
5. Catherine Guicherd, 'International Law and the War in Kosovo', *Survival*, 41/2 (Summer 1999), pp. 26–7. A majority of states were not prepared to accept a doctrine of implied authorization (although this resurfaced in connection with the Iraq War in 2003). On this debate see Christine Gray, *International Law and the Use of Force* (Oxford: Oxford University Press, 2008), pp. 341–3.
6. Nicholas J. Wheeler, 'The Humanitarian Responsibilities of Sovereignty', in Jennifer M. Welsh (ed.), *Humanitarian Intervention and International Relations* (Oxford: Oxford University Press, 2004), p. 42.
7. Foreign and Commonwealth paper circulated to NATO capitals, October 1998, cited in Adam Roberts, 'NATO's "Humanitarian War" over Kosovo', *Survival*,

41/3 (1999), p. 106. The NATO Secretary-General Javier Solana similarly justified NATO's threat of military action by the 'imminent risk of humanitarian catastrophe', as well as by former Security Council resolutions. Summary of North Atlantic Council consultations of 9 October 1998, cited in Guicherd, 'International Law and the War in Kosovo', pp. 27–8.

8. US representative in Security Council 3988th Meeting, 24 March 1999, S/PV.3988, pp. 4–5, http://daccess-dds-ny.un.org/UNDOC/PRO/N99/852/09/PDF/N9985209.pdf; UK representative in Security Council 3989th Meeting, 26 March 1999, Press Release SC/6659, http://www.un.org/News/Press/docs/1999/19990326.sc6659.html.
9. President Clinton, Address to the Nation, 24 March 1999, in Krieger (ed.), *The Kosovo Conflict and International Law*, pp. 415–16.
10. US Senate, NATO's 50th Anniversary Summit, hearing before the Committee on Foreign Relations, 106th Congress, first session, 21 April 1999, in Krieger (ed.), *The Kosovo Conflict and International Law*, pp. 422–3.
11. Abraham D. Sofaer, 'International Law and Kosovo', *Stanford Journal of International Law*, 36/1 (2000), p. 13.
12. Interview in Konstantin Eggert, 'Only a Miracle Can Stop a New Balkan War', *Izvestiya*, 4 June 1998, p. 3.
13. James Headley, *Russia and the Balkans: Foreign Policy from Yeltsin to Putin* (New York: Columbia University Press, 2008), pp. 336–45.
14. Statement by Sergei Lavrov at 3988th meeting of the UN Security Council, 24 March 1999, also quoting statement by President Yeltsin of same day, http://daccess-dds-ny.un.org/UNDOC/PRO/N99/852/09/PDF/N9985209.pdf.
15. These Russian statements are discussed fully in Wheeler, *Saving Strangers*, p. 263.
16. Statement by Sergei Lavrov at 4011th meeting of the Security Council, 10 June 1999, http://www.un.org/News/Press/docs/1999/19990610.SC6686.html.
17. Lavrov at 3988th meeting of the UN Security Council, 24 March 1999, http://daccess-dds-ny.un.org/UNDOC/PRO/N99/852/09/PDF/N9985209.pdf.
18. Foreign Minister Igor Ivanov at press conference, 2 April 1999; the Permanent Mission of Russia to the OSCE, Vienna, 23 April 1999, set out in detail Russia's claims of NATO's mass violations of human rights and humanitarian commitments in the FRY and went so far as to describe NATO actions as inducing 'the greatest humanitarian disaster in Europe after the end of the second world war', in Krieger (ed.), *The Kosovo Conflict and International Law*, pp. 486, 487–9.
19. Statement by official representative of the Ministry of Foreign Affairs, 3 April 1999, in Krieger (ed.), *The Kosovo Conflict and International Law*, p. 487.
20. Ivanov at press conference, 2 April 1999, in Krieger (ed.), *The Kosovo Conflict and International Law*, p. 485.
21. Statement by Sergei Lavrov at 3989th meeting of the UN Security Council, 26 March 1999, http://daccees-dds-ny.un.org/doc/UNDOC/PRO/N99/852/15/PDF/N9985215.pdf.
22. Michael E. Aleprete Jr., 'Democratic Politics and Russian Foreign Policy: Russia's Domestic Debate and the Conflict in Kosovo', *Journal of International Relations and Development*, 3/4 (December 2000), pp. 10–15 (online version).

23. Statement by Sergei Lavrov at 4000th meeting of UN Security Council, 8 May 1999, Press Release SC/6674/Rev.1, http://www.un.org/News/Press/docs/1999/19990508.SC6674.R1.html.
24. These responses were proposed, for example, by Colonel-General Leonid Ivashov, director of the Department for International Military Cooperation of the Russian Ministry of Defence and Gennady Zyuganov, leader of the Russian Communist Party, Dmitri Gornostayev, 'West Gives Belgrade Ultimatum', *Nezavisimaya gazeta*, 13 October 1998, pp. 1, 6; 'Russian Deputies Eager to Defend Serbs', *Segodnya*, 13 October 1998, p. 3.
25. Gennady Sysoyev, 'Time Running Out on Ultimatum to Belgrade', *Kommersant-Daily*, 13 October 1998, p. 4.
26. Dmitri Gornostaev and Viktor Sokolov, 'Boris Yeltsin announces that "we will not allow Kosovo to be touched"', *Nezavisimaya gazeta*, 19 February 1999, p. 1.
27. Alex J. Bellamy, 'Lessons Unlearned: Why Coercive Diplomacy Failed at Rambouillet', *International Peacekeeping*, 7/2 (Summer 2000), p. 110.
28. Aleprete, 'Democratic Politics and Russian Foreign Policy', p. 11.
29. For the spectrum of political debate on how Russia should respond to OAF and on its implications for international order, see Andrei P. Tsygankov, 'The Final Triumph of the Pax Americana? Western Intervention in Yugoslavia and Russia's Debate on the Post-Cold War Order', *Communist and Post-Communist Studies*, 34/2 (June 2001), pp. 133–56.
30. Viktor Litovkin, 'Our Armoured Train to Belgrade is Already at the Siding', *Obshchaya gazeta*, 13, 1–7 April 1999, p. 2.
31. Dmitri Gornostayev, 'NATO's Invasion of Yugoslavia May Happen as Soon as this April', *Nezavisimaya gazeta*, 9 April 1999, pp. 1, 6.
32. Vladimir Atlasov, 'Will NATO Start Inspecting Russian Oil Tankers?', *Nezavisimaya gazeta*, 29 April 1999, pp. 1, 6.
33. Irina Borogan, 'Volunteers are Going to Fight in the Balkan War', *Segodnya*, 24 May 1999, pp. 1–2.
34. Cited in Gennady Sysoev, 'Only Madmen Would Want to Deliver Arms to Yugoslavia', *Kommersant-Daily*, 7 April 1999, p. 3. See also Headley, *Russia and the Balkans*, pp. 372–80.
35. Paul Latawski and Martin A. Smith, *The Kosovo Crisis and the Evolution of Post-Cold War Security* (Manchester: Manchester University Press, 2003), pp. 104–5.
36. In the words of the Commander of Russian Airborne Troops, Colonel General Georgi Shpak, 'we pride ourselves on that operation—by means of it we forced NATO to reckon with the Russian military', interview in Rosa Tsvetkova, 'We are Going into a War', *Vremya*, June 1999, pp. 1–2. In reality the Russian forces at Slatina found themselves isolated and ineffective as reinforcements failed to arrive. For a solid analysis of the whole affair, see Headley, *Russia and the Balkans*, pp. 410–16.
37. Speech by Sergei Lavrov at 3989th Meeting of the Security Council, 26 March 1999, Press Release SC/6659, http://www.un.org/News/Press/docs/1999/19990326.sc6659.html.
38. For a breakdown of the arguments by those states opposing this resolution see Wheeler, *Saving Strangers*, pp. 275–81.

39. Vladimir Baranovsky, 'The Kosovo Factor in Russia's Foreign Policy', *International Spectator*, 35/2 (April–June 2000), p. 116.
40. Chinese representative at 4000th meeting of the Security Council, 8 May 1999, Press Release SC/6674/Rev.1, http:www.un.org/News/Press/docs/1999/19990508.SC6674.R1.html. China had also threatened to veto any Security Council resolution authorizing force against the FRY in October 1998 and condemned OAF in March 1999 in similar terms to Russia; see Kieger (ed.), *The Kosovo Conflict and International Law*, p. 491.
41. For the context of this re-engagement of Russia with NATO over Kosovo, see Dov Lynch, '"Walking the Tightrope": The Kosovo Conflict and Russia in European Security, 1998–August 1999', *European Security*, 8/4 (Winter 1999), pp. 57–83.
42. Archil Gegeshidze, Chief Georgian Presidential Aide. He suggested that military operations similar to the Balkan campaign should be launched in Abkhazia, Karabakh, and the Transdniester region. Yuri Chubchenko, 'The Balkan War has Increased Differences among the CIS Armies', *Kommersant-Daily*, 26 March 1999, p. 4.
43. Sally N. Cummings, 'Perceptions in the Commonwealth of Independent States', in Mary Buckley and Sally N. Cummings (eds.), *Kosovo: Perceptions of War and its Aftermath* (London: Continuum, 2001), pp. 182–6.
44. Cummings, 'Perceptions in the Commonwealth of Independent States', pp. 177–82, 186–7. James Sherr and Steven Main, *Russian and Ukrainian Perceptions of Events in Yugoslavia* (Camberley: Conflict Studies Research Centre, 1999), pp. 18–21.
45. Declaration adopted on 3 April 1999, in Krieger (ed.), *The Kosovo Conflict and International Law*, p. 487.
46. Baranovsky, 'The Kosovo Factor in Russia's Foreign Policy', p. 116.
47. For an overview of Russia–NATO relations from this point, see Vicktor Gobarev, 'Russia–NATO Relations after the Kosovo Crisis: Strategic Implications', *The Journal of Slavic Military Studies*, 12/3 (September 1999), pp. 1–17.
48. Lynch, '"Walking the Tightrope"', pp. 63, 66–7.
49. Igor Ivanov, interview by Konstantin Eggert, *Izvestiya*, 28 October 1998, pp. 1, 6.
50. Alliance's Strategic Concept, 24 April 1999, http://www.nato.int/cps/en/natolive/official_texts_27433.htm.
51. Igor Ivanov in *Nezavisimaya gazeta*, 25 June 1999, pp. 1, 6. Boris Kazantsev (Deputy Director of the European Cooperation Department of the Russian Foreign Ministry), 'NATO: Obvious Bias to the Use of Force', *International Affairs* (Moscow), 45/4 (1999), pp. 38–9.
52. Mikhail Gorbachev, 'The US Tested its New Doctrine in Kosovo', *Nezavisimaya gazeta*, 8 July 1999, p. 3. See also his article 'A Greeting to Arms?' *Argumenty i fakty*, April 1999, p. 4.
53. 'Kosovo Crisis, One Year On', Igor Ivanov, *Nezavisimaya gazeta*, 23 March 2000, and *Nezavisimaya gazeta—diplomaticheskiy kurier*, No. 5, March 2000, p. 9.
54. 'A Dangerous Precedent for International Security', Marshal Igor Sergeev, *Krasnaya zvezda*, 25 March 2000, pp. 1, 3.
55. Baranovsky, 'The Kosovo Factor in Russia's Foreign Policy', p. 125.
56. Yu. V. Morozov, V. V. Glushkin, and A. A. Sharavin, *Balkany segodnya i zavtra: voennopoliticheskie aspekty mirotvorchestva* (Moscow: Centre of Military Strategic

Studies of the Russian General Staff and Institute of Political and Military Analysis, 2001), p. 308.

57. 'Russia and NATO Council's Statement on Chechnya', Russian Foreign Ministry Statement, 3 December 1999, Press Release of Russian Embassy, London, 6 December 1999. Dmitri Gornostaev, 'Vollebaek Complains to Albright about Russia', *Nezavisimaya gazeta*, 4 December 1999, pp. 1, 6.
58. 'On the NATO Council's Statement of December 15, 1999', undated Russian Foreign Ministry Statement, Press Release of Russian Embassy, London, 17 December 1999.
59. 'On the NATO Council's Statement of December 15, 1999'. However, for an analysis of the international legal context to a theoretical humanitarian intervention in Chechnya, see Geoff Larson, 'The Right of International Intervention in Civil Conflicts: Evolving International Law on State Sovereignty in Observance of Human Rights and Application to the Crisis in Chechnya', *Transnational Law and Contemporary Problems*, 11 (Spring 2001), pp. 251–75.
60. Grigori Vazhin and Alexander Zhilin, 'Outcome of the Balkans War is Already Evident', *Nezavisimaya gazeta*, 10 April 1999, p. 6; Morozov et al., *Balkany segodnya i zavtra*, p. 303.
61. Morozov et al., *Balkany segodnya i zavtra*, p. 305.
62. For the prior debate on justified intervention, see Laura W. Reed and Carl Kaysen (eds.), *Emerging Norms of Justified Intervention* (Cambridge, MA: American Academy on Arts and Sciences, 1998).
63. For brief summaries of this variation in legal opinion, see Steven Haines, 'The Influence of Operation Allied Force on the Development of the *jus ad bellum*', *International Affairs*, 85/3 (May 2009), pp. 477–80; Kosovo (House of Commons Select Committee on Foreign Affairs, HC 28, 2 vols., Fourth Report of Session 1999–2000, 7 June 2000), summarized evidence of witnesses on international law, http://www.publications.parliament.uk/pa/cm199900/cmselect/cmfaff/28/2813.htm.
64. Kofi Annan, speech on 7 April 1999. Cited by Ove Bring, 'Should NATO Take the Lead in Formulating a Doctrine on Humanitarian Intervention?', *NATO Review*, 3 (Autumn 1999), p. 25. For a careful discussion of legality and normative evolution in the context of Kosovo, see Nicholas J. Wheeler, 'Reflections on the Legality and Legitimacy of NATO's Intervention in Kosovo', in Ken Booth (ed.), *The Kosovo Tragedy: The Human Rights Dimensions* (London: Frank Cass, 2001), pp. 145–63.
65. Wheeler, *Saving Strangers*, p. 281.
66. Marc Weller, 'Forcible Humanitarian Action: The Case of Kosovo', in Michael Bothe, Mary Ellen O'Connell, and Natalino Ronzitti (eds.), *Redefining Sovereignty: The Use of Force after the Cold War* (Ardsley, NY: Transnational Publishers, 2005), p. 313.
67. Corneliu Bjola, *Legitimising the Use of Force in International Politics: Kosovo, Iraq and the Ethics of Intervention* (London: Routledge, 2009), pp. 107–9.
68. Richard Falk, 'Legality and Legitimacy: The Quest for Principled Flexibility and Restraint', *Review of International Studies*, Special Issue (December 2005), p. 36.

69. Independent International Commission on Kosovo, *The Kosovo Report: Conflict; International Response; Lessons Learned* (Oxford: Oxford University Press, 2000). The Commission recommended a framework of principles, which allowed for considerable interpretative discretion in their application to actual situations, to guide and assess legitimacy undertakings. *The Kosovo Report*, p. 39.
70. Falk, 'Legality and Legitimacy', p. 37, referring to Michael J. Glennon, *Limits of Law, Prerogatives of Power: Interventionism after Kosovo* (New York: Palgrave Macmillan, 2001).
71. Guicherd, 'International Law and the War in Kosovo', p. 30.
72. R. H. Jackson, *The Global Covenant: Human Conduct in a World of States* (Oxford: Oxford University Press, 2000), pp. 289–90.
73. Wheeler, 'Reflections on the Legality and Legitimacy of NATO's Intervention in Kosovo', p. 161.
74. Vladimir Baranovsky, 'Humanitarian Intervention: Russian Perspectives', *Pugwash Occasional Papers*, 2/1 (January 2001), pp. 11–12; http://pugwash.org/reports/rc/como_russia.htm.
75. United Nations General Assembly Fifth-fourth Session, *Official Records* A/54/PV.4, in Headley, *Russia and the Balkans*, p. 496; *Monitor* (Jamestown Foundation), 5/175, 23 September 1999.
76. Sergey Lavrov, Russian Permanent Representative to the UN, 'The Russian Approach: The Fight against Genocide, War Crimes and Crimes against Humanity', *Fordham International Law Journal*, 23/2 (1999), p. 421.
77. Address by Foreign Minister Tang Jiaxuan, at UN General Assembly Fifty-fourth Session, 22 September 1999, http://www.fmprc.gov.cn/eng/ziliao/3602/3604/t18058.htm.
78. Such analyses may reflect or impact on debate in official circles. For an outstanding non-official Russian analysis, see Baranovsky, 'Humanitarian Intervention: Russian Perspectives', pp. 1–14.
79. Anatolii Torkunov, Rector of the Moscow State Institute of International Relations, 'International Relations in the Post-Kosovo Context', *International Affairs* (Moscow), 46/1 (2000), p. 78.
80. Stanislav Chernichenko, Professor at the Diplomatic Academy of the Russian Foreign Ministry, 'NATO's Operation in Yugoslavia and International Law', *International Affairs* (Moscow), 46/1 (2000), pp. 172–3.
81. The official Foreign Policy Concept of the Russian Federation, approved by Putin on 28 June 2000, simply described humanitarian intervention as promoted in order 'to justify unilateral forceful actions circumventing the UN Security Council'. The section entitled 'human rights and international relations' did not mention humanitarian intervention, but defined Russia's goal broadly as 'searching for respect of human rights and freedoms all over the world on the basis of observing the norms of international law'. See http://www.fas.org/nuke/guide/russia/doctrine/econcept.htm.
82. Statement by Vladimir Putin after Security Council meeting held by President Yeltsin, 12 May 1999, Interfax news agency, Moscow, 12 May 1999, in *BBC Monitoring Online*, BBC Mon FS1 FsuPol gar.

83. Address by Putin, 1 February 2000 after multilateral Middle East Peace talks in Moscow, *Monitor* (Jamestown Foundation), 7/23, 2 February 2000.
84. Statement by Vladimir Putin after Security Council meeting held by President Yeltsin, 12 May 1999.
85. Itar-Tass news agency, Moscow, 25 July 2000, *BBC Summary of World Broadcasts. Former Soviet Union* (henceforth SU) 3902 B/3, 26 July 2000.
86. Draft of military doctrine, *Krasnaya zvezda*, 9 October 1999, pp. 3–4.
87. As argued, for example, in a monograph by military analysts on threats to Russia and the development of the Russian armed forces; described by Sergei Orlov, 'On Military Threats to Russia', *Krasnaya zvezda*, 29 September 2000, p. 3.
88. Morozov et al., *Balkany segodnya i zavtra*, pp. 272–3.
89. Russian Foreign Ministry statement, Press Release, Russian Embassy, London, 10 June 2000.
90. 'On the second anniversary of NATO aggression against the FRY', Russian Foreign Ministry statement, Press Release, Russian Embassy, London, 27 March 2001. To stop this spread of conflict, in this statement Moscow even called for decisive action by the international community, under Security Council leadership, 'if necessary, by use of force'. Russia sought to turn the tables on OAF, in calling for an international intervention against Albanian militants. See the similar demand by Putin, *Kommersant*, 20 March 2001, p. 3.
91. Baranovsky, 'Humanitarian Intervention: Russian Perspectives', p. 4.
92. Baranovsky, 'Humanitarian Intervention: Russian Perspectives', p. 4.
93. For a discussion of this in terms of different Russian and NATO conceptions of security, see Vincent Pouliot, *International Security in Practice: The Politics of NATO–Russia Diplomacy* (Cambridge: Cambridge University Press, 2010), pp. 207–8.
94. This process is carefully examined in Alex J. Bellamy, 'The Responsibility to Protect and the Problem of Military Intervention', *International Affairs*, 84/4 (2008), pp. 620–30.
95. See Francis M. Deng et al., *Sovereignty as Responsibility* (Washington, DC: Brookings Institution, 1996). Bellamy, 'The Responsibility to Protect and the Problem of Military Intervention', pp. 618–20.
96. Among the large and expanding literature on this topic, see Alex J. Bellamy, *Responsibility to Protect: The Global Effort to End Mass Atrocities* (Cambridge and Malden, MA: Polity Press, 2009); Richard H. Cooper (ed.), *Responsibility to Protect: The Global Moral Compact for the 21st Century* (Basingstoke: Palgrave Macmillan, 2009); the journal launched in 2009 *Global Responsibility to Protect*; Philip Alston, *Human Rights, Intervention, and the Use of Force* (Oxford: Oxford University Press, 2008).
97. *The Responsibility to Protect: Report of the International Commission on Intervention and State Sovereignty* (Ottawa: International Development Research Centre, 2001), also at http://www.iciss.ca/report2-en.asp.
98. Most states have pledged to protect their respective populations from genocide under the 1948 Convention on the Prevention and Punishment of the Crime of Genocide.
99. *The Responsibility to Protect*, para. 6.21.

100. Haines, 'The Influence of Operation Allied Force on the Development of the *jus ad bellum*', p. 485. More ambitiously, in the case of a veto in the Security Council, the commission proposed that the matter could still be taken, in a descending hierarchy of empowered actors, by the UN General Assembly, under the Uniting for Peace mechanism, regional and sub-regional actors, and finally 'concerned states'.
101. Jennifer M. Welsh, 'Conclusion: The Evolution of Humanitarian Intervention in International Society', in Welsh (ed.), *Humanitarian Intervention and International Relations*, pp. 184–5.
102. Alex J. Bellamy, 'Realizing the Responsibility to Protect', *International Studies Perspectives*, 10/2 (2009), pp. 112–13.
103. On this discourse, see statement of the Russian State Duma and Federation Council, 4 July 2004, that 'Disregard for the fundamental rules of international law...have turned into a rejection of the "humanitarian intervention" by Iraqi society'. At http://www.mid.ru.
104. See Yevgeny Primakov, 'Rather the United Nations than US Unilateralism', *New Perspectives Quarterly*, 21/2 (March 2004), p. 51.
105. Speech on 27 June 2005, cited in Sergei Yu. Marochkin, 'On the Recent Development of International Law: Some Russian Perspectives', *Chinese Journal of International Law*, 8/3 (2009), p. 712.
106. Russian Foreign Minister spokesman Mikhail Kamynin, 12 September 2005, http://www.mid.ru.
107. Russian Foreign Minister spokesman Mikhail Kamynin, 12 September 2005, http://www.mid.ru.
108. UN General Assembly 60th Session, A/RES/60/1, paragraphs 138–40, http://daccess-dds-ny.un.org/doc/UNDOC/GEN/NO5/487/60/PDF/NO548760.pdf.
109. Bellamy, 'The Responsibility to Protect and the Problem of Military Intervention', pp. 622–3. For an argument, however, that opportunistic nations may still use the rhetoric of the summit agreement to justify unilateral interventions, that it is likely that 'future unilateral actors will make arguments drawing on the duty to prevent genocide and other atrocities in addition to claims of self-defence or international security', see Alicia L. Bannon, 'The Responsibility to Protect: The U.N. World Summit and the Question of Unilateralism', *Yale Law Journal*, 115 (2006), pp. 1157–65. As we show in chapter 7, Russia made just such opportunistic arguments over its intervention in Georgia in 2008. See also Nicholas J. Wheeler, 'A Victory for Common Humanity? The Responsibility to Protect after the 2005 World Summit', *International Law and International Relations*, 95/2 (2005–6), pp. 95–105.
110. Bellamy, 'Realizing the Responsibility to Protect', pp. 113–15.
111. UN Security Council Resolution 1674, 28 April 2006, paragraph 4, http://www.un.org/Docs/scres/2006/sc2006.htm.
112. Haines, 'The Influence of Operation Allied Force', pp. 485–6.
113. Bellamy, 'Realizing the Responsibility to Protect', p. 115.
114. Russian representative Mikhail Margelov, Sixty-third General Assembly Plenary, 28 July 2009, GA/10850, at http://www.un.org/News/Press/docs/2009/ga10850.doc.htm. However, as we note in chapter 7, Russia abusively referred to the R2P in the context of the 2008 Russia–Georgia war.

115. 'The Powerless UN Security Council', *Nezavisimaya gazeta*, 28 September 2007, p. 2.
116. Despite these cases, China has sought to constrain and shape the elaboration of R2P as a global norm rather than simply to block its potential for elaboration. See Rosemary Foot, 'The Responsibility to Protect (R2P) and its Evolution: Beijing's Influence on Norm Creation in Humanitarian Areas', *St Antony's International Review*, 6/2 (February 2011), pp. 47–66; Rosemary Foot and Andrew Walter, *China, the United States, and Global Order* (Oxford: Oxford University Press, 2011), pp. 46–51.
117. Draft resolution, Security Council 5933rd meeting, 11 July 2008, S/2008/447, http://daccess-dds-ny.un.org/doc/UNDOC/GEN/NO8/420/69/PDF/NO842069.pdf; statement by UK representative, John Sawers, S/PV.5933, http://daccess-dds-ny.un.org/doc/UNDOC/PRO/NO8/419/47/PDF/NO841947.pdf.
118. Russian UN Representative Vitaly Churkin, Security Council 5933rd meeting, 11 July 2008, http://daccess-dds-ny.un.org/doc/UNDOC/GEN/NO8/420/69/PDF/NO842069.pdf.
119. S. Neil MacFarlane, Carolyn J. Thielking, and Thomas G. Weiss, '*The Responsibility to Protect*: Is Anyone Interested in Humanitarian Intervention?', *Third World Quarterly*, 25/5 (2004), pp. 983–5.
120. States could argue that the human rights crisis in Sudan was such that it could not yet reasonably be claimed that Sudan was failing in its responsibilities. In effect R2P language 'allowed opponents of intervention to replace largely discredited "sovereignty-as-absolute" type arguments against intervention in supreme humanitarian emergencies with arguments about who had the primary responsibility to protect Darfur's civilians'. Alex J. Bellamy, 'Responsibility to Protect or Trojan Horse? The Crisis in Darfur and Humanitarian Intervention after Iraq', *Ethics and International Affairs*, 19/2 (September 2005), pp. 51–2.
121. Alex J. Bellamy, 'The Responsibility to Protect—Five Years On', *Ethics and International Affairs*, 24/2 (2010), pp. 160–2.
122. For a critical view of the consequences of OAF see David N. Gibbs, *First Do No Harm: Humanitarian Intervention and the Destruction of Yugoslavia* (Nashville, TN: Vanderbilt University Press, 2009).
123. Ian Johnstone, 'Discursive Power in the UN Security Council', *Journal of International Law and International Relations*, 2/1 (Winter 2005), pp. 78–9.
124. Edward C. Luck, 'Sovereignty, Choice and the Responsibility to Protect', *Global Responsibility to Protect*, 1/1 (2009), pp. 10–21.

Chapter 4 Afghanistan and the 'Global War on Terror': A New Basis for Consensus?

1. Citha D. Maass, 'The Afghanistan Conflict: External Involvement', *Central Asian Survey*, 18/1 (1999), pp. 65–78.
2. Reports that Russian pilots flew Northern Alliance aircraft or that unmarked Russian fighters bombed Taliban positions have never been substantiated. See Pavel Felgenhauer, 'A Vicious Circle of Terror', *Moscow Times*, 27 September 2001. However, special forces of Tajikistan's interior ministry, which fought in units of the Northern Alliance, may have received Russian military training; see Vladimir Georgiev, 'Tajik Commander in Afghanistan', *Nezavisimaya gazeta*, 26 December 2001.

3. 'Putin Warns G8 of "Terrorist Arc", Afghanistan', *Russia Today*, 24 July 2000. The Taliban movement officially recognized the Chechen government of Aslan Maskhadov on 16 January 2000.
4. SC Res.1333, adopted by the Security Council on 19 December 2000, available at http://www.un.org/Docs/scres/2000/sc2000.htm. See Oleg Odnokolenko, 'Russia Joins Anti-Talib Sanctions', *Segodnya*, 19 January 2001, p. 3.
5. Tarcisio Gazzini, *The Changing Rules on the Use of Force in International Law* (Manchester: Manchester University Press, 2005), pp. 102–3.
6. Statements by Igor Ivanov, 24 May 2000, at CIS Collective Security Council, and Sergei Ivanov, 25 May 2000; *Inside Central Asia*, BBC Monitoring, 15–21 May 2000, issue 325, p. 6; Interfax news agency, 25 May 2000, *BBC Summary of World Broadcasts. Former Soviet Union* (henceforth SU), 3851 B/5, 27 May 2000. These statements reportedly gave rise to concerns in the Russian Foreign Ministry, where officials claimed that preventive air raids would be contrary to international law and the UN Charter without irrefutable proof of Afghanistan's aggression against Russia or its neighbours and confirmation by independent sources; Vladimir Skosyrev, 'Russia: To Bomb or Not to Bomb Afghanistan?', *Moscow News*, 21, 31 May– 6 June 2000, p. 2.
7. Andrei Mikhailov, 'Taliban Will Be Difficult to Get', *Nezavisimaya gazeta*, 24 May 2000; Sergei Sokut et al., 'It Will Be Hard to Fulfill the Threat', *Nezavisimoe voennoe obozrenie*, 19, 2–8 June 2000, p. 2.
8. 'Russia May Strike Terrorists in Afghanistan', *The Times of Central Asia*, 2/21 (54), 25 May 2000; 'Russia Begins to Back-track on Afghan Threats', *Russia Today*, 25 May 2000; 'China Urges Talks to End Afghan Conflict', *Russia Today*, 4 July 2000; 'New Puzzle Awaiting Russia', Alan Kasaev et al., *Nezavisimaya gazeta*, 26 May 2000, p. 1.
9. See Gennadi Charodeyev, *Izvestiya*, 23 November 2000; and Yuri Sigov, *Novye izvestiya*, 26 May 2001.
10. The fullest analysis of this topic to date is by Myra Williamson, *Terrorism, War and International Law: The Legality of the Use of Force Against Afghanistan in 2001* (Farnham: Ashgate, 2009).
11. SC Res. 1368, SC Res. 1373; both available at http://www.un.org/Docs/scres/2001/sc2001.htm.
12. Here and for the following argument see Michael Byers, 'Terrorism, the Use of Force and International Law after 11 September', *International and Comparative Law Quarterly*, 51 (April 2002), pp. 401–14.
13. Byers, 'Terrorism, the Use of Force and International Law after 11 September', pp. 409–10. But it has also been argued that, despite the widespread support among writers and governments for the US use of force against Afghanistan and more general support for an expanded right of self-defence to counter terrorism by many, this did not create new customary law. Most states are unlikely to accept an action like the invasion of Afghanistan again except perhaps if a similar spectacular incident like 9/11 occurs. Belinda Helmke, *Under Attack: Challenges to the Rules Governing the International Use of Force* (Farnham: Ashgate, 2010), pp. 193–5. For further discussion on the legal limits on using force against 'haven states' arising from this case, see 'The Invasion and Occupation of Afghanistan', in Thomas Michael McDonnell, *The United States, International Law, and the Struggle against Terrorism* (London: Routledge, 2010), pp. 259–74.

14. Foreign Minister Sergei Lavrov, 'We Have No Right to Risk the United Nations', *Rossiyskaya gazeta*, 204 (September 2005), p. 11.
15. Byers, 'Terrorism, the Use of Force and International Law after 11 September', p. 410. See also Michael Byers, 'Not Yet Havoc: Geopolitical Change and the International Rules on Military Force', *Review of International Studies*, 31 (2005), 58–9.
16. 'On the start of the USA's and Great Britain's counterterrorist operation on the territory of Afghanistan', Russian Foreign Ministry statement, 7 October 2001, Embassy of Russian Embassy, London, Press Release, 8 October 2001.
17. Presentation by Sergei Ivanov to NATO officials on 25 September 2001. Author's notes of summary of this meeting by a NATO participant.
18. Speeches and statements cited in Gazzini, *The Changing Rules on the Use of Force in International Law*, p. 191.
19. Ambassador Leonid Skotnikov, Permanent Representative of the Russian Federation to the UN Office, 'The Right of Self-Defence and the New Security Imperatives', *International Affairs* (Moscow), 50/6 (2004), pp. 18–19.
20. Skotnikov, 'The Right of Self-Defence and the New Security Imperatives', pp. 19–20.
21. For discussion of the requirements of 'necessity' and 'proportionality' in this case see Gazzini, *The Changing Rules on the Use of Force in International Law*, pp. 193–9.
22. This legal case is made, for example, by Christopher Greenwood, 'International Law and the Pre-emptive Use of Force: Afghanistan, Al-Qaida and Iraq', *San Diego International Law Journal*, 4 (2003), 24–5.
23. Helmke, *Under Attack*, p. 194.
24. Address to Joint Session of Congress and the American People. The White House, at http://whitehouse.gov/news/releases/2001/09/20010916-2.html.
25. *Radio Free Europe/Radio Liberty Central Asia Report*, 1/9 (20 September 2001), at http://www.rferl.org/centralasia/2001/09/9-200901.asp.
26. 'New Poll Suggests Russians Do Not Support U.S. Retribution', *Monitor* (Jamestown Foundation), 7/178, 28 September 2001, at http://www.eurasia.net.org; 'Publics in Moscow and Kiev Oppose Attacks against Countries Harbouring Terrorists', *Opinion Analysis*, Office of Research, Department of State, Washington, DC, 18 September 2001, citing the then reputable pollster VTsIOM.
27. Embassy of Russian Federation, London, Press Release, 25 September 2001; *Izvestiya*, 24 September 2001, p. 2.
28. Presentation by Sergei Ivanov to NATO officials on 25 September 2001.
29. Statement of the State Duma of the Federal Assembly 'In connection with the military operation against international terrorism on the territory of Afghanistan', 9 November 2001, Embassy of Russian Federation, London, Press Release, 27 November 2001.
30. Presentation by Sergei Ivanov to NATO officials on 25 September 2001.
31. Reports by Aleksei Smirnov, *Novye izvestiya*, 6 November 2001, p. 3; Vladimir Urban, *Novye izvestiya*, 3 November 2001, pp. 1, 5.
32. *Izvestiya*, 19 November 2001, p. 2.
33. 'Russia Returns Stealthily to Afghanistan', *Monitor* (Jamestown Foundation), 7/228, 12 December 2001, at http://www.eurasia.net.org.

34. SC Res.1386, adopted by the Security Council on 20 December 2001, at http://www.un.org/Docs/scres/2001/sc2001.htm. The ISAF mandate was expanded to areas of Afghanistan outside Kabul by SC Res. 1510, on 13 October 2003, at http://www.un.org/Docs/scres/2003/sc2003.htm.
35. Vadim Solovyov, 'Russia Returning to Afghanistan', *Nezavisimaya gazeta*, 8 December 2001, pp. 1, 6; Yuri Golotyuk, 'Humanitarian Occupation', *Vremya novostei*, 10 December 2001, p. 1.
36. *Radio Free Europe/Radio Liberty Central Asia Report*, 1/9 (20 September 2001), at http://www.rferl.org/centralasia/2001/09/9-200901.asp.
37. For the initial reaction of Central Asian states see *Radio Free Europe/Radio Liberty Central Asia Report*, 1/9 (20 September 2001), as well as 'Russia Says Nyet, Others Say Yes to America', *Eurasia Daily Monitor* (Jamestown Foundation), 7/170, 18 September 2001, at http://www.eurasianet.org.
38. 'President Niyazov Offers to Mediate over Afghanistan', 'President Karimov Defends Decision to Assist US Operation', BBC Monitoring, *Inside Central Asia*, Issue 394, 24–30 September 2001. 'Kazakh President Reiterates Support for US Strikes', *Inside Central Asia*, Issue 398, 22–28 October 2001. 'Bishkek Gives Backing to US Strikes on Afghanistan' *Inside Central Asia*, Issue 396, 8–14 October 2001. 'Tajikistan Ready to Help US War on Terrorism', *Inside Central Asia*, Issue 395, 1–7 October 2001.
39. Foreign Minister Yerlan Idrisov, speaking in Almaty, 14 September 2001, cited in *Eurasia Insight* (Jamestown Foundation), 17 September 2001, at http://www.eurasia.net.org/departments/insight/articles/pp091701. The states in the SCO were Russia, China, Kazakhstan, Kyrgyzstan, Tajikistan, and Uzbekistan.
40. See Simon Chesterman, 'Humanitarian Intervention and Afghanistan', in Jennifer M. Welsh (ed.), *Humanitarian Intervention and International Relations* (Oxford: Oxford University Press, 2004), pp. 163–75.
41. Fatima Ayub and Sari Kouvo, 'Righting the Course? Humanitarian Intervention, the War on Terror and the Future of Afghanistan', *International Affairs*, 84/4 (2008), pp. 647–8.
42. Christine Gray, *International Law and the Use of Force* (3rd edn.) (Oxford: Oxford University Press, 2008), p. 207.
43. Press release by the Russian Foreign Ministry on the adoption of UNSC Resolution 1890 on renewing the mandate of ISAF, 10 October 2009, at www.mid.ru.
44. At the outset of Operation Enduring Freedom top generals, including former commanders of Soviet forces in Afghanistan Viktor Yermakov and Boris Gromov and the deputy head of Soviet General Staff during 1979–84 Valentin Varennikov, wrote scathing articles about the likelihood of US success in introducing ground forces into Afghanistan, 'Ex-Soviet Generals Doubt America Can Prevail in Afghanistan', *Monitor* (Jamestown Foundation), 7/172, 20 September 2001; 'Soviet Generals Warn of "Sea of Bloodshed": Veterans Recall Failure in Afghanistan', *Washington* Post, 19 September 2001; Mikhail Khodarenok, 'An interview with General of the Army Viktor Yermakov', *Nezavisimoe voennoe obozrenie*, 39, 19–25 October 2001, 1–3.
45. Colonel-General Georgiy Shpak, former Commander of the Airborne Troops, Interfax-AVN military news agency website, Moscow, 24 December 2009,

BBC Summary of World Broadcasts Former Soviet Union, at http://www.bbc.monitoringonline.com (henceforth BBC), Mon FS1 FsuPol SA1 AAsPol gyl.

46. AFP report 6 June 2010, in *Johnson's Russia List*, 110, 7 June 2010.
47. Aspects of the debate are summarized by R. Streshnov, *Krasnaya zvezda*, 24 January 2002.
48. Mikhail Khodarenok, 'Russia Surrounded by US Military Bases', *Nezavisimoe voennoe obozreniya*, 10, 27 March–4 April 2002.
49. I. Zviagelskaya and D. Makarov, 'Vospriyatie Rossiey politiki zapada v Tstentral'noy Azii', in M. Narinskiy and A. Mal'gin (eds.), *Yuzhniy flang SNG* (Moscow: Logos, 2003), p. 120.
50. Noted by Russian First Deputy Minister of Foreign Affairs and former Foreign Intelligence Service head, Vyacheslav Trubnikov, 'The Unity of the Antiterrorist Coalition in Danger', *Vremya novostei*, 10 September 2002.
51. As argued, for example, by Viktor Ivanov, director of Russia's Federal Drug Control Service, at a meeting in the General Staff Military Academy, Interfax-AVN military news agency website, Moscow, 23 October 2009, BBC Mon FS1 FsuPol va.
52. 'Russia Heads Back to Afghanistan', *The Times*, 27 October 2010, p. 29; Pavel Felgenhauer, 'Russia is Demanding One-Sided Western Concession', *Eurasia Daily Monitor* (Jamestown Foundation), 7/195, 28 October 2010. Russian drug raids in Afghanistan were controversial as they were condemned by the Afghan government as a violation of the country's sovereignty. Bilateral cooperation prospects were boosted by a visit of President Hamid Karzai to Moscow in January 2011, 'Russia Prepares to Re-enter Afghanistan', *Eurasia Daily Monitor* (Jamestown Foundation), 8/17, 25 January 2011.
53. Speeches by Foreign Minister Lavrov at international conferences on Afghanistan in Kabul, 20 July 2010, and Bonn, 5 December 2011, at http://www/mid.ru.
54. 'US and Kabul in Secret Negotiations over Long-Term Bases in Afghanistan', *The Guardian*, 14 June 2011, p. 17; Dmitry Babich, 'Permanent American Bases in Afghanistan?', *Russia Profile*, 19 February 2011.
55. For an appraisal of how various aspects of the 'global war on terror' in the 2000s may have affected the development of international law on the use of force, see Eric A. Heinze, 'The Evolution of International Law in Light of the "Global War on Terror"', *Review of International Studies*, 37 (2011), pp. 1069–94.
56. Speech at the Nixon Centre, Itar-Tass news agency, 20 September 2001, BBC Mon FS1 FsuPol tp.
57. Presentation by Sergei Ivanov on 25 September 2001.
58. 'Russia Has Its Own Path', Boris Volkhonsky, *Kommersant*, 5 February 2002, p. 10.
59. 'Partners are Ceasing to Understand Each Other', *Nezavisimoe voennoe obozreniye*, 4, 8 February 2002, p. 1; 'Putin Walks Careful Line on US Antiterror Policy', *Monitor* (Jamestown Foundation), 8/32, 14 February 2002.
60. 'Russia is Out to Help the Rogue States', Aleksei Nikolsky, *Vedomosti*, 18 February 2002, p. A3.
61. Colonel A. S. Abramyan, 'Pravovye aspekty primeneniya voennoy sily v bor'be s terrorizmom', *Voennaya mysl'*, 12 (December 2003), pp. 27–34. See also B. S. Krylov, 'Mezhdunarodnoe pravo i problemy sozdaniya pravovogo akta o bor'be s mezhdunarodnym terrorizmom', in V. N. Kudryavtsev (ed.), *Bor'ba s Terrorizmom* (Moscow: Nauka, 2004), pp. 195–204.

62. Aleksei Arbatov, 'Anti-Ballistic Missile Defence Treaty and Terrorism', *Nezavisimaya gazeta*, 26 December 2001, p. 11.
63. Arbatov, 'Anti-Ballistic Missile Defence Treaty and Terrorism', p. 11.
64. BBC Monitoring, *Inside Central Asia*, 1–7 October 2001, Issue 395, p. 6.
65. Army General Anatoly Kulikov, 'How Not to Fall into the Crime Trap', *International Affairs* (Moscow), 48/1 (January 2002), pp. 72–7. However, with regard to domestic counter-terrorism in Russia, Kulikov, with responsibilities in the State Duma on the issue, proceeded to argue that the army should play a greater role in combating terrorism, that in every military district there should be a brigade specially organized to carry out counter-terrorist operations; Anatoly Kulikov, 'Conception. The Army Cannot Stand on the Side in the Anti-Terrorist Struggle', *Nezavisimoe voennoe obozrenie*, 3 (31 January–6 February 2003), p. 5.
66. Address on 12 September 2002, at http://www.mid.ru. See Iurii Fedotov (Russian Deputy Foreign Minister), 'Challenges to Multilateralism and the UN', *International Affairs* (Moscow), 50/3 (2004), pp. 6–11.
67. For the obligation of states in relation to the Committee, see SC Res. 1456, adopted by the Security Council on 20 January 2003, and SC Res. 1566, adopted on 8 October 2004, at http://www.un.org/Docs/scres/2003/sc2003.htm and http://www.un.org/Docs/scres/2004/sc2004.htm.
68. A UNSC definition in 2004, for example, failed to bridge differences over the targets of terrorism, referring to acts 'including against civilians'. See SC Res. 1566, adopted by the Security Council on 8 October 2004, at http://www.un.org/Docs/scres/2004/sc2004.htm.
69. For a useful evaluation see Gail W. Lapidus, 'Putin's War on Terrorism: Lessons from Chechnya', *Post-Soviet Affairs*, 18/1 (2002), pp. 41–8.
70. Interview with Putin, 'We Will Reach Agreement with the Chechens', *Nezavisimaya gazeta*, 8 July 2000.
71. Statement by Deputy Foreign Minister Yevgenny Gusarov at EU Conference, 20 October 2001, cited in Mark Smith, *Russian Perspectives on Terrorism* (Conflict Studies Research Centre, Defence Academy of the United Kingdom, January 2004), p. 10.
72. Sergei Lavrov, Press Release for Security Council 4497th Meeting, 26 March 2002, SC/7338, at http://www.un.org/News/Press/docs/2002/SC7338.doc.htm.
73. Author's transcript of meeting with Putin on 6 September 2004 in Novo-Ogarevo, with members of the Valdai Discussion Club.
74. For analysis of Russian allegations of al-Qaeda–Chechen links see Graeme P. Herd, 'The Russo-Chechen Information Warfare and 9/11: Al-Qaeda through the South Caucasus Looking Glass?', *European Security*, 11/4 (Winter 2002), pp. 110–30; John Russell, 'Exploitation of the "Islamic Factor" in the Russo-Chechen Conflict before and after 11 September 2001', *European Security*, 11 (Winter 2002), pp. 96–109.
75. Pavel Baev, 'Putin's Counter-Terrorism: The Parameters of a Strategic Dead-End', *Small Wars and Insurgencies*, 17/1 (2006), pp. 1–21.
76. James Hughes, 'The Chechnya Conflict: Freedom Fighters or Terrorists?', *Demokratizatsiya*, 15/3 (Summer 2007), p. 307. See also John Russell, *Chechnya—Russia's 'War on Terror'* (London: Routledge, 2007), especially chapter 6, '9/11, Chechnya and the War on Terror', pp. 89–110.

77. US State Department spokesman Richard Bouchner at press briefing on 10 January 2002, as reported critically in Maxim Yusin and Alexander Shumilin, 'United States Breaking Moratorium on Criticizing Russia over Chechnya', *Izvestiya*, 12 January 2002, p. 2.
78. Statement by US Ambassador Alexander Vershbow in July 2002; Smith, *Russian Perspectives on Terrorism*, p. 11.
79. Tuomas Forsberg and Graeme Herd, 'The EU, Human Rights and the Russo-Chechen Conflict', *Political Science Quarterly*, 120/3 (2005), pp. 467–71.
80. Among the substantial literature on the *jus in bello* with regard to Chechnya, see Miriam Kosmehl, 'Rechsgewalt oder Gewaltrecht: Das internationale Recht unter die Menschenrechte in Tschetschenien', *Osteuropa*, 53/8 (August 2003), pp. 1066–83; Svante Cornell, 'International Reactions to Massive Human Rights Violations: The Case of Chechnya', *Europe-Asia Studies*, 51/1 (1999), pp. 85–100; 'War Crimes and Russia's International Standing', chapter 7 in Matthew Evangelista, *The Chechen Wars. Will Russia Go the Way of the Soviet Union?* (Washington, DC: Brookings Institution, 2002), pp. 139–77; Anatol Lieven, 'Morality and Reality in Approaches to War Crimes: The Case of Chechnya', *East European Constitutional Review*, 10/2–3 (Spring/Summer 2001), pp. 72–8.
81. Andrei Nikolaev, Chairman of the Defence Committee of the Russian State Duma, 'A Terrorist War in Russia', *Nezavisimaya gazeta*, 15 November 2002, p. 2. For Russian studies of terrorism in the period to 2004, which include consideration of the domestic legal regulation of counter-terrorist operations and the international context, see A. Kol'tyukov (ed.), *Terrorizm: kak ugroza natsional'noy bezopasnosti gosudarstva* (Moscow: Main Command of the Russian Ministry of Internal Affairs, Institute of Military History of the Russian Ministry of Defence, 2003); Ye. Stepanov (ed.), *Sovremennyy terrorizm: sostoyanie i perspectivy* (Moscow: URSS, 2000); V. Kudryavtsev (ed.), *Bor'ba s terrorizm* (Moscow: Nauka, 2004); R. Rybakov (ed.), *Terrorizm: ugroza chelovechestvu v XXI veke* (Moscow: Kraft, 2003).
82. Mikhail Khodarenok, 'Victory, as before, is not round the corner', *Nezavisimoe voennoe obozrenie*, 23–29 March 2001, pp. 1–2.
83. Evangelista, *The Chechen Wars*, pp. 139–77, 156–61; Robert Garwood, 'The Second Russo-Chechen Conflict (1999 to Date): "A Modern Military Operation"', *Journal of Slavic Military Studies*, 15/3 (September 2002), pp. 60–80. It should be acknowledged, however, that US counter-terrorist operations in Iraq post-2003 raised serious, if not quite analogous, questions about the treatment of civilian populations.
84. 'We are obliged to have a war without fronts or borders', interview, *Izvestiya*, 5 November 2002, p. 2.
85. 'The unity of the antiterrorist coalition in danger', interview, *Vremya novostei*, 19 September 2002, at http://www.mid.ru.
86. Interview, *Vremya novostei*, 5 February 2003, pp. 1, 5. We should note that Rumyantsev had an interest in downplaying such nuclear weapon capabilities since his ministry was interested in promoting Russian civilian nuclear trade.
87. Andrei Kokoshin, 'In a Nuclear Ring', *Argumenty i fakty*, 12 March 2003, p. 4.
88. Presentation by Sergei Ivanov on 25 September 2001.
89. Defence Minister Sergei Ivanov's statement to the 40th international security conference, in Munich, *Krasnaya zvezda*, 10 February 2004, pp. 1, 3.

90. Vladimir Nazarov, deputy chief of the Russian Security Council, maintained in February 2010 that the possibility of nuclear weapons falling into the hands of extremists in Pakistan was viewed by Russia as a 'big potential threat'. In his view extremists could gain such weapons either by legally coming to power or as a result of a terrorist action. Interfax 14 February 2010. *Johnson's Russia List*, 30, 15 February 2010, at http://www.cdi.org/russia/johnson.
91. As revealed in revelations from leaked US diplomatic reports by WikiLeaks, summarized in 'Biggest Fear Was Terrorists Seizing Nuclear Arsenal', *The Times*, 1 December 2010, p. 9; 'Suspicion and Mistrust Reign Amid US Fears of Nuclear Theft', *The Guardian*, 2 December 2010, p. 13. A particular concern is the allegation that Pakistani intelligence has continued to covertly support the Afghan Taliban and the Pakistan-based militant group Lashkar-e-Taiba.

Chapter 5 Pre-emption, the Iraq War, and the Spectre of Unconstrained Force

1. Jose Alvarez, 'Hegemonic International Law Revisited', *American Journal of International Law*, 97 (2003), p. 879. The author suggests that the US sought to rework international law to include new rights of intervention by means of the 'hegemonic capture' of the UN Security Council. Cited in Christopher J. Borgen, 'Whose Public, Whose Order? Imperium, Region and Normative Friction', *Yale Journal of International Law*, 22 (2007), p. 346.
2. See Jutta Brunnée and Stephen J. Toope, 'The Use of Force: International Law after Iraq', *International and Comparative Law Quarterly*, 53/4 (October 2004), p. 795.
3. This is the language of the right of self-defence used in 1841 in connection with the celebrated case around the British destruction of the steamboat *Caroline*.
4. Adam Roberts, 'Law and the Use of Force after Iraq', *Survival*, 45/2 (Summer 2003), pp. 45–7. For a legal analysis of this challenge, see Mary Ellen O'Connell, *The Myth of Preemptive Self-Defense*, The American Society of International Law Task Force on Terrorism, August 2002, at http://www.asil.org/taskforce/oconnell.pdf.
5. Tarcisio Gazzini, *The Changing Rules on the Use of Force in International Law* (Manchester: Manchester University Press, 2005), p. 199.
6. Remarks by President George W. Bush at 2002 Graduation Exercise of the US Military Academy West Point, New York, at http://www.whitehouse.gov/news/releases/2002/06/20020601-3.htm.
7. White House, *The National Security Strategy of the United States of America* (17 September 2002), at http://georgebush-whitehouse.archives/gov/nsc/nss/2002, and 'U.S Adoption of New Doctrine on the Use of Force', *American Journal of International Law*, 97/1 (January 2003), pp. 203–5. In this context see Christine Gray, 'The US *National Security Strategy* and the New "Bush Doctrine" on Preemptive Self-Defence', *Chinese Journal of International Law*, 1 (2002), pp. 437–47. For a balanced appraisal of the pre-emption quandary see Belinda Helmke, *Under Attack: Challenges to the Rules Governing the International Use of Force* (Farnham: Ashgate, 2010), chapter 8, 'Bolt from the Blue: The Pre-emptive Use of Force', pp. 149–67. For a clear argument favouring the use of pre-emptive force undertaken in the absence of imminence only with the approval of the UN Security Council, which 'would likely prevent the opening of the floodgates to unilateral preemptive action

by other states', see Anthony Clark Arend, 'International Law and the Preemptive Use of Military Force', *The Washington Quarterly*, 26/2 (Spring 2003), pp. 89–103.

8. 'After the exhaustion of peaceful remedies and a careful, deliberate consideration of the consequences, in the face of overwhelming evidence of an imminent threat, a nation may take preemptive action to defend its nationals from unimaginable harm', William H. Taft IV, 'The Legal Basis for Preemption', published by the Council on Foreign Relations, 18 November 2002, available at http://www.cfr.org/publication.php?id=5250.
9. Jane E. Stromseth, 'Law and Force after Iraq: A Transitional Moment', *The American Journal of International Law*, 97/3 (July 2003), p. 635.
10. Michael Byers, 'Not Yet Havoc: Geopolitical Change and the International Rules on Military Force', *Review of International Studies*, 31 (2005), p. 62.
11. Brunnée and Toope, 'The Use of Force', pp. 791–2.
12. W. Michael Reisman and Andrea Armstrong, 'Claims to Pre-Emptive Uses of Force: Some Trends and Projections and their Implications for World Order', in Michael N. Schmitt and Jelena Pejic (eds.), *International Law and Armed Conflict: Exploring the Faultlines* (Leiden: Martinus Nijhoff, 2007), pp. 80–1.
13. Christine Gray, 'The US *National Security Strategy* and the New "Bush Doctrine" on Preemptive Self-Defense', *Chinese Journal of International Law*, 1 (2002), p. 446.
14. As summarized in Julie Wilhelmsen and Geir Flikke, 'Evidence of Russia's Bush Doctrine in the CIS', *European Security*, 14/3 (September 2005), pp. 397–403.
15. UN Document S/2002/1012, cited in Christine Gray, *International Law and the Use of Force* (3rd edn.) (Oxford: Oxford University Press, 2008), p. 230.
16. Interview with Foreign Minister Igor Ivanov in New York, 9 September 2002, at http://www.mid.ru, 1757-10-09-2002. Putin's remarks in Gennady Sysoyev et al., 'Russian General Staff is Drawing Up Plans for Special Operations', *Kommersant*, 12 September 2002, pp. 1–2. For the Georgian president Eduard Shevardnadze's response to Putin that Russia had no right to invoke Article 51 of the UN Charter in this context, see *Kommersant*, 16 September 2002, p. 11.
17. Gray, *International Law and the Use of Force*, pp. 230–1.
18. Wilhelmsen and Flikke, 'Evidence of Russia's Bush Doctrine in the CIS', pp. 398–402.
19. Vladimir Ivanov, 'Defence Minister Sergei Ivanov Promises that Russia Will Not Carry Out Preventive Nuclear Strikes', *Nezavisimoe voennoe obozrenie*, 37, 17–23 October 2003; Sophie Lambroschini. 'Moscow Struggles to Clarify Stance on Preemptive Force', *Radio Free Europe/Radio Liberty*, feature article, available at http://www.rferl.org/features/2003/10/14102003171155.asp; Svetlana Babayeva, 'Reforms Over', *Izvestiya*, 14 October 2003, p. 4.
20. Mikhail Vorobyev, 'We Have Enough Missiles to Take On Everyone', *Vremya novostei*, 3 October 2003, p. 1.
21. In this sense the Russian use of the term 'preventivny' (preventive) is indeed more accurate than 'uprezhdayushchiy' (pre-emptive), though these terms are not always distinguished in translations into English.
22. This followed initial suggestions, probably aimed at a Russian audience, that Russian nuclear weapons might be used preventively 'to stop acts of aggression'.

Pavel Felgenhauer, 'Ivanov's Defence Manifesto', *The Moscow Times*, 9 October 2003.

23. Article by Colonel-General Leonid Ivashov, *Nezavisimaya gazeta*, 21 September 2004.
24. Article by Colonel-General Leonid Ivashov, *Nezavisimaya gazeta*, 21 September 2004. As Ivashov put it elsewhere, 'proclaiming our right—illegitimate, that is—to strike at other countries, we give them the right—legitimate—to strike back'; interview in *Nezavisimoe voennoe obozrenie*, 17 September 2004.
25. Author's transcript of meeting with President Putin at Novo-Ogarevo, 6 September 2004, with members of the Valdai Discussion Club.
26. Statements by CSTO Deputy Secretary-General, Valeriy Semerikov, and first deputy head of the Joint Staff of the CSTO, Lieutenant-General Oleg Latypov, Interfax-AVN military news agency website, 26 August 2009, at http://www.bbc.monitoringonline.com (henceforth BBC) Mon FS1 FsuPol sv.
27. Interview with President Putin on 3 November 2003, at http://eng.kremlin.ru.text/speeches. See also B. R. Tukmukhamedov, 'Uprezhdayushchee primenenie sily: vozmozhnye kriteriii dopustimosti', *Rossiyskiy ezhegodnik mezhmunarodnogo prava* (St Petersburg), 2005, pp. 50–2.
28. For a detailed analysis of the whole subject by a senior Russian academic international lawyer, see Tukmukhamedov, 'Uprezhdayushchee primenenie sily: vozmozhnye kriteriii dopustimosti', pp. 36–55.
29. Ambassador Leonid Skotnikov, Permanent Representative of the Russian Federation to the UN Office and other International Organizations in Geneva and to the Conference on Disarmament, 'The Right of Self-Defense and the New Security Imperatives', *International Affairs* (Moscow), 50/6 (2004), pp. 15–17. See also Leonid Skotnikov, 'The Use of Force: Legal Aspects', *International Affairs* (Moscow), 50/4 (2004), pp. 44–7.
30. Steve Gutterman, 'Russian defence Chief Reserves Right to Conduct Preemptive Strikes', *Associated Press*, 10 December 2004, cited in Wilhelmsen and Flikke, 'Evidence of Russia's Bush Doctrine in the CIS', p. 396.
31. Interview with Yuri Fedotov, *Novoye izvestiya*, 20 September 2004, pp. 1, 4.
32. Reisman and Armstrong, 'Claims to Pre-Emptive Uses of Force', p. 109.
33. Sergei Ivanov, 'Russia Must Be Strong', *Wall Street Journal*, 11 January 2006, cited in Ivo H. Daalder (ed.), *Beyond Preemption; Force and Legitimacy in a Changing World* (Washington, DC: Brookings Institution, 2007) p. 6.
34. However, the Russian State Duma and Federation Council only amended Russian legislation to allow the president to exercise such powers in 2006 and Russia continued to have very limited capabilities for such operations. See Andrei Soldatov, 'The FSB Can't Hunt Down Terrorists Behind Enemy Lines', *Novaya gazeta*, 10 July 2006, p. 9.
35. The issue was complicated for the Russian military by its reluctance to renounce pre-emption wholly as part of national nuclear strategy, especially at a time of seriously weakened conventional military capabilities. In this sense, a security logic at the systemic level continued to influence the regulation of force, for all the talk of the world having changed after 9/11.
36. For official statements along these lines, see Reisman and Armstrong, 'Claims to Pre-Emptive Uses of Force', pp. 96–109.

37. *China Defense Daily*, 8 February 2006, cited in Reisman and Armstrong, 'Claims to Pre-Emptive Uses of Force', p. 108. These authors suggest, however, that the Chinese government appears to support a limited version of the right to pre-emptive action in the context of its claims to Taiwan.
38. Miriam Sapiro, 'Iraq: The Shifting Sands of Preemptive Self-Defence', *The American Journal of International Law*, 97/3 (July 2003), pp. 599–603.
39. *Izvestiya*, 29 June 1993, cited in Helen Belopolsky, *Russia and the Challengers: Russian Alignment with China, Iran and Iraq in the Unipolar Era* (Basingstoke: Palgrave Macmillan, 2009), p. 161. The ambiguous legal position of this unilateral American action is discussed in W. Michael Reisman, 'The Raid on Bagdad: Some Reflections on its Lawfulness and Implications', *European Journal of International Law*, 5/1 (1994), pp. 120–33.
40. Belopolsky, *Russia and the Challengers*, p. 167, *Rossiyskaya gazeta*, 18 December 1998, p. 3.
41. Michael N. Schmitt, 'Responding to Transnational Terrorism Under the *Jus ad Bellum*: A Normative Framework', in Schmitt and Pejic (eds.), *International Law and Armed Conflict*, p. 189.
42. For the US justification, see letter dated 20 March 2003 from the Permanent Representative of the US to the UN addressed to the President of the Security Council, UN, SCOR, 58th session, S/2003/351, at http://daccess-dds-ny.un.org/doc/UNDOC/GEN/N03/290/79/PDF/N0329079.pdf.
43. White House, *The National Security Strategy of the United States of America* (17 September 2002), at http://georgebush-whitehouse.archives.gov/nsc/nss/2002.
44. Schmitt, 'Responding to Transnational Terrorism', pp. 188–9.
45. US Ambassador John Negroponte, Security Council, 4726th Meeting, Press Release SC/7707, 27 March 2003, at http://www.un.org/News/Press/docs/2003/sc7707.doc.htm.
46. 'The unity of the antiterrorist coalition in danger', interview with First Deputy Minister of Foreign Affairs Vyacheslav Trubnikov, *Vremya novostei*, 19 September 2002, at http://www.mid.ru. Colonel-General Yuri Baluevsky, first deputy chief of the Russian General Staff expressed the same view, 'Yuri Baluevsky: War is Inevitable', *Nezavisimaya gazeta*, 21 February 2003.
47. Statement, 20 March 2003, at http://www.mid.ru.
48. Interview with Foreign Minister Igor Ivanov, 8 November 2003, at http://www.mid.ru. A Russian specialist argued at the time, however, that by moving potential objects of attack (US and coalition military forces and civilian personnel) to the conflict area itself the US-led occupation 'has thus far stimulated mainly the import of terrorism into Iraq rather than the export of terrorism', Ekaterina Stepanova, 'The Challenge of Terrorism in Post-Saddam Iraq: A View from Russia', PONARS Policy Memo 325, April 2004, at http://gwu.edu/~ieresgwu/assets/docs/ponars/pm_0325.pdf.
49. Gray, *International Law and the Use of Force*, pp. 217–18.
50. For an argument by the US State Department Legal Adviser in 2003 that pre-emptive use of force in Iraq was in fact lawful, based on the past actions of Iraq and the threat it posed over a protracted period of time, see William H. Taft IV and Todd F Buchwald, 'Preemption, Iraq and International Law', *The American Journal of International Law*, 97/3 (July 2003), pp. 557–63.

51. Gray, *International Law and the Use of Force*, pp. 219–20.
52. Security Council 4721st Meeting, Press Release SC/7696, 19 March 2003, at http://www.un.org/News/Press/docs/2003/sc7696.doc.htm.
53. Jutta Brunnée and Stephen J. Toope, 'The Use of Force: International Law after Iraq', *International and Comparative Law Quarterly*, 53/4 (October 2004), p. 803.
54. For the specialist debate see Fernando R. Tesón, 'Ending Tyranny in Iraq', *Ethics and International Affairs*, 19/2 (2005), pp. 1–20; and arguing against humanitarian depictions of the Iraq invasion, Terry Nardin, 'Humanitarian Imperialism', *Ethics and International Affairs*, 18/2 (September 2005), pp. 21–2, Kenneth Roth, 'Was the Iraq War a Humanitarian Intervention?', *Journal of Military Ethics*, 5/2 (2006), pp. 84–92.
55. Statement on 20 March 2003, available at http://www.mid.ru.
56. Statement at the Security Council, 27 March 2003, available at http://www.mid.ru.
57. Sergei Lavrov, 'The Iraq Crisis and the Struggle for a New World Pattern', *Yearbook of the Russian Diplomatic Academy*, 2003, 19 January 2004, at http://www/mid.ru.
58. Press conference, 11 April 2003, at http://www.kremlin.ru.
59. For a critical view that in the Iraq case 'the facts did not support the case for preemption, as there was neither *imminence* nor *necessity*', see Richard A. Falk, 'What Future for the UN Charter System of War Prevention?', *The American Journal of International Law*, 97/3 (July 2003), p. 598.
60. Ambassador John Negroponte, Security Council 4726th Meeting, Press Release SC/7707, 27 March 2003, at http://www.un.org/News/Press/docs/2003/sc7707.doc.htm.
61. For defence of the American position and criticism of the French, German, and Russian view as treating Council resolutions 'as if they merely recorded temporary diplomatic agreement rather than enacted enduring legal texts', see John Yoo (Deputy Assistant Attorney General, US Department of Justice), 'International Law and the War in Iraq', *The American Journal of International Law*, 97/3 (July 2003), pp. 567–8.
62. Adam Roberts, 'Law and the Use of Force after Iraq', *Survival*, 45/2 (Summer 2003), pp. 43–4. Roberts argues, p. 43, however, that the guiding principle should be that a resolution once passed remains in effect, unless repudiated by a new resolution, which would be hard to achieve given the existence of the veto in the Security Council. For a forthright defence of the implied authorization rationale, see Christopher Greenwood, 'The Legality of the Use of Force in Iraq in 2003', in Michael Bothe, Mary Ellen O'Connell, and Natalino Ronzitti (eds.), *Redefining Sovereignty: The Use of Force after the Cold War* (Ardsley, NY: Transnational Publishers, 2006), pp. 387–415; Christopher Greenwood, 'International Law and the Pre-Emptive Use of Force: Afghanistan, al-Qaida, and Iraq', *San Diego International Law Journal*, 4 (2003), pp. 26–37. However, in the large literature around the subject many other Western international lawyers have rejected the legitimacy of the implied authorization rationale. The head of the legal department of the British Foreign Office at the time of the invasion, Sir Michael Wood, repeatedly told ministers that there was no basis in international law for regime change in Iraq without a second UN Security Council resolution (beyond Resolution 1441) specifically authorizing force, 'I told ministers Iraq war was illegal', *Evening Standard*, 26 January 2010, p. 5.

63. Gazzini, *The Changing Rules on the Use of Force in International Law*, p. 229.
64. Statement by Putin, 20 March 2003, at http://www.mid.ru; Foreign Minister Igor Ivanov, Security Council 4721st Meeting, Press Release SC/7696, 19 March 2003, at http://www.un.org/News/Press/docs/2003/sc7696.doc.htm; speech by Igor Ivanov, 26 March 2003, at http://www.mid.ru.
65. Sergei Lavrov, 'My Years on East River: Apropos the 60th Anniversary of the Global Organization', *International Affairs* (Moscow), 4 (2005), at http://www.mid.ru, 9 September 2005.
66. Galia Golan, 'Russia and the Iraq War: Was Putin's Policy a Failure?', *Communist and Post-Communist Studies*, 37 (2004), pp. 430–7.
67. The Deputy Chairman of the Defence Committee of the Russian State Duma, Vladimir Volkov, noted that Russian leaders were not telling the Russian public about this treaty, although Russia as the successor to the USSR 'ought to honour its terms and provisions', *Rossiyskie vesti*, 5, February 2003, p. 4. When Operation Iraqi Freedom commenced, Foreign Minister Igor Ivanov informed that Iraq had not requested assistance from Russia under this treaty and that 'Russia's assistance consists of its clear stance in favour of a political settlement', interview on 21 March 2003, at http://www.mid.ru. Article 8 of the treaty stipulates that in the event of a threat to either party they should 'coordinate their positions to remove the threat that has arisen or … restore peace', Zafar Imam, *Towards a Model Relationship: A Study of Soviet Treaties with India and other Third World Countries* (New Delhi: ABC Publishing House, 1983), p. 120.
68. Sergei Solodovnik, 'Geopolitical Bargaining', *Vremya*, 13 September 2002, p. 1. The author argues that such a bargain was unworkable.
69. Golan, 'Russia and the Iraq War', p. 438.
70. 'Chirac Promises to Use Veto but Putin Faces Dilemma', *The Guardian*, 11 March 2003. Putin himself kept silent, perhaps still considering his options to the last minute.
71. For this UN diplomacy see Golan, 'Russia and the Iraq War', pp. 437–42.
72. 'On open meeting of UN Security Council on Iraq', 28 March 2003; statement by Lavrov at meeting of the Security Council, 27 March 2003, at http://www.mid.ru.
73. Statement by Lavrov, 27 March 2003.
74. Sergei Karaganov, 'Lessons of the War in Iraq', *Izvestiya*, 14 May 2003, p. 4.
75. UNSC Resolution 1483, adopted on 22 May 2003, at http://www.un.org/Docs/scres/2003/sc2003.htm. The resolution begins, in line with Lavrov's appeal, by stressing the Iraqi people's right to determine their own political future and control their own natural resources.
76. Alexei Arbatov, 'Iraq Lessons', *Moscow News*, 23, 18–24 June 2003, p. 4. For Ivanov's assessment of Resolution 1483, see Igor Ivanov, 'The Iraq Problem Returns to the United Nations', *Nezavisimaya gazeta*, 30 May 2003.
77. UNSC Resolution 1511, adopted on 16 October 2003, http://www.un.org/Docs/scres/2003/sc2003.htm.
78. Interview, 3 November 2003, http://www.kremlin.ru.
79. Georgy Stepanov, 'Moscow and Paris Revolt against UK–US Resolution on Iraq', *Izvestiya*, 4 June 2004, p. 5.
80. UNSC Resolution 1546, adopted on 8 June 2004, http://www.un.org/Docs/scres/2004/sc2004.htm.
81. *Izvestiya*, 30 August 2004.

82. Sergei Karaganov, 'Lessons of the War in Iraq', *Izvestiya*, 14 May 2003, p. 4.
83. 'Tomahawks and Scuds in the Sights', Vladimir Urban, *Novye izvestiya*, 31 January 2003, pp. 1, 6; Yury E. Fedorov, 'Russia's Foreign Policy: Basic Trends under President Putin', in Hanna Smith (ed.), *Russia and its Foreign Policy: Influences, Interests and Issues* (Säärijärvi: Kikimora Publications, 2005), p. 21.
84. See interview with General Vladimir Lobov, 'Strategy of Starvation Used Against Iraq', *Krasnaya zvezda*, 12 April 2003, p. 3; meeting of Science Council of the Academy of Military Sciences to discuss the war in Iraq, Oleg Falichev, 'Hidden Springs of the Iraqi War', *Krasnaya zvezda*, 28 June 2003, p. 3; Major General G. A. Berezkin, 'Lessons of the Iraq War', *Military Thought*, 12/3 (2003), pp. 139–82.
85. *Izvestiya*, 4 April 2004, p. 1.
86. 'Putin Hints Solution on Iraq Possible', *The Moscow Times*, 22 September 2003, pp. 1–2; Andrei Zlobin, 'Iraq: The Russians Are Coming', *Vremya novostei*, 5 September 2003, p. 1.
87. Putin at press conference, 5 November 2003 and interview with Foreign Minister Igor Ivanov, 8 November 2003, at http://www.mid.ru.
88. Author's transcript of meeting with Putin on 6 September 2004, at Novo-Ogarevo, with members of the Valdai Discussion Club.
89. 'More Iraqis to Learn from NATO', *International Herald Tribune*, 23 September 2004.
90. Vladimir Mukhin, 'CIS Readies for Defence', *Nezavisimaya gazeta*, 20 March 2003, p. 4.
91. Statement of Sixth Meeting of Secretaries of the Security Councils of the CST Member States, 20 March 2003, at http://www.mid.ru.
92. Yelena Baikova, 'An Advantageous "Swamp" Status', *Nezavisimaya gazeta*, 21 March 2003, p. 7; 'Five Degrees of Separation: The Central Asia States' Positions towards War in Iraq', *RFE/RL Central Asia Report*, 3/12, 21 March 2003. Moldova, Kyrgyzstan, Tajikistan, and Turkmenistan emphasized rather the need to resolve the crisis through the UN.
93. 'Five Degrees of Separation'.
94. Helmke, *Under Attack*, p. 161. For the positions taken and claims made by these states, see Reisman and Armstrong, 'Claims to Pre-Emptive Uses of Force', pp. 96–108.
95. Kofi Annan, 'Address to the General Assembly', 23 September 2003, at http://www.un.org/webcast/ga/58/statements/sg2eng030923. Cited in Daalder (ed.), *Beyond Preemption*, p. 7.
96. Report of the Secretary General's High Level Panel on Threats, Challenges and Change, *A More Secure World: Our Shared Responsibility*, UN Doc. A/59/565, 2 December 2004, p. 63, at http://www.un.org/secureworld/report/pdf. Reisman and Armstrong, 'Claims to Pre-Emptive Uses of Force', pp. 88–9. The Panel included senior former American and Russian officials. For contrasting claims that the legal prohibition of intervention in another state must be adjusted to reflect the fact that the most serious threats to international security today arise within states, in particular threats posed by WMD in repressive states, see L. Feinstein and A. M. Slaughter, 'A Duty to Prevent', *Foreign Affairs*, 83/1 (2004), p. 137; as criticized in Brunnée and Toope, 'The Use of Force: International Law after Iraq', pp. 802–3.

97. *National Security Strategy of the United States of America*, White House (March 2006), at http://georgebush-whitehouse.archives.gov/nsc/nss/2006.
98. Thomas M. Franck, 'What Happens Now? The United Nations after Iraq', *The American Journal of International Law*, 97/3 (July 2003), p. 616.
99. Tom J. Farer, 'The Prospect for International Law and Order in the Wake of Iraq', *The American Journal of International Law*, 97/3 (July 2003), p. 628.
100. Statement on 20 March 2003, at http://www.mid.ru. For a Russian anthology which argues overall that the Iraq crisis marked a general crisis in world order and revealed the US as seeking to establish global hegemony and introduce a system of 'limited national sovereignty', see V. A. Guseinov and S. V. Kortunov (eds.), *Iraksky krizis i stanovlenie novogo mirovogo poryadka* (Moscow: Institute of Strategic Studies and Analysis, Friedrich Ebert Foundation).
101. Foreign Minister Igor Ivanov, 'The Iraq Crisis and the Struggle for a New World Pattern', 19 January 2004, at http://www/mid.ru.

Chapter 6 Contested Norms in the CIS Regional Order

1. Major studies on Russian-style peacekeeping that confirm this point include Dov Lynch, *Russian Peacekeeping Strategies in the CIS: The Cases of Moldova, Georgia and Tajikistan* (Basingstoke: Macmillan, 2000); Lena Jonson and Clive Archer (eds.), *Peacekeeping and the Role of Russia in Eurasia* (Boulder: Westview Press, 1996); John Mackinlay and Peter Cross (eds.), *Regional Peacekeepers: The Paradox of Russian Peacekeeping* (Tokyo: United Nations University Press, 2003); Roy Allison, *Peacekeeping in the Soviet Successor States* (Paris: Institute for Security Studies, Western European Union, Chaillot Paper No. 18, November 1994); Lena Jonson, *Keeping the Peace in the CIS: The Evolution of Russian Policy* (London: Royal Institute of International Affairs, Discussion Paper No. 81, 1999).
2. Interview in *Nezavisimya gazeta*, 8 December 1992.
3. Speech to the Federation Council, *Rossiyskaya gazeta*, 12 January 1994; cited in Elizabeth Teague, 'Yeltsin: Russia "First among Equals" in Commonwealth', *RFE/RL Daily Report*, 7, 20 January 1994.
4. See Roy Allison, 'Military Factors in Foreign Policy', in Neil Malcolm, Alex Pravda, Roy Allison, and Margot Light (eds.), *Internal Factors in Russian Foreign Policy* (Oxford: Oxford University Press, 1996), pp. 263–77.
5. Andrew Bennett, *Condemned to Repetition? The Rise, Fall and Reprise of Soviet-Russian Military Interventionism, 1973–1996* (Cambridge, MA: MIT Press, 1999), pp. 305–10.
6. Russia TV, 28 February 1993, in *BBC Summary of World Broadcasts. Former Soviet Union* (henceforth SU), 1626 B/1, 2 March 1993. For details of the reaction of the Russian Foreign Ministry see SU/1629, Section B. See also *Izvestiya*, 4 March 1993.
7. Kozyrev at press conference, RIA news agency, 20 November 1993, in SU/1853 B/9, 23 November 1993; interview, *Nezavismaya gazeta*, 24 November 1993, pp. 1, 3.
8. Deputy Defence Minister Georgy Kondratiev, *Krasnaya zvezda*, 21 June 1994, pp. 1–2.

9. See Allison, 'Military Factors in Foreign Policy', pp. 271–5.
10. Reported by Pavel Felgengauer, 'Old Borders and New Bases', *Segodnya*, 16 September 1993. As revealed by Defence Minister Pavel Grachev in an internal briefing on 14 September 1993.
11. Interview with Andrey Nikolaev, Channel 1 TV, 25 August 1994, in SU/2087 G/3, 30 August 1994.
12. Directive of 5 April 1994, in *Rossiiskie vesti*, 7 April 1994. For controversy about this directive see *Segodnya*, 16 September 1993.
13. Colonel-General Mikhail Kolesnikov, first deputy chief of the Russian General Staff, *Nezavisimaya gazeta*, 1 August 1992.
14. *Krasnaya zvezda*, 23 June 1992 (the CIS Joint Forces structure failed to develop any real autonomy from Russian national forces). One reason why Russian military conservatives opposed NATO military intervention under the UN mandate to support peacekeeping operations in the former Yugoslavia at the time appears to have been to avoid establishing a precedent for any possible future NATO intervention on the Russian periphery.
15. Interview in *Nezavisimaya gazeta*, 24 November 1993, pp. 1, 3.
16. Report of press conference, Radio Moscow World Service, 20 May 1992, in SU/1387 C2/1, 22 May 1992.
17. Colonel Sergei Pechurov, 'Pentagon engages in implementation of "Clinton Doctrine"', *Krasnaya zvezda*, 19 October 1993, p. 3.
18. 'US to Intervene in ex-Soviet Union', *The Guardian*, 6 August 1993.
19. Suzanne Crow. 'Russia Asserts its Strategic Agenda', *Radio Free Europe/Radio Liberty Research Report*, 2/50, 17 December 1993, p. 5; Russian Foreign Ministry statement on 13 August 1993, in *RFE/RL News Brief*, 16–20 August 1993.
20. Statement by Strobe Talbott, special adviser to the US Secretary of State, *Washington Times*, 20 August 1993.
21. 'Russia Warned To Respect Borders', *Financial Times*, 7 February 1994.
22. US special envoy (and later Secretary of State) Madeleine Albright in talks with Azerbaijani president Heydar Aliyev, Itar-Tass news agency, 3 September 1994, in SU/2098 F/1, 12 September 1994. The 'Caucasus' here clearly denotes the South Caucasus.
23. S. Neil MacFarlane and Albrecht Schnabel, 'Russia's Approach to Peacekeeping', *International Journal*, 55, 2 (Spring 1995), p. 314.
24. See 'Boris Yeltsin Presents Russian "Monroe Doctrine" in New York', *Izvestiya*, 28 September 1994, p. 3; *The Times*, 27 September 1994. The section on conflicts was similar to the paragraphs on the same subject in a Russian Foreign Intelligence Service analytical report published the previous week; see 'Russia's Foreign Intelligence Service Predicts Scenarios for Events in the CIS', *Nezavisimaya gazeta*, 22 September 1994.
25. 'US and Russia Carve Out 'Spheres of Influence', *The Times*, 27 July 1994; 'US and Russia Broker Haiti Invasion Deal', *The Times*, 1 August 1994; *Komsomolskaya Pravda*, 2 August 1994, p. 1, *Foreign Broadcast Information Service* (henceforth FBIS) SOV-94-148, 2 August 1994.
26. 'Osnovy voennoi doktriny Rossii', *Voennaya mysl*, Special Issue, May 1992, pp. 1–2. This was not just a radical military perspective. A Russian deputy foreign minister suggested that a rapid deployment force be created specifically to protect the rights of

Russian-speaking people outside the Russian Federation; Sergei Krylov, 3 December 1993, Itar-Tass, report in *RFE/RL News Briefs*, 6–10 December 1993, p. 2.

27. 'Basic Provisions of the Military Doctrine of the Russian Federation', *Izvestiya*, 18 November 1993, pp. 1, 4.
28. As cited MacFarlane and Schnabel, 'Russia's Approach to Peacekeeping', p. 312.
29. Sergei Stankevich, Russian State Adviser on Political Questions, *Rossiyskaya gazeta*, 23 June 1992, p. 1.
30. Speech at 48th session of UN General Assembly, 28 September 1993, Itar-Tass news agency, 28 September 1993, in SU/1807 B/3, 30 September 1993. Here Kozyrev also had in mind Russian minorities in the Baltic States. See also his article 'United Nations: The World's Hopes and Fears', *Rossiyskaya gazeta*, 30 October 1993, pp. 1 and 7.
31. See Andrei Zagorski, 'Regional Structures of Security Policy Within the CIS', in Roy Allison and Christoph Bluth (eds.), *Security Dilemmas in Russia and Eurasia* (London: Royal Institute of International Affairs, 1998), pp. 281–300.
32. Nicole Jackson, *Russian Foreign Policy in the CIS: Theories, Debates and Actions* (London: Routledge, 2003), pp. 153–5; Lena Jonson, *The Tajik War: A Challenge to Russian Policy* (London: The Royal Institute of International Affairs, Discussion Paper No. 74, 1998), pp. 12–13.
33. Russian Defence Ministry statement, Itar-Tass news agency, 9 August 1993, in SU/1765 C1/1, 12 August 1991. Rather at odds with this, Kozyrev, in a speech to Russian deputies, stressed that Russia has a certain 'zone of special responsibility and special interests' in Tajikistan; *Nezavisimaya gazeta*, 29 April 1993, p. 3. For his definition of Russian national interests in Tajikistan see *Izvestiya*, 4 August 1993.
34. Article by Kozyrev, *Nezavisimaya gazeta*, 22 September 2003, p. 1. A joint statement by the Russian ministries of foreign affairs and defence repeated this formulation later word for word; see Itar-Tass news agency, 29 March 1994, in BBC SU/1963 S1/1, 5 April 1994.
35. Among the large literature on the 'peacekeeping doctrine' that was developed by the Russian military command out of the experience of these operations, see James M. Greene, 'The Peacekeeping Doctrines of the CIS', *Jane's Intelligence Review*, 5/4 (April 1993), pp. 156–9; Pavel K. Baev, *The Russian Army in a Time of Troubles* (London: Sage, 1996), pp. 135–41; Allison, *Peacekeeping in the Soviet Successor States*, pp. 22–30; Lena Jonson, 'In Search of a Doctrine: Russian Interventionism in Conflicts in its "Near Abroad"', *Low Intensity Conflicts and Law Enforcement*, 5/3 (Winter 1996), pp. 440–65. For Russia's formal military regulations see *Programma podgotovki chastey mirotvorcheskikh sil* (Moscow: Russian Ministry of Defence, 1992); *Vremennaya instruktsiya po podgotovke voinskikh kontingentov, privlekaemykh dlya formirvaniya grupp voennykh nablyudateley i kollektivnykh sil po podderzhaniyu mira gosudarstv-uchastnikov sodruzhestva nezavisimykh gosudarstv* (Moscow: Russian Ministry of Defence, 1993).
36. Kozyrev, *Nezavisimaya gazeta*, 22 September 2003, p. 1.
37. Deputy defence minister, Colonel-General Georgiy Kondratyev, 'Russia's Blue Helmets', *Krasnaya zvezda*, 16 February 1994, p. 2.
38. 'US to Intervene in ex-Soviet Union', *The Guardian*, 6 August 1993.
39. Kozyrev, 'United Nations: The World's Hopes and Fears'.

40. NTV, Moscow, interview with Boutros Boutros-Ghali and Foreign Minister Kozyrev, 3 April 1994, SU/1963 B/9–10.
41. Joint statement by Russian Ministry of Defence and Ministry of Foreign Affairs, statement by Deputy Foreign Minister Sergei Lavrov, *Sevodnya*, 6 April 1994, p. 1; Itar-Tass news agency, 5 April 1994, SU/1971 B/5, 14 April 1994.
42. 'U.N. Security Council Establishes Observer Mission in Tajikistan', *Segodnya*, 20 December 1994, p. 4.
43. Martha Finnemore 'Constructing Norms of Humanitarian Intervention', in Peter J. Katzenstein (ed.), *The Culture of National Security: Norms and Identity in World Politics* (New York: Columbia University Press, 1996), p. 182.
44. Baev, *The Russian Army in a Time of Troubles*, pp. 110–14; Jonson, 'In Search of a Doctrine: Russian Interventionism in Conflicts in its "Near Abroad"', pp. 450–2.
45. Among many analyses of this role of the CIS, see for example S. Neil MacFarlane, 'On the Front Lines in the Near Abroad: The CIS and the OSCE in Georgia's Civil Wars', *Third World Quarterly*, 18/3 (1997), pp. 512–23. See also Dov Lynch, *The Conflict in Abkhazia: Dilemmas in Russian 'Peacekeeping' Policy* (London: Royal Institute of International Affairs, Discussion Paper No. 77, 1998).
46. 'Agreement on Collective Peacemaking Forces and Joint Measures on the Material and Technical Supply', *Military News Bulletin*, 10 October 1993, pp. 1–2.
47. The Kazakh President Nursultan Nazarbayev explicitly opposed this option during a visit to Britain in March 1994. *Financial Times*, 23 March 1994.
48. Address by foreign ministers of the five countries, circulated as a document of the UN Security Council. Itar-Tass news agency, 3 November 1993, SU/1848 A/1, 17 November 1993.
49. Baev, *The Russian Army in a Time of Troubles*, p. 113.
50. Jonson, *Keeping the Peace in the CIS*, p. 14.
51. Statement by President Nazarbayev to Kazakhstan's Supreme Soviet, 23 December 1991, SU/1264 B/4, 28 December 1991. Charter of the Commonwealth of Independent States, reproduced in *International Peacekeeping*, 6/1 (2000), p. 55.
52. 'Agreement on Groups of Military Observers and Collective Peacekeeping Forces in the CIS', signed on 20 March 1992, Itar-Tass, 23 March 1992, in SU/1339 C2/2–3. Also in *Diplomaticheskiy vestnik*, 7 (April 1992). This was signed by eleven states, although Azerbaijan and Ukraine made conditions.
53. Meeting of CIS defence ministers, 18 July 1994, Itar-Tass 18 July 1994, SU/2053 A/1, 21 July 1994. Russian defence minister Pavel Grachev criticized the representatives of some states like Uzbekistan for telling him that Georgia is a long way away and had nothing to do with them; interview on NTV, 19 July 1994, SU/2053 A2/2, 21 July 1994.
54. It begins with the CIS leaders promising to refrain 'from military, political or economic and other forms of pressure on each other'. They affirmed their opposition to any moves to undermine the stability of each other's existing borders. They undertook not to support separatist movements or to establish links with or assist separatist regimes that may arise. Memorandum adopted at meeting of CIS heads of states, Almaty, 10 February 1995, Itar-Tass, 10 February 1995, in FBIS-SOV-95-029, 13 February 1995.
55. 'Kontseptsiya preodotvrashcheniya i ureglulirovaniya konfliktov na territorii gosudarstv—uchastnikov Sodruzhestva nezavisimykh Gosudarstv'. 'Polozhenie

o Kollektivnykh silakh po podderzhannyu mira v Sodruzhestve Nezavisimykh Gosudarstv', *Diplomaticheskiy vestnik*, 2, February (1996), pp. 38–52. See Jonson, 'In Search of a Doctrine', pp. 445–57.

56. This raised the problem of how consent would be identified and the role of coercion in reaching such consent in the hierarchical regional order described in this chapter.
57. Jonson, *Keeping the Peace in the CIS*, p. 14.
58. This was illustrated by the political battleground in the post-Soviet region over international election observer missions. See Rick Fawn, 'Battle over the Box: International Election Observation Missions, Political Competition and Retrenchment in the Post-Soviet Space', *International Affairs*, 82/6 (2006), pp. 1133–53.
59. Envoy Extraordinary and Plenipotentiary Yuri Sharkov, '"Color Revolutions": Uniformity in Diversity', *International Affairs* (Moscow), 54/4 (2008), p. 26.
60. Cited in Julie Wilhelmsen and Geir Flikke, 'Evidence of Russia's Bush Doctrine in the CIS', *European Security*, 14/3 (2005), p. 394.
61. Interview in *Profil*, 22, 13–19 June 2005.
62. Sergei Ivanov. 'Russia Must Be Strong', *Wall Street Journal*, 11 January 2006, as cited in *Eurasia Daily Monitor* (Jamestown Foundation), 8/9, 13 January 2006, at http://www.eurasia.org.
63. For assessment of these contrary interpretations see Sharkov, '"Color Revolutions"', pp. 25–31; Stephen F. Jones, 'The Rose Revolution: A Revolution Without Revolutionaries?', *Cambridge Review of International Affairs*, 19/1 (March 2006), pp. 40–3; Andrew Wilson, 'Ukraine's Orange Revolution, NGOs and the Role of the West', *Cambridge Review of International Affairs*, 19/1 (March 2006), pp. 21–31; Thomas Ambrosio, *Authoritarian Backlash: Russian Resistance to Democratization in the Former Soviet Union* (Farnham: Ashgate, 2009), pp. 131–57; Donnacha Ó Beacháin and Abel Polese, 'What Happened to the Colour Revolutions? Authoritarian Responses from Former Soviet Spaces', *Journal of International and Area Studies*, 17/2 (2010), pp. 31–51.
64. Andrey Makarychev, 'Russia, NATO and the "Color Revolutions": Discursive Traps', *Russian Politics and Law*, 47/5 (September–October 2009), pp. 40–51.
65. The concept was popularized after a speech by Vladislav Surkov, deputy director of the Russian presidential administration and a leading ideologue for the Kremlin, *Nezavisimaya gazeta*, 13 July 2005, pp. 1, 3. See Ambrosio, *Authoritarian Backlash*, pp. 71–86; Andrey Makarychev, 'Russia's Search for International Identity through the Sovereign Democracy Concept', *The International Spectator*, 43/2 (June 2008), pp. 49–62. Putin himself retained some distance from the concept, not wishing to present it as a model competing with Western liberal democracy.
66. Despite this anxiety, formally Russian officials claimed that for various reasons 'the components that [American] organizers of the "color revolutions" in Georgia and Ukraine relied on are completely or partially absent in Russia', as elaborated by Sharkov, 'Color Revolutions', pp. 30–1.
67. Thomas Ambrosio, 'Insulating Russia from a Colour Revolution: How the Kremlin Resists Regional Democratic Trends', *Democratization*, 14/2 (April 2007), pp. 232–52; Ambrosio, *Authoritarian Backlash*. See also Vitali Silitski, '"Survival

of the Fittest": Domestic and International Dimensions of the Authoritarian Reaction in the former Soviet Union Following the Colored Revolutions', *Communist and Post-Communist Studies*, 43/4 (December 2010), pp. 339–50.

68. US secret diplomatic memorandum, 14 November 2005, Secret Dushanbe 001812, published by WikiLeaks website, available at http://www.guardian.co.uk/world/us-embassy-cables-documents/45022.
69. *Eurasia Daily Monitor* (Jamestown Foundation), 7/68, 8 April 2010; *Eurasia Daily Monitor* (Jamestown Foundation), 7/69, 9 April 2010, at http://www.eurasia.org.
70. Army General Nikolay Makarov, Interfax-AVN military news agency, 25 May 2010, in BBC Mon FS1 MCU 250510 ib/ats. The commander of Russian airborne troops had noted that the duration of the paratroopers' stay would depend on the situation in Kyrgyzstan; Lt-General Vladimir Shamanov, Interfax-AVN military news agency, 15 April 2010, in BBC Mon FS1 MCU 150410 aby.
71. For such a comparative perspective on second-tier states see Andrew Hurrell, 'Hegemony, Liberalism and Global Order: What Space for Would-Be Great Powers?', *International Affairs*, 82/1 (2006), p. 8.
72. This argument is developed in Roy Allison, 'Virtual Regionalism, Regional Structures and Regime Security in Central Asia', *Central Asian Security*, 27/2 (June 2008), pp. 185–90.
73. Articles 9 and 7 in the Charter of the Collective Security Treaty Organization, at http://untreaty.un.org/unts/144078-158780/5/913289.pdf.
74. See Roy Allison, 'Strategic Reassertion in Russia's Central Asia Policy', *International Affairs*, 80/2 (March 2004), pp. 286–8.
75. This process of political bonding is a probable function, for example, of the CSTO Parliamentary Assembly, which had its inaugural session in St Petersburg in March 2007. More specific measures are likely to be considered at the six-monthly meetings of the Committee of Secretaries of the Security Councils of the CSTO.
76. Moscow described the Kant base in Kyrgyzstan as a component of a CSTO rapid reaction force, although in terms of its structure and personnel it is part of the Russian Urals Air Force. As noted by Lt-General Yevgeny Yurev, Commander of the Urals Air Force and Air Defence Army, 'Russia Returns to Central Asia', *Nezavisimaya gazeta*, 24 October 2003, p. 2.
77. Pavel Baev, *Russian Energy Policy and Military Power: Putin's Quest for Greatness* (London: Routledge, 2008), p. 71.
78. Silitski, 'Survival of the Fittest', p. 349. See also Erica Marat, *The Military and the State in Central Asia* (London: Routledge, 2010), pp. 94–5.
79. *Eurasia Daily Monitor* (Jamestown Foundation), 8/177, 27 September 2011; *Eurasia Daily Monitor* (Jamestown Foundation), 8/180, 30 September 2011, at http://www.eurasianet.org.
80. Bordyuzha could not formally speak for the Russian leadership, but his views seemed to express well the thinking of the Russian security elite. Interview in *Nezavisimaya gazeta*, 13 January 2006, p. 9.
81. See communiqué of the 2006 Shanghai SCO Summit, 15 June 2006, *Nezavisimaya gazeta*, 16 June 2006, pp. 1, 6. For further discussion, see Allison, 'Virtual Regionalism, Regional Structures and Regime Security', pp. 185–7; Thomas

Ambrosio, 'Catching the "Shanghai Spirit": How the Shanghai Cooperation Organization Promotes Authoritarian Norms in Central Asia', *Europe-Asia Studies*, 60/8 (October 2008), pp. 1321–44.

82. It has been claimed that Russia aired a proposal at the time of the Astana SCO summit in July 2005 to prevent such regime change through some 'mechanism of mutual assistance', legitimized by the SCO, that would provide Moscow permission to carry out special operations in Central Asian countries, as 'requested' by their regimes. See Sergei Strokan, 'The Shanghai Verdict', *Kommersant*, 5 July 2005, p. 9.
83. For an argument that the SCO has focused on intra-regional transnational security challenges perceived as a threat to regime security by its member states' leaderships, see Stephen Aris, *Eurasian Regionalism: The Shanghai Cooperation Organisation* (Basingstoke: Palgrave Macmillan, 2011).
84. Marcel de Haas, *The 'Peace Mission 2007' Exercises: The Shanghai Cooperation Organisation Advances*, Defence Academy of the United Kingdom, September 2007, p. 11. See also Ambrosio, *Authoritarian Backlash*, p. 171.
85. Aleksandr Gabuyev, 'China's Got Money in the Bank', *Kommersant*, 16 June 2011, p. 1; Interfax-Kazakhstan news agency, Almaty, 6 June 2012, BBC Mon CAU 060612 ak/qu.
86. Fyodor Lukyanov, 'Russia's Zone of Responsibility', *Moscow Times*, 16 June 2010.
87. A Kazakh presidential adviser on political issues urged 'Kyrgyzstan's people to find a way out of this difficult situation themselves' as there was no need for an intervention of CSTO third forces. In contrast, deposed president Bakiyev advocated sending in such forces to restore order. Interfax-Kazakhstan news agency, 14 June 2010, BBC Mon CAU 140610 ak/akh; *Eurasia Daily Monitor* (Jamestown Foundation), 7/124, 28 June 2010, at http://www.eurasia.org.
88. Bordyuzha as reported by Interfax-AVN military news agency, 26 January 2011, BBC Mon FS1 FsuPol jp.
89. *Eurasia Daily Monitor* (Jamestown Foundation), 8/165, 9 September 2011, at http://eurasia.org.
90. Proposals for the CSTO to develop a legal basis for responding to domestic crises were circulated in a report by the Institute for Contemporary Development (INSOR), a think tank with connections to President Medvedev, Igor Yurgens (ed.), *Collective Security Treaty Organization: Responsible Security* (synopsis of report), Moscow, August 2011, pp. 4–6, at http://www.insor-russia.ru/files/CSTO%Synopsis.pdf.
91. The December 2010 CSTO summit resulted in documents intended to amend the Collective Security Treaty and the CSTO Charter. But Uzbekistan did not consent to these amendments and questioned their legality since they do not have the consent of all CSTO members. See *Radio Free Europe Radio Liberty* report, 4 September 2011, at http://www.rferl.org/articleprintview/24317363.html.
92. Arkady Dubnov, 'Who Needs the Bulky and Unreliable CSTO?', *Yezhednevnyy zhurnal*, 22 August 2011, cited in *Johnson's Russia List*, 25 August 2011, issue 145, at http://www.cdi.org/russia/johnson.
93. Marat, *The Military and the State in Central Asia*, p. 89.

94. Uzbekistan set out conditions for its participation in the CRRF in June 2009, which included prohibiting their use in setting conflicts between the CSTO member states; Interfax-Kazakhstan news agency, 4 June 2009, in BBC Mon Alert CAU 040609 nu/mio. See also *Eurasia Daily Monitor* (Jamestown Foundation), 8/98, 20 May 2011, at http://www.eurasia.org; undated session of Legislative Chamber of Uzbekistan's parliament, commenting on CSTO Security Council session of 14 July 2011, at http://parliament.gov.uz/en/events/chamber/1334.
95. As pointed out by the Russian analyst Dubnov, 'Who Needs the Bulky and Unreliable CSTO?'
96. Vladimir Mukhin, 'Achilles Heel of Collective Defence', *Nezavisimaya gazeta*, 13 December 2010, p. 1.
97. Report of roundtable meeting by military news agency Interfax-AVN, 27 April 2011, in BBC Mon FS1 MCU 270411 et.
98. Bordyuzha's description of the discussions at an informal CSTO meeting in August 2011, Kazakh Khabar TV, 12 August 2011, BBC Mon Alert CAU 120811 ak/hsh.
99. Bordyuzha's description of the discussions at an informal CSTO meeting in August 2011, Kazakh Khabar TV, 12 August 2011, BBC Mon Alert CAU 120811 ak/hsh; Tai Adelaja, 'Brotherhood in Resistance', *Russia Profile*, 15 August 2011.
100. Roundtable meeting reported by military news agency Interfax-AVN, 27 April 2011, in BBC Mon FS1 FsuPol kdd. The force was described as 4,200 strong.
101. Interfax-AVN website, 17 March 2010, in BBC Mon FS1 FsuPol gyl.
102. A senior Kazakh defence official described Kazbat as 'the most well-prepared peacekeeping unit in Central Asia' after exercises with servicemen from Kazakhstan, the USA, the UK, Lithuania, and Kyrgyzstan, in August 2011. Interfax-Kazakhstan news agency, 18 August 2011, BBC Mon CAU 180811 sg/akm. For the interaction of Central Asian states with NATO, see Marat, *The Military and the State in Central Asia*, pp. 104–15.
103. *Eurasia Daily Monitor* (Jamestown Foundation), 9/10, 16 January 2012, at http://www.eurasianet.org.
104. Yelena Chernenko, 'CSTO Member States Will Have to Learn to Coordinate Their Foreign Political Positions and Rhetoric', *Kommersant*, 2 November 2011.
105. Neil Melvin, 'Eurasian Security Arrangements Face Reality Check after Kyrgyzstan Crisis', *SIPRI Newsletter*, July/August 2010, at http://www.sipri.org/media/newsletter/essay/julyaugust10.

Chapter 7 Russian Intervention in Georgia 2008

1. For analysis of these conflicting narratives see Roy Allison, 'Russia Resurgent? Moscow's Campaign To "Coerce Georgia to Peace"', *International Affairs*, 84/6 (November 2008), pp. 1145–71; Svante E. Cornell and S. Frederick Starr (eds.), *The Guns of August 2008: Russia's War in Georgia* (Armonk, NY: M. E. Sharpe, 2008), especially chapters 8 and 9; Wolfgang Richter, 'Initial Military Operations during the War in Georgia in August 2008', *Caucasus Analytical Digest*, 10 (2 November 2009), pp. 5–9, http://www.res.ethz.ch/analysis/cad; Ruslan Pukhov

(ed.), *The Tanks of August* [online] (Moscow: Centre for Analysis of Strategies and Technologies, 2010), http://www.cast.ru/files/The_Tanks_of_August_sm_Eng_pdf; Rick Fawn and Robert Nalbandov, 'The Difficulties of Knowing the Start of War in the Information Age: Russia, Georgia and the War over South Ossetia, August 2008', *European Security*, 21/1 (March 2012), pp. 57–89. See also the European Union's special commission on the conflict, although only a part of one chapter (5) addresses the disputed timeline and conduct of operations, *Independent International Fact-Finding Mission on the Conflict in Georgia*, Vol. 2 (September 2008), pp. 200–17, at http://www.ceiig.ch.

2. Statement on 8 August 2008, at http://www.mid.ru.
3. Letter by Russia's permanent representative at the UN, Vitaliy Churkin, Ministry of Foreign Affairs website, 13 August 2008, *BBC Summary of World Broadcasts Former Soviet Union*, available at http://www.bbc.monitoringonline.com (henceforth BBC), Mon FS1 MCU 140808 hb/ats.
4. See speech by President Medvedev at ceremony honouring Russian servicemen, 8 August 2009, Vladikavkaz, at http://www.kremlin.ru/eng/text/speeches.2009/08/08/1845. For the General Assembly definition see http://www.un.org/documents/ga/res/29/ares29.htm. For an overview of the legal issues see Christopher P. M. Waters, 'The Caucasus Conflict and the Role of Law', in James A. Green and Christopher P. M. Waters (eds.), *Conflict in the Caucasus: Implications for International Legal Order* (Basingstoke: Palgrave Macmillan, 2010), pp. 8–25.
5. Major-General Vyacheslav Borisov, interview on Ekho Moskvy radio, 6 June 2009, BBC Mon FS1 FsuPol gv. See also Angelika Nussberger, 'The "Five-Day War" in Court: Russia, Georgia and International Law', *Osteuropa*, 58/11 (November 2008), pp. 19–39.
6. Similar conclusions are reached in the EU fact-finding report; *Independent International Fact-Finding Mission*, Vol. 2, p. 221.
7. We may note in this respect that the 1974 UN General Assembly (in Article 3 (g)) defines 'The sending by or on behalf of a State of armed bands, groups, irregulars or mercenaries, which carry out acts of armed force against another State' as aggression.
8. In this discussion one side has argued that the legal prohibition of the aggressive use of force reflects a definition of aggression as the conduct of one state against another, whereas the secessionist enclave of South Ossetia was not recognized as a state, even by Russia at the time of its intervention. Hence Georgia undertook an enforcement operation by the central government against a separatist entity (albeit one that many have claimed raised serious issues of international humanitarian law—a separate issue). It has also been argued in this context that the application of the *jus ad bellum* to non-state entities remains aspirational or at best an emerging principle in legal terms; Christian Henderson and James A Green, 'The *jus ad bellum* and Entities Short of Statehood in the Report on the Conflict in Georgia', *International and Comparative Law Quarterly*, 59 (January 2010), pp. 129–39. This is contrary to the analysis of the EU fact-finding mission, which did not uphold the legality of the Georgian offensive against the city of Tskhinvali in the form that it was undertaken.
9. *Independent International Fact-Finding Mission*, Vol. 2, pp. 280–3.

10. International law essentially regards secessionist conflicts as matters of domestic law and politics. Regardless of Russia's extensive involvement as mediator, as the provider of economic and military support to South Ossetia as well as other forms of intervention, Russia has been a 'third-party state' in relation to this secessionist conflict. Formally, the rights and duties of third-party states regarding such domestic conflicts are rooted in the concept of sovereignty, which enjoins states not to intervene in the resolution of the conflict by the recognized government of the state.
11. Russian letter to the UN Security Council, 13 August 2008, http://www.mid.ru. This is examined by James A. Green, 'Passportisation, Peacekeepers and Proportionality: The Russian Claim of the Protection of Nationals Abroad in Self-Defence', in Green and Waters (eds.), *Conflict in the Caucasus*, pp. 64–6.
12. Georgia argued that Georgian troops entering Tskhinvali were fired at from the Russian peacekeepers' compound and that they had to return fire. No reliable independent reports on these different allegations have yet surfaced; see *Independent International Fact-Finding Mission*, Vol. 2, p. 221. For a Russian account see Pukhov (ed.), *The Tanks of August*, pp. 51–3.
13. The EU fact-finding mission concluded that Russian peacekeepers could still be regarded as representative of Russian official state structures, that an attack on their base would equal an attack on an ordinary Russian base in a foreign country. But a Russian military response as self-defence could be justified in the sense of Article 51 only if the other conditions for self-defence under that article were met as well, which they were not. *Independent International Fact-Finding Mission*, Vol. 2, pp. 264–76.
14. Significantly, the requirement of proportionality 'functions as a barrier against retaliatory or punitive actions that are meant to be a sanction or to teach the attacker a "lesson"', *Independent International Fact-Finding Mission*, Vol. 2, p. 271.
15. Russian letter to the UN Security Council, 13 August 2008, http://www.mid.ru.
16. Interview with Lavrov for Abkhaz magazine *Apsny*, 1 February 2009, at http://www.mid.ru. Green, 'Passportisation, Peacekeepers and Proportionality', pp. 68–70.
17. Statement by Foreign Minister Lavrov, 8 August 2008. See also Green, 'Passportisation, Peacekeepers and Proportionality'.
18. *Independent International Fact-Finding Mission*, Vol. 2, pp. 285–8.
19. For a debate between Russian legal specialists on the options for the defence of Russian nationals abroad and whether the August 2008 campaign might be a case of 'preventive humanitarian intervention', see 'Humanitarian Intervention and Protection of Nationals Abroad', *International Affairs* (Moscow), 55/5 (2009), pp. 83–97. See also Sergei Markedonov, *Turbulentnaya Yevraziya* (Moscow: Akademia, 2010), pp. 219–20; Green, 'Passportisation, Peacekeepers and Proportionality', pp. 66–70.
20. See Natalie Wild, 'Does a State Have the Right to Protect its Citizens Abroad?', *Radio Free Europe/Radio Liberty*, 22 August 2008.
21. *Independent International Fact-Finding Mission*, Vol. 2, pp. 288–9.
22. For an excellent analysis of the context to these issues and Russian instrumentalization of its citizenship policy, see Scott Littlefield, 'Citizenship, Identity and Foreign Policy: The Contradictions and Consequences of Russia's Passport Distribution

in the Separatist Regions of Georgia', *Europe-Asia Studies*, 61/8 (October 2009), pp. 1461–82.

23. Andreas Umland, 'A Shield of a Passport: Moscow Uses Russian Citizenship as a Tool for Recollecting the Empire's Lands', *Russia Profile*, 21 August 2008.
24. Statement on 8 August 2008, http://www.mid.ru; see also statement by Russia's envoy to the OSCE, Vladimir Voronkov, RIA Novosti news agency, Moscow, 8 August 2008, BBC Mon FS1 FsuPol yy.
25. Interview with Vladimir Voronkov, acting Russian permanent representative to the OSCE, *Rossiyskaya gazeta*, 20 August 2008. The deputy head of the Russian General Staff, Col.-General Anatoliy Nogovitsyn argued that since at the start of the conflict Georgian troops outnumbered the Russian peacekeepers there by twelve to one, the Russian side to 'eliminate this inequality, was forced to increase the peacekeepers strength'; NTV Mir television, 10 August 2008, BBC Mon FS1 FsuPol gv.
26. This is claimed, for example, in an analysis of the role of these 'peacekeepers' in the Russian Defence Ministry newspaper; report by Pavel Gerasimov, *Krasnaya zvezda*, 24 September 2008.
27. The EU fact-finding mission came to a similar conclusion based on its reading of the Sochi agreement, and noted also that 'the status of a victim of an armed attack is incompatible with the neutral status of a peacekeeper'; *Independent International Fact-Finding Mission*, Vol. 2, pp. 275–6.
28. The analysis here is backed up by the EU report's unequivocal assertion that the peacekeeping mission 'could not be reinforced or replaced by heavily armed "fresh reinforcement units". Greater use of force was not only against the spirit of the Sochi Agreement, but also against the very idea of peacekeeping'; *Independent International Fact-Finding Mission*, Vol. 2, p. 276.
29. *The Foreign Policy Concept of the Russian Federation*, 12 July 2008, at http://www.kremlin.ru/eng/text/docs/2008/07/204750.shtml.
30. Prime Minister Gordon Brown urged his EU colleagues 'to intensify our support to Georgia and others who may face Russian aggression', *The Times*, 1 September 2008, p. 33; US Defence Minster Robert Gates referred to Russia's 'aggressive posture and actions in Georgia', *International Herald Tribune*, 15 August 2008.
31. After visiting the North Caucasus Putin claimed 'we are seeing elements of a kind of genocide against the Ossetian people'; meeting between Medvedev and Putin, 10 August 2008, http://www.mid.ru. See also Medvedev's interview with the BBC, 26 August 2008, http://www.mid.ru.
32. Lavrov in press conference, 12 August 2008, http://www.mid.ru; Medvedev in meeting with leaders of parliamentary factions of the State Duma, 11 August 2008, http://www.mid.ru.
33. Foreign Minister Sergei Lavrov, Interfax news agency, Moscow, 9 August 2008, BBC Mon FS1 FsuPol iz/sw.
34. In December 2008 the Investigations Committee under the Russian Prosecutor-General's Office reported precise data 'based on documents' that only 162 South Ossetian civilians were killed during the military conflict; Ekho Moskvy radio, 23 December 2008, BBC Mon Alert FS1 231208 yk/oz.
35. As pointed out by former Russian government official Andrey Illarionov, who argues that the Russian genocide investigation has clearly been politicized; interview on Ekho Moskvy news, 4 July 2009, BBC Mon FS1 FsuPol iz.

36. Aleksandr Bastrykin in Interfax news agency report, 3 July 2009, BBC Mon Alert FS1 FsuPol gyl.
37. Satellite photos showing that Georgian villages ceased to exist on the territory of South Ossetia and similar 'marauder activities' in Georgian villages in the buffer zone were published early in *Novaya gazeta*, 8 September 2008, and became more comprehensibly available on the UNOSAT portal. See 'Village Damage Summary: Kekhvi to Tskhinvali, South Ossetia, Georgia', UNOSAT, 29 August, http://unosat.web.cern.ch/unosat/freeproducts/Georgia/Russia_ConflictAug08/UNOSAT_GEO_Village_Damage_Summary_Tskhinvali_19aug08_Lowres.pdf.
38. *Civilians in the Firing Line: The Georgia–Russia Conflict* (London: Amnesty International Publications, 2008), especially pp. 60–1. For the Russian Foreign Ministry response, see www.mid.ru, 26 January 2009. The key conclusions of the Amnesty International report are supported by the EU fact-finding mission (including serious evidence of ethnic cleansing committed against ethnic Georgians in South Ossetia), which concluded that 'allegations of genocide against Ossetians are not substantiated by evidence'; *Independent International Fact-Finding Report*, Vol. 2, pp. 430–1.
39. S. N. MacFarlane, 'The Crisis in Georgia', *Strategic Datalink*, 3 (August 2008), Canadian International Council, http://www.igloo.org/canadianinternational.
40. Interview with Foreign Minister Lavrov by BBC, 9 August 2008, http //www.mid.ru.
41. UNGA, 'Delegates Weigh Legal Merits of Responsibility to Protect', GA/10850, 28 July 2009, at http://www.unorg/News/Press/docs/2009/ga10850.doc.htm. Address by Lavrov, 27 September 2008, http://www.mid.ru.
42. Interview with Lavrov 9 August 2008, http://mid.ru. First Deputy Russian Foreign Minister Andrey Denisov, Interfax news agency, 26 September 2008, BBC Mon FS1 MCU 260908 sw/er. Interview with Lavrov, Abkhaz magazine *Apsny*, http://www.mid.ru, 5 February 2009.
43. 'The Georgia–Russia Crisis and the Responsibility to Protect: Background Note', the Global Centre for the Responsibility to Protect, http://www.globair2p.org/pdf/related/GeorgiaRussia.pdf. See also *Russia vs Georgia: The Fallout* (International Crisis Group, Europe Report), 195 (22 August 2008), pp. 28–9.
44. Article by Lavrov, 15 September 2008, at http://www.mid.ru.
45. Statement at press conference, 8 August 2008, at http://www.mid.ru.
46. Interview with Dmitriy Rogozin on Zvezda TV, Moscow, 12 August 2008, BBC Mon FS1 MCU 130808 im/js.
47. 'The Georgia–Russia Crisis and the Responsibility to Protect'. This is one of a number of reasons also why the effort by many Russians to draw an analogy between their intervention in Georgia and NATO collective intervention against Serbia over Kosovo in 1999 is unconvincing. On this see, for example, James P. Rubin, 'Russia's Poor Excuse for Invading Georgia', *The New Republic*, 8 November 2008; Russian Foreign Ministry 'Commentary on the 10th Anniversary of the NATO Bombing of Yugoslavia', http://www.mid.ru, 24 March 2009.
48. Gareth Evans, former Australian foreign minister, cited in 'Russia's Reversal: Where Next for Humanitarian Intervention?', *Financial Times*, 23–24 August 2008, p. 9. He argues that a number of criteria articulated in major reports advocating acceptance of R2P, in the lead-up to the 2005 UN World Summit, were not satisfied in the case of Russian military action in Georgia, Gareth Evans, 'Russia,

Georgia and the Responsibility to Protect', *Amsterdam Law Forum*, 1/2 (2009), pp. 25–8.

49. For Russian policy in the 1990s, see Pavel Baev, 'Russia's Stance against Secessions: From Chechnya to Kosovo', *International Peacekeeping*, 6/3 (Autumn 1999), pp. 73–94.
50. For example, see Noelle Shanahan Cutts, 'Enemies through the Gates: Russian Violations of International Law in the Georgia/Abkhazia Conflict', *Case Western Reserve Journal of International Law*, 44/281 (2007–9), pp. 281–310.
51. These activities as well as other Russian covert actions in Georgia are detailed in a leaked classified cable drawn up by the US Embassy in Tbilisi, 'Russian Active Measure in Georgia', Tbilisi 001732, 20 July 2007, at http://www.guardian.co.uk/world/us-embassy-cables-documents/116089.
52. Statements by Putin in Itar-Tass Daily, 14 February 2008, 22 February 2008.
53. For the role of Russian legal argumentation in this case, see Christopher J. Borgen, 'The Language of Law and the Practice of Politics: Great Powers and the Rhetoric of Self-Determination in the Cases of Kosovo and South Ossetia', *Chicago Journal of International Law*, 10/1 (Summer 2009), pp. 769–88.
54. Statement by Russian Foreign Ministry and by Lavrov, 26 August 2008; statement by Lavrov in the Federation Council, 18 September 2008, both at http://www.mid.ru. Regardless of how one interprets the Declaration of Principles of International Law concerning Friendly Relations and Cooperation among States (especially the so-called saving clause), it is only in a non-binding General Assembly resolution and is not in itself hard law, nor has it become customary law and it deviates from state practice. See *Independent International Fact-Finding Mission*, Vol. 2, pp. 137–9.
55. For the wider context, see Bruno Coppieters and Richard Sakwa (eds.), *Contextualizing Secession* (Oxford: Oxford University Press, 2003). For an argument that contemporary minority groups can achieve external self-determination exclusively through the support of the most powerful states in the system, see Milena Sterio, *The Right to Self-determination Under International Law* (Basingstoke: Palgrave Macmillan, 2012).
56. Heiko Krueger, 'Implications of Kosovo, Abkhazia and South Ossetia for International Law: The Conduct of the Community of States in Current Secession Conflicts', *Caucasian Review of International Affairs*, 3/2 (Spring 2009), pp. 122–3, online at http://www.cria-online.org.
57. For analysis of the case of South Ossetia and Abkhazia for external self-determination, see Robert McCorquodale and Kristin Hausler, 'Caucuses in the Caucasus: The Application of the Right of Self-Determination', in Green and Waters (eds.), *Conflict in the Caucasus*, pp. 26–53; Angelika Nussberger, 'The War between Russia and Georgia: Consequences and Unresolved Questions', *Göttingen Journal of International Law*, 1/2 (2009), pp. 343–64.
58. Jure Vidmar, 'Remedial Secession in International Law: Theory and (Lack of) Practice', *St. Antony's International Review*, 6/1 (May 2010), pp. 37–56.
59. Commenting on South Ossetia and Abkhazia in 2006, for example, Lavrov argued that 'the right to self-determination . . . is exercised through expressions of the will of the people'; Yulia Petrovskaya, 'Sergei Lavrov after Vienna', *Nezavisimaya gazeta*, 5 June 2006, pp. 1, 8.

60. 'Press conference by President Obama and President Medvedev of Russia', 6 July 2009; 'Remarks by the President at the New Economic School Graduation', 7 July 2009, both available at http://www.whitehouse.gov/.
61. Interview for TV Channel One, *Rossiya*, NTV, 31 August 2008, http://www.kremlin.ru/eng/text/speeches/2008/08/31/1150.
62. Sergey Lavrov, 'Russian Foreign Policy and a New Quality of the Geopolitical Situation', *Diplomatic Yearbook*, Moscow (2008), online at http://www.mid.ru, 29 December 2008.
63. Responding to a question on this, Russian Deputy Foreign Minister Grigoriy Karasin observed that he 'would rather not talk about either the precedential nature of that decision or its exclusiveness', http://www.mid.ru, 4 August 2009.
64. Azerbaijan claimed that Armenia became more intransigent in discussions over Nagorno-Karabakh separatism, which was encouraged by the precedent of 'statehood' for South Ossetia and Abkhazia.
65. Address to the Federal Assembly, 5 November 2008, at http://www.kremlin.ru.
66. The risks in this scenario, if Russia codified the right to protect its nationals abroad, were stressed by Russian legal specialist Vladimir Kotlyar in roundtable discussion, 'Humanitarian Intervention and Protection of Nationals Abroad', p. 96.
67. Statement by the Investigations Committee under the Russian Prosecutor's Office, Interfax news agency, 24 August 2009, BBC Mon Alert FS1 FsuPol gyl/jp. This followed an open highly critical letter from President Medvedev to President Yushchenko and earlier claims that Ukrainian crews manned Georgian air defence systems: Interfax, 13 August 2008, BBC Mon Alert FS1 FsuPol ib.
68. Interfax news agency, 2 October 2008, BBC Mon Alert FS1 FsuPol sv.
69. Comments by Air Force Commander-in-Chief Colonel-General Aleksandr Zelin, RIA Novosti news agency, 5 August 2009, BBC Mon FS1 FsuPol osc.
70. As confirmed in a broad-ranging interview with the leader of the Crimean Tatar Majlis, Mustafa Dzhemilyev, *Kontrakty*, Kiev, 20 September 2008, pp. 12–14, BBC Mon KVU 300908 gk/dk.
71. *Military Doctrine of Russia*, 5 February 2010, at http://news.kremlin.ru/ref_notes/461.
72. Text of joint SCO declaration, Tajik president's website, Dushanbe, 28 August 2008, BBC Mon CAU 280808 nu/fm/abm/mk.
73. After initial hesitation, for example, see supportive statement by Kazakhstan; report by RIA news agency, Moscow, 28 August 2008, BBC Mon Alert CAU 280808 abm/akh. Author's interviews of senior Central Asian officials, September 2008.
74. Statement of CSTO foreign ministers, 4 September 2008, at http://www.mid.ru.
75. Interview with Lavrov in Abkhaz magazine *Apsny*, 1 February 2009, at http://www.mid.ru.
76. As cited on http://www.politkom.ru, Moscow, 6 October 2008.
77. In this respect a 1995 Federal Act defining the participation of Russian servicemen in peacekeeping and other operations abroad was ignored (it was claimed no decision was needed on just increasing the strength of the peacekeeping contingent). Such servicemen could also only have been sent to South Ossetia on a voluntary basis and on the conclusion of a contract. As for 'coercion to peace', according to the act, such actions could only be carried by decision of the UN Security

Council. Boris Vishnevsky, 'Peacekeeping Forces', *Novaya gazeta*, 25 August 2008; Aleksandr Golts, 'Tonkin Legislation', *Yezhednevnyy zhurnal*, 12 August 2009. For detailed analysis of Russian domestic accountability in deploying its forces abroad in the 1990s, see Bakhtiyar Tuzmukhamedov, 'Russian Federation: The Pendulum of Powers and Accountability', in Charlotte Ku and Harold K. Jacobson (eds.), *Democratic Accountability and the Use of Force in International Law* (Cambridge: Cambridge University Press, 2002), pp. 257–79.

78. Proekt federal'nogo zakona 'O vnesenii izmeneniy v Federal'nyy zakon "Ob oborone"', 10 August 2009, at http://www.kremlin.ru/text/docs/2009/08/220710.shtml, 10 August 2009. Armed forces could be used beyond Russia's borders for the following purposes: 'To counter an attack against the Russian Armed Forces or other troops deployed beyond Russia's borders; to counter or prevent an aggression against another country; to protect Russian citizens abroad; to combat piracy and ensure safe passage of shipping.'
79. For an assessment of Russian motivations in the conflict, see Allison. 'Strategic Reassertion', pp. 1161–6.
80. Leaked US State Department confidential cable, EO 12958, 20 October 2008, of discussion with UK FCO Russia, Caucasus and Central Asia Director, at http://www.guardian.co.uk/world/us-embassy-cables-documents/174440.
81. Dmitri Trenin, 'Russia in the Caucasus: Reversing the Tide', *Brown Journal of World Affairs*, 15/2 (Spring/Summer 2009), p. 149.
82. For the claim that Russia applied these rationales in August 2008 after observing Western interventions, see Vladislav Inozemtsev, 'Coercion to Peace: A Legitimate Measure', *Nezavisimaya gazeta*, 13 August 2008.
83. 'Medvedev Gets Caught Telling the Truth', *Radio Free Europe/Radio Liberty*, 22 November 2011, at http://www.rferl.org/articleprintview/24399004.html.
84. Green, 'Passportisation, Peacekeepers and Proportionality', pp. 72–3.

Chapter 8 Russian Global Perspectives and Contemporary Military Intervention

1. See Russian Foreign Minister Igor Ivanov, 'The Iraq Crisis and the Struggle for a New World Pattern', in *Diplomatic Yearbook*, Russian Diplomatic Academy, 2003, listed 19 January 2004 at http://www.mid.ru.
2. For example, see Russian reference to the Final Document of the summit of the Non-Aligned Movement in February 2003, in which the non-aligned states 'expressed their rejection of unilateralism, which is increasingly leading to the erosion and violation of international law, to the use and threat of use of force ...'. A. Orlov, 'Nonalignment Aligns with Antiwar', *International Affairs* (Moscow), 49/3 (2003), p. 71.
3. Speech on 10 February 2007, at http://www.mid.ru.
4. Address by Sergei Lavrov on 20 February 2007, at http://www.mid.ru.
5. Sergei Lavrov, 'The Present and Future of Global Politics', *Russia in Global Affairs*, 2 (April–June 2007), p. 3.
6. Statement by Lavrov, Interfax 7 March 2007, at http:/www.cdi.org/russia/johnson/2007-56-20.cfm.
7. Speech by Sergei Lavrov at MGIMO University, 3 September 2007, at http://www.mid.ru.

8. *The Foreign Policy Concept of the Russian Federation*, 12 July 2008, at http://www.kremlin.ru/eng/text/docs/2008/07/204750.shtml.
9. Deputy Foreign Minister Yuri Fedotov, opening a conference on the role of international law, 24 June 2003, at http://www.mid.ru.
10. As related by Mikhail Margelov, chairman of the International Affairs Committee of the Federation Council, in Svetlana Babayeva, 'Voice of Russia', *Izvestiya*, 26 September 2003, pp. 1 and 3.
11. Babayeva, 'Voice of Russia', pp. 1 and 3.
12. Deputy Foreign Minister Yuri Fedotov, 24 June 2003, at http://www.mid.ru.
13. Report on plenum of the Russian Supreme Court, Alexander Shashkov, 'Russia Supreme Court for Use of Norms of International Law', Itar-Tass, 18 September 2003, at http://dilb.eastview/com/browse/doc/53011709.
14. President Dmitry Medvedev, speech at World Policy Conference, Evian, 8 October 2008, at http://eng.kremlin.ru/text/speeches/2008/10/08/2159
15. For different Russian interpretations of this period, see Mikhail Troitskiy, 'Going "Relativistic": The Changing Vision of "Just International Order" in Russian Foreign Policy', in Douglas W. Blum (ed.), *Russia and Globalization: Identity, Security and Society in an Era of Change* (Washington, DC: Woodrow Wilson Center Press, 2008), pp. 207–31; Konstantin Kosachev, 'Russia and the West: Where the Differences Lie', *Russia in Global Affairs*, 4 (October–December 2007), pp. 1–8, at http://eng.globalaffairs.ru/numbers/21/1149.html.
16. Andrei Zagorski, 'Multilateralism in Russian Foreign Policy Approaches', in Elana Wilson Rowe and Torjesen, Stina (eds.), *The Multilateral Dimension in Russian Foreign Policy* (London: Routledge, 2009), pp. 47–8. See pp. 46–57 for an excellent overview of contemporary Russian approaches to multilateralism.
17. Sergei Karaganov, chairman of the Council on Foreign and Defence Policy in Moscow, *RIA Novosti*, 14 August 2006, *Johnson's Russia List*, 183 (2006), at http://www.cdi.org/russia/johnson.
18. Gennady Gatilov, Director of the Department of International Organizations, Russian Foreign Ministry, 'Blue Berets: The UN's Peacekeepers', *International Affairs* (Moscow), 56/6 (2010), p. 118.
19. Gatilov, 'Blue Berets: The UN's Peacekeepers', p. 115. See also Robert Legvold, 'The Role of Multilateralism in Russian Foreign Policy', in Rowe and Torjesen (eds.), *The Multilateral Dimension in Russian Foreign Policy*, p. 27.
20. For this point and analysis in this paragraph, see Zagorski, 'Multilateralism in Russian Foreign Policy Approaches', pp. 52–4.
21. Pavel Baev, 'Leading in the Concert of Great Powers: Lessons from Russia's G8 Chairmanship', in Rowe and Torjesen (eds.), *The Multilateral Dimension in Russian Foreign Policy*, pp. 58–68.
22. Soon after the attack on Iraq Russia explicitly rejected the view heard among some Western politicians that 'the G8 states might undertake to resolve some priority global problems' as 'impossible' from the point of view of international law, noting that the G8 lacked the UN's 'expertise, experience and mechanisms', Russian Representative to the UN Sergei Lavrov. 'The New Iraq Will Not Come About without United Nations Support', *Nezavisimaya gazeta*, 18 April 2003.

23. Sergei Karganov, 'The World Crisis: A Time for Creation', *Russia in Global Affairs*, 4 (October–December 2008), p. 4, at http://eng.globalaffairs.ru/numbers/25/1235.html.
24. Document addressed to G20 London summit, 'Russia unveils G20 plan to reform "obsolescent" world order', AFP, 16 March 2009, in *Johnson's Russia List*, 16 March 2009, at http://www.cdi.org/russia/johnson.
25. We use the acronym BRICs or BRIC nations in referring to the grouping before South Africa joined.
26. Alexander Kramarenko, Director of Russian Foreign Ministry Policy Planning, 'Russia and the Rise of the Dialogue Mechanism in the BRIC Format', 16 January 2009, at http://www.mid.ru.
27. For a discussion of the responses of these states to US hegemony and to the changing character of international society, see Andrew Hurrell, 'Hegemony, Liberalism and Global Order: What Space for Would-Be Great Powers?', *International Affairs*, 82/1 (2006), pp. 1–19.
28. *Eurasia Daily Monitor* (Jamestown Foundation), 2/108, 3 June 2005, at http://www.jamestown.org.
29. Roy Allison, 'Virtual Regionalism, Regional Structures and Regime Security', *Central Asian Survey*, 27/2 (June 2008), pp. 196–7.
30. Joint heads of states declaration signed at the end of Jiang Zemin's visit to Russia in July 2001; in Legvold, 'The Role of Multilateralism in Russian Foreign Policy', p. 39.
31. See Rosemary Foot, 'The Responsibility to Protect (R2P) and its Evolution: Beijing's Influence on Norm Creation in Humanitarian Areas', *St Antony's International Review*, 6/2 (February 2011), pp. 59–63.
32. Hiski Haukkala and Linda Jakobson, 'The Myth of a Sino-Russian Challenge to the West', *International Spectator*, 44/3 (September 2009), pp. 59–76. For a comprehensive analysis of Chinese normative preferences, see Rosemary Foot and Andrew Walter, *China, The United States, and Global Order* (Cambridge: Cambridge University Press, 2011).
33. Roy Allison, 'Russian Security Engagement with the European Union', in Roy Allison, Margot Light, and Stephen White, *Putin's Russia and the Enlarged Europe* (London: Blackwell and Royal Institute for International Affairs, 2006), pp. 73–5, 83–5.
34. Allison, 'Russian Security Engagement with the European Union', pp. 85–91. Nicu Popescu, *EU Foreign Policy and Post-Soviet Conflicts* (London: Routledge, 2011).
35. See, for example, Derek Averre, 'Competing Rationalities: Russia, the US and the "Shared Neighbourhood"', *Europe-Asia Studies*, 61/10 (December 2009), pp. 1689–713; Hiski Haukkala, 'The Russian Challenge to EU Normative Power: The Case of European Neighbourhood Policy', *The International Spectator*, 43/2 (June 2008), pp. 35–47.
36. Viktor Ivanov, director of Russia's Federal Drug Control Service, Interfax-AVN military news agency website, Moscow, 23 October 2009, BBC Mon FS1 FsuPol va.
37. 'The Istanbul Declaration: Our Security in a New Era', press release 2004 (097), 28 June 2004, at http://www.nato.int/docu/pr/2004/p04-097e.htm.
38. Vladimir Kuzar, 'NATO's Global Aims', *Krasnaya zvezda*, 22 November 2006, p. 3.

39. Press statement after meeting of the NATO–Russia Council, 4 April 2008, at http://www.kremlin.ru.
40. *Strategic Concept for the Defence and Security of the Members of the North Atlantic Treaty Organization*, adopted 19–20 November 2010, at http://www.nato.int/strategic-concept/pdf/strat_Concept_web_en.pdf. This reaffirmed the role of the Alliance's expeditionary forces and of its crisis management activities beyond its borders.
41. Interview with Lavrov, 22 June 2010, at http://telegraph.co.uk/sponsored/russianow/politics/7847648.
42. *Voennaya doktrina Rossiyskoy Federatsii* (Military Doctrine of the Russian Federation), 5 February 2010, at http://news.kremlin.ru/ref_notes/461. Lavrov has not been shy to repeat this; see, for example, joint press conference with NATO Secretary General Anders Rasmussen on 4 July 2011, at http://www,mid.ru. NATO efforts to assume 'global functions counter to the norms of international law' were branded as unacceptable in Russia's National Security Strategy to 2020, *Strategiya natsional'noy bezopasnosti Rossiyskoy Federatsii do 2020 goda*, 12 May 2009, at http://www.scrf.gov.ru/documents/99.html. Overall, these documents reflect to a large extent Putin's security policy documents of 2007 and 2008, suggesting that Medvedev as president carried forward the security thinking of his predecessor.
43. A Russian Defence Ministry 'White Paper', presented in October 2003, and perhaps drafted in large part by the General Staff, demanded that 'anti-Russian components' be removed from NATO military planning and from the political declarations of Alliance member states, but overall envisaged reduced direct competition with NATO. See *Aktual'nyye zadachi razvitiya Vooruzhennykh Sil Rossiyskoy Federatsii* (The priority tasks of the development of the armed forces of the Russian Federation), Interfax, Moscow, 2 October 2003, BBC Mon Alert FS1 FsuPol kp/jh; Matthew Bouldin, 'The Ivanov Doctrine and Military Reform: Reasserting Stability in Russia', *Journal of Slavic Military Studies*, 17/4 (2004), pp. 631–2.
44. Statement by Ivanov to journalists, 17 August 2004. Vadim Solovyov, 'Moscow Not Frightened by NATO Advance', *Nezavisimaya gazeta*, 18 August 2004, p. 2.
45. Solovyov, 'Moscow Not Frightened by NATO Advance', p. 2.
46. Aleksei Bogaturov, 'Bush's Two-Pronged Strategy', *Nezavisimaya gazeta*, 26 August 2004, p. 5.
47. Vladimir Kuzar, 'The Pentagon's Rearrangement', *Krasnaya zvezda*, 6 June 2006, p. 3.
48. Alexander Bartosh, 'Russia–NATO strategy', *Nezavisimoe voennoe obozrenie*, 10 (19 March 2010).
49. A provocative extension of this belief in energy-related conflict is the argument that a continued energy crisis and high oil and gas prices 'will create in the United States and Europe the determination to weaken Russia's military might by fostering permanent controlled conflicts in the southern parts of the country'. Aleksei Matveyev, 'Return into Instability is a Possibility', *Voenno-promyshlennyy kurier*, 1 (9–15 January 2008).
50. *Strategiya natsional'noy bezopasnosti Rossiyskoy Federatsii do 2020 goda.*

51. Makarov's comments on 17 November 2011 extended to the potential for nuclear conflict erupting close to Russian borders. As reported in *Moskovskiy komsomolets*, 28 November 2011; *Eurasia Daily Monitor* (Jamestown Foundation), 8/221, 6 December 2011, at http://www.eurasia.net.org.
52. *Strategiya natsional'noy bezopasnosti Rossiyskoy Federatsii do 2020 goda.*
53. *National Security Strategy of the United States of America* (16 March 2006), at http://georgebush-whitehouse.archives.gov/nsc/nss/2006.
54. Cited in Abraham D. Sofaer, 'The Best Defense: Preventive Force and International Security', *Foreign Affairs*, 89/1 (2010), p. 110.
55. Nicholas Kerton-Johnson, *Justifying America's Wars: The Conduct and Practice of US Military Intervention* (London: Routledge, 2011), pp. 153–9.
56. For a particularly *Realpolitik* assessment of arguments for and against an attack on Iran, by a former adviser on defence strategy on Iran in the Office of the US Secretary of Defense, see Matthew Kroenig, 'Time to Attack Iran', *Foreign Affairs*, 91/1 (January/February 2012), pp. 76–86.
57. Speech by Obama to the American Israel Public Affairs Committee, on 4 March 2012, at http://www.guardian.co.uk/world/2012/mar/04/obama-aipac-speech-read-text. See also *The Times*, 5 March 2012, p. 26.
58. As argued by Bruce Ackermann, criticizing claims made by Anthony D'Amato and Alan Dershowitz; see 'Iran's Nuclear Programme: Legal Debate Stirs over Basis for US or Israeli Attack', at http://www.guardian.co.uk/world/2012/apr/12/iran-military-attack-legal-debate.
59. For example, in a meeting with Putin in February 2007, Foreign Minister Lavrov confirmed that this is not just a hypothetical scenario. Dmitri Sidorov, 'Pre-war Iran', *Kommersant*, 27 February 2007, p. 9.
60. Indeed Moscow has tried to claim that Iranian territorial integrity is reinforced since 'security guarantees are provided to Iran under the UN Security Council resolution passed after the Iran–Iraq war', approved on the basis of Article VII of the UN Charter. Lavrov in response to questions at symposium in Moscow, 20 June 2008, at http://mid.ru.
61. In the debates preceding these resolutions Russia pointed out that their language excluded the use of force. Gray, *International Law and the Use of Force*, pp. 225–6.
62. Resolution 1929, 9 June 2010, at http://www.un.org/Docs/scres/2010/sc2010.htm; statement by Vitaly Churkin, at http://daccess-dds-ny.un.org/doc/UNDOC/PRO/N10/395/96/PDF/N1039596/pdf.
63. Lavrov in response to questions at symposium in Moscow, 20 June 2008, http://www.mid.ru.
64. Comment by Russian Foreign Ministry, 9 November 2011, at http://www.mid.ru.
65. Alexander A. Pikayev, 'Russia's Attitude Towards Nuclear Non-Proliferation Regimes and Institutions: An Example of Multilateralism?', in Rowe and Torjesen (eds.), *The Multilateral Dimension in Russian Foreign Policy*, pp. 80–1.
66. Robert S. Litwak, 'Living with Ambiguity: Nuclear Deals with Iran and North Korea', *Survival*, 50/1 (February–March 2008), pp. 111–14.
67. In November 2011 Russian Deputy Foreign Minister Gennady Gatilov told that Moscow would veto new UN sanctions and 'the world community will see all additional sanctions against Iran as an instrument of regime change in Tehran'; *Wall Street Journal*, 14 November 2011.

68. British officials also noted that if Washington were to press ahead with strikes against Iran it would seek and receive UK military help for any mission, and that the UK had 'a lot of plans in the locker' to strike Iran if it became a threat; *The Guardian*, 3 November 2011, p. 5; *The Times*, 14 November 2011, p. 15.
69. For example, Vladimir Vanin, 'Strikes from Four Directions', *Nezavisimoe voennoe obozrenie*, 15, 12–18 May 2006, p. 2; Maksim Yusin, 'The United States versus Iran: Air Strikes or Invasion?', *Izvestiya*, 19 September 2007, pp. 1–2; Mikhail Lukanin, 'Five Weeks Will Be Enough for a War with Iran', *Trud*, 9 February 2011, p. 4. Obviously the Russian General Staff has developed its own analyses.
70. Yuri Fedorov, in oral evidence; *Global Security: Russia* (House of Commons Select Committee on Foreign Affairs, HC 51, Second Report of Session 2007–8), 25 November 2007, p. 114.
71. Nikolai Patrushev, Secretary of the Russian Security Council, *Izvestiya*, 14 October 2009, and Interfax news agency, 13 October 2009, BBC Mon FS1 FsuPol ME1 MEPol ibg.
72. Taking account of Iranian intentions, Russian Deputy Foreign Minister Anatoly Antonov observed in June 2011 that 'I cannot say that Iran is a threat'; Military news agency Interfax-AVN, 11 June 2011, BBC Mon FS1 FsuPol va.
73. Interview with President Nursultan Nazarbayev, Interfax, 19 November 2011, BBC Mon Alert CAU ME1 MEPol 191111 ad/ar.
74. Nikolai Patrushev, Secretary of the Russian Security Council, *Izvestiya*, 14 October 2009. Similar views have been expressed by the Chief of the Russian General Staff, Army General Nikolai Makarov, Interfax-AVN military news agency website, 12 April 2010, BBC Mon FS1 FsuPol ydy.
75. Interview with Vladimir Nazarov, Deputy Secretary of the Russian Security Council, 'Strike at Iran will be Colossal Mistake', *Kommersant*, 15 February 2010.
76. Assessment of threats by US and Russian extended interagency delegations in Moscow, 22 December 2009; secret US diplomatic memorandum, published by WikiLeaks. *Eurasia Daily Monitor* (Jamestown Foundation), 7/215, 2 December 2010, at http://www.jamestown.org. Russian Space Troops Deputy Commander Lt-General Sergei Lobov reaffirmed that Iran has no ballistic missiles that could target European countries; Interfax-AVN military news agency, 15 February 2011, BBC Mon FS1 FsuPol ME1 MEPol gyl.
77. 'Israel's Warning to Obama: If You Don't Sort Out Tehran, We Will', *The Times*, 29 November 2010.
78. SC/10180, AFR/2120, issued on 22 February 2011, at http://www.un.org/News/Press/docs/2011/sc10180.doc.htm.
79. Russia–EU statement on 24 February 2011, at http://www.mid.ru; also Interfax, 24 February 2011, BBC Mon FS1 FsuPol va. Presidential statement on 25 February 2011, at http://eng.news.kremlin.ru/news/1821.
80 See executive order on sanctions against Libya, 10 March 2011, at http://eng.news.kremlin.ru/news/1878.
81. *The Times*, 17 March 2011, p. 3.
82. As cited in Jennifer Welsh, 'Civilian Protection in Libya: Putting the Coercion and Controversy Back into RtoP', *Ethics and International Affairs*, 25/3 (Fall 2011), p. 3.
83. *The Guardian*, 12 March 2011, p. 28.

84. *The Times*, 11 March 2011, p. 6; *The Guardian*, 19 March 2011, p. 7.
85. UNSC Resolution 1973, adopted on 17 March 2011, at http://www.un.org/Docs/scres/2011/sc2011.htm.
86. For example, the UK Attorney General, Dominic Grieve, in his legal advice to the cabinet, noted that UN resolutions provided a 'clear and unequivocal' legal basis for UK military deployments for the Libya operation. *The Guardian*, 22 March 2011, p. 5.
87. Speech by Obama on Libya, 23 February 2011, *New York Times*, 24 February 2011.
88. Speeches at UN Security Council 6498th meeting, 17 March 2011, S/PV.6498, http://daccees-dds-ny.un.org/doc/UNDOC/PRO/N11/267/18/PDF/N1126718.pdf.
89. Speech by William Hague on 22 March 2011, *The Times*, 23 March 2011, p. 21.
90. Address to the Nation on Libya, 28 March 2011, at http:/www.whitehouse.gov/the-press-office/2011/03/28/remarks-president-address-nation-libya.
91. Address to the Nation on Libya, 28 March 2011. See also Bruce D. Jones, 'Libya and the Responsibilities of Power', *Survival*, 53/3 (June–July 2011), pp. 51–60.
92. Welsh, 'Civilian Protection in Libya', p. 5.
93. Western international lawyers quickly took varying positions on what the use of 'all necessary means' to protect Libyan civilians from the threat of attack could mean in practice. See 'Coalition Bombing May Be in Breach of Legal Limits', *The Guardian*, 29 March 2009.
94. Speech at UN Security Council 6498th meeting, 17 March 2011, S/PV.6498, at http://daccees-dds-ny.un.org/doc/UNDOC/PRO/N11/267/18/PDF/N1126718.pdf.
95. Speech at UN Security Council 6498th meeting, 17 March 2011.
96. Interview in *Moskovskie novosti*, 12 May 2011, and at http://www.mid.ru, 12 May 2011.
97. Speeches in Security Council debate, 17 March 2011. Interview in *Moskovskiye novosti*, 12 May 2011, and at http://www.mid.ru, 12 May 2011.
98. Statement by Medvedev on the situation in Libya, 21 March 2011, at http://eng.news.kremlin.ru/transcripts/1933.
99. Statement by Russian Foreign Ministry spokesman Alexander Lukashevich, 20 March 2011, at http://www.mid.ru.
100. Viktor Zavarzin, chairman of the State Duma Defence Committee and a retired Colonel-General, Inferfax-AVN military news agency, 21 March 2011, BBC Mon FS1 Fsu tm.
101. An opinion poll published on 24 March 2011 by the VTsIOM public opinion research agency found that 64% of Russians did not support the operation in Libya. RIA-Novosti news agency, *Johnson's Russia List*, 55, 25 March 2011, at http://www.cdi.org/russia/johnson.
102. Interview with Putin, 21 March 2011, at http://premier.gov.ru/events/news/14542.
103. For the debate on this statement see Ivan Rodin, 'United Russia Backs Medvedev's Position on Libya', *Nezavisimaya gazeta*, 24 March 2011, p. 3.
104. Olga Kryshtanovskya, head of the Centre for the Study of Elites of the Russian Academy of Sciences Institute of Sociology, argued that Medvedev seeks to

redeem Russia's image 'as the more liberal politician who takes his cue from the most influential forces of the global community', while Putin 'plays up to the Russian electorate', 'Tandem Tests Strength before 2012 Election', *Nezavisimaya gazeta*, 23 March 2011, p. 1. Putin's remarks were politically shrewd. According to an opinion poll carried out by the Levada Centre on 15–16 April, Putin's position on Libya had the support of 53% of Russians, while only 13% supported Medvedev on this issue. Of those who replied, 62% believed that Resolution 1973 was wrong and saw it as 'aggression against a sovereign country'. Interfax, 18 May 2011, BBC Mon FS1 FsuPol ME1 MEPol kdd.

105. Just before the draft Resolution 1973 was passed, Medvedev observed that it 'proposes permitting ground operations', Reuters, 16 March 2011, *Johnson's Russia List*, 49, 17 March 2011, at http://www.cdi.org/russia/johnson. According to the Russian Chief of General Staff, Army General Nikolai Makarov, 'If they have set themselves the goal of overthrowing al-Qadhafi's rule, then, probably, they will not be able to avoid a ground phase', Interfax-AVN military news agency, 26 March 2011, BBC Mon FS1 MCU 260311 Is/ed.
106. News conference after G8 summit, at 28 May 2011, at http://www.kremlin.ru.
107. Address to the Nation on Libya, 28 March 2011, at http:/www.whitehouse.gov/the-press-office/2011/03/28/remarks-president-address-nation-libya.
108. Sergei Lavrov at press conference in Tskhinvali, 26 April 2011, BBC Mon FS1 FsuPol sv.
109. See remarks by Putin on 26 April 2011, at http://premier.gov.ru; Russian Foreign Ministry press release, 1 May 2011, http://www.mid.ru; statement by the new Russian Foreign Ministry human rights envoy, Konstantin Dolgov, RIA Novosti news agency, 3 May 2011, BBC Mon FS1 FsuPol stu; interview with Sergei Lavrov, *Moskovskiye* novosti, 12 May 2011, and at http://www.mid.ru; statement by Konstantin Dolgov, Interfax, 25 May 2011, BBC Mon Alert FS1 MCU ME1 MEPol 250511 ib.
110. *The Guardian*, 30 March 2011; *The Times*, 30 March 2011.
111. Statement by Sergei Lavrov, Interfax, 21 April 2011, BBC Mon FS1 FsuPol ME1 MEPol sw.
112. Despite initial claims that the UN arms embargo would cost the Russian arms export agency some $4 billion, it soon transpired that Russian arms sales contracts with Libya had not come into force, Russian enterprises had not started production, and it was only an issue of potential future lost profits. Yekaterina Zabrodina et al., 'Revolution Will Pay', *Izvestiya*, 2 March 2011; Interfax-AVN military news agency, 9 March 2011, BBC Mon Alert FS1 MCU ME1 MEPol 090311 evg. One real material loss seemed to be the contract involving Russian Railways Corporation to construct a railway from Benghazi to Sirte.
113. Address to the Nation on Libya, 28 March 2011, at http:/www.whitehouse.gov/the-press-office/2011/03/28/remarks-president-address-nation-libya.
114. This sense of legitimacy was dented when Amr Moussa, the head of the Arab League, criticized the coalition early in its operations for killing civilians and overstepping the Security Council mandate. *The Times*, 21 March 2011, p. 10.
115. Konstantin Kosachev, Chairman of the Foreign Affairs Committee of the Russian State Duma. 'Russia's Choice', *Rossiyskaya gazeta*, 25 March 2011.
116. Lavrov, 12 May 2011, and 17 May 2011, at http://www/mid.ru.

117. Statement by Nikolai Bordyuzha, 13 April 2011, Interfax-AVN military news agency, 13 April 2011, BBC Mon FS1 MCU ME1 MEPol 130411 ib/nm.
118. Lavrov, 12 May 2011, and 17 May 2011, at http://www/mid.ru.
119. Lavrov, Centre TV, 30 April 2011, BBC Mon Alert FS1 FsuPol tm. Vladimir Chizhov, Russia's representative at the EU, Interfax, 23 May 2011, BBC Mon Alert FS1 FsuPol ME1 MEPol EU1 EuroPol kdd.
120. News conference after G8 summit, 28 May 2011, at http://www.kremlin.ru.
121. Mikhail Margelov, Interfax, 8 June 2011, *Johnson's Russia List*, 101, 9 June 2011, at http://www.cdi.org/russia/johnson; Viktor Ozerov, chairman of the Committee on Security and Defence Issues, Federation Council, Interfax-AVN military news agency, 7 June 2011, BBC Mon FS1 MCU ME1 MEPol 070611 ib/vg. See also Lavrov's call for a UN peacekeeping operation in Libya, in meeting UN Secretary General Ban ki-moon, Press Release, 27 September 2011, at http://www.mid.ru.
122. Interfax, Brussels, 15 November 2011, *Johnson's Russia List*, 201, 16 November 2011, at http://www.cdi.org/russia/johnson.
123. Russian Chief of General Staff, Army General Nikolai Makarov, Interfax-AVN military news agency, 4 May 2011, BBC Mon FS1 FsuPol sv.
124. Lavrov at press conference, 8 December 2011, http://www.mid.ru. NATO Secretary-General Anders Fogh Rasmussen had suggested earlier already that the Libya operation 'could set a template', since 'we have demonstrated ability to act in support of the UN and we have demonstrated an ability to include partners outside NATO in such an operation', *The Guardian*, 2 September 2011, pp. 4–5.
125. Fedor Lukyanov, 'Devaluation of Legitimacy', 27 October 2011, at http://www.gazeta.ru, cited in *Johnson's Russia List*, 195, 28 October 2011, at http://www.cdi.org/russia/johnson. More assertively, Russia's NATO envoy Dmitri Rogozin took the view that the Libya war 'means the end of the alliance's eastward enlargement and the beginning of the southward enlargement'; 16 June 2011, http://www.russiatoday.com, cited in *Johnson's Russia List*, 106, 16 June 2011, at http://www. cdi.org/russia/johnson.
126. Lavrov, *Moskovskie novosti*, 12 May 2011, and 12 May 2011, at http://www.mid.ru.
127. Lavrov, 1 June 2011, at http://www.mid.ru.
128. Lavrov, Rossiya 24 TV Channel, 27 September 2011, at http://www.mid.ru.
129. Lavrov, Interfax, 13 May 2011, BBC Mon Alert FS1 MCU ME1 MEPol 130511 et.
130. Lavrov, 1 June 2011, http://www.mid.ru.
131. Lavrov, 23 December 2011, http://www.mid.ru.
132. Medvedev, Russia Today TV, Interfax, 4 August 2011, *Johnson's Russia List*, 140, 5 August 2011, at http://www.cdi.org/russia/johnson.
133. For the Russian explanation of its vote see Vitaly Churkin, 5 October 2011, http://www.mid.ru and S/2011/612, 4 October 2011, at http://www.un.org/Depts/dhl/resguide/scact2011.htm. For joint positions with BRICS states, see BRICS Foreign Ministers' Meeting, 24 September 2011, Joint Communiqué of Meeting of BRICS deputy foreign ministers, 24 November 2011, at http://www.mid.ru.
134. Statement by Vitaly Churkin, Security Council 6710th meeting, 31 January 2012, S/PV.6710, at http://daccess-dds-ny.un.org/UNDOC/PRO/N12/219/19/PDF/N1221919.pdf.

135. Security Council 6711th meeting, 4 February 2011, S/PV.6711, at http://daccess-dds-ny.un.org/doc/UNDOC/PRO/N12/223/56/PDF/N1222356.pdf.
136. Statement by President Nursultan Nazarbayev, Interfax, 19 November 2011, BBC Mon Alert CAU ME1 MEPol 191111 ad/ar. Kazakhstan chaired the Organization of Islamic Conference (OIC) at the time, which stated that OIC states would not tolerate any foreign intervention in Syria; Interfax-Kazakhstan, 1 December 2011, BBC Mon CAU ME1 MEPol 011211 ad/sg.
137. Security Council 6711th meeting.
138. As noted by Welsh, 'Civilian Protection in Libya', p. 1.
139. Addressing the NATO Parliamentary Assembly, 30 May 2011, *Eurasia Daily Monitor* (Jamestown Foundation), 8/107, 3 June 2011, at http://www.eurasia.org.
140. Statement by Vitaly Churkin, 4 October 2011, http://www.mid.ru; his explanation of the Russian veto of the draft Security Council resolution the same day, S/2011/612, at http://www.un.org/Depts/dhl/resguide/scact2011.htm.
141. Russian Foreign Minister spokesman Alexander Lukashevich, 12 November 2011, at http://www.mid.ru.
142. Interview with Putin, RIA Novosti news agency, Moscow 27 April 2011, in BBC Mon Alert FS1 MCU ME1 MEPol 270411 evg.
143. Lavrov, 10 October 2011, and 1 November 2011, at http://www.mid.ru.
144. Jones, 'Libya and the Responsibilities of Power', p. 57.
145. Resolution 1975, adopted on 30 March 2011, at http://www.un.org/Docs/scres/2011/sc2011.htm.

Chapter 9 Conclusion

1. The 12 July 2008 *Foreign Policy Concept of the Russian Federation* restated the Russian view that Article 51 of the UN Charter was viewed as an adequate legal basis, not subject to revision 'for the use of force in self-defence, including in the face of existing threats to peace and security such as international terrorism and proliferation of weapons of mass destruction', at http://www.kremlin.ru/eng/text/docs/2008/07/204750.shtml.
2. See Christopher Browning, 'Reassessing Putin's Project: Reflections on IR Theory and the West', *Problems of Post-Communism*, 55/5 (September/October 2008), pp. 9–12.
3. For discussion of this wider global normative contestation, see Ramesh Thakur, *The Responsibility to Protect: Norms, Laws and the Use of Force in International Politics* (London: Routledge, 2011).
4. See Jennifer M. Welsh, 'Taking Consequences Seriously: Objections to Humanitarian Intervention', in Jennifer M. Welsh (ed.), *Humanitarian Intervention and International Relations* (Oxford: Oxford University Press, 2004), pp. 64–6.
5. Mohammed Ayoob, 'Humanitarian Intervention and State Sovereignty', *The International Journal of Human Rights*, 6/1 (Spring 2002), p. 99.
6. Statement by Vitaly Churkin, Russian Permanent Representative to the UN, 23 September 2011, at Security Council meeting on conflict resolution, at http://www.mid.ru.
7. Martha Finnemore, *The Purpose of Intervention: Changing Beliefs about the Use of Force* (Ithaca and London: Cornell University Press, 2003), pp. 50–5.

8. See Bakhtiar Tuzmukhamedov, Vice President of the Russian Association of International Law, 'Law and Force', *International Affairs* (Moscow), 55/2 (2009), pp. 100–2.
9. Sergei Lavrov, interviewed in *Moskovskie novosti*, 12 May 2011, at http://www.mid.ru.
10. For these different understandings of international law and their implications for humanitarian intervention, see James Pattison, *Humanitarian Intervention and the Responsibility to Protect: Who Should Intervene?* (Oxford: Oxford University Press, 2010), pp. 45–51.
11. Interview with Lavrov, 'We Can't Say That NATO Presents a Threat to Us', *Kommersant*, 11 June 2010, as at 11 June 2010, http://www.mid.ru.
12. See Sergei Lavrov, *Rossiyskaya gazeta*, 10 November 2010, and at http://www.mid.ru.
13. Alex J. Bellamy, 'The Responsibility to Protect—Five Years On', *Ethics and International Affairs*, 24/2 (2010), p. 166.
14. Rosemary Foot and Andrew Walter, *China, the United States and Global Order* (Oxford: Oxford University Press, 2011), pp. 13–14.
15. Christopher J. Borgen, 'Whose public, Whose Order? Imperium, Region and Normative Friction', *Yale Journal of International Law*, 32 (2007), p. 340.
16. Alex J. Bellamy, 'Normative Innovation and the Great Powers', in Alex J. Bellamy (ed.), *International Society and its Critics* (Oxford: Oxford University Press, 2005), pp. 266–9.
17. S. Neil MacFarlane, 'Russian Perspectives on Order and Justice', in Rosemary Foot, John Gaddis, and Andrew Hurrell (eds.), *Order and Justice in International Relations* (Oxford: Oxford University Press, 2003), pp. 184–206.
18. Bellamy, 'Normative Innovation and the Great Powers', p. 268.
19. Foot and Walter, *China, the United States and Global* Order, pp. 280–4.
20. Report by General Nikolai Makarov to the Russian Public Chamber on 17 November 2011; *Kommersant*, 18 November 2011, p. 2.
21. See the defence of pluralism by John Vincent, R. J. Vincent, *Human Rights and International Relations* (Cambridge: Cambridge University Press for the Royal Institute of International Affairs, 1986), pp. 117–18; as discussed by Jennifer M. Welsh, 'A Normative Case for Pluralism: Reassessing Vincent's Views on Humanitarian Intervention', *International Affairs*, 87/5 (September 2011), pp. 1201–2.

Bibliography

Principal official documents

The Alliance's Strategic Concept, 24 April 1999, at <http://www.nato.int/cps/en/natolive/official_texts_27433.htm>.

The Foreign Policy Concept of the Russian Federation, 28 June 2000, at <http://www.fas.org/nuke/guide/russia/doctrine/econcept.htm> and *Nezavisimaya gazeta*, 11 July 2000, pp. 1, 6.

The Foreign Policy Concept of the Russian Federation, 12 July 2008, at <http://www.kremlin.ru/eng/text/docs/2008/07/204750.shtml>.

Global Security: Russia (House of Commons, Select Committee on Foreign Affairs, HC 51, Second Report of Session 2007–8), 25 November 2007.

Kosovo (House of Commons Select Committee on Foreign Affairs, HC28, 2 vols., Fourth Report of Session 1999–2000), 7 June 2000, at <http://www.publications.parliament.uk/pa/cm199900/cmselect/cmfaff/28/2813.htm>.

A More Secure World: Our Shared Responsibilities, Report of the Secretary General's High Level Panel on Threats, Challenges and Change, UN Doc A/59/565, 2 December 2004, at <http://www.un.org/secureworld/report/pdf>.

The National Security Strategy of the United States of America, White House, 17 September 2002, at <http://georgewbush-whitehouse.archives.gov/nsc/nss/2002>.

The National Security Strategy of the United States of America, White House, 16 March 2006, at <http://georgewbush-whitehouse.archives.gov/nsc/nss/2006>.

'Osnovy voennoi doktriny Rossii', *Voennaya mysl'*, Special Issue, May (1992), pp. 1–16

Russia: A New Confrontation? (House of Commons, Defence Committee, HC276, Second Report of Session 2008–9), 10 July 2009.

Strategic Concept for the Defence and Security of the Members of the North Atlantic Treaty Organization, adopted 19–20 November 2010, at <http://www.nato.int/strategic-concept/pdf/Strat_Concept_web_en.pdf>.

Strategiya natsional'noy bezopasnosti Rossiyskoy Federatsii do 2020 goda, 12 May 2009, at <http://www.scrf.gov.ru/documents/99.html>.

United Nations General Assembly Resolutions, at <http://www.un.org/documents/resga.htm>.

United Nations General Assembly Sessions, at <http://www.un.org/en/ga/sessions>.

United Nations Security Council Meetings (meetings records, press releases on meetings, and Security Council action/vote) at <http://www.un.org/Depts/dhl/resguide/scact.htm>.

United Nations Security Council Resolutions (just resolutions adopted), at <http://www.un.org/documents/scres.htm>.

Voennaya doktrina Rossiyskoy Federatsii, 5 February 2010, at <http://news.kremlin.ru/ref_notes/461>.

Russian newspapers and periodicals

Argumenty i fakty
Izvestiya
Kommersant-Daily
Komsomolskaya pravda
Krasnaya zvezda
Moscow News
Moskovskie novosti
Nezavisimaya gazeta
Nezavisimoe voennoe obozrenie
Novaya gazeta
Novoye vremya
Novye izvestiya
Obshchaya gazeta
Pravda
Profil
Rossiiskie vesti
Rossiyskaya gazeta
Russia Profile
Russia Today
Segodnya
Sovetskaya Rossiya
Vedomosti
Voenno-promyshlennyy kurier
Vremya
Vremya novostei
Yezhednevnyy zhurnal

Western newspapers

Financial Times
The Guardian
International Herald Tribune
New York Times
The Times
The Times of Central Asia
Wall Street Journal
Washington Post
Washington Times

News bulletins and news reports

BBC Monitoring Online, at <http://wwww.bbc.monitoringonline.com>.

BBC Summary of World Broadcasts. Former Soviet Union, at <http://www.bbc.monitoringonline.com>.

BBC Summary of World Broadcasts. Soviet Union.

Eurasia Daily Monitor (Jamestown Foundation), at <http://www.eurasia.net.org>.
Eurasia Insight (Jamestown Foundation), at <http://www.eurasia.net.org>.
Foreign Broadcast Information Service (FBIS).
Johnson's Russia List, at <http://www.cdi.org/russia/johnson>.
Inside Central Asia, BBC Monitoring.
Military News Bulletin.
Monitor (Jamestown Foundation), at <http://www.eurasia.net.org>.
Joint Publication Research Service (JPRS).
Radio Free Europe/Radio Liberty Central Asia Report, at <http://www.rferl.org/centralasia>.
Radio Free Europe/Radio Liberty Daily Report, at <http://www.rferl.org>.
Radio Free Europe/Radio Liberty News Brief, at <http://www.rferl.org>.
Radio Free Europe/Radio Liberty Research Report, at <http://www.rferl.org>.

Books, articles, reports, and collections of documents

Abakov, M. M. (ed.), *Narusheniya SShA norm mezhdunarodnogo prava* (Moscow: Mezhdunarodnye otnosheniya, 1984).

Abramyan, A. S., 'Pravovye aspekty primeneniya voennoy sily v bor'be s terrorizmom', *Voennaya mysl'*, 12 (2003), 24–37.

Aleprete, Michael E. Jr., 'Democratic Politics and Russian Foreign Policy: Russia's Domestic Debate and the Conflict in Kosovo', *Journal of International Relations and Development*, 3/4 (2000), 1–24.

Allison, Roy, 'New Thinking on Defence Policy in the Soviet Union', in Ken Booth (ed.), *New Thinking about Strategy and International Security* (London: Unwin Hyman, 1991), pp. 215–43.

Allison, Roy, *Peacekeeping in the Soviet Successor States* (Paris: Institute for Security Studies, Western European Union, Chaillot Paper 18, November 1994).

Allison, Roy, 'Military Factors in Foreign Policy', in Neil Malcolm, Alex Pravda, Roy Allison, and Margot Light, *Internal Factors in Russian Foreign Policy* (Oxford: Oxford University Press, 1996), 220–85.

Allison, Roy, 'Strategic Reassertion in Russia's Central Asia Policy', *International Affairs*, 80/2 (2004), 277–93.

Allison, Roy, 'Russia Resurgent? Moscow's Campaign to "Coerce Georgia to Peace"', *International Affairs*, 84/6 (2008), 1145–71.

Allison, Roy, 'Virtual Regionalism, Regional Structures and Regime Security in Central Asia', *Central Asian Survey*, 27/2 (2008), 185–202.

Allison, Roy, 'The Russian Case for Military Intervention in Georgia: International Law, Norms and Political Calculation', *European Security*, 18/2 (2009), 173–200.

Allison, Roy, Margot Light, and Stephen White, *Putin's Russia and the Enlarged Europe* (Oxford: Blackwell, 2006).

Allison, Roy and Phil Williams (eds.), *Superpower Competition and Crisis Prevention in the Third World* (Cambridge: Cambridge University Press, 1990).

Alston, Philip and Euan Macdonald (eds.), *Human Rights, Intervention and the Use of Force* (Oxford: Oxford University Press, 2008).

Ambrosio, Thomas, 'Insulating Russia from a Colour Revolution: How the Kremlin Resists Regional Democratic Trends', *Democratization*, 14/2 (2007), 232–52.

Ambrosio, Thomas, 'Catching the "Shanghai Spirit": How the Shanghai Cooperation Organization Promotes Authoritarian Norms in Central Asia', *Europe-Asia Studies*, 60/8 (2008), 1321–44.

Ambrosio, Thomas, *Authoritarian Backlash: Russian Resistance to Democratization in the Former Soviet Union* (Farnham: Ashgate, 2009).

Antonenko, Oksana, 'Russia, NATO and European Security after Kosovo', *Survival*, 41/4 (1999–2000), 124–44.

Arend, Anthony Clark, 'International Law and the Preemptive Use of Military Force', *The Washington Quarterly*, 26/2 (2003), 89–103.

Aris, Stephen, *Eurasian Regionalism: The Shanghai Cooperation Organization* (Basingstoke: Palgrave Macmillan, 2011).

Armstrong, David, 'Introduction', *Review of International Studies*, 31, Special Issue, 'Force and Legitimacy in World Politics' (2005), 1–13.

Armstrong, David, Theo Farrell, and Hélène Lambert, *International Law and International Relations* (Cambridge: Cambridge University Press, 2007).

Asmus, Ronald D., *A Little War that Shook the World: Georgia, Russia, and the Future of the West* (New York: Palgrave Macmillan, 2010).

Aspaturian, Vernon, 'Soviet Global Power and the Correlation of Forces', *Problems of Communism*, 29 (May–June 1980), 1–18.

Averre, Derek, 'Russian Foreign Policy and the Global Political Environment', *Problems of Post-Communism*, 55/5 (2008), 28–39.

Averre, Derek, 'Competing Rationalities: Russia, the US and the "Shared Neighbourhood"', *Europe-Asia Studies*, 61/10 (2009), 1689–713.

Averre, Derek, 'From Pristina to Tskhinvali: The Legacy of Operation Allied Force in Russia's Relations with the West', *International Affairs*, 85/3 (2009), 575–87.

Ayoob, Mohammed, 'Humanitarian Intervention and State Sovereignty', *The International Journal of Human Rights*, 6/1 (2001), 81–102.

Ayub, Fatima and Sari Kouvo, 'Righting the Course? Humanitarian Intervention, the War on Terror and the Future of Afghanistan', *International Affairs*, 84/4 (2008), 641–57.

Bacon, Edwin 'Military Reform and Soviet Analysis of the Gulf War', *The Journal of Soviet Military Studies*, 5/2 (1992), 169–86.

Baev, Pavel K., *The Russian Army in a Time of Troubles* (London: Sage, 1996).

Baev, Pavel K., 'Russia's Stance against Secessions: From Chechnya to Kosovo', *International Peacekeeping*, 6/3 (1999), 73–94.

Baev, Pavel, 'Putin's Counter-Terrorism: The Parameters of a Strategic Dead-End', *Small Wars and Insurgencies*, 17/1 (2006), 1–21.

Baev, Pavel, *Russian Energy Policy and Military Power: Putin's Quest for Greatness* (London: Routledge, 2008).

Baev, Pavel K. 'Leading in the Concert of Great Powers: Lessons from Russia's G8 Chairmanship', in Elana Wilson Rowe and Stina Torjesen (eds.), *The Multilateral Dimension in Russian Foreign Policy* (London: Routledge, 2009), 58–68.

Bannon, Alicia L., 'The Responsibility to Protect: The U.N. World Summit and the Question of Unilateralism', *Yale Law Journal*, 115 (2006), 1157–65.

Baranovsky, Vladimir, 'Russia's Interests are Too Important', *International Affairs* (Moscow), 45/3 (1999), 4–14.

Baranovsky, Vladimir, 'The Kosovo Factor in Russia's Foreign Policy', *International Spectator*, 35/2 (2000), 113–30.

Baranovsky, Vladimir, 'Russia: Reassessing National Interests', in Albrecht Schnabel and Ramesh Thakur (eds.), *Kosovo and the Challenge of Humanitarian Intervention: Selective Indignation, Collective Action and International Citizenship* (Tokyo: United Nations University Press, 2000), 101–15.

Baranovsky, Vladimir, 'Humanitarian Intervention: Russian Perspectives', *Pugwash Occasional Papers*, 2/1 (2001), 1–14, at <http://pugwash.org/reports/rc/como_russia.htm>.

Barkin, Samuel J. and Bruce Cronin, 'The State and the Nation: Changing Norms and the Rules of Sovereignty in International Relations', *International Organization*, 48/1 (1994), 107–30.

Barynkin, V. M., 'Russian Armed Force and Peacekeeping', *Military Thought*, 7/6 (1998), 14–22.

Bass, Gary Jonathan, *Freedom's Battle: The Origins of Humanitarian Intervention* (New York: Alfred A. Knopf, 2008).

Beacháin, Donnacha Ó and Abel Polese, 'What Happened to the Colour Revolutions? Authoritarian Responses from Former Soviet Spaces', *Journal of International and Area Studies*, 17/2 (2010), 31–51.

Bellamy, Alex J., 'Lessons Unlearned: Why Coercive Diplomacy Failed at Rambouillet', *International Peacekeeping*, 7/2 (2000), 95–114.

Bellamy, Alex J., *Kosovo and International Society* (Basingstoke: Palgrave Macmillan, 2002).

Bellamy, Alex J. (ed.), *International Society and its Critics* (Oxford: Oxford University Press, 2005).

Bellamy, Alex J., 'Responsibility to Protect or Trojan Horse? The Crisis in Darfur and Humanitarian Intervention after Iraq', *Ethics and International Affairs*, 19/2 (2005), 31–53.

Bellamy, Alex J., 'The Responsibility to Protect and the Problem of Military Intervention', *International Affairs*, 84/4 (2008), 615–39.

Bellamy, Alex J., 'Realizing the Responsibility to Protect', *International Studies Perspectives*, 10/2 (2009), 111–28.

Bellamy, Alex J., *Responsibility to Protect: The Global Effort to End Mass Atrocities* (Cambridge and Malden, MA: Polity Press, 2009).

Bellamy, Alex J., *Politics, Law and the Responsibility to Protect: From Concept to Practice* (London: Routledge, 2010).

Bellamy, Alex J., 'The Responsibility to Protect—Five Years On', *Ethics and International Affairs*, 24/2 (2010), 143–69.

Bellamy, Alex J., 'Libya and the Responsibility to Protect: The Exception and the Norm', *Ethics and International Affairs*, 25/3 (2011), 1–7.

Belopolsky, Helen, *Russia and the Challengers: Russian Alignment with China, Iran and Iraq in the Unipolar Era* (Basingstoke: Palgrave Macmillan, 2009).

Bennett, Andrew, *Condemned to Repetition? The Rise, Fall and Reprise of Soviet–Russian Military Interventionism, 1973–1996* (Cambridge, MA: MIT Press, 1999).

Bennett, Andrew, 'The Guns That Did Not Smoke: Ideas and the Soviet Non-Use of Force in 1989', *Journal of Cold War Studies*, 7/2 (2005), 81–109.

Berezkin, G. A., 'Lessons from the War in Iraq', *Military Thought*, 12/3 (2003), 139–82.

Bessmertnykh, Aleksandr, 'The Iraq War and its Implications', *International Affairs* (Moscow), 49/4 (2003), 24–36.

Bjola, Corneliu, *Legitimising the Use of Force in International Politics: Kosovo, Iraq and the Ethics of Intervention* (London and New York: Routledge, 2009).

Borgen, Christopher J., 'Whose Public, Whose Order? Imperium, Region and Normative Friction', *Yale Journal of International Law*, 32 (2007), 333–74.

Borgen, Christopher J., 'The Language of Law and the Practice of Politics: Great Powers and the Rhetoric of Self-Determination in the Cases of Kosovo and South Ossetia', *Chicago Journal of International Law*, 10/1 (2009), 769–88.

Bothe, Michael, Mary Ellen O'Connell, and Natalino Ronzitti (eds.), *Redefining Sovereignty: The Use of Force after the Cold War* (Ardsley, NY: Transnational Publishers, 2006).

Bouldin, Matthew, 'The Ivanov Doctrine and Military Reform: Reasserting Stability in Russia', *Journal of Slavic Military Studies*, 17/4 (2004), 619–41.

Boyle, Francis A. et al., 'International Lawlessness in Grenada', *The American Journal of International Law*, 78 (1984), 172–5.

Bring, Ove, 'Should NATO Take the Lead in Formulating a Doctrine on Humanitarian Intervention', *NATO Review*, 3 (1999), 24–7.

Browning, Christopher, 'Reassessing Putin's Project: Reflections on IR Theory and the West', *Problems of Post-Communism*, 55/5 (2008), 3–13.

Brunnée, Jutta and Stephen J. Toope, 'The Use of Force: International Law after Iraq', *International and Comparative Law Quarterly*, 53/4 (2004), 785–806.

Buckley, Mary and Sally N. Cummings (eds.), *Kosovo: Perceptions of War and its Aftermath* (London: Continuum, 2001).

Buzan, Barry, 'The Middle East through English School Theory', in Barry Buzan and Ana Gonzalez-Pelaez (eds.), *International Society and the Middle East: English School Theory at the Regional Level* (Basingstoke: Palgrave Macmillan, 2009), 24–44.

Buzan, Barry and Ana Gonzalez-Pelaez (eds.), *International Society and the Middle East: English School Theory at the Regional Level* (Basingstoke: Palgrave Macmillan, 2009).

Byers, Michael, 'Terrorism, the Use of Force and International Law after 11 September', *International and Comparative Law Quarterly*, 51 (2002), 401–14.

Byers, Michael, 'Not Yet Havoc: Geopolitical Change and the International Rules on Military Force', *Review of International Studies*, 31 (2005), Special Issue, 'Force and Legitimacy in World Politics', 51–70.

Cassese, A. (ed.), *The Current Legal Regulation of the Use of Force* (Dordrecht: Martinus Nijhoff, 1986).

Chernichenko, Stanislav, 'NATO's Operation in Yugoslavia and International Law', *International Affairs* (Moscow), 46/1 (2000), 168–77.

Chesterman, Simon, 'Humanitarian Intervention and Afghanistan', in Jennifer M. Welsh (ed.), *Humanitarian Intervention and International Relations* (Oxford: Oxford University Press, 2004), 163–75.

Chesterman, Simon, '"Leading from Behind": The Responsibility to Protect, the Obama Doctrine, and Humanitarian Intervention in Libya', *Ethics and International Affairs*, 25/3 (2011), 1–7.

Civilians in the Firing Line: The Georgia-Russia Conflict (London: Amnesty International Publications, 2008).

Clark, Ian, *Legitimacy in International Society* (Oxford: Oxford University Press, 2005).

Clark, Ian, *International Legitimacy and World Society* (Oxford: Oxford University Press, 2007).

Cooper, Richard H. (ed.), *Responsibility to Protect: The Global Moral Compact for the 21st Century* (Basingstoke: Palgrave Macmillan, 2009).

Coppieters, Bruno and Richard Sakwa, *Contextualizing Secession* (Oxford: Oxford University Press, 2003).

Cordovez, Diego and Selig Harrison, *Out of Afghanistan: The Inside Story of the Soviet Withdrawal* (Oxford: Oxford University Press, 1995).

Cornell, Svante, 'International Reactions to Massive Human Rights Violations: The Case of Chechnya', *Europe-Asia Studies*, 51/1 (1999), 85–100.

Cornell, Svante E. and S. Frederick Starr (eds.), *The Guns of August 2008: Russia's War in Georgia* (Armonk, NY: M. E. Sharpe, 2008).

Crow, Suzanne, 'Primakov and the Soviet Peace Initiative', *Radio Free Europe/Radio Liberty Report on the USSR*, 3/9 (1 March 1991), 14–17.

Crow, Suzanne, 'Russia Seeks Leadership in Regional Peacekeeping', *Radio Free Europe/Radio Liberty Research Report*, 2/15 (1993), 28–32.

Cummings, Sally N., 'Perceptions in the Commonwealth of Independent States', in Mary Buckley and Sally N. Cummings (eds.), *Kosovo: Perceptions of War and its Aftermath* (London: Continuum, 2001), 176–92.

Cutts, Noelle Shanahan, 'Enemies Through the Gates: Russian Violations of International Law in the Georgia/Abkhazia Conflict', *Case Western Reserve Journal of International Law*, 44/281 (2007–9), 281–310.

Daalder, Ivo H. (ed.), *Beyond Preemption: Force and Legitimacy in a Changing World* (Washington, DC: Brookings Institution, 2007).

Danchev, Alex and Dan Keohane (eds.), *International Perspectives on the Gulf Conflict, 1990–91* (Basingstoke: Palgrave Macmillan, 2003).

Damrosch, Lori F. and David J. Scheffer (eds.), *Law and Force in the New International Order* (Boulder: Westview Press, 1991).

Dawisha, Karen, *The Kremlin and the Prague Spring* (Berkeley: University of California Press, 1984).

Deng, Francis M. et. al. *Sovereignty as Responsibility* (Washington, DC: Brookings Institution, 1996).

Etzioni, Amitai. 'The "Secret" Matrix', *The World Today*, 66/7 (July 2010), 11–14.

Evangelista, Matthew, *The Chechen Wars. Will Russia go the Way of the Soviet Union?* (Washington, DC: Brookings Institution, 2002).

Evans, Gareth, 'Russia, Georgia and the Responsibility to Protect', *Amsterdam Law Forum*, 1/2 (2009), 25–8.

Falk, Richard A., 'What Future for the UN Charter System of War Prevention?', *The American Journal of International Law*, 97/3 (2003), 590–8.

Falk, Richard, 'Legality and Legitimacy: The Quest for Principled Flexibility and Restraint', *Review of International Studies*, 31, Special Issue 'Force and Legitimacy in World Politics' (2005), 33–50.

Farer, Tom J., 'The Prospect for International Law and Order in the Wake of Iraq', *The American Journal of International Law*, 97/3 (2003), 621–28.

Fawn, Rick, 'Battle over the Box: International Election Observation Missions, Political Competition and Retrenchment in the Post-Soviet Space', *International Affairs*, 82/6 (2006), 1133–53.

Fawn, Rick and Robert Nalbandov, 'The Difficulties of Knowing the Start of War in the Information Age: Russia, Georgia and the War over South Ossetia, August 2008', *European Security*, 21/1 (2012), 57–89.

Fedotov, Iurii, 'Challenges to Multilateralism and the UN', *International Affairs* (Moscow), 53/3 (2004), 6–11.

Feinstein, L. and A. M. Slaughter, 'A Duty to Prevent', *Foreign Affairs*, 83/1 (2004), 136–51.

Feste, Karen E. *American and Soviet Intervention: Effects on World Stability* (New York: Crane Russak, 1990).

Finnemore, Martha, 'Constructing Norms of Humanitarian Intervention', in Peter J. Katzenstein (ed.), *The Culture of National Security: Norms and Identity in World Politics* (New York: Columbia University Press, 1996), 153–85.

Finnemore, Martha, *The Purpose of Intervention: Changing Beliefs about the Use of Force* (Ithaca and London: Cornell University Press, 2003).

Finnemore, Martha, 'Fights about Rules: The Role of Efficacy and Power in Changing Multilateralism', *Review of International Studies*, 31, Special Issue, 'Force and Legitimacy in World Politics' (2005), 187–206.

Finnemore, Martha and Kathryn Sikkink, 'International Norm Dynamics and Political Change', *International Organization*, 52/4 (1998), 887–917.

Foot, Rosemary, 'The Responsibility to Protect (R2P) and its Evolution: Beijing's Influence on Norm Creation in Humanitarian Areas', *St Antony's International Review*, 6/2 (2011), 47–66.

Foot, Rosemary and Andrew Walter, *China, the United States and Global Order* (Cambridge: Cambridge University Press, 2011).

Foot, Rosemary, John Gaddis, and Andrew Hurrell (eds.), *Order and Justice in International Relations* (Oxford: Oxford University Press, 2003).

Forsberg, Tuomas and Graeme Herd. 'The EU, Human Rights and the Russo-Chechen Conflict', *Political Science Quarterly*, 120/3 (2005), 455–78.

Franck, Thomas M., 'What Happens Now? The United Nations after Iraq', *The American Journal of International Law*, 97/3 (2003), 607–20.

Franck, Thomas and Edward Weisband, *World Politics: Verbal Strategies among the Superpowers* (New York: Oxford University Press, 1971).

Freedman, Lawrence and Efraim Karsh, *The Gulf Conflict 1990–1991: Diplomacy and War in the New World Order* (Princeton, NJ: Princeton University Press, 1993).

Fuller, Graham E., 'Moscow and the Gulf War', *Foreign Affairs*, 70/3 (1991), 55–76.

Garwood, Robert, 'The Second Russo-Chechen Conflict (1999 to Date): "A Modern Military Operation"', *Journal of Slavic Military Studies*, 15/3 (2002), 60–80.

Gatilov, Gennady, 'Blue Berets: The UN's Peacekeepers', *International Affairs* (Moscow), 56/6 (2010), 119–27.

Gazzini, Tarcisio, *The Changing Rules on the Use of Force in International Law* (Manchester: Manchester University Press, 2005).

George, Alexander L., 'US–Soviet Global Rivalry: Norms of Competition', *Journal of Peace Research*, 23/3 (1986), 247–62.

Gibbs, David N., *First Do No Harm: Humanitarian Intervention and the Destruction of Yugoslavia* (Nashville, TN: Vanderbilt University Press, 2009).

Glennon, Michael J., *Limits of Law, Prerogatives of Power: Interventionism after Kosovo* (New York: Palgrave Macmillan, 2001).

Glennon, Michael J., 'Why the Security Council Failed', *Foreign Affairs*, 82/3 (2003), 16–35.

Gobarov, Vicktor, 'Russia–NATO Relations after the Kosovo Crisis: Strategic Implications', *The Journal of Slavic Military Studies*, 12/3 (1999), 1–17.

Gokov, A. V., 'Vvod sovetskikh voysk v Afganistan v 1979 godu', *Voenno-istoricheskiy zhurnal*, 12 (2009), 43–4.

Golan, Galia, 'Gorbachev's Difficult Time in the Gulf', *Political Science Quarterly*, 107/2 (1992), 213–30.

Golan, Galia, 'Russia and the Iraq War: Was Putin's Policy a Failure?', *Communist and Post-Communist Studies*, 37 (2004), 429–59.

Goodman, Melvin A. (ed.), *The End of Superpower Conflict in the Third World* (Boulder: Westview Press, 1992).

Gorbachev, Mikhail, *Perestroika: New Thinking for our Country and the World* (2nd edn.) (London: Fontana Collins, 1988).

Gray, Christine, 'The US National Security Strategy and the new "Bush Doctrine" on Preemptive Self-Defence', *Chinese Journal of International Law*, 1 (2002), 437–47.

Gray, Christine, *International Law and the Use of Force* (Cambridge: Cambridge University Press, 2008).

Green, James A., 'Passportisation, Peacekeepers and Proportionality: The Russian Claim of the Protection of Nationals Abroad in Self-Defence', in James A. Green and Christopher P. M. Waters (eds.), *Conflict in the Caucasus: Implications for the International Legal Order* (Basingstoke: Palgrave Macmillan, 2010), 54–79.

Green, James A. and Christopher P. M. Waters (eds.), *Conflict in the Caucasus: Implications for the International Legal Order* (Basingstoke: Palgrave Macmillan, 2010).

Greene, James M., 'The Peacekeeping Doctrines of the CIS', *Jane's Intelligence Review*, 5/4 (1993), 156–9.

Greenwood, Christopher, 'International Law and the Pre-emptive Use of Force: Afghanistan, Al-Qaida and Iraq', *San Diego International Law Journal*, 4 (2003), 7–37.

Greenwood, Christopher, 'The Legality of the Use of Force in Iraq in 2003', in Michael Bothe, Mary Ellen O'Connell, and Natalino Ronzitti (eds.), *Redefining Sovereignty: The Use of Force after the Cold War* (Ardsley, NY: Transnational Publishers, 2006), 387–415.

Guicherd, Catherine, 'International Law and the War in Kosovo', *Survival*, 41/2 (1999), 19–34.

Gushev, A., 'Voenno-politicheskie posledstviya voyny v zone Persidskogo zaliva', *Zarubezhnoe voennoe obozrenie*, 8 (1991), 3–7.

Haines, Steven, 'The Influence of Operation Allied Force on the Development of the *Jus ad Bellum*', *International Affairs*, 85/3 (2009), 477–90.

Halliday, Fred, 'Soviet Foreign Policymaking and the Afghanistan War: From "Second Mongolia" to "Bleeding Wound"', *Review of International Studies*, 25/4 (1999), 675–91.

Haslam, Jonathan, 'The UN and the Soviet Union: New Thinking?', *International Affairs*, 65/4 (1989), 677–84.

Haukkala, Hiski, 'The Russian Challenge to EU Normative Power: The Case of European Neighbourhood Policy', *The International Spectator*, 43/2 (2008), 35–47.

Haukkala, Hiski and Linda Jakobson, 'The Myth of a Sino-Russian Challenge to the West', *International Spectator*, 44/3 (2009), 59–76.

Headley, James, *Russia and the Balkans: Foreign Policy from Yeltsin to Putin* (New York: Columbia University Press, 2008).

Heinze, Eric A., 'The Evolution of International Law in Light of the "Global War on Terror"', *Review of International Studies*, 37 (2011), 1069–94.

Helmke, Belinda, *Under Attack: Challenges to the Rules Governing the International Use of Force* (Farnham: Ashgate, 2010).

Henderson, Christian and James A. Green, 'The Jus ad Bellum and Entities Short of Statehood in the Report on the Conflict in Georgia', *International and Comparative Law Quarterly*, 59 (2010), 129–39.

Herd, Graeme P., 'The Russo-Chechen Information Warfare and 9/11: Al-Qaeda through the South Caucasus Looking Glass?', *European Security*, 11/4 (Winter 2002), 110–30.

Herman, Robert G., 'Identity, Norms and National Security: The Soviet Foreign Policy Revolution and the End of the Cold War', in Peter J. Katzenstein (ed.), *The Culture of National Security: Norms and Identity in World Politics* (New York: Columbia University Press, 1996), 271–316.

Hilali, A. Z., 'The Soviet Decision-Making for Intervention in Afghanistan and its Motives', *The Journal of Slavic Military Studies*, 16/2 (2003), 113–45.

Hughes, James, 'The Chechnya Conflict: Freedom Fighters or Terrorists?', *Demokratizatsiya*, 15/3 (2007), 293–311.

'Humanitarian Intervention and the Protection of Nationals Abroad', Roundtable discussion, *International Affairs* (Moscow), 55/5 (2009), 83–97.

Hurrell, Andrew, 'Legitmacy and the Use of Force: Can the Circle be Squared?', *Review of International Studies*, 31, Special Issue, 'Force and Legitimacy in World Politics' (2005), 15–32.

Hurrell, Andrew, 'Hegemony, Liberalism and Global Order: What Space for Would-be Great Powers?', *International Affairs*, 82/1 (2006), 1–19.

Ikenberry, John G., *After Victory: Institutions, Strategic Restraint and the Rebuilding of Order after Major Wars* (Princeton, NJ: Princeton University Press, 2001).

Imam, Zafar, *Towards a Model Relationship: A Study of Soviet Treaties with India and other Third World Countries* (Delhi: ABC Publishing House, 1983).

Independent International Commission on Kosovo. The Kosovo Report: Conflict; International Response; Lessons Learned (Oxford: Oxford University Press. 2000).

Independent International Fact-Finding Mission on the Conflict in Georgia, 3 vols. (Brussels: IIFFMCG, 2008), at <http:www.ceiig.ch>.

Jackson, Nicole, *Russian Foreign Policy in the CIS: Theories, Debates and Actions* (London: Routledge, 2003).

Jackson, R. H., *The Global Covenant: Human Conduct in a World of States* (Oxford: Oxford University Press, 2000).

Johnstone, Ian, 'Security Council Deliberations: The Power of the Better Argument', *European Journal of International Law*, 14/3 (2003), 437–80.

Johnstone, Ian, 'Discursive Power in the UN Security Council', *Journal of International Law and International Relations*, 2/1 (2005), 73–94.

Jones, Bruce D., 'Libya and the Responsibilities of Power', *Survival*, 53/3 (2011), 51–60.

Jones, Christopher D., 'Soviet Hegemony in Eastern Europe: The Dynamics of Political Autonomy and Military Intervention', *World Politics*, 29/2 (1977), 216–41.

Jones, Robert A., *The Soviet Concept of Limited Sovereignty: From Lenin to Gorbachev* (Basingstoke: Macmillan, 1990).

Jones, Stephen F., 'The Rose Revolution: A Revolution without Revolutionaries?', *Cambridge Review of International Affairs*, 19/1 (2006), 33–48.

Jonson, Lena, 'In Search of a Doctrine: Russian Interventionism in Conflicts in its "Near Abroad"', *Low Intensity Conflicts and Law Enforcement*, 5/3 (1996), 440–65.

Jonson, Lena, *The Tajik War: A Challenge to Russian Policy* (London The Royal Institute of International Affairs, Discussion Paper 74, 1998).

Jonson, Lena, *Keeping the Peace in the CIS: The Evolution of Russian Policy* (London: Royal Institute of International Affairs, Discussion Paper 81, 1999).

Jonson, Lena and Clive Archer (eds.), *Peacekeeping and the Role of Russia in Eurasia* (Boulder: Westview Press, 1996).

Joyner, Christopher C., 'The United States Action in Grenada: Reflections on the Lawfulness of Invasion', *The American Journal of International Law*, 78 (1984), 131–44.

Kahn, Paul W., 'Lessons for International Law from the Gulf War', *Stanford Law Review*, 45/2 (1993), 425–41.

'Kak prinimalos' reshenia', *Voenno-istoricheskiy zhurnal*, 7 (1991), 40–52.

Kalinovsky, Artemy, 'Decision-Making and the Soviet War in Afghanistan: From Intervention to Withdrawal', *Journal of Cold War Studies*, 11/4 (2009), 46–73.

Karaganov, Sergei. 'The World in Crisis: A Time for Creation', *Russia in Global Affairs* 4, (2008), at <http://eng.globalaffairs.ru/numbers/25/1235/html>.

Katz, Mark N., 'The Evolution of the Brezhnev Doctrine under Gorbachev', in Kurt M. Campbell and S. Neil MacFarlane (eds.), *Gorbachev's Third World Dilemmas* (London: Routledge, 1989), 36–66.

Katzenstein, Peter J. (ed.), *The Culture of National Security: Norms and Identity in World Politics* (New York: Columbia University Press, 1996).

Katzenstein, Peter J. (ed.), *Civilizations in World Politics: Plural and Pluralist Perspectives* (London: Routledge, 2009).

Kazantsev, Boris, 'NATO: Obvious Bias to the Use of Force', *International Affairs* (Moscow), 45/4 (1999), 38–42.

Kerton-Johnson, Nicholas, *Justifying America's Wars: The Conduct and Practice of US Military Intervention* (London: Routledge, 2011).

Kol'tyukov, A., *Terrorizm: kak ugroza natsional'noy bezopasnosti gosudarstva* (Moscow: Main Command of the Russian Ministry of Internal Affairs, Institute of Military History of the Russian Ministry of Defence, 2003).

Kosachev, Konstantin, 'Russia and the West: Where the Differences Lie', *Russia in Global Affairs*, 4 (2007), 1–8, at <http://eng.globalaffairs.ru/numbers/21/1149/html>.

Kosmehl, Miriam, 'Rechsgewalt oder Gewaltretcht: Das internationale Recht unter die Menschenrechte in Tschetschenien', *Osteuropa*, 53/8 (2003), 1066–83.

Kratochwil, Friedrich V., 'How Do Norms Matter?', in Michael Byers (ed.), *The Role of Law in International Politics* (Oxford: Oxford University Press, 2000), 35–68.

Krieger, Heike (ed.), *The Kosovo Conflict and International Law: An Analytical Documentation 1974–1999* (Cambridge: Cambridge University Press, 2001).

Kroenig, Matthew, 'Time to Attack Iran', *Foreign Affairs*, 91/1 (2012), 76–86.

Krueger, Heiko, 'Implications of Kosovo, Abkhazia and South Ossetia for International Law', *Caucasian Review of International Affairs*, 3/2 (2009), 121–42, at <http://www.cria-online.org>.

Krylov, B. S., 'Mezhdunarodnoe pravo i problemy sozdaniya pravovogo akta o bor'be s mezhdunarodnym terrorizmom', in V. N. Kudryavtsev (ed.), *Bor'ba s Terrorizmom* (Moscow: Nauka, 2004), 195–204.

Kudryavtsev, V. (ed.), *Bor'ba s terrorizmom* (Moscow: Nauka, 2004).

Kulikov, Anatoly, 'How Not to Fall into the Crime Trap', *International Affairs* (Moscow), 48/1 (2002), 72–7.

Kull, Steven, *Burying Lenin: The Revolution in Soviet Ideology and Foreign Policy* (Boulder: Westview Press, 1992).

Kuzmin, Eduard, 'International Law at a Crossroads', *International Affairs* (Moscow), 53/5 (2007), 77–90.

Lambeth, Benjamin J., *Desert Storm and its Meaning: The View from Moscow* (Santa Monica: RAND Report, 1992).

Lang, Jr., Anthony F., 'The Violence of Rules? Rethinking the 2003 War Against Iraq', *Contemporary Politics*, 13/3 (2007), 257–76.

Lapidus, Gail W., 'Putin's War on Terrorism: Lessons from Chechnya', *Post-Soviet Affairs*, 18/1 (2002), 41–8.

Larson, Geoff, 'The Right of International Intervention in Civil Conflicts: Evolving International Law on State Sovereignty in Observance of Human Rights and Application to the Crisis in Chechnya', *Transnational Law and Contemporary Problems*, 11 (2001), 251–75.

Latawski, Paul and Martin A. Smith, *The Kosovo Crisis and the Evolution of Post-Cold War Security* (Manchester: Manchester University Press, 2003).

Lavrov, Sergei, 'The Present and Future of Global Politics', *Russia in Global Affairs*, 2 (2007), 1–7, at <http://eng.globalaffairs.ru/numbers/19/1102.html>.

Lavrov, Sergey, 'The Russian Approach: The Fight Against Genocide, War Crimes and Crimes Against Humanity', *Fordham International Law Journal*, 23/2 (1999), 415–28.

Legvold, Robert, 'The Revolution in Soviet Foreign Policy', *Foreign Affairs*, 68/1 (1989), 82–98.

Legvold, Robert (ed.), *Russian Foreign Policy in the 21st Century and the Shadow of the Past* (New York: Columbia University Press, 2007).

Legvold, Robert, 'The Role of Multilateralism in Russian Foreign Policy', in Elana Wilson Rowe and Stina Torjesen (eds.), *The Multilateral Dimension in Russian Foreign Policy* (London: Routledge, 2009), 21–45.

Levitkin, Oleg, 'Inside Moscow's Kosovo Muddle', *Survival*, 42/1 (2000), 130–40.

Lider, Julian, 'The Correlation of Forces: The Soviet Concept', *Journal of Peace Research*, 17/2 (1980), 151–71.

Lider, Julian, *Correlation of Forces: An Analysis of Marxist-Leninist Concepts* (Aldershot: Gower, 1986).

Lieven, Anatol, 'Morality and Reality in Approaches to War Crimes: The Case of Chechnya', *East European Constitutional Review*, 10/2–3 (2001), 72–8.

Light, Margot, 'Soviet Policy in the Third World', *International Affairs*, 67/2 (April 1991), 263–80.

Littlefield, Scott, 'Citizenship, Identity and Foreign Policy: The Contradictions and Consequences of Russia's Passport Distribution in the Separatist Regions of Georgia', *Europe-Asia Studies*, 61/8 (2009), 1461–82.

Litwak, Robert S., 'Living with Ambiguity: Nuclear Deals with Iran and North Korea', *Survival*, 50/1 (2008), 91–118.

Luck, Edward C., 'Sovereignty, Choice and the Responsibility to Protect', *Global Responsibility to Protect*, 1/1 (2009), 10–21.

Lynch, Dov, *The Conflict in Abkhazia: Dilemmas in Russian 'Peacekeeping' Policy* (London: The Royal Institute of International Affairs, Discussion Paper 77, 1998).

Lynch, Dov, '"Walking the Tightrope": The Kosovo Conflict and Russia in European Security, 1998–August 1999', *European Security*, 8/4 (1999), 58–83.

Lynch, Dov, *Russian Peacekeeping Strategies in the CIS: The Cases of Moldova, Georgia and Tajikistan* (Basingstoke: Macmillan, 2000).

Maass, Citha D., 'The Afghanistan Conflict: External Involvement', *Central Asian Survey*, 18/1 (1999), 65–78.

McCorquodale, Robert and Kristin Hausler, 'Caucases in the Caucasus: The Application of the Right of Self-Determination', in James A. Green and Christopher P. M. Waters (eds.), *Conflict in the Caucasus: Implications for the International Legal Order* (Basingstoke: Palgrave Macmillan, 2010), 26–53.

McDonnell, Michael, *The United States, International Law, and the Struggle against Terrorism* (London: Routledge, 2010).

MacFarlane, S. Neil, 'On the Front Lines in the Near Abroad: The CIS and the OSCE in Georgia's Civil Wars', *Third World Quarterly*, 18/3 (1997), 509–25.

MacFarlane, S. Neil, *Intervention in Contemporary World Politics* (Oxford: International Institute for Strategic Studies, 2002), Adelphi Paper 350.

MacFarlane, S. Neil, 'Russian Perspectives on Order and Justice', in Rosemary Foot, John Gaddis, and Andrew Hurrell (eds.), *Order and Justice in International Relations* (Oxford: Oxford University Press, 2003), 176–206.

MacFarlane, S. Neil, 'The "R" in BRICs: Is Russia an Emerging Power?', *International Affairs*, 82/1 (2006), 41–57.

MacFarlane, S. Neil and Albrecht Schnabel, 'Russia's Approach to Peacekeeping', *International Journal*, 55/2 (1995), 294–324.

MacFarlane, S. Neil, Carolyn J. Thielking, and Thomas G. Weiss, 'The Responsibility to Protect: Is Anyone Interested in Humanitarian Intervention?', *Third World Quarterly*, 25/5 (2004), 977–92.

Mackinlay, John and Peter Cross (eds.), *Regional Peacekeepers: The Paradox of Russian Peacekeeping* (Tokyo: United Nations University Press, 2003).

Makarychev, Andrey S., 'Russia's Search for International Identity through the Sovereign Democracy Concept', *The International Spectator*, 43/2 (2008), 49–62.

Makarychev, Andrey, 'Russia, NATO and the "Color Revolutions": Discursive Traps', *Russian Politics and Law*, 47/5 (2009), 40–51.

Malcolm, Neil, Alex Pravda, Roy Allison, and Margot Light, *Internal Factors in Russian Foreign Policy* (Oxford: Oxford University Press, 1996).

Malone, David, *The International Struggle over Iraq: Politics in the UN Security Council, 1980–2005* (Oxford: Oxford University Press, 2006).

Marat, Erica, *The Military and the State in Central Asia* (London: Routledge, 2010).

Markedonov, Sergei, *Turblentnaya Yevraziya* (Moscow: Akademia, 2010).

Marochkin, Sergei Yu., 'On the Recent Development of International Law: Some Russian Perspectives', *Chinese Journal of International Law*, 8/3 (2009), 698–714.

Matthews, Ken, *The Gulf Conflict and International Relations* (London: Routledge, 1993).

Melvin, Neil, 'Eurasian Security Arrangements Face Reality Check after Kyrgyzstan Crisis', *SIPRI Newsletter* (July/August 2010), at <http://www.sipri.org/media/newsletter/essay/julyaugust10>.

Melzer, Nils, *Targeted Killing in International Law* (Oxford: Oxford University Press, 2008).

Meyer, Stephen M., 'The Sources and Prospects of Gorbachev's New Political Thinking on Security', *International Security*, 13 (1988), 124–63.

Moore, John Norton and Robert F. Turner, *International Law and the Brezhnev Doctrine* (Lanham, MD: University Press of America, 1987).

Morris, Justin, 'Normative Innovation and the Great Powers', in Alex Bellamy (ed.), *International Society and its Critics* (Oxford: Oxford University Press, 2005), 265–80.

Morozov, Yu. V., V. V. Glushkin and A. A. Sharavin, *Balkany segodnya i zavtra: voenno-politicheskie aspekty mirotvorchestva* (Moscow: Centre of Military Strategic Studies of the Russian General Staff and Institute of Political and Military Analysis, 2001).

Mullerson, Rein, 'Self-Defense in the Contemporary World', in Lori F. Damrosch and David J. Scheffer (eds.), *Law and Force in the New International Order* (Boulder: Westview Press, 1991), 13–25.

Mullerson, Rein, 'Precedents in the Mountains: On the Parallels and Uniqueness of the Cases of Kosovo, South Ossetia and Abkhazia', *Chinese Journal of International Law*, 8/1 (2009), 2–25.

Nanda, Ved P., 'The Validity of the United States Intervention in Panama under International Law', *The American Journal of International Law*, 84 (1990), 494–503.

Nardin, Terry, 'Humanitarian Imperialism', *Ethics and International Affairs*, 19/2 (2005), 21–6.

Narinskiy, M. and A. Mal'gin (eds.), *Yuzhniy Flang SNG* (Moscow: Logos, 2003).

Norris, John, *Collision Course: NATO, Russia and Kosovo* (Westport, CT: Praeger, 2005).

Nussberger, Angelika, 'The "Five-Day War" in Court: Russia, Georgia and International Law', *Osteuropa*, 58/11 (2008), 19–39.

Nussberger, Angelika, 'The War between Russia and Georgia: Consequences and Unresolved Questions', *Göttingen Journal of International Law*, 1/2 (2009), 341–64.

O'Connell, Mary Ellen, *The Myth of Preemptive Self-Defense* (The American Society of International Law Task Force on Terrorism, August 2002), 1–21, at <http://www.asil.org/taskforce/oconnell.pdf>.

Orlov, A., 'Nonalignment Aligns with Antiwar', *International Affairs* (Moscow), 49/3 (2003), 70–76.

Pattison, James, *Humanitarian Intervention and the Responsibility to Protect: Who Should Intervene?* (Oxford: Oxford University Press, 2010).

Payne, Keith, 'Are they Interested in Stability? The Soviet View of Intervention', *Comparative Strategy*, 3/1 (1983), 1–24.

Petrovskii, Vladimir, 'International Humanitarian Law', *International Affairs* (Moscow), 46/1 (2000), 161–7.

Pikayev, Alexander A., 'Russia's Attitude Towards Nuclear Non-Proliferation Regimes and Institutions: An Example of Multilateralism?', in Elana Wilson Rowe and Stina Torjesen (eds.), *The Multilateral Dimension in Russian Foreign Policy* (London: Routledge, 2009), 69–82.

Popescu, Nicu, *EU Foreign Policy and Post-Soviet Conflicts* (London: Routledge, 2011).

Pouliot, Vincent, *International Security in Practice: The Politics of NATO–Russia Diplomacy* (Cambridge: Cambridge University Press, 2010).

Primakov, Yevgeny M., 'Rather the United Nations than US Unilateralism', *New Perspectives Quarterly*, 21/2 (2004), 49–59.

Programma podgotovki chastey mirotvorcheskikh sil (Moscow: Russian Ministry of Defence, 1992).

Pukhov, Ruslan (ed.), *The Tanks of August* (Moscow: Centre for Analysis of Strategies and Technologies, 2010), at <http://www.cast.ru/files/The_Tanks_of_August_sm_eng_pfd>.

Quigley, John, 'Perestroika and International Law', *American Journal of International Law*, 82/4 (1988), 788–97.

Reed, Laura W. and Carl Kaysen (eds.), *Emerging Norms of Justified Intervention* (Cambridge, MA: American Academy of Arts and Sciences, 1998).

Reisman, Michael, 'The Raid on Bagdad: Some Reflections on its Lawfulness and Implications', *European Journal of International Law*, 5/1 (1994), 120–33.

Reisman, W. Michael and Andrea Armstrong, 'Claims to Pre-emptive Uses of Force: Some Trends and Projections and their Implications for World Order', in Michael N. Schmitt and Jelena Pejic (eds.), *International Law and Armed Conflict: Exploring the Faultlines* (Leiden: Martinus Nijhoff, 2007), 79–112.

The Responsibility to Protect: Report of the International Commission on Intervention and State Sovereignty (Ottawa: International Development Research Centre, 2001).

Reus-Smit, Christian, 'International Law', in John Baylis, Steve Smith, and Patricia Owens (eds.), *The Globalization of World Politics: An Introduction to International Relations* (New York: Oxford University Press, 2008), 279–94.

Reuveny Rafael and Aseem Prakash, 'The Afghanistan War and the Breakdown of the Soviet Union', *Review of International Studies*, 25/4 (1999), 693–708.

Rich, Paul (ed.), *Crisis in the Caucasus: Russia, Georgia and the West* (London: Routledge, 2011).

Richter, Wolfgang, 'Initial Military Operations During the War in Georgia in August 2008', *Caucasus Analytical Digest*, 10 (2 November 2009), 5–9, at <http://www.res.ethz.ch/analysis.cad>.

Ringmar, Erik, 'The Recognition Game: Soviet Russia against the West', *Cooperation and Conflict*, 37/2 (2002), 115–36.

Roberts, Adam, 'NATO's "Humanitarian War" over Kosovo', *Survival*, 41/3 (1999), 102–23.

Roberts, Adam, 'Law and the Use of Force after Iraq', *Survival*, 45/2 (2003), 31–56.

Roslowski, Rey and Friedrich Kratochwil, 'Understanding Change in International Politics: The Soviet Empire's Demise and the International System', *International Organization*, 48/2 (1994), 215–47.

Roth, Kenneth, 'Was the Iraq War a Humanitarian Intervention?', *Journal of Military Ethics*, 5/2 (2006), 84–92.

Rowe, Elana Wilson and Stina Torjesen (eds.), *The Multilateral Dimension in Russian Foreign Policy* (London: Routledge, 2009).

Rowe, Peter (ed.), *The Gulf War 1990–91 in International and English Law* (London: Routledge, 1993).

Rubinstein, Alvin Z., 'Moscow and the Gulf War: Decisions and Consequences', *International Journal*, 49 (1994), 301–27.

Russell, John, 'Exploitation of the "Islamic Factor" in the Russo-Chechen Conflict before and after 11 September 2001', *European Security*, 11 (2002), 96–109.

Russell, John, *Chechnya: Russia's 'War on Terror'* (London: Routledge, 2007).

Russia vs. Georgia: The Fallout (International Crisis Group, Europe Report 195, 2008).

Rybakov, R. (ed.), *Terrorizm: ugroza chelovechestvu v XXI veke* (Moscow: Kraft, 2003).

Sapiro, Miriam, 'Iraq: The Shifting Sands of Preemptive Self-Defence', *The American Journal of International Law*, 97/3 (2003), 599–607.

Schmid, Alex P., *Soviet Military Interventions since 1945* (New Brunswick and Oxford: Transaction Books, 1985).

Schmitt, Michael N., Responding to Transnational Terrorism under the *Jus ad Bellum*: A Normative Framework', in Michael N. Schmitt and Jelena Pejic (eds.), *International Law and Armed Conflict: Exploring the Faultlines* (Leiden: Martinus Nijhoff, 2007), 157–95.

Schmitt, Michael N. and Jelena Pejic (eds.), *International Law and Armed Conflict: Exploring the Faultlines* (Leiden: Martinus Nijhoff, 2007).

Schnabel, Albrecht and Ramesh Thakur (eds.), *Kosovo and the Challenge of Humanitarian Intervention: Selective Indignation, Collective Action and International Citizenship* (Tokyo: United Nations University Press, 2000).

Sharkov, Yuri, '"Color Revolutions": Uniformity in Diversity', *International Affairs* (Moscow), 54/4 (2008), 25–31.

Sherr, James and Steven Main, *Russian and Ukrainian Perceptions of Events in Yugoslavia* (Camberley: Conflict Studies Research Centre, 1999).

Silitski, Vitali, '"Survival of the Fittest": Domestic and International Dimensions of the Authoritarian Reaction in the Former Soviet Union Following the Colored Revolutions', *Communist and Post-Communist Studies*, 43/4 (2010), 339–50.

Skotnikov, Leonid, 'The Right of Self-Defence and the New Security Imperatives', *International Affairs* (Moscow), 50/6 (2004), 13–21.

Skotnikov, Leonid, 'The Use of Force: Legal Aspects', *International Affairs* (Moscow), 50/4 (2004), 33–49.

Smith, Hanna (ed.), *Russia and its Foreign Policy: Influences, Interests and Issues* (Säärijärvi: Kikimoro Publications, 2005).

Smith, Mark, *Russian Perspectives on Terrorism* (Conflict Studies Research Centre, Defence Academy of the United Kingdom, January 2004).

Smith, Mark, 'Russian Policy during the Kosovo Conflict', in Stephen Badsey and Paul Latawski (eds.), *Britain, NATO and the Lessons of the Balkan Conflicts 1991–1999* (London: Frank Cass, 2004), 139–52.

Sofaer, Abraham D., 'International Law and Kosovo', *Stanford Journal of International Law*, 36/1 (2000), 1–21.

Sofaer, Abraham D., 'The Best Defense? Preventive Force and International Security', *Foreign Affairs*, 89/1 (2010), 109–18.

Stefes, Christoph H. and Julie A. George, 'The Battle after the Battle: International Law and the Russia–Georgia Conflict', in James A. Green and Christopher P. M. Waters (eds.), *Conflict in the Caucasus: Implications for the International Legal Order* (Basingstoke: Palgrave Macmillan, 2010), 153–76.

Steffek, Jens, 'Legitimacy in International Relations: From State Compliance to Citizen Consensus', in Achim Hurrelman, Steffen Schneider, and Jens Steffek (eds.), *Legitimacy in an Age of Global Politics* (Basingstoke: Palgrave Macmillan, 2007), 175–92.

Stepanov, Ye. (ed.), *Sovremennyy terrorizm: sostoyanie i perspektivy* (Moscow: URSS, 2000).

Stepanova, Ekaterina, 'The Challenge of Terrorism in Post-Saddam Iraq: A View from Russia', PONARS Policy Memo 325 (April 2004), 1–6, at <http://www.gwu.edu/~ieresgwu/assets/docs/ponars/pm_0325.pdf>.

Sterio, Milena, *The Right to Self-Determination under International Law* (Basingstoke: Palgrave Macmillan, 2012).

Stewart, Brandon M. and Yuri M. Zhukov, 'Use of Force and Civil–Military Relations in Russia: An Automated Content Analysis', in Paul Rich (ed.), *Crisis in the Caucasus: Russia, Georgia and the West* (London: Routledge, 2011), 69–93.

Stromseth, Jane E., 'Law and Force after Iraq: A Transitional Moment', *The American Journal of International Law*, 97/3 (2003), 638–42.

Taft IV, William, H., 'The Legal Basis for Preemption' (Council on Foreign Relations, 18 November 2002), 1–3, at <http://www.cfr.org/publication.php?id=5250>.

Taft IV, William H. and Todd F. Buchwald, 'Preemption, Iraq and International Law', *The American Journal of International Law*, 97/3 (2003), 557–63.

Talentino, Andrea Kathryn, 'US Intervention in Iraq and the Future of the Normative Order', *Contemporary Security Policy*, 25/2 (2004), 312–38.

Tesón, Fernando R., 'Ending Tyranny in Iraq', *Ethics and International Affairs*, 19/2 (2005), 1–20.

Thakur, Ramesh, *The Responsibility to Protect: Norms, Laws and the Use of Force in International Politics* (London: Routledge, 2011).

Thomas, Caroline, *New States, Sovereignty and Intervention* (Aldershot: Gower, 1985).

Torkunov, Anatolii, 'International Relations in the Post-Kosovo Context', *International Affairs* (Moscow), 46/1 (2000), 74–81.

Trenin, Dmitri, 'Russia and Global Security Norms', *The Washington Quarterly*, 27/2 (2004), 63–77.

Trenin, Dmitri, 'Russia in the Caucasus: Reversing the Tide', *Brown Journal of World Affairs*, 15/2 (2009), 143–55.

Troitskiy, Mikhail, 'Going "Relativistic": The Changing Vision of a "Just International Order" in Russian Foreign Policy', in Douglas W. Blum (ed.), *Russia and Globalization: Identity, Security and Society in an Era of Change* (Washington, DC: Woodrow Wilson Center Press, 2008), 207–31.

Tsygankov, Andrei P., 'The Final Triumph of the Pax Americana? Western Intervention in Yugoslavia and Russia's Debate on the Post-Cold War Order', *Communist and Post-Communist Studies*, 34/2 (2001), 133–56.

Tsygankov, Andrei P., 'Russia's International Assertiveness: What Does it Mean for the West?', *Problems of Post-Communism*, 55/2 (2008), 38–55.

Tukmukhamedov, Bakhtiyar, 'Russian Federation: The Pendulum of Powers and Accountability', in Charlotte Ku and Harold K. Jacobson (eds.), *Democratic Accountability and the Use of Force in International Law* (Cambridge: Cambridge University Press, 2002), 257–79.

Tukmukhamedov, B. R., 'Uprezhdayushchee primenenie sily: vozmozhnye kriterii dopustimosti', *Rossiyskiy ezhegodnik mezhdunarodnogo prava* (St Petersburg, 2005), 36–55.

Tukmukhamedov, Bakhtiar, 'Law and Force', *International Affairs* (Moscow), 55/2 (2009), 92–102.

Valenta, Jiri, *Soviet Intervention in Czechoslovakia, 1968* (Baltimore: Johns Hopkins University Press, 1979).

Valenta, Jiri, 'From Prague to Kabul: The Soviet Style of Invasion', *International Security*, 5/2 (1980), 114–41.

Valenta, Jiri, 'Revolutionary Change, Soviet Intervention and "Normalization" in East-Central Europe', *Comparative Politics*, 16/2 (1984), 127–51.

Valenta, Jiri and Frank Cibulka (eds.), *Gorbachev's New Thinking and Third World Conflicts* (New Brunswick and London: Transaction Publishers, 1990).

Valkenier, Elizabeth, K., 'New Soviet Thinking about the Third World', *World Policy Journal*, 4/4 (1987), 651–74.

Veselov, V. A., D. G. Yevstaf'ev, and P. P. Skorospelov, 'Geopoliticheskiy aspekt voyny v zone Persidskogo zaliva', *Voennaya mysl*, 3 (1993), 20–9.

Vidmar, Jure, 'Remedial Secession in International Law: Theory and (Lack of) Practice', *St Antony's International Review*, 6/1 (2010), 37–56.

Vincent, John, *Nonintervention and International Order* (Princeton, NJ: Princeton University Press, 1974).

Vincent, R. J., *Human Rights and International Relations* (Cambridge: Cambridge University Press for the Royal Institute of International Affairs, 1986).

Vremennaya instruktsiya po podgotovke voinskikh kontingentov privlekaemykh dlya formirovaniya grupp voennykh nablyudateley i kollektivnykh sil po podderzhaniyu mira gosudarsvt-uchastnikov sodruzhestva nezavisimykh gosudarstv (Moscow: Russian Ministry of Defence, 1993).

Wallander, Celeste A., 'Lost and Found: Gorbachev's "New Thinking"', *The Washington Quarterly*, 25/1 (2002), 117–29.

Waters, Christopher P. M., 'The Caucasus Conflict and the Role of Law', in James A. Green and Christopher P. M. Waters (eds.), *Conflict in the Caucasus: Implications for the International Legal Order* (Basingstoke: Palgrave Macmillan, 2010), 8–25.

Weiss, Thomas G. and Meryl A. Kessler, 'Moscow's UN Policy', *Foreign Affairs*, 79 (1990), 94–112.

Weller, Marc, 'The United Nations and the *jus ad bellum*', in Peter Rowe (ed.), *The Gulf War 1990–91 in International and English Law* (London: Routledge, 1993), 23–45.

Weller, Marc, 'Forcible Humanitarian Action: The Case of Kosovo', in Michael Bothe, Mary Ellen O'Connell, and Natalino Ronzitti (eds.), *Redefining Sovereignty: The Use of Force after the Cold War* (Ardsley, NY: Transnational Publishers, 2005), 299–314.

Weller, Marc, *Contested Statehood: Kosovo's Struggle for Independence* (Oxford: Oxford University Press, 2009).

Welsh, Jennifer M. (ed.), *Humanitarian Intervention and International Relations* (Oxford: Oxford University Press, 2004).

Welsh, Jennifer M., 'Taking Consequences Seriously: Objections to Humanitarian Intervention', in Jennifer M. Welsh (ed.), *Humanitarian Intervention and International Relations* (Oxford: Oxford University Press, 2004), 52–68.

Welsh, Jennifer, 'Civilian Protection in Libya: Putting the Coercion and Controversy Back into RtoP', *Ethics and International Affairs*, 25/3 (2011), 1–8.

Welsh, Jennifer M., 'A Normative Case for Pluralism: Reassessing Vincent's Views on Humanitarian Intervention', *International Affairs*, 87/5 (2011), 1193–204.

Westad, Odd Arne, 'Concerning the Situation in "A": New Russian Evidence on the Soviet Intervention in Afghanistan', *Cold War International History Project Bulletin*, 8–9 (1996/7), 128–32.

Westad, Odd Arne, *The Global Cold War: Third World Interventions and the Making of our Times* (Cambridge: Cambridge University Press, 2005).

Wheeler, Nicholas, 'Pluralist and Solidarist Conceptions of International Society: Bull and Vincent on Humanitarian Intervention', *Millennium: Journal of International Studies*, 21/3 (1992), 463–87.

Wheeler, Nicholas J., *Saving Strangers: Humanitarian Intervention in International Society* (Oxford: Oxford University Press, 2000).

Wheeler, Nicholas J., 'Reflections on the Legality and Legitimacy of NATO's Intervention in Kosovo', in Ken Booth (ed.), *The Kosovo Tragedy: The Human Rights Dimensions* (London: Frank Cass, 2001), 145–63.

Wheeler, Nicholas J., 'The Humanitarian Responsibilities of Sovereignty', in Jennifer M. Welsh (ed.), *Humanitarian Intervention and International Relations* (Oxford: Oxford University Press, 2004), 29–51.

Wheeler, Nicholas J., 'A Victory for Common Humanity: The Responsibility to Protect after the 2005 World Summit', *International Law and International Relations*, 95/2 (2005–6), 95–105.

White, Stephen, 'The Domestic Management of Russia's Foreign and Security Policy', in Allison Roy, Margot Light, and Stephen White, *Putin's Russia and the Enlarged Europe* (Oxford: Blackwell, 2006), 21–44.

Wihelmsen, Julie and Geir Flikke, 'Evidence of Russia's Bush Doctrine in the CIS', *European Security*, 14/3 (2005), 387–417.

Williamson, Myra, *Terrorism, War and International Law: The Legality of the Use of Force Against Afghanistan in 2001* (Farnham: Ashgate, 2009).

Wilson, Andrew, 'Ukraine's Orange Revolution, NGOs and the Role of the West', *Cambridge Review of International Affairs*, 19/1 (2006), 21–32.

Yoo, John, 'International Law and the War in Iraq', *The American Journal of International Law*, 97/3 (2003), 563–76.

Yurgens, Igor (ed.), *Collective Security Treaty Organization: Responsible Security* (Moscow: Institute for Contemporary Development, 2011), 1–21, at <http://www.insor-russia.ru/files/CSTO%Synopsis.pdf>.

Zagorski, Andrei, 'Regional Structures of Security Policy Within the CIS, in Roy Allison and Christoph Bluth (eds.), *Security Dilemmas in Russia and Eurasia* (London: Royal Institute of International Affairs, 1998), 281–300.

Zagorski, Andrei, 'Multilateralism in Russian Foreign Policy Approaches', in Elana Wilson Rowe and Stina Torjesen (eds.), *The Multilateral Dimension in Russian Foreign Policy* (London: Routledge, 2009), 46–57.

Zmeyevsky, Alexander, 'International Law and the Struggle Against Terrorism', *International Affairs* (Moscow), 51/5 (2005), 80–4.

Index